Black Yeats:
Eric Roach and the Politics of Caribbean Poetry

Black Yeats:
Eric Roach and the Politics of Caribbean Poetry

Laurence A. Breiner

PEEPAL TREE

First published in Great Britain in 2008
Peepal Tree Press Ltd
17 King's Avenue
Leeds LS6 1QS
UK

ISBN13: 9781845230470

ARTS COUNCIL ENGLAND Peepal Tree gratefully acknowledges Arts Council support

Table of Contents

for Anson Gonzalez and Danielle Gianetti

pioneers
who make the necessary
possible

PREFACE

For readers of West Indian literature, a study of Eric Roach requires no justification. He is the most significant poet in the English-speaking Caribbean between Claude McKay (who spent nearly all of his life abroad) and Derek Walcott. Roach would be celebrated as the leading poet of Trinidad, were he not overshadowed by Walcott, a native of Saint Lucia strongly associated with Trinidad.[1] Roach began publishing in the late 1930s and continued, with a few interruptions, until 1974, the year of his suicide. His career thus spans an extraordinary period of Anglophone Caribbean history, from the era of violent strikes that led to the formation of most of the region's political parties, through the process of decolonization, the founding and subsequent failure of the Federation of the West Indies (1958-1962), and the coming of Independence in the 1960s.

This book presents a critical analysis of all of Roach's published poetry, but it presents that interpretation as part of a broader study of the relations between his poetic activity, the political events he experienced (especially West Indian Federation, Independence, the Black Power movement, the "February Revolution" of 1970 Trinidad), and the seminal debates about art and culture in which he participated. He is particularly important for his thinking about the relation between poetry as "High Art" and the products and elements of popular culture, and his sense of the place of the folk, their language and customs in Caribbean life. Throughout his career, as we will see, Roach steadily reflected on the salient issues of West Indian life in poetry of vigour and authority.

This is impressively crafted poetry, worthy of discussion in its own right, but it is especially valuable because of its engagement with the events and forces that shaped the societies of the contemporary Caribbean. His total poetic output is comparable in scale to that of Dylan Thomas, Philip Larkin, or Elizabeth Bishop, and his poems have been well known in the Caribbean since the 1940s through periodicals and anthologies. Several of them are regarded as classics, yet there has been relatively little critical attention to his work (see Bibliography). The reason is not far to seek: largely as consequence of the conditions in which he lived and worked, he never published a volume of poems during his lifetime, and the first collection of his poems was published only in 1992, nearly twenty years after his death. By exploring his work within its conditions, this book aims above all to confirm Roach's rightful place among West Indian and metropolitan poets of comparable gifts and accomplishments.

Eric Roach published poetry for nearly forty years. Born in rural Tobago in 1915 to a family of peasant farmers, educated there at Grammar School, Scarborough, then a schoolteacher, he began by publishing locally (and often pseudonymously) in 1938-39, but this beginning was interrupted by the outbreak of World War II. Roach saw military service in Trinidad from 1939 to 1946, at which time he returned to Tobago as a civil servant. Now thirty years old, he was writing prolifically, publishing poetry, stories, and articles primarily in the *Trinidad Guardian*. In 1949, Roach had a sort of second debut, when he achieved international exposure and began relationships with the BBC "Caribbean Voices" programme (from 1949 to 1955) and the literary magazine *Bim* (from 1949 to 1962). Roach married in 1952, and for a short time tried to live by his writing. Throughout the 1950s (his most prolific period – about 30 poems published in 1952-55) his poetry appeared regularly in the major regional journals, *Caribbean Quarterly* and *Kyk-over-al* as well as *Bim*. The first critical attention to his poetry appears during this period.

In 1958, however, British colonial administration in the Caribbean gave way to the founding of the Federation of the West Indies, a goal in which Roach had invested considerable political and intellectual capital. The events which led to its failure a few years later, and the default solution of independence for Trinidad and Tobago in 1962, contributed to a profound disillusionment. From 1961 until just before his death he worked as a journalist in Trinidad, producing hundreds of articles first for *The Nation* (the party organ of the People's National Movement (PNM), led by Eric Williams) and then for the *Trinidad Guardian* and *The Evening News*. During the 1960s Roach also cultivated links with politically active intellectual circles in Port of Spain, particularly the Pivot, New World and Tapia groups.[2] He published no new poems between 1962 and 1970, though his considerable reputation was sustained through reprints in anthologies, and by a new local celebrity as a playwright. During that period there were performances and publications of three plays: *Belle*

Fanto (1967), *Letter from Leonora* (1968), *A Calabash of Blood* (1971). When he resumed publishing poetry later (1970-74) it was in different venues, some obscure (*The Black I* and *Studio Arts Group*), others new to the scene, such as *Tapia* and *Savacou*. It was almost as if he were starting over – a third debut, this time local and "relevant". In 1973 he again left his job to devote his time to writing (as he had done in the 1950s). He committed suicide on Apr. 18, 1974,[3] leaving as literary legacy more than a dozen blue folders of published and unpublished material, prose and drama as well as verse, now preserved at the University of the West Indies, St. Augustine. Newspaper reports of his death invariably identified him as a playwright, but it is as a poet that Roach is commemorated in poems and other pieces by several West Indian writers.[4]

This book is not a biography or a "life and letters", but a study of Roach as an author; that is, of his construction of himself as a poet in his published work, and of the aesthetic politics inherent in that construction. In periods of discouragement, Roach was all too conscious of the obstacles he faced when he envisioned himself as a minor poet, from a racial minority, living in a place marginal politically as well as geographically, and working in an unpopular medium. His beleaguered poetic ambition expressed itself as a programmatic effort to become representative, to speak for a people rather than merely for himself, out of their shared situation of ambiguously defined nationhood in the period of transition from colonialism to a sort of independence.

Roach had a career in Trinidad as a public figure – playwright, journalist, even something of a politician – but that is not my subject here. The arena of action constituted by the poems is different: not society itself but the illusorily liberating page. For him as for many writers the blank page is a transcendental space of competition with the literary tradition, not with his personal situation. But it is also the space in which he comes to himself as colonial subject – he can make himself on paper someone it is impossible to be in his colonial society, a figure of assurance and authority. In effect, this is an account of an ambitious and anxious writer's efforts to make a poet of himself, shouldering the burden that the word "poet" bore for one educated in the schools of colonial Tobago. Roach was no stranger to controversy in his life, and his positions on race, gender, and politics invite heated discussion. To maintain focus on Roach's pages, however, I have tried not to pursue such large issues too far from the texts into the realms of biography or psychology. On the assumption that a spirit of advocacy must characterise any initial study of a significant but marginalized author, my perspective on Roach here is inclined to be curatorial rather than critical or deconstructive.

Since this is about Roach as a publishing poet, you will find only glancing attention to his plays, or his fiction (much of that in any case still unpublished), or his voluminous journalistic work. In the interests of concentrating on how Roach in fact presented himself – or found himself presented – before the world of his contemporaries, I have purposely referred only sparingly to the twenty or so previously unpublished poems which Ramchand's edition made available in 1992.

A study like this cannot succeed without treating the accumulated body of his work as sequential career, as conscious self-making, responding to events with some immediacy. Even so, it should be borne in mind that the notion of a career is problematic for (post-) colonial writers, who are nearly always amateur and intermittent writers. At some periods of his life Roach functioned like a professional, and I will characterize some of his gestures, for example the trope of palinode, in a way that presumes we can regard his work as a self-conscious career, with a self-consciousness about the persona he has created on paper over time. Even so, the coherence of effort implied by the term "career" can be misleading.

Some of Roach's habits, such as his tendency to redesign the same poem several times, suggest that he strove not to be a great poet, a Caribbean Milton, but more (and in a way less) modestly to write individual poems of such evident quality that they would be anthologized for posterity even if anonymous, sustaining themselves without the glitter of a biography or even a reputation. To write poems which speak so convincingly for themselves that their particular origins are irrelevant or at best of purely anecdotal interest is an agenda fairly common among writers in colonial settings (it applies for example to the so-called "tracing paper" poets). These are writers engaged in the process of demonstrating that their work is indistinguishable from, and therefore as good as, metropolitan work; poets you "cannot tell" are black, or colonial or non-native speakers. In Roach's case this is not, strictly speaking, a universalist agenda, since it is less concerned with making subject matter accessible than with making aesthetic value patent.

Bear in mind too that the array of venues where Roach published meant that few readers would have been likely to see all of his poems as they appeared during his lifetime. Until the publication of the collected poems few would have a sense of his career, because no real overview of the poetry was possible without great effort. As V. S. Naipaul shrewdly warns, "people doing research in university libraries, where everything is accessible, sometimes see progressions that didn't exist at the time."[5]

With those limitations stated, this book begins with a study of the earliest published poems, which appeared only locally between 1938 and 1949. Along with the common anxieties of apprentice poets, these poems of Roach's first decade of publishing betray more specialized anxieties about whether a "real" poet can arise and function in the physical and cultural climate of a tropical colony. Roach here defensively insists that the impulse to write poetry comes from human nature, not culture. At the same time, these poems illustrate, by their forms as much as their content, the ways in which Roach negotiates his relationship with the received tradition of poetry in English. The chapter also offers some account of the essential biographical and socio-historical context, especially of the milieu for the production and consumption of poetry in Trinidad and Tobago during this period.

The second and third chapters examine the international dissemination of Roach's work, which began in 1949 through BBC radio and through the journal *Bim*. Between World War II and the founding of the Federation of the West Indies in 1958, the BBC "Caribbean Voice" radio programme regularly broadcast West Indian writing back to the Caribbean. The programme opened an important breach in the barrier of colonialism, enabling Caribbean writers to be heard in and from the metropolis. His first group of broadcast poems constitutes a self-conscious declaration of vocation, and articulates what will prove to be lifelong themes, such as the relation of a West Indian poet to his community and to poetic antecedents in the tradition. Roach explores his alternatives through conflicting images of rooted ancestral figures and free-ranging adventurers. At the same time that Roach's work first began to be heard on the BBC, he stopped publishing in local Trinidadian venues and began to appear in *Bim*, the widely-read literary magazine, based in Barbados, which had become by 1949 the preeminent regional publication for the Anglophone Caribbean, fostering regional consciousness and West Indian nationalism. This chapter examines Roach's preoccupation with the roles of the poet, his claims to authority, and his relationship with West Indian society. The poems of this period introduce and develop what will become Roach's signature imagery: the flowering rock, the nurturing village, the bardic bird that soars above earthbound humans.

The next three chapters explore the poems of the productive 1950s. One treats the poems about his home, family and friends. Most obvious here is his programmatic transformation of life into art rather than autobiography. These are Roach's most intimate poems, but his revisions invariably make the poems *less* personal – evidence of his effort to establish himself as a representative regional voice, rather than a confessional writer. The poems about his parents reveal little about his family-life but much about his developing sense of himself as a poet. Both of his parents are in a sense mythologized, but the poems about his mother are remarkably different from those about his father. His father becomes an ancestral spirit of place, while his mother is not idealized, but treated with brutal realism. Her barely literate devotion to the Bible is presented as a challenge to her son's secular literary ambitions.

The following chapter surveys poems from the 1950s about various men and women of the Caribbean. Consistent with the role of gender in differentiating the poems about his parents, this body of work divides cleanly along gender lines into two quite different projects. The male figures are named individuals, heroic (if often severely flawed) leaders, and ancestral figures rooted in the land. They are associated with issues of nationhood, identity, and race. The female figures are associated with themes of obsession and jealousy. Almost always unnamed, they are either victims or victimizers, depicted as immortal goddesses or demons, rather than historically specific persons.

The third of these chapters treats the overtly political poems from the years 1952 to 1962 – poems in which Roach presents himself as the poet of the peasantry, and as a self-conscious spokesman for political federation and related issues. During this period, West Indians generally felt the increasing tension between the demands of local island allegiances and regional nationalism, along with the temptation to migrate (a course chosen by many of his contemporaries, but not Roach). These concerns are addressed in the poems under the aegis of Roach's preoccupation with defining (and exemplifying) the West Indian poet's relationship to his own little island, his "eyot."

A brief chapter dramatizes the transformation of Roach's outlook in response to the failure of the Federation by explicating the extensive revision in 1965 of a poem originally published in 1953. Chapter Eight then examines the strongly political poems that appeared when Roach resumed publishing in the 1970s. These poems delineate his increasingly sophisticated (and bitter) conception of history as a victimizing force in the light of Trinidad's "February Revolution" and its aftermath. They also exemplify the changing roles of folk figures and concerns in his poetry, reflecting and responding to rapid social changes in Trinidad associated with independence and fortuitous prosperity. There is a personal as well as a political dimension to these texts. In them the depth of Roach's disillusionment as a poet is patent; many of these poems amount to palinodes, explicitly repudiating or undoing earlier works.

At the same time that Roach found himself politically marginalized in the aftermath of the Federation, he was further shocked to find himself apparently cut off from developments in West Indian poetry itself. The catalyst was the publication of an anthology of new writing by the journal *Savacou* in Jamaica. The debate about this anthology unfolded in terms of highly charged oppositions between high art and popular art, literacy and orality, "Europe" and "Africa". Roach's vociferous participation in the debate leads to a natural conclusion for this book, a study of his conflicted conceptions of the poetic artifact, as expressed in his poetry and in the critical writing he produced in the context of the *Savacou* debate. This discussion is complemented by a concluding examination of Roach's extraordinary last poems, searching revaluations of himself and his work written in the face of what had become an almost pathological sense of marginality.

Chapter 1 - Home Work: The First Decade

"Did ever season murder song?"

In 1965, Eric Roach's reputation was at its zenith. He had finally achieved metropolitan recognition, with first appearances in a British periodical (*London Magazine*) and a British anthology (*Young Commonwealth Poets '65*). His poems were beginning to be reprinted frequently in anthologies on both sides of the Atlantic, and his only "chapbook," a pamphlet entitled *A Collection of Poems by a Poet of Tobago E. M. Roach*, would appear two years later in conjunction with the Conference of Heads of Caribbean Universities.[1] But it was in 1965 that he composed this hair-raising autobiographical note for a British anthology:

> Now a newspaperman in Port of Spain, Trinidad. He has been a soldier, teacher, civil servant and failed writer. Born nearly fifty years ago in the tiny, little known island of Tobago where his family are peasants, Roach hoped to become a poet, but his talent for verse did not develop beyond his native dooryard, and after a few years he abandoned the writing of verse. He has never left the West Indies, and is now living and working in Trinidad. None of his verse has been published except in small regional magazines. In the fifties he used to be a contributor to B. B. C.'s 'Caribbean Voices'.[2]

It is terrible to read, and knowing that he had in fact been publishing for 25 years before he "abandoned the writing of verse" only makes it worse. This is by far the most negative account of him ever written by anyone. What brought him to take such a view of himself? There were personal demons no doubt, but to the extent that this is the despair of a poet as a poet, it is rooted in his sensitivity to the marginal status of his medium, of his race, of his nationality, and of his relationship to the literary tradition in English. As Chamberlin puts it, "The career of the poet and critic Eric Roach . . . is a tragic illustration of the pressures on West Indians in the period since the Second World War."[3] More broadly, the case of Roach is also representative of, and revelatory about, the condition of many postcolonial writers in the period straddling national independence.

Are poets made, or born? Roach repeatedly insists that he was born a poet, and that the impulse to poetry is natural rather than culturally determined. Yet throughout his life he expended great effort to make himself a poet, and cultivated his craft assiduously. Indeed, images of cultivation are recurrent in the poems, as we will see. Even at the end of his career this ambivalence persists; the poems in which he asserts that poetry is a natural effusion are themselves not effusive at all, but very self-consciously constructed. His earliest poems already express anxiety about whether a "real" poet can arise and function in the physical and cultural climate of a tropical colony. Might the Caribbean itself be inimical to poetry? "Did ever season murder song?" – that is how he states the question in 1953, in a poem for Cecil Herbert, one of several talented colleagues (including the likes of George Lamming and Wilson Harris) who quickly gave up writing poetry.

Roach fought long to overcome that anxiety in himself, but he saw that it had to be overcome also in others, in his potential audience. However sure he was that he had been born a poet, it was equally important to be recognized as such, to be seen as a poet. This objective was complicated in the Caribbean by the very different characters and expectations of one's potential metropolitan and local audiences. Roach's dedication to craft was the means by which he hoped to establish his credentials and gain a hearing. His ambition was to demonstrate through his own work that poetry from the West Indies could bear comparison to the best in the world, and moreover that the region and especially its people provided worthy subjects for poetry of the highest order.

My title – *Black Yeats* – reflects a contemporaneous characterization of his work, but it also foregrounds the irony (of which Roach was not unaware) that either the first word *or* the second would attract more potential readers than the poet's own name. During his career he was criticized for being too much like Yeats, and for being first too black and then not black enough. Indeed Roach's poetic career might be said to play itself out between the poles of "black" and "Yeats" and along the trajectory of decolonization, a kind of Gulf Stream that carried him from labour unrest to independence and its aftermath.

The relationship with Yeats is obvious and need not receive sustained attention here, but it provides a very direct entry into central issues of Roach's self-fashioning. Roach's literary education depended upon the resources of a small island high school library, and so it is dominated by Shakespeare, Milton, Wordsworth, and the lyrics of the familiar anthologies. He naturally had less exposure to living writers. He knew of Eliot, and one of his poems, "Christmas Eclogue" (1950) is a blatant imitation of Eliot's "Journey of the Magi" (perhaps a factor: Eliot had just won the Nobel Prize in 1948). Otherwise there is almost no trace of Eliot in Roach's output. Roach read Yeats early, however, and attached himself to that model in a remarkable way. Walcott was critical of the relationship: "Roach exhausted his themes through an almost total dependence on Yeats, and it is interesting to explore why he found such sympathy from that oracle. Yeats's later poems have a directness of address that Roach, who needed to exhort his folk into realising their dignity and their use, found appropriate."[4] Walcott is right that Roach felt an affinity with Yeats first of all as a writer about the peasantry, whose poems could both ennoble and criticize them. But his status as an Irishman, a colonial, is also crucial. Roach associates himself with Yeats, a nearly contemporary man in a parallel situation, rather than a canonized British "master," as gesture of protection against literary colonization. For Roach the relationship with Yeats is not dialogic or revisionary at all, there is no "writing back," such as we will find in Roach's rewriting of Tennyson. Instead the relationship is fraternal (much like the role of Synge for Yeats).

The earliest traces of Yeats's influence occur in these lines from "Death on Sunday" of 1938, the first year Roach was publishing and the year before Yeats died:

> . . . death is right,
> For age had looked his coming overlong;
> Age being in pain, more than old flesh could bear. (FR 30)

Here the absolute construction "age being in pain"[5] in conjunction with the neighbouring phrase "death is right" recalls specifically the opening of Yeats's "After Long Silence" of about five years before: "Speech after long silence; it is right, / All other lovers being estranged or dead."[6] In that setting Roach's later use of the phrase "to cleanse in Holy Fire" (line 16) cannot help but recall "Sailing to Byzantium" (1928). This is one of several instances where what Roach takes from Yeats is an original bit of diction.

Similarly Roach sometimes stole distinctive rhythms. His "Carib and Arawak" (1945) is a short poem that plays with some curious rhythmic shifts. At the heart of the metamorphoses is the rhythm of this line: "Oh, the *bright stain* is the *loud blood*" (FR 40). It seems likely that this peculiar rhythm came from a line in a poem of Yeats's of about the same length which is also given to rhythmic play, "Who Goes with Fergus" (1893).

The particular rhythm of Yeats's corresponding line – "and the white breast of the dim sea" (49) – is memorable in part because it occurs only once in his poem.

More than any other poem, "He Juggles Images" (1961) bears the aura of late Yeats, not only for its priapic treatment of old age, but for rhythms and rhymes associated with the specific kind of jaunty, scandalous iambic tetrameter couplets which derive from Blake by way of Yeats. This is Roach:

> The carnal eye's delighted in
> The frenzy of original sin,
> Grins as the seed in its wet sack
> Hollows the prim virgin's back. (FR 143)

There are some occasions when Roach stoops to pastiche, merely mimicking diction, imagery and even sentiment. "Troy World" (1955) shuffles together "The Second Coming" and "No Second Troy" while both "Tree" (1952) and "Hawk Heart" (1955) shamelessly parrot lines like "I take this tree for symbol." A more pervasive and productive kind of lesson learned from Yeats had to do with innovations in rhyming, especially the use of slant, false, and half rhymes which becomes prominent in Yeats's poems of the 1930s – that is, in what would have been the newest poems for young Roach. The most consequential lesson Roach learned from Yeats, however, was a format or template for loosely stanzaic poems that begin with observation and conclude with exhortation (as Walcott noted). This model appears in several poems of Yeats, but Roach was especially drawn to those in a certain register of diction and tone. The manner of Roach's exhortations in particular can best be traced to Yeats's "Under Ben Bulben" (1939), which commands poets to undertake the cultural work of singing "whatever is well made," whether it be found among the peasantry, the gentry, the clergy, or the nobility, so that the nation can forever retain its character as "the indomitable Irishry" (400).

In poems like this one, Yeats celebrates a certain nobility of the folk without abandoning that of the aristocracy, and without surrendering either his own aristocratic affiliations or the license he claimed for himself to speak quite critically indeed of the peasantry. For Roach, on an island without even the pretence of a planter aristocracy, the only nobility could be that of the folk and the soil. His license to speak critically is thus quite different. As Walcott memorably phrased it, Roach "has a proprietary candour, the salutary contempt of a man speaking about his own people. . . It is the tone of Yeats, . . . but its moral fury is not aristocratic."[7] Roach shared Yeats's anticolonial politics, his interest in folk culture (typical of so many artists undergoing decolonization), and his dedication to high diction. But having grown up in rural Tobago his relation to West Indian folk life was intimate and profound. The example of Yeats enabled Roach to forge an exalted language for speaking from a position among the peasantry about the peasantry – a position to which he had of course a secure claim, as his predecessor did not. Roach was drawn to places in Yeats in which he recognized his own voice and situation. From "Ben Bulben" and similar poems he took a form and a sound that suited his own project and situation as a poet even better than they had suited the position of its creator.

Roach was a black man who grew up on a small, homogeneously black island colony. His relationship to the politics and culture of "blackness" as they evolved during his lifetime is naturally complex, and will be an important theme of this study. As in the case of other West Indian writers, it needs to be emphasized that he is *not* an African-American poet. African-American experience in the United States is not a reliable model for his history, his politics, the structure of his society, or his formulations of identity. Even the word "black" is sometimes problematic for him – the intonations of that adjective in his poems (such as " Haitian Trilogy") can be surprising. The note that he composed to accompany the 1968 version of "Homestead" provides a good reference point:

> Generally, the West Indian today is blundering around in a twilight world, half loving, half scornful of himself. All he knows of his heritage is that he was hauled in as cargoes and dumped on islands to raise sugar for Europe's desperate need. The slave ancestry disgusts him and he attempts to flee from himself but is trapped in the world outside his islands. Europe resents him. Africa does not recognise the long absent, much changed prodigal with his European language and attitudes. He is condemned to plod along the limbo edges of the world, rootless, displaced, marginal. My whole history is my immediate family, and dimly seen behind the parents, the generations of heavy slave folk trampled into the clay where the sweet cane prospered in our bitter sweat. [8]

Characteristically, Roach here links race, national identity and class, while discriminating between African and Caribbean identity, and the palpable anger flashes in several directions at once. These traits are recurrent in the poems as well.

Besides poetic affiliation, and issues of race and class, the crucial third register of identity for Roach is literally and figurative his location. As a poet, Roach's home was the books he devoured, and he regarded himself as vying for a place in the tradition of poetry in English, in the same kind of anthologies that he read as a youth and in the eyes of what he called "the savants". Yet at the same time he was a poet with a complex vision of the social responsibilities of poetry and of poets, and especially of the black West Indian poet in a pluralistic society.

Considering his situation in the process of decolonization, it would have been plausible for Roach to present himself as the poet of his own Tobago (in the way that Walcott despite his trans-nationalism remains the 'voice of St. Lucia'). For him, the villages of Tobago always epitomized life in the Caribbean, and he is the island's most important poet. But in the poetry he programmatically turned his village into a generalized, representative model for something much larger. Shifting his allegiance early on, Roach chose to fashion himself as the voice of an imagined regional community, the Federation of the West Indies, the actuality of which he advocated passionately and the failure of which he grieved furiously. It is a central dramatic irony of his tragedy that he strove to become the poet of a country that never quite came into existence. If the Federation had succeeded, there would be parks and libraries named after Roach. But it did not, and there are not. The Anglophone Caribbean, reorganized as a scattering of independent nations, does not quite have a place for him in its poetic landscape – especially as long as that landscape is defined by the too-hasty polarization of Brathwaite and Walcott. In the end he was the uncrowned laureate of a lost country – unaccommodated archipelagic man. Indications are his ambitions were most nearly achieved in the years of the BBC programmes, when he was a disembodied voice broadcast throughout the region. Rohlehr chooses his verb with the utmost precision when he laments "Eric Roach, who above all had had a vision of the archipelago as something potentially one."[9]

*

Roach's first appearance as a poet was very local. His earliest published poems appeared pseudonymously (as Merton Maloney) during 1938 in *The Teachers' Herald*, a professional magazine of limited circulation and no literary pretensions; he first ventured to publish under his own name in the *Trinidad Guardian* during the following year.[10] If a bit shy, Roach in his early twenties was certainly resolute about making his way as a poet; at least a dozen poems appeared in print in the space of a year and a half. But events in Europe aborted this beginning. For the duration of the war, while Roach was in military service in Trinidad, he published only a handful of poems. With the coming of peace, he made a new – if somewhat slower – start, and published another dozen poems in the *Guardian* from 1947 through 1950. The appearance of these poems was one of several factors that lead up to his first exposure outside Trinidad and Tobago, in 1949/50. Thereafter he published no further original work in either *The Teachers' Herald* or the *Guardian*. This chapter will examine what must therefore be regarded as the work of Roach's apprenticeship: the thirty-odd locally published poems of the years 1938-1950.

First, a word about the setting. At the turn of the century, just before Roach's birth in 1915, his native Tobago was a colony of perhaps 15,000 people, mostly peasant farmers and fisherman, predominantly black and Protestant, living on 116 square miles of hilly terrain. Virtually bankrupt, the island had become a ward of the Crown Colony of Trinidad in 1889. Trinidad itself, an island about half the size of Jamaica or Connecticut, had been named by Columbus in 1498, but remained an unimportant and sparsely populated Spanish outpost until the end of the eighteenth century, when it came under British control. It was belatedly transformed into a sugar island thanks to an influx of refugees from the French islands, planters and their slaves fleeing the real or anticipated effects of the revolutions in Haiti and France. The period of plantation slavery in Trinidad was thus quite short, ending in 1838 after less than fifty years. At the time of emancipation, two-thirds of the island's population spoke French or Spanish exclusively, and the new demand for labour initiated the importation of indentured workers from West Africa, China, and especially India. By the time the practice ended in 1917, just two years after Roach's birth, nearly 150,000 Indians had been transported to Trinidad and settled there, bringing their own languages and cultures. For Trinidad, the 1920s were years of rapid economic and social development; oil had been discovered in 1910, and when the Royal Navy and Air Force converted from coal to oil in 1912, Trinidad was assured a buyer for as much as it could produce.[11] Trinidad's favourable labour market during this period attracted immigrants from other Caribbean islands in considerable numbers, who further diversified the culture of the island as a whole and of the capital, Port of Spain, in particular.

It was in that city, with its uniquely "provincial, yet cosmopolitan environment",[12] that the earliest concentration of significant literary talent anywhere in the British West Indies materialized in the late 1920s as an informal circle of intellectuals centred around Alfred Mendes and C. L. R. James.[13] In 1929 /30 they together brought out what they considered the first literary magazine in the island's history (*Trinidad*), of which only two issues were published. Albert Gomes, then a young man studying in New York, made contact with the circle when he returned to Port of Spain in 1930, and the result was a new magazine, *The Beacon*, which between 1931 and late 1933 published 28 issues of creative writing and political commentary (there was one more issue in November 1939). The magazine was regarded – not least by its organizers – as dangerously provocative; an ordinance framed in 1935 expressly to limit small political periodicals was probably aimed at *The Beacon* in particular.[14] The acuity of its editorials on such topics as black consciousness, federation, and Church/State relations is still impressive, and the impression they made on their first readers is reflected in a circulation that reached five thousand, a huge number by the standards of the time and place. On its literary pages, *The Beacon* introduced poetry by a number of hands, and while most of this verse was negligible, the relatively large number of contributors was in itself a good omen.

The momentum of the group continued even after publication of *The Beacon* ceased, and there is ample evidence of literary activity in Trinidad throughout the 1930s.[15] Though James had emigrated to England in 1932, and Mendes to the United States in 1933, Gomes remained at home, laying the groundwork for a long political career in Trinidad, and editing what appears to be the island's very first anthology, *From Trinidad: Fiction and Verse* (1937). Here again the poetry is disappointing. As a collection, *From Trinidad* might need no further characterization than the fact that it contains a poem entitled "Exquisite Hour".

In fact two sorts of poetry dominated the Trinidad literary scene in the period between the world wars. Gomes and his circle favoured "poems of ideas", with abstract nouns for titles and much reliance on words like "love", "death", and "eternity". Gomes himself produced a great deal of such verse, and his influence may be responsible for its prominence as a kind of house style during this era. The titles in *From Trinidad* are nearly all of this kind: e.g. "Dreams", "Beyond", "Ecstasy", "Reverie", "Despair", "Reality". There is also a high proportion of pretentious Latin titles: "Hora in excelsis", "Apologia", "Consumatum Est [sic]", "Requiem". It is a relief to note that among Roach's poems only the negligible "Folly" (1939) much resembles this *Beacon* manner. At the same time there is an abundant body of poetry in a very different style of effusive natural description. This is quite similar to that of the contemporaneous Jamaica Poetry League, which was more widely known through publications such as the

1929 anthology characteristically entitled *Voices from Summerland*. Though perceived even at the time as rather old-fashioned, this blandly lyrical nature poetry was still being produced by leading writers of the day. In Roach's oeuvre, "Dusk" (1948), with its "wooded dells", is probably the worst instance of several among the earliest poems. The work of Alfred Mendes sometimes exemplifies the genre (e.g. "Tropical Lines" [1929]: "The hummingbirds were busy with the flowers" and so on), but Mendes also participated in the subsequent modernist sabotage of it, for instance in "Tropic Night" (1932), which describes the night as a hairy tarantula crawling over the city, or in the opening of "Lines" [1933]: "The dusty haunts of men make my belly sick".[16] There are certainly traces of this hard-boiled modernism in Roach's poems, but it rarely appears when his subject is nature.

That was the milieu in which Roach began to make a place for himself. It comes as no surprise that Roach's earliest poems are generally tentative, sometimes insecure, exploratory works, very diverse in style; he attempts various voices, forms, and subjects, and along with the successes there are certainly failures, false starts, and mere fizzles. Yet there are significant harbingers here. Among the poems that appeared in *The Teachers' Herald* and *Trinidad Guardian* just before the outbreak of war, the most notable fall into two broad categories: poems about poetry, and poems concerned with national history and identity. These poems consider fundamental matters: the value of poetry (and of poets), and the relation of poetry to nature, to society, to its tradition. Many of them are engaged in developing appropriately public forms of expression. Such poems as "Immortelles (I)" and "A Poet Passes" constitute ventures in establishing something obviously important to Roach at this stage: the existence of a secure, unequivocal link between physical nature and poetic expression in what he usually called "song". At issue is his own access, as a country boy from Tobago, to the same wellsprings that nourished a Homer or a Milton; for Roach as for many of his coevals, Caribbean society itself was as problematic a matrix for poetry as was Caribbean nature. Elsewhere in this early work "New Loaves" is the first of many poems concerned to recognize and celebrate the poetry inherent in everyday life (as distinct from nature). "Stair of Song" is at heart about the relation of his poetry to the literary tradition, and in "Tribute to Winifred Atwell" Roach is at pains to identify the particular immortality that poetry confers as a source of its *value* (just as elsewhere he asserts the value of its "naturalness"). The place of the poet in Caribbean society is also at issue, if somewhat less explicitly, in two groups of poems: those on historical or political subjects (such as "Tragedy", "For Freedom", "Song of the Sleepers-Out", "Carib and Arawak", and "Sounds Live"), as well as those that begin Roach's livelong dedication to representing idealized West Indian personages ("To Learie", "A Lover Speaks", "Anacaona", "She", and "Dancer").

1938 – *THE TEACHERS' HERALD*

One of the very first published poems illustrates how Roach sets about extricating himself from the cliches of his poetic milieu, and displaying his particular sensibility and skills. From its opening lines, "Immortelles"[17] sounds like the Jamaican Poetry League work of the same era:

> The forest flames! Look yonder in the vale.
> The forest flames! Look over the green hill. (FR 25)

But the poem's formal ambitions, if modest, reach beyond that style. This is one of several sonnets Roach produced in the early years; in this instance iambic pentameter with a somewhat simplified rhyme scheme: ABCB DEFE GHIH JJ. Despite the Shakespearean pattern of the rhymes, there is a fully Petrarchan break after the octave, which has done little more than remark, overexcitedly, that it is January and the immortelles are blooming. But the last line of the octave with fine poetic instinct begins to lead from the observation itself to its significance, first hinted at only vaguely: "The turning days a welcome magic hold". The "magic" involved might be nothing more than the weather: the burst of flowerings, especially of immortelles and pouis, that signals the coming of dry season, with its clear air and cooler breezes. That was a common approach in other West Indian poems of this sort. But Roach has something more interesting in mind. The next line, the first of the sestet, joins together two phrases of the same length and rhythm:

> *The forest flames! Burst forth my song*,
> And bound along the pathways of the sky
> Warbling high honour to the floral fire
> That loosed thee from thy mute captivity! [emphasis added]

"The forest flames!" is the phrase which initially set the entire poem in motion, and which has been repeated to indicate the beginning of each new quatrain. The second phrase – "Burst forth my song" – after its introduction here will eventually supplant the first, taking its metrical and structural place in the final couplet:

> *Burst forth my song*! Let tropic beauties own
> A queen is now ascended to her throne. [emphasis added]

The couplet's insistence on repeating "Burst forth" establishes it as a replacement for the previous refrain, but it also draws attention to the fact that the substitution is brought about by the *action* of the initial refrain itself. Thus, by an economical juxtaposition, the first line of the sestet encapsulates the entire action of the poem, as it summarizes the magical *act* that justifies the poem: the flowering of the trees, by its natural "magic", sets the song free from captivity and gives it voice (just as the emergence of the blooms gives the forest colour). This is only the first of many places where Roach meditates on poetry in terms of birds and flowering trees, but here he is careful to keep his images distinct. Apart from being called a "wonder", the immortelle is figured throughout only as fire: it is a glory that flames and blazes. The song is figured not as a bloom but as a bird, whose music honours the "floral fire" that loosed it. Precisely how Roach conceived the song's initial "captivity" is left vague, but there seems to be an implication that what inspires poetry is not nature as such, but its brazen exceptional flowerings.

In a very simple way – which analysis cannot help exaggerating – this is a poem that moves beyond conceptions of poetry as the result of mere natural observation to insist that the production of poetry not only mirrors but somehow *corresponds* to nature's own expression in flowers, bird-song, and the like. Roach shares this insistence with the poets who used to be called "pre-Romantic", and who like him assert the legitimacy of local springs of inspiration – that is, the worthiness of the local as poetic subject *but also* (something distinctly different) its crucial ability to provide the energy for poetic "song". This is a very ordinary poem; but so are many of Blake's *Poetical Sketches*, in which this project has been abundantly demonstrated.[18] It is the instinct of the poet to make certain gestures, to clear certain sorts of space in certain sorts of ways, that is notable here.

While Roach must have encountered a great deal of insipid nature poetry, in a poem like "Immortelles" he does more than strive to avoid insipidity. If on the one hand he asserts wellsprings of authentic poetry in the local, on the other he successfully avoids the defensive tic endemic to many West Indian poems of the period: there is no comparison (favourable or unfavourable) with European seasons. In the present poem the closing couplet makes a point of describing the pre-eminence of the immortelle *vis a vis* "tropic beauties", avoiding any comparison with the trees of the received literary tradition. Roach comes closest to exemplifying the defensive reflex in the second and third lines of another early sonnet also called "Immortelles": "A mountain top with cap of silver snow \ I have not seen, but heard it lovely; here . . ." (FR 26). One hears, however, a healthy superciliousness in the tone of that "heard it lovely" which introduces the catalogue of local attractions, and in any case the implied unequal comparison has already been defused by the poem's levelling first line: "Earth decks herself with beauty *everywhere*" [emphasis added]. Roach produced none of those apologetic poems, so typical of pre-Independence work from throughout the region, which seem capable of making a space for themselves only by acknowledging their inability to compete directly with European literature and experience.[19]

Of course, Roach is by no means free of that tradition and its burdens, and another poem of 1938 illustrates something of his vulnerability to the Trinidadian poetic milieu. "Death on Sunday" begins like this:

> Death is my next-door neighbour in this dawn;
> He came upon the old man in the night
> On some most holy hour; death is right;
> For age had looked his coming overlong;
> Age being in pain, more than old flesh could bear. (FR 30)

Unnaturally stiff diction infects several of these early poems. Roach seems to have resorted to it as a technique for asserting the kind of aesthetic distance that he felt could support serious and authoritative utterance. Self-consciousness about his own marginality not only with respect to the tradition but even to the Trinidadian literary establishment drove him to seek technical and stylistic (rather than personal) grounds for authority. As noted earlier, this passage also bears the earliest traces of Yeats's powerful influence on Roach. Yeats died on Jan. 28, 1939, a few months after the publication of "Death on Sunday", and the appreciation that Gomes wrote for the *Guardian* a few days later conveniently indicates the pitch of Yeats's reputation at that moment. Gomes praises especially the most recent poems, noting that Yeats had become "in the last few years, the arch-rebel. His verse became less exuberant, more austere and ripened. Indeed, some of his very recent poems show that quality of tenuity found only in works of art of the very highest."[20] By way of context, Gomes had earlier in the essay called Eliot and Auden merely "rebels". It is surprising to us, though it would not have been to contemporary readers, that the complex, even "post-colonial" relation of each of the three to the British tradition goes unmentioned. That relation was not lost on Roach, however, and it constitutes an important part of the grounds for his affinity with the Irish poet.

No one seems to have known quite what Gomes meant by the word "tenuity" in his remarks about Yeats,[21] but the term probably describes for Gomes the austere and sinewy philosophical manner he himself aspired to achieve. In any case, the blustering "modernism" of the *Beacon* poets and the stoic toughness of contemporaneous late Yeats combine and assert themselves throughout Roach's career. They do so – with unfortunate results – at the end of "Death on Sunday":

> And who shall sing a dirge or lay a wreath
> For this most joyously departed breath?
> I'll write his epitaph sans name and date,
> "Here lies a man who loved his present state."

The tonal failure seems a matter of not leaving well enough alone. The first two lines of the above quotation are wholly consistent with the mildly provocative stance of the whole, and constitute a couplet which concludes the formal shape we have been led to expect in this third and final stanza. Indeed, the open question constitutes an effective summation of the poem's resistance to conventional pieties. Yet Roach has gone out of his way to tack on a second couplet, though both argument and form were complete without it, and the flippant banality contributes nothing.

While Roach is self-consciously rude about death, here and elsewhere,[22] at this stage of his life he almost invariably romanticizes poetry, and when the two subject cross, it is the romance that dominates. This is illustrated by the very different atmosphere of another early elegy, "A Poet Passes" (1938), which mourns the death of a local poet (Levi Darlington) at age 32 – young, yet older than Roach. The frame of reference for both the form and the style of this poem – four quatrains of lofty iambic pentameters, virtually blank verse – is Elizabethan pastoral elegy and its progeny down to Milton's "Lycidas". In the first quatrain the dead poet is described as a fountain of song which once flowed through the land. In the roughly parallel second stanza, the poet is a harp that charmed Iëre's ear.[23] The conclusion is then conventional: sorrow may be short-lived (as was the poet), but "what he has done" will make him live forever. Like "Immortelles", this is another poem in which Roach insists on the *natu-*

ralness of poetic activity. But at the same time there is a self-serving progression in the background: now that the fountain (nature) and the harp (artifact) are gone with the loss of Darlington, we have access to the unmediated *human* sounds of a new poet: "Hear you Iëre the deep sigh I breathe?" (FR 31). It is conventional to intrude the self of the *surviving* poet into the poem supposedly about the dead one (the message of such elegies is often "the poet is dead, long live the poet"). True to form, the second half of this poem is more concerned with Roach's tears, and especially with whether Iëre hears his sighs and moans, his poem – *his*, not Darlington's. In its small way this is an announcement of a new poet's presence on the scene; but that poet is still known as Merton Maloney.

The idyllic aura of "A Poet Passes" contrasts unrealistically with the Trinidad of that historical moment (though surely no more than parallel Renaissance lyrics contrasted with their own political contexts). In the late 1930s the end of the *Beacon* period coincided with Trinidad's political awakening, precipitated when chronic labour unrest climaxed in the oilfield strikes led by Uriah Butler in Fyzabad.[24] The 1937 riots had racial as well as economic dimensions. There was revulsion at racist attitudes attributed to Americans and South Africans among the expatriate managers,[25] but race was a factor among the workers as well: oil workers were predominantly black, while sugar workers were Indian. The European failure to resist the Italian invasion of Ethiopia in 1935 had set off protest marches and other public demonstrations in Trinidad.[26] A concurrent revival of interest in Marcus Garvey and pan-Africanism during the 1930s nourished an increasing racial consciousness that tended to set black and East Indian Trinidadians at odds. So Butler had emerged, as early as 1935, as a black leader for black workers. It was out of these strikes that Trinidad's political parties (and its racial politics) evolved, and they developed amid concurrent movements toward universal suffrage, decolonization, and regional federation. It was the Trinidad strikes, in conjunction with disturbances in Jamaica during May-June 1938, that stirred Britain to send out the Moyne Commission to investigate. The Commission's recommendations about constitutional reform (not made public until after the war),[27] ultimately led to the Montego Bay Conference which in 1947 initiated the process of building a Federation within the Commonwealth.

Roach's creative life unfolds between these social upheavals of 1937-38 and those of the early 1970s, and is in many respects shaped by them, as his politics is shaped by the hope for a West Indian Federation. Yet it cannot be said that his voice emerges out of those events, as George

Campbell's voice comes out of (and is formed by) the parallel events in Jamaica or Martin Carter's from later unrest in Guyana. For the most part, Roach comes to address these events only retrospectively, in the poems of the 1970s. As a young poet, however, he did write one curious poem, "The Tragedy" (1938), on the events of the late 1930s. This is his first overtly political poem, and it is characteristic that he works to dignify the topical and potentially ephemeral subject matter by imposing both the formal frame of a fairly tight sonnet (ABAB CACA DEDE FF), and the figurative frame of a nearly allegorical relation to *The Merchant of Venice*, established from the outset:

> The old year was a Shylock in its threat
> To cut a foolish forfeit of our flesh,
> But Britain sent a gallant advocate
> To steer us cleanly through the evil mesh. (FR 32)

Shakespeare's play is a puzzling choice for the allegorical vehicle here; it has the effect of obscuring the poem's relation to the events that motivated it. Nothing in the play corresponds to Roach's notions that the defeated Shylock passes his threats on to his "heir," the new year, and that the new year "who greets us now with visage sternly set" seems less than promising. Given the plot of the play, it is particularly mystifying that the poem includes two advocates: one sent already from Britain, and another whom the poem ends by invoking:

> We seek with sighs Bassanio's bride of peace
> To haste from Belmont to our high release.

What can this Portia correspond to in the political allegory? It is tempting to speculate that the reference here is to some very specific detail of local politics: in Port of Spain, Belmont is a district with a reputation as something of a cradle of politicians. But the idea that this might amount to an elaborate political campaign jingle founders on the unlikelihood that, in 1938, any such candidate could be female.

Actually, this poem was published as a sort of coda to an essay, "Human Progress", also by "Merton Maloney", which immediately precedes it in *The Teachers' Herald*. Writing there about the recent strikes in the Caribbean in 1938, Roach says:

> These are but the expressions of a discontented people. And what has been so long amiss is the lack of leadership among the people. But still we strive on. It is our Age of Achievement. We are staging the age-old drama of

> Progress here in the West Indies. None should be blind to the end to which our striving moves. It is no mere struggle between Labour and Capital. It tends to the social and economic uplift of all. It tends to a truer representative government in the various colonies. It tends in the latter end to Federation and a true democratic government to which we shall come after a lapse of years.[28]

This can stand as a representative statement of the federation politics that persisted through his life, but for our present purposes the tone is of greater interest. This starchy diction, which corresponds to the stiffness in some of the poems, seems to be the means by which Roach assumes a position of authority. Yet the tone is mixed. There is an air of wise condescension in the opening sentences and the final one; at the same time the body of the passage harps repeatedly on the solidarity expressed by the second person plural pronoun. The juxtaposition of those two features – distance and familiarity – is the earliest indication of Roach's "proprietary candour", his complex relationship to the peasant people whom he so frequently wrote about.

Roach's willingness to pontificate in this essay also owes something to the nature of his relationship with *The Teachers' Herald*. It must have been very favourable and supportive, considering the ad hoc nature of the poems he published there. These were not manuscripts pulled from a drawer; evidently they were being written as the occasions arose. Thus he published "New Year" in the January issue, two seasonal poems (both entitled "Immortelles") in February and March, "Discovery" in August to mark Discovery Day (i.e., the naming of Trinidad by Columbus), and finally "The Tragedy", which explicitly sums up the events of the year. So it appears that, for a crucial period at the beginning of his career, he enjoyed something like unconditional access to the *Herald* and could publish what he wrote promptly and without fear of rejection. Following "The Tragedy", he published only one more poem there, much later ("Carib and Arawak", 1945); after his year with the *Herald* he was ready for pastures new, in the more widely circulated pages of the *Trinidad Guardian*.

1939 – *THE TRINIDAD GUARDIAN*

It would be a mistake to underestimate the *Guardian* of those days; it was a dignified newspaper of record, comparable to the *Gleaner* in Jamaica, with high editorial standards (higher then than now), a model of crisp editing, enlightened and cosmopolitan. In 1939, when the first of Roach's poems appeared there, the *Guardian* was regularly publishing news about the war in Asia *in Chinese* for Trinidadian readers. Parallel with "A Page of Indian News" and "A Page of Chinese News," there was "A Page of Literary News" appearing on Thursdays and edited by Gomes. The space was mostly taken up with information about debating societies and the like, but there were poems, stories, and essays as well, and occasional articles on painting and music. There were generally also some literary items in the Sunday edition. While some of the verse is trivial, the (relatively) major poets of the era also appeared there, and they did not necessarily write down for this venue.

Of the four poems Roach published in that setting during 1939, two are trite examples of the prevailing local style; they can serve to illustrate his affinity with his surroundings – both the society of poets around him and his literal surroundings on the poetry page of the *Guardian*. "Folly" and "Tonight, Tomorrow" (the only poem to appear under the name "Merton Roach") resemble the poems of Gomes, and even more A. M. Clarke's earnest lyrics. It is just conceivable that they were tailored to appeal to the taste of the editor, Gomes, though such opportunism seems out of character for Roach. In any case, Roach, even at his least distinctive, compared favourably with much of what the *Guardian* printed; his "Folly" shared its page with "Just a Dream" ("Tell them, oh tell them, Love, / That it was just a dream") and "Sleep" ("Gently falling, sleep down calling,/ Gently, eyelids drooping fall").[29]

The other two *Guardian* poems of 1939, however, are both directly concerned with Roach's aspirations as a poet; the very first to appear in the *Guardian* seems distinctly calculated to make an impression in several ways at once. "To Learie" is a celebration of the Trinidadian cricketer Learie Constantine, then at the height of his international fame. The subject matter alone would have attracted the contemporary eye, and the first-name familiarity of the title would also have had its effect on readers – it is one of several small ways in which Roach here pulls himself up, as it were, by other people's bootstraps. The choice of poetic form is significant too. This is a sonnet – a time-honoured arena in which new poets prove technical assurance – and so it makes claims both about the poet and about his subject:

> Of famous father a most famous son
> Wherever cricket has been greatly played
> Wherever men discourse of wonders done
> By wisden wizards – of fine feats displayed

In the great Empire game, – there in renown
Is known the name of Learie Constantine
Who won and wears now cricket's triple crown.[30]

The impression of strength here derives from the long arch of the syntax, but also from the initial echo of Milton's sonnet to Edward Lawrence (which begins: "Lawrence, of virtuous father virtuous son"). The two poems resemble one another in no other way, but this echo in combination with the latinate syntax invokes a specifically Miltonic sense of the seriousness of the sonnet, and of its function as a form of public utterance. This poem illustrates one solution – albeit a borrowed one – to the problem of achieving the kind of impersonal, even hieratic, diction that Roach aspired to command.

The public tone supports the poem's role as a contribution to the project of shaping a national consciousness. "To Learie" does not construct the kind of idealized icon (of which we will encounter several shortly) that was common throughout the West Indies in the pre-Independence period; instead it celebrates a local hero who has made good abroad, with special emphasis on the point that Constantine achieved this not by leaving his roots behind, but by playing a distinctively *West Indian* style of cricket without compromise even at the heart of Empire. The poem expresses an amazed delight at the continuity, the integrity, of Constantine's progress from local cricket pitch to the height of the sport, and therefore, too, a corresponding sense of every West Indian's real participation in the final victory:

Here have we seen him hit a hundred, take
A grandest catch, and give the thundering crowd
A smile as though he's done it for our sake.

The phrase "we have seen him" occurs twice in the poem, with an almost incantatory force that evokes priority of possession, and the player's final smile signals the reciprocal nature of the link between the colony and the greater world which Constantine's success provides: somehow even from England the hero returns the admiration of the Trinidadian crowd.

This poem aspires to make a very public gesture (however much or little attention it actually received), and Roach's reach for the highest available poetic style here is particularly notable because he is writing in direct competition with demotic celebrations of figures like Constantine (and Joe Louis) in contemporaneous calypsos.[31] On the common turf of public utterance, Roach asserts his sense of the difference between lasting poetry and ephemeral popular verse, and at the same time insists on equal access for poets like himself to the nation's business. In its effort to constitute a civic – almost Pindaric – poetry, "To Learie" anticipates the subjects and objectives of the poems about various Caribbean figures which we will consider in Chapter 5, and it stands in surprisingly close relation to "At Guaracara Park", a late poem which expresses a very similar sense of the presence of the crowd, of an athlete's direct relation to it, and of the poet's own presence as participant and testifying witness. "To Learie" is concise, but it manages to convey two interdependent messages: first, that "our" local hero is worthy to be praised in Miltonic cadences, since to be preeminent in cricket (which the poem identifies as "the great Empire game") is to be preeminent in the Empire itself; and secondly that the poet best qualified to praise him in such cadences is E. M. Roach, who with this substantial poem first publishes under his own name.

In sharp tonal contrast to the Constantine sonnet, Roach's next poem in the *Guardian*, "The Stair of Song" (1939), with its seven quatrains of simple song-like diction and downright naive rhyming, seems intentionally unpretentious, even disarming. As the stanza which both opens and closes the poem illustrates, only the even-numbered lines rhyme, and of fourteen such lines, five end with the word "go" and five with the word "ago":

> Tread lightly on the stair, stranger,
>   Lightly as you go;
> Ionian Homer hammered it
>   Two thousand years ago. (FR 33)

In Roach's little myth the stair of song is built by Homer, and trodden by poets ever since. Rather strangely, poets through the ages are described as going up *and* down on the stair; one wonders what that two-way traffic can refer to as a poetic activity, since success is measured in this poem not by advancement but by whether the footprints fade or endure "in a golden glow". Roach is probably remembering Jacob's ladder with its angels going up and down. Consciously or not, the image of the stair of song itself may come to Roach from Chaucer:

> Go, litel book: . . .
> But subjet be to alle poesye,
> And kiss the steppes wher-as thou seest passe
> Virgil, Ovid, Homer, Lucan and Stace.[32]

As that possible allusion highlights, this is a poem about the burden of the past; "tread lightly on the stair, stranger" is an admonition motivated by reverence for those who have passed here before. But (as even the self-effacing form suggests) this is not a poem that *grapples* with the burden of the past in any way; it is not about Roach's own climbing of the stair, but addressed to anyone who might approach. The poem has an air of reverence and decorum. It emphasizes the seriousness of the poetic undertaking even as its own mien seems too naive to engage such attitudes. Roach enunciates no program or ambition; this is more like a medal struck to commemorate the selection of a vocation. It is indeed a kind of inscription. The initial address to a "stranger" locates the poem squarely in the genre of gravestone elegy or other monumental poetry, so that while one face of this poem is an actual (and viable) song, another is an inscription on the stair itself. But the word "stranger" is also almost deviously self-referential. Despite the fiction that these are the words of the stair and not of Roach, there is a distinct emphasis on the idea that those who pass upon the stair come "from many lands . . . where'er the wild winds blow." The underlying hope that there is access to the stair for outlanders (say, for example, Tobagonians) is even stronger in the text as originally printed: "from many lands they come strangers where'er the wild winds blow."[33] Here it looks as if the word "strangers" refers not to a disinterested passer-by, but to the poets themselves. Perhaps, however, the plural form of "strangers" is a typographical error, a comma misread as an "s".

Given the subject of this poem, Roach's way of positioning himself with respect to the stair of song without including himself in the poem is significant. He is not to be identified with either the passing stranger or a climbing poet, and even if we choose to construe the words as spoken rather than inscribed, their awed tone characterizes him as an acolyte or newly initiated adept – a figure with a tentative, distant, or merely potential relationship to the stair. Since several poets are mentioned by name, we can fairly take them as exemplary, at least of what Roach valued in poetry, if not of what he aspired to write. Homer is traditionally the great original, but Roach makes a point of referring to Homer as "Ionian", and while the poem is too simple to justify making very much of this, it seems to invoke the *archipelagic* context of Homer, and so of his special value for any Caribbean island poet, in terms of the "American Mediterranean" analogy that was current at the time among advocates of cultural federation. Any inclination to call Roach's own poetry Homeric would have to do with the self-consciously "bardic" image of the poet he later develops, and with his attraction to heroic subjects. Yet Roach has no interest at all in narrative, and his conception of the "bard" is thoroughly Romantic, not ancient.

In addition to Homer, the poem mentions only Dante and Wordsworth. We cannot know that Roach recalled the Chaucer passage in sufficient detail that his replacement of Chaucer's other four poets (Virgil, Lucan, Ovid, Statius) is intentional. Whether he did or not, his is a curious enough selection – the absence of any Latin writer is especially strange in the context of British colonial education – and interesting too for its remoteness from our sense of the nature of Roach's own aspirations as a poet. At no point in Roach's career would one spontaneously think of Dante in connection with the forms of his work, or his persona as a poet, or his subject matter. Some of Roach's poems about peasant-farmers have been called Wordsworthian, but they recall the Wordsworth of *Lyrical Ballads*, while the characterization in "Stair of Song" suggests the blank-verse Wordsworth of pensive epic, whom Roach in no way resembles. It is in many respects a strangely ill-assorted trinity.

THE WAR YEARS

World War II was not a remote event for Trinidad; there were mines and U-boats in the Gulf of Paria, at least two ships were torpedoed inside the harbour at Port of Spain, and Vichy France was as close as Martinique. The domestic crises of the 1930s were for the most part suspended during the war; there was for example a "no strike" agreement for the duration.[34] Specifically economic problems were to some extent resolved as a result of the virtual invasion of Trinidad by thousands of American troops and American dollars, ushering in a period of rapid growth for the society as a whole. But the boom brought new social problems of its own (prostitution, an epidemic of venereal diseases, a new kind of racism), and had as one of its most enduring effects an irrevocable shift from British to American cultural hegemony. Ambivalence about the American presence is very close to the surface in this contemporaneous account from the Colonial Office:

> 1941. This was perhaps the most epochal year in the history of the Colony. It marked the commencement of a change in the economic and social life and outlook of the people. United States personnel began to arrive. . . . A new El Dorado loomed on the horizon. This small and distant outpost had become the seat for one of the greatest experiments in international relationships. Despite the lure of the American dollar, and, in fact, perhaps to a great extent, because of it, the inhabitants remained loyal to the cause of Empire, manifestly deeply conscious of the life and death struggle in which the British nation was engaged.[35]

The transformation of Trinidadian society in the aftermath of the war had a profound effect on Roach's poetry and indeed on his life, but he did not write about the war itself. During the war years, Roach seems to have written very little, and he published only a handful of poems, though some of his work did appear (again under the name "Merton Maloney") in the most important anthology of that era, *Best Poems of Trinidad* (1943), which was edited (and like so many West Indian books, privately printed) by one of the newer writers, A. M. Clarke. The collection is anchored by names familiar from *The Beacon*: Gomes, Stollmeyer, Carr, Thomasos, and Mendes. The younger poets included particularly Harold Telemaque (with whom Clarke soon published a joint collection of poetry), Edgar Mittelholzer (who had moved to Trinidad in 1941), and "Maloney". To the extent that his pseudonym was recognized in the small circle, this confirmed for Roach a place on the local map, and in the local tradition, linking him with the previous generation as well as with the best of his contemporaries. The association with his like-minded contemporaries Clarke and Telemaque was particularly important for the next phase of his career (as we know from *Burnt Bush*, both Clarke and Telemaque made a point of taking a regional perspective; like Roach both were teachers at the time).[36]

Roach was represented in the anthology by "Death on Sunday" (considered earlier) and "New Loaves", In spite of its inclusion in this volume, "New Loaves" is an awkward poem, inferior to much of what Roach had already published at that point. The idea is simple and appealing: a woman brings fresh-baked bread to the table, and the poet rhapsodizes about the antiquity of the fragrance and of our emotional response to it. Roach's procedure, too, is interesting; he poeticizes the experience by noting that this is "an old fragrance . . . /which everybody knows. /The Assyrian and Egyptian knew it..." Roach maximizes the value of his references here, since these examples evoke not just antiquity, but specifically a Biblical context, which helps to ritualize and sanctify the event. Soon, however, in the little poem's oddest and least successful move, Roach stretches to provide a full stanza each for Homer and Shakespeare, with no hint why they, or any authors as such for that matter, ought to be mentioned here; his point is not even that they wrote about bread, but merely that they smelled it. Images of bread and worked dough are developed more successfully in later poems, as we shall see, but "New Loaves" deserves mention as an early example of Roach's devotion to the poetry inherent in the simplest elements of everyday Caribbean experience, and also of his inclination to make that poetry patent by the imputation of specifically *historical* significance.

Only four other poems appeared during the war. Stylistically they still bear the marks of their era, and Roach is still freely exploring voices and subjects. But there is evidence in all four that Roach is thinking about relations between art, politics, and history. "Tribute to Winifred Atwell" (1944), for example, expresses gratitude for Atwell's performance: "You wrought us there a world within our world / Of stress and strife and traffic; an hour of charm."[37] Roach's anxiety about how poetry might celebrate accomplishment, which lies unspoken beneath the form and style of "To Learie", here comes to the surface – though it *appears* without quite being *addressed*:

> For this, bouquets of roses are no price:
> Beauty that perishes may not requite
> The imperishable hour. Grace is not dead.
> What tribute too, this wreath of windy words,
> This light inodorous flowering of the spirit,
> This shoddy sonnet writ by half a poet? (FR 38)

In contrast to the control of the medium which Roach projects in "To Learie", that final line goes far beyond mere modesty topos into the realm of self-laceration. He might be berating himself for managing to produce only the right length and meter for a sonnet, with no rhyme except the final "spirit / poet." Perhaps he is experiencing something more like stage-fright, at finding himself unexpectedly committed to addressing publicly the old question of the immortality of poetry within the constraints of a sestet. Certainly as soon as the issue emerges, Roach shies away from it and the poem becomes tongue-tied. Instead of the expected argument that poems are (or are not) more lasting than roses, we get the verbal equivalent of blushing confusion.

We will see in Chapter 9, in the context of vociferous debate about the role of oral performance in West Indian poetry, how seriously Roach regarded the dilemma of art's evanescence and its permanence. In the present text he maintains that the apparently transient hour of the performance is less perishable than the congratulatory roses, because "It[']s a golden graving on our thought" by "the burin of your heart". Then there is this poem itself: a wreath, a "flowering" like the roses, but "light", "inodorous", "windy" – somehow less substantial than even the roses, though it has in fact (whatever its quality) outlasted the performance, and the roses, and the "thought" of the now dead poet. A poem can be regarded as a performance with exactly the same paradoxical ontological status as

Atwell's: an imperishable couple of minutes. That notion is not in play here, but the possibility has implications for this topic as it develops later in Roach's career, when he is thinking about the extent to which poetry is both a performance ("windy") and an inscription ("a golden graving").[38]

"Tribute" concludes with a rare date-line ("Piarco"), the site of Roach's military service in Trinidad; so does "Song of the Sleepers-Out" (1944) the first and most explicit of three political poems published during the war. This is a poem about urban homelessness – something Roach encountered for the first time when he came to Trinidad. Though the poem is not explicit, he may well be responding to the homeless Indians who camped in Woodford Square during the early 1940s.[39] This was a social problem not only visible but much talked about in that period – there had been many calypsos on homelessness and hunger during the depression of the mid-1930s.[40] But such subject-matter is highly unusual for Roach, who rarely wrote about *any* aspect of urban society until the 1970s. The poem is one of Roach's many formal exercises: it is composed of long seven-foot iambic lines, rhyming AAX, BBX, CCX, etc., where X is the entire phrase "sidewalk sleepers-out." But the poem's primary aesthetic venture ends in failure; the "song" begins "*We* are the last lees of the city's sub-communities" (emphasis added), but Roach cannot bring off the attempt to sing convincingly in the voice of the homeless. While the problem of finding an appropriate diction is foremost, the poem also draws attention to the fact that Roach, though he went on to write effective plays in the 1960s, seldom attempts dramatic poetry, poetry in a voice that is distinctly not one of his own.

"For Freedom" (1944) is another frankly political poem, in this case celebrating the imminence of universal adult suffrage. Considering that subject-matter, Roach's choice of free verse as his medium certainly has thematic implications. The poem demonstrates great technical assurance in its effective handling of rhythms and line lengths (though the diction wobbles a bit when it resorts to "Lo," "'twas," and "enceinte"). Roach's free verse ingeniously achieves closure without any sense of formal constraint by grouping assonances in the second strophe in a way that merely suggests rhyme (the sequence of terminal words "dawns" / "gone" / "free" / "song" / "harmony" / "intensity" / "freedom" / "dawn" / "born" implying AAB ABB AAA). Yet here as in the previous poem the voice is untypical of Roach:

Look brother, the day dawns!
Look how the edges of the vast dun clouds
        Are tipped with silver!
Look how one shaft of light climbs up the sky!
The island stirs and shudders in her sleep
        As when within the womb
        The enceinte woman feels
The urge and surge of birth. (FR 39)

This sounds very much like what the Jamaican George Campbell was writing in the 1940s, and it could easily be mistaken for the work of several among the politically aware Jamaican poets of the period, the poets that is of *Focus* magazine, edited by Edna Manley and intimately associated with the People's National Party led by her husband Norman. The *Focus* writers were engaged in a conscious turn away from the manner of the Jamaican Poetry league, but the political directness and the high, oratorical style are quite *un*like what was being written in Trinidad at this time. If the first issue of *Focus* (1943) had found its way to Port of Spain fairly quickly, it is possible that Roach in "For Freedom" was exploiting the resources of this new influence.

What *is* typical of Roach here, however, is the insistently imperative mood of his poem, and its central rhetorical gesture, the resuscitation, in response to this dawn, of another earlier dawning, that of emancipation:

'Twas such a dawning when a century gone
The slave men were set free,
When fields were cradles rocked with song
And woods were hung with a wild harmony,
And the winds hummed joy's deep intensity.

This is the first rural *scene* in Roach's poetry, and the passage offers a first glimpse of the entirely characteristic images and atmosphere of Roach's "village" poems of a few years later. "For Freedom" begins by addressing a solitary "brother" situated in a pared-down, symbolic landscape; this setting, along with the coordinated images of the phallic shaft of light and the pregnant woman, suggest the problematized terms of poems like "Transition", "The Flowering Rock", and "Beyond" (all 1950). In this poem, as in some of those, the stark opening is contrasted with the warm domesticity of the settlement. Here the actual depiction of a human society is doubly distanced: set a century in the past, and described, with striking indirection, entirely in terms of the music that accompanied these unrecounted events. The natural music of wind through the trees is confused or commingled with the human music of jubilee; these images, along with that of cradles of song, will recur prominently in other poems.

We will find that Roach does not usually write poems on historical subjects; the only early example is "Discovery" (1938), an occasional poem that celebrates the heroism of Columbus. The poem is ambitious – over sixty lines long and wrestling with an awkward anapaestic meter in an effort at suitably heroic tone. Yet the treatment of Columbus is iconic rather than historical; as usual, Roach's emphasis is on his adventuring spirit, and the poem ends with image of Columbus as "the deathless Colossus / Bestriding our world, our rising New World" (FR 29). Much more frequently, as in "For Freedom", Roach evokes history as a way of giving depth to the experience of the present. History intrudes upon, or is discerned behind, the present object of attention. While the title of "Carib and Arawak" (1945) seems to indicate an historical subject, the poem is (strictly speaking) about the colour of hibiscus flowers. This is the last poem Roach published in *The Teachers' Herald*, immediately after V-J Day and the end of the war. Like all the other work published there seven years earlier, this is signed "Merton Maloney" – it is the last pseudonymous poem – and in many respects it rounds off the first phase of Roach's career. The deceptively simple expressiveness of this 21-line poem masks considerable technical craft, and it pointedly draws attention to the lurking immediacy of Caribbean history in a way that suggests (but does not investigate) strong political implications. The timing is significant. Published right after a war which on both fronts (though in different ways) was about nationhood and race, this poem almost literally digs up old *regional* ethnic animosities. The Spanish victimization of Amerindians is only part of the poem's business; the title makes a point of invoking both Carib and Arawak: *pre*-Columbian antagonists. The poem's claim is simple: the hedge hibiscus – that is, the domestic, the commonplace, the plain – blooms red because of the buried blood of the Amerindians, and thus signifies how that history is everywhere around us in the islands. Such an idea will come to constitute a master-trope in Roach for the insistence with which suppressed local history impinges upon present Caribbean consciousness. The notion is hinted at in "Hurricane Hill" (1948), where the wind tells the story of an unquiet Carib ghost, and in "Sounds Live" (1948), a poem whose premise is that "Sounds live eternally,/ forevermore wandering / like ghosts . . . / in the land of their birth" (FR 45); among the ghostly sounds are Carib songs ("arietoes"), noises of battles, sobs and screams. This trope quite literally blossoms in the slightly-earlier "Carib and Arawak", and is then developed along various lines in poems of the 1950s: for example, in terms of buried blood in "Haitian Trilogy", buried ancestors in poems like "The Old Man" and "Shallow Underground", or legends which the wind draws up from the roots of trees in "Invocation", "The Old Man", and elsewhere.

POST-WAR POEMS

After the war the long ascendancy of the Trinidadian novel began in earnest, fuelled by the great postwar migration of West Indians to London which included many young and talented writers. But poetry lay fallow – not only abroad, where promising poets like Harris and Lamming turned to fiction, but even to some extent on the local scene. There was one post-war anthology, *Papa Bois*, in 1947. There are no poems by Roach in it, but not much should be made of that, since the collection presented work from a particular literary club that met during the 1940s, organized by an Englishman, Judge Ernest Hallinan, at his home in Port of Spain.[41] It included older writers who had been associated with the *Beacon* (Carr, Thomasos, Farrell) as well as younger writers (Telemaque, Mittelholzer and Lamming). Several of these writers had appeared in Gomes' anthology of 1937 and even in *The Beacon*, and most of the poetry is predictable. In any case, *Papa Bois* marks the end of an era.

The lack of local journals during this period was also an impediment – when Clifford Sealy's *Voices* began publication in 1964 it was the first significant literary magazine in Trinidad since *The Beacon*, which had ceased publication thirty years earlier. A few poets (Gomes, Thomasos, Clarke) managed to publish volumes of their own work, and in the aftermath of the war alternatives to local publication were soon to be provided by the BBC and the emerging regional magazines. But poetic activity was circumscribed, and there was little recognition at this point from the outside world, where for the most part "West Indian poetry" still meant "Jamaican poetry." The *Life and Letters* anthology of 1948 for example included only three poems from Trinidad, while Langston Hughes' *The Poetry of the Negro* (1949) offered just two.[42] Even among the collections that appeared a decade later to celebrate Federation, only that of *Caribbean Quarterly* adequately represented Trinidadian efforts, including as it did the work of nine poets.[43] Thus, during the years between the end of the war and Independence, even when Roach's own work was appearing abroad, there were hardly any local outlets for poetry. Throughout this period the *Guardian* newspaper continued to play a supportive role; it not only occasionally published but actually hired important creative writers. Among the writers who worked there at one time or another were Lamming, Mittelholzer, Selvon, Ismith Khan, Michael Anthony, Roach, and Walcott.[44] It was in the *Guardian* that Roach made his "new start" as a writer; he published another dozen poems there from 1947 through 1950, along with twenty-eight stories and a number of articles during approximately the same period.

Roach's poem "Colour" (1947) appeared in considerable isolation: two years after the previous poem in the *Guardian* ("For Freedom"), a year and a half after the previous poem anywhere ("Carib and Arawak" in the *Herald*), and a year and a half before the next poem anywhere ("Hurricane Hill") which in August 1948 finally began a new, steadily accelerating stream of publication. "Colour" is dedicated to Roach's friend Telemaque, and it is likely that the imminent publication of Telemaque's own collection of poems during 1947 was an incentive for the composition of "Colour". Even the isolation of its appearance marks it as something of a liminal poem, and its concluding exhortation to Caribbean poets and painters, though plainly modelled on Yeats, is very much in the spirit of Telemaque's dedication of his own collection to "the New West Indian." Such exhortations will be common in Roach's poems from this time on.

"Colour" begins with twenty lines of very visual, or more precisely *painterly*, description:

> The island world is filled
> With the sky's blues and ocean's,
> With the earth's green and ocean's,
> The cloud's white and the wave's. (FR 41)

Roach's striking economy of diction in these lines – his meagre palette – conveys vividly the experience of unmediated visual perception, the disturbingly shifty relation between colour and form in the natural world. The poem goes on to offer other instances of the disorienting ways in which nature presents itself to an observer. The notion that "Day's light within, upon, / Makes star-dance on the water" is typical; here the bright sunlight which both shines through the clear water and glints off its surface produces the spangling effect of twinkling stars, but these stars are *below* us, not above, and though they evoke night the scene is in bright daylight. The visual impressionism of Roach's approach to the play of colour and ambiguity of outline in this poem is occasionally recapitulated on the level of shifting sound effects, as in these lines:

> Day passing on a pall
> Of paling colours, ends
> Like embers.

Such a detail has the aural subtlety of Tennyson, and harmonizes with the unexpectedly Impressionist atmosphere of the poem's opening, the lucid yet vibrant atmosphere of a beach scene painted by Eugene Boudin or Maurice Prendergast. Yet in spite of their successful deployment in this poem, these effects are not particularly thematized, and are so uncharacteristic of Roach that they may indeed constitute a stylistic homage to the dedicatee, whose poems are generally much more attentive to colour than Roach's; this is certainly the only extant poem in which he seems to be working in watercolours.

The initial emphasis, however, on the intermingling of colours (and sounds) in the natural world provides a base for Roach's characteristic view of the Caribbean artists' mission. Though the text does not make this explicit, the impressionism of the opening seems to suggest something like bewilderment, the inarticulateness of a West Indian aesthetics still in its infancy – still speechless in the face of its own experience. The objective of the poem is to summon artists to interpret the Caribbean sensorium, to give names to the confusion and bring it into focus. Thus the ending calls upon both poet and painter to use the materials immediately at hand, "the sun's hot ardour", "the earth's rich rhythms", to interpret this beauty for "us". Reasonably enough, it is the painter whom Roach first summons to elucidate the scene: "Come / Down on the sun's long road, / Down the great rainbow's arch." But at once the poet, too, is called upon – at much greater length, to accommodate a little myth about what poets are:

> Come poet, come,
> Up through a chasm of earth,
> Up from that darkness
> Where life sleeps and dreams,
> And breathes her great rare dreams,
> Through golden corridors,
> Whence their splendours come,
> As poets among men.

The painter's colours come from above, from the sun and the rainbow, but language here comes from the earth – from a sort of underground. Poetic *rhythms* too come from the earth, from the pulses and seasons of earth conceived as an organism, as either the embodiment or the container of life. The poet is summoned to rise from the dark place where life *produces* poets, with the strong implication that the task of a poet is not to describe nature but rather to convey a graspable impression of the environment and indeed somehow to constitute the expression of natural forces. Carrying forward an idea first introduced as early as "Immortelles", Roach here describes poets as themselves manifestations in the world of the splendours dreamed by "life". Roach's management of the unusual style of this poem underscores its liminality. But the poem's movement from observation to injunction, along with its investment in the value of forces asserting themselves from below, links "Colour" directly with the poems of Roach's imminent maturity.

I have already mentioned in passing some of the poems that appeared in the *Guardian* during 1948-1950; most noteworthy among them is a group of poems which present various female figures as in some way emblematic of national identity. Poems in which a peasant girl, or dancer, or unselfconscious beauty is treated as an erotic image for the nation or even for the land itself are standard accoutrements of awakening nationalism throughout the Caribbean. Abundant during the 1920s in the context of Afro-Cubanism and even of the Harlem Renaissance, such poems come into vogue in the Anglophone Caribbean after World War II, and almost immediately replace nature poetry of the Poetry League sort as the primary medium in which poets worked out issues of identity, nationalism and relation to the land. Roach, who had previously produced no poem of this kind, published four of them during this three-year period: "A Lover Speaks", "She", and "Dancer" (all of which celebrate black or creole identity), and the more significant "Anacaona", which rehabilitates the image of a dancing Amerindian queen.

In "A Lover Speaks" (1948), a charmingly jingoistic lover assures his lady that he could resist her if she decked herself in all the natural beauty of the rainbow, the moon, and the stars (stanza I), or even if she were to "become all legend beauty" of Greek, Egyptian, Germanic, or Irish mythology (stanza II). What *can't* he resist? He lets her know in the third and final stanza:

> But, when your bright imaginings shall end
> And you are your black hair,

Black eyes, deep lips and dark complexion;
When you are native to this time and island; . . .
Your beauty maddening in the moment's dusk,
Your Naiad nakedness in the clean sea;
When you are you
Then shall my fancy be not free
But slave and bound to what I love to see. (FR 44)[45]

In its light-hearted way, this is a call to West Indian self-consciousness (and self-worth) on a par with Archie Lindo's "Bronze" ("You sat there \ Quite unconscious of your charm \ . . . You turned your head")[46] or H. A. Vaughan's familiar "Revelation" ("Turn sideways now and let them see . . .").[47] Yet the implications of the phrase "slave and bound" are a little distracting in their context, and it seems ironic that the poem itself cannot resist covering its nakedness – and indeed the actual word "nakedness" – with a scrap of Greek mythology ("Naiad") even in this final stanza; we know what this lover means, but he doesn't seem to hear quite all of what he himself actually says.

The simple argument of "A Lover Speaks" is structured like a very prolix sonnet, with "quatrains" of eight lines each, and a "sestet" of ten. Quite a few of the best-known of these "nationalist pin-up" poems from the West Indies are in fact sonnets, for the same kinds of reasons that led Roach to write "To Learie" as a sonnet: the prestige of the form, the technical challenges it offers, and its traditional association with demonstrations of the worthiness of an author or a subject-matter.[48] Roach shapes his own "She" (1949) as a strict Petrarchan sonnet (ABBA ABBA CDECDE) with an especially subtle and impressive octave:

She is Caribbean. She is the meaning,
Flower and fruit of our four centuries
Of ruthless traffic, of dark uneasy peace
Among ourselves, of reckless greedy gleaning
From old continents, and the commingling
Of our blood with wanton, lustful ease.
She's Europe, Africa and Asia, these
And the native Carib disappearing. (FR 49)[49]

Once again Roach reveals a talent for significant formal detail, as in the series of very effective enjambements, which revise and deepen the unfolding meaning of the lines in a way that might have been learned from his friend Telemaque's complexly ironic poem "In Our Land". The metrical play that echoes the disappearance of the Caribs in line 8 is also notable: a shift to trochaic rhythm produces an apparently normal pentameter line of ten syllables in which we are made to feel the absence of the "extra" eleventh syllable that the obviously feminine ending leads us to expect (an expectation which has been fulfilled – and thus reinforced – in lines 1 and 4). For the purposes of "A Lover Speaks", Roach sets aside historically-determined identity to insist on the appeal of the bare physical self in intimate and harmonious relation with the most immediately local setting, "this time and island". A more serious poem, "She" takes pride in pan-Caribbean *mulatez* – though to call this a celebration would misrepresent the tone. Even in the West Indies, "She" is much less familiar than Adolphe Roberts's widely-anthologized (and almost exactly contemporaneous) "The Maroon Girl" (1950), but it is a measure of the limitations of this genre that the two poems share many common elements. Both are sonnets that describe an idealized woman of mixed blood posed virtually motionless in a "rare frame" of tropical flowers and foliage, and both include a note of proud defiance.

Roach's "Dancer" (1950) presents a more mobile icon of identity than "She", but the central image is not so sharp. The presentation of an Afro-Caribbean dancer is dominated by the image of ancestral drums pounding in her blood – already a cliché in the 1920s. More specifically, Roach's "Dancer" bears a family resemblance to the better and better known "Harlem Dancer" of Claude McKay, in which similarly the occluded history of the (female) dancer is recognized by the (male) viewer in the know, but not dealt with by either party, so that the recognition has no consequence. Still, Roach's sensitivity to her "grief-marrowed gaieties" and his vision of ghostly "torrid dancers" in their "dark kraals" places this among the earliest instances of attention to the implications of African ancestry in West Indian poetry. This imagery in "Dancer" anticipates "The Fighters", in which the grief that remains hidden here will be faced and worked through.

In contrast to "A Lover Speaks", "She", and "Dancer", the central figure of "Anacaona" (1949) is not an idealized pin-up of national pride, but an historical personage who epitomizes instead colonial victimization and the devastation of the Indies. The poem is based on fact. One of the very few Antillean Amerindians whose name is recorded, Anacaona was the *cacica* of part of Hispaniola, betrayed and murdered by the Spaniards she had welcomed.[50] But it was not the tragic story alone which motivated Roach to write. His inspiration for this poem is almost certainly an early and little-encountered poem of Tennyson's with the same title, written while Tennyson was still a student at Cambridge. It might seem improbable that Roach could have known this text. Yet the two poems both use the unusual place-name Xaraguay, and another poem, "Sounds Live", which Roach published a few months earlier, refers to the Caribs' "arietoes", a term (gone slightly Italianate in Roach's ear) that appears in Tennyson's description of Anacaona as "Naked, without fear, moving / To her Areyto's mellow ditty" (lines 61-62).[51] Conceivably these words might merely happen to appear in some common source consulted (directly or indirectly) by both poets; but the link between the two poems seems to me to be clinched by the programmatically revisionary nature of the relation that emerges if we hypothesize that Roach knew Tennyson's poem.

Roach's opening, for example, is a powerful and imaginative evocation of a vanished race, which emphasizes their sense of themselves as a people, with a culture and a history:

> They wrote their names,
> Their race, their pride,
> Their dancing figures,
> All their history
> Upon flats of stone
> Kept clean in wind and sunlight.[52]

This particular gambit certainly looks like a rejoinder to Tennyson: Tennyson's poem is gaudy with local colour and overflowing with tropical flora (he mentions among others pineapple, orange, cocoa, palm, canna, cedar, cinchona, ebony, and guava). Roach has no objection in principle to such opulent framing of female beauty – we have just seen him exploit the effect in "She" – but he seems to make a point of avoiding it here. In reaction against Tennyson, Roach wants to make it clear that Anacaona is not just a wild "golden flower" loose in the woods, but the representative of a civilization.[53] For this reason, Roach emphasizes that the Amerindians have a high culture and a recorded history. The importance of this recorded history for the vitality of the future is acknowledged particularly in the phrase "dancing figures", which refers not only to pictures of themselves dancing, but to the figures of the dance itself, the choreography, by which it could be re-enacted, brought back to life. In Tennyson's poem, Anacaona and her handmaidens spend all their time dancing on the beach of a tropical paradise; no building or interior space of any kind is mentioned. As an antidote to that, Roach envisions the sort of urban setting we usually associate with the Aztecs and the Maya: *his* Anacaona lives among households with hearths, courtyards, chambers, courtiers, draperies, palace doors, and a central plaza. Cultivated fields are mentioned once, but there are no jungles, and the *only* flora (there is no other vegetation at all except that implicit in the word "fields") is the queen's red roses – confined in a vase, indoors.

Tennyson recounts the arrival of the white men, and Anacaona's innocent greeting, but he is circumspect about the outcome. She is last seen showing them the island, but there is no account of what happens next. It is tempting to interpret this aversion of the poem's gaze as an instance of Victorian imperial bad conscience, but it at least also urges us to read the poem more effectually as an emblem of what happens ("inevitably" perhaps, in the logic of colonialism) to the Americas as a whole, rather than as the lurid story of an isolated particular crime. And the demurral is certainly also an instance of something much more particular, Tennyson's own "art of the penultimate".[54]

Roach's dialogue with this poem – his own efforts must be interpreted as such, if we accept the close relation of the texts – is among other things (a refusal of the merely decorative, for example) an insistence that it is no allegorical Innocence that suffers, but a concrete historical person, along with the distinctive culture she inhabits. So in Roach the transgression of the Europeans is not social but cultural; not a breach of hospitality but part of a programmatic dismantling:

> They shattered the stone records
> And they scattered household goods
> And gods and blood
> Across the hearths and fields.

When Roach goes on to envision the details of the Spanish attack on the Amerindian queen the poem becomes lurid and banal, the verse awkward ("The voices cried "Ho!" / The courtiers screamed / Woe!"); yet this excess may be Roach's hypercorrection of Tennyson's excessive discretion about the crime. In any case Roach's later version of this poem, broadcast on the BBC as "The Legend of Anacaona" (Aug. 14, 1955), eliminates such awkward melodramatic elements as those lines just quoted. The revision shuffles the sequence of some lines and fine-tunes a word here or there (in the spirit of Roach's insistence on specificity, "queen" becomes the more precisely evocative "cacica", the anonymous "don" is fingered as "Don Fernan", and the invading "paladins" inexplicably become "vikings"). The first version of the poem ends with Anacaona's death; the later version adds an epilogue which more effectively rounds off the poem by returning to the imagery of the opening. In the *Guardian* version it is not especially clear why the poem should begin with an account of Amerindian record-keeping; this added stanza makes full sense of that opening gesture:

Her bones are grains of sand;
And the white stones
On which she wrote her beauty
Are lost as her loins
That thrummed love's hot canzones
Among her maidens. (FR 51)

Her own beauty, its expression in her dance and songs, and the record of all that, are lost. Anacaona has been reduced to sand; the stones of record reduced to shards. The phrase "stones on which she wrote her beauty" plausibly also alludes to the stones of the dancing floor where she performed – apt symbol of the entire material culture of the Caribbean Amerindians which this poem treats as exaggeratedly urban and substantial. In Roach's hands, Tennyson's exoticist poem is rewritten as an evocation of a lost world – in the vacated space of which West Indians now live. Such a parodic rewriting, or re-vision, of a specific British poem is unique in Roach's work. He engages in no such sustained dialogue with Eliot in the "Eclogue" of the following year or even with Yeats. Thus it is notable that the poem's publication coincides with the date of another important intervention in the stream of the British literary tradition: the debut of Roach's poetry on the BBC "Caribbean Voices" programme, which will be the subject of the next chapter.

*

This present chapter has been concerned with a very diverse and uneven body of work. There are scattered foreshadowings (and foreglintings) of later work in these poems, but only limited conclusions can be drawn about the apprenticeship itself. No distinct profile of poetic habits or themes emerges, and there is certainly no salient poetic program. The poets of the *Beacon* group dominate the immediate context in which he wrote, but Roach seems to be guided, first, by the standard anthology pieces of English tradition (a dependency reflected especially in his self-conscious efforts at formal mastery), and secondly by an attraction to –

and impatience with – the example of Poetry League verse. It is shocking, really, to reflect that in over a decade a young poet from the countryside should have written no poems of *specific* local description, and no poems about the landscape of Tobago. Roach seems bent on recuperating nature poetry as a genre by turning away from slack description; instead, in poems like "Immortelles", "Hurricane Hill", and "Carib and Arawak", he prefers to read the psychic and historical values inscribed in the landscape of the Caribbean as a whole. His early work along this line is clearly affected by his interest in contemporaneous models for nationalistic iconography; in poems as diverse as "Discovery", "To Learie", "She", "Anacaona", and "Dancer", we have seen how his sensitivity to the intrusions of history finds expression by studying the example of contemporaneous "national icon" poems.

Readers familiar with the "flowering rock" images in Roach's later poetry cannot help but notice the scattered instances among these early poems where history or heritage is envisioned as forcing its way into the light. The image of blood that comes to the surface, central to "Carib and Arawak", also appears in "Dancer" and, much less prominently, in "She" (ll. 2-3); but it is as if Roach has not yet noticed how frequently he comes back to this idea. It is hindsight, too, that enables us to recognize a related idea in the image of the poet as a "sweet-voiced fountain" ("A Poet Passes"), or of poetry as springing irresistibly from the force of life itself ("Colour"). But there can be no question that Roach from the beginning invests heavily in the belief that the production of poetry is a natural phenomenon, and that a talent for it springs up quite involuntarily. This insistence that writing poetry is fundamentally a matter of nature, not culture, is, of course, a thinly veiled insistence that he himself can be a poet in the fullest sense of the term, despite his marginality with respect to the cultural tradition of the language in which he writes. Such protestation only draws attention to his anxiety – but this anxiety itself motivates the production of poems, as demonstrations of the validity of his claim. This peculiar psychological condition can be chronic for colonial writers, and it often expresses itself in a complex interplay of cockiness and timidity, as when Roach in "A Poet Passes" follows the traditional trope of elegy, but only so far, taking over the mantle not from a master but from another apprentice poet. There is a related interplay between technical assurance and abject apology in "Tribute".

At the same time there are fairly confident poems that either explicitly declare the poet's vocation ("Colour") or attempt to demonstrate it ("To

Learie"). And it seems clear that for Roach confidence is most intimately involved with sound, with command of voice. This, even more than form, seems to be in his view the locus of poetic authority. Although the poems we have considered in this chapter experiment with many different voices and dictions, Roach is never confessional, meditative, or conversational. The voices in his ear are those of very public poets: of Milton, Yeats, Marlowe, Shakespeare. There are a few isolated and diverse assays at political poetry ("The Tragedy", "Song of the Sleepers-Out", "For Freedom", "Eclogue for Christmas"); some of them succeed, some fail, but in terms of Roach's development all are dead-ends. He felt the urge to take up topical issues – felt indeed, the urgency of such issues for a West Indian poet of his era. But it was his habit to look beyond any immediate audience to the permanence of art, the embodiment of voice in form. The early poems investigate public speech and the positions to make it from, but apart from the revealing failure of "Song for the Sleepers-Out", he did not attempt demotic public speech, and as I have suggested already, "To Learie", in its raid on the subject matter of calypso, makes a claim for the authenticity of an alternative, a public speech that can transcend its occasion.

In this context, one of the last poems Roach published in the *Guardian* proves illustrative. "Poem (He plucked a burning stylus)" (1950) is the most frequently reprinted of the early poems, and a fine example of nearly oratorical public speech in the act of transcending its occasion – though the occasion here is erotic, not political. Presumably the reprintings indicate that "Poem" was regarded not only as excellent in itself, but as representative of Roach. It is not in fact much like the rest of his earliest work, but rather looks forward to work of the 1950s in such striking features as its elemental *mise en scene*, its reach for the sublime, and the incantatory power of its parallelisms. All these features are manifest in the opening stanza:

> He plucked a burning stylus from the sun
> And wrote her name across the endless skies
> And wrote her name upon the waxing moon
> And wrote her name among the thronging stars. (FR 67)

Because of their very high level of redundancy, the weight of these lines falls (perhaps disproportionately) on the changing prepositions and adjectives, but the passage sets the pattern for the entire poem, which relies heavily upon this kind of rapt repetition. As in the lines just quoted, a set of key words ("sun", "moon", "stars", "skies") re-echoes throughout, and every line of the second stanza ends with the word "remember".[55] All these are techniques for representing the heroic persistence of a lover in the face of failed love; by means of those key words, heavenly bodies are drawn into the poem, in order, as it were, to implicate them in the text, and so to sustain the assertion that nothing can "blot the legend from the ageless stars". Moreover, the expectation within the poem that structures and words will recur functions like a magic spell, aimed at inducing in the real world the return of love itself.

Though Roach had been writing off and on for a decade without producing any erotic poetry, "Poem" (along with some poems we will encounter in the next chapter, especially the similar but inferior "Token") readily invites the biographical speculation that Roach's career is ignited by an unhappy love. But we cannot ignore the extent to which this poem (like some of the others) is also an exercise in style. The characteristic redundancy certainly calls to mind the style of Yeats's poetry of the 1890s, and the opening lines especially seem to evoke the idiosyncratic fustian of Marlowe's blank verse. The impotent self-glorification of the unsuccessful suitor is a persistent trope of love poetry, but another factor here may be the very West Indian taste for preposterous boasting – a feature of public oratory and of the so-called "Midnight Robber" diction associated with Carnival, which we will have reason to consider more extensively in connection with some later poems.

If in this poem Roach presents for us a Tamurlane of the heart, there is still a characteristic insecurity in the bombast; Marlowe after all would certainly have written in the first person: "*I* plucked . . . and wrote *my* name." While some of the earliest poems in the *Herald* are written in the first person singular, we have encountered several instances in this chapter where Roach loses himself in the crowd of a "we" (e.g. "To Learie"), or interposes some figure between himself and the business of the poem (for example the "stranger" of "Stair of Song", the "poet and painter" of "Colour" – not to mention his pseudonyms). In "Tribute", where the central issue is the very value of poetry, Roach insulates himself behind *both* the communal "us" and the impersonal "half a poet". Whether or not Roach can be described in conventional terms as having found a voice and made a name for himself as early as 1949, we will see in the next two chapters that the new availability of robust media for the international dissemination of his work coincides with a surer sense of the range of his voice and the scope of his poetic agenda. At this point, Eric Roach does begin to write his *own* name across the sky – or at least across the trans-Atlantic airwaves of the BBC.

Chapter 2 – Going Public I: The BBC "Caribbean Voices" programme

As we have seen, Roach published a dozen poems locally in Trinidad and Tobago during 1938-1939. This early productivity had been cut off by the war, but once the tide of the war had turned in late 1944, his work began to appear occasionally in the *Guardian* again. It is easy to look back and dismiss *The Teachers' Herald* as a union house organ, and the *Guardian* as a setting for mere "newspaper verse". But there were virtually no alternatives; these were the best placements available.[1] The great fragility of the West Indian literary scene, its lack of material and financial resources, its reliance often on the initiative and energy of single individuals like Frank Collymore, A. J. Seymour, Edna Manley, Anson Gonzalez – these conditions are always in the background of Roach's career, and of his thinking about his career.

It is in the 1940s and particularly after the war that the West Indies came to recognize itself as both a political and a cultural entity. This recognition in turn encouraged a number of initiatives to comprehend Anglophone Caribbean literature on a regional rather than an island scale. Two were entirely local inventions – the magazines *Bim* (from 1942) and *Kyk-over-al* (from 1945) – and two originated in England: the "Caribbean Voices" programme of the BBC (1945-58), and the founding of the University College of the West Indies in 1948 as a branch of London University. Even before it was reorganized as the independent University of the West Indies, UCWI began publication of *Caribbean Quarterly* in 1949, a journal that from the start embodied a regional perspective. All of these were cultural anticipations of the idea of West Indian Federation, an idea whose political manifestation was destined to fail shortly after its institution in 1958. The coincidence of cultural and political federation had long been an ideal of West Indian visionaries like C. L. R. James and before him W. Adolphe Roberts, who took note of the topographical analogy between the American archipelago of the Caribbean and the Mediterranean archipelago of the Greek islands and from that basis projected a cultural analogy. They saw great creative potential, akin to that of ancient Greece, in the region's dialectic of proximity and isolation – the dialectic inherent, for example, in the situation of small islands within sight of one another but without a common language. Colonialist diction had saturated plantation realities with a bucolic aura; that falsifying vision was in the process of being preempted by the colonized and transformed into a positive programme, in much the same way that Négritude attempted to co-opt colonialist perceptions of the "darkness" of Africa for its own antithetical purposes.[2] Many were dubious of the viability of political and especially of economic federation, but belief in the value of cultivating cultural affinities between the islands was much more widespread; for example, an editorial in the *West Indian Review* as early as 1934, in the course of arguing that there could be "no kind of uniformity of political outlook" in the Caribbean, had stated categorically that "there is a Federation of the mind, and of the spirit" in the region.[3] At about the same time, the phrase "West Indian literature" begins to appear in print, though at first it refers to something expected to emerge in the future.[4]

It was against this background that Roach's work began to appear regularly and frequently in the Barbadian magazine *Bim* and on the weekly BBC "Caribbean Voices" programme – fourteen different poems in the short period between August 1949 and December 1950. This breakthrough depended on his contacts with several of the best local writers of his generation, particularly Telemaque, a fellow Tobagonian whose book had just been published (and then favourably reviewed in *Bim*, in Dec. 1948), and whose poems were featured on the BBC. George Lamming, who had been living in Trinidad, was an important link between Trinidadian writers and *Bim*. With the support of such colleagues, Roach achieved and retained access to the most prestigious regional media just at the time when the term "West Indian" was taking on new meanings and associations.

To say that Roach thus became a "West Indian" poet might amount to saying no more than that he appeared in *Bim* and on the BBC, but that identification has more meaningfully to do with the particular contours of his sense of subject and his sense of audience. As we saw in Chapter 1, Roach's earliest work had included its share of "universalist" poems, and its share of poems on stereotypically tropical subjects (immortelles, hibiscus, and the like), but none of the apologetic poems so typical of pre-Independence work from throughout the region, poems which seem capable of making a space for themselves only by acknowledging their inability to compete directly with European literature and experience. On the contrary, Roach began very early to distance himself from the paths of much contemporaneous work with poems on local events ("The Tragedy") and regional history ("Carib and Arawak"), and with poems which celebrate local heroes specifically for their ability to compete on the international stage and yet remain West Indians. His paean to the cricketer Learie Constantine is an obvious example. It celebrates a Trinidadian not as such, but specifically for his achievements as a representative of the region, and so serves also as a reminder that the West Indian cricket team was one of the earliest and most visible transnational ventures.[5]

What is most West Indian (apart from explicitly articulated themes) is his imagery, at every level of scale from momentary metaphor through controlling symbol to the fictive setting of an entire poem. The roots of his poetry are in rural Tobago, but his work routinely avoids specifically local detail for the sake of an expression that will be resonantly accessible to inhabitants of any of these islands. At the centre is what Walcott would call a "race-containing symbol": the peasant, his village, and his plot of ground, which for Roach together constitute the essential unit of West Indian identity.[6] Even the archetypal fisherman of so much West Indian poetry rarely makes an appearance in Roach; while there are, as we shall see, many similar images of isolation, independence and brute survival in the poems, Roach's emotional investment is in the freehold peasant – perhaps because that figure reflects the personal experience of a wider regional audience, but certainly because it communicates Roach's life-long insistence that, after a history of deracination, slavery, and exile, West Indian identity must begin in the intimate relationship to the land.[7]

The rest of this and the following chapter will look closely at the poems of 1949 and 1950, in which Roach emerges as a West Indian poet who addresses more than his own island. The emphasis will be on identifying the poet's resources of form, theme, style, and diction; tracing his early exploration and development of those resources; and considering how he chooses to present himself as a mature poetic voice and sensibility.

*

The BBC "Caribbean Voices" programme evolved at the end of World War II out of "Calling the West Indies," a programme produced during the war by the Jamaican poet and journalist Una Marson; "Caribbean Voices" was eventually discontinued in 1958 in conjunction with the transfer of political power from London to the West Indian Federation. Under the direction of Henry Swanzy and then V. S. Naipaul (after Swanzy's departure to Ghana in 1954), the programme broadcast to the Caribbean readings of fiction and poetry by West Indians. Many of the region's leading writers first became known in this way, and it is particularly important in the light of later developments that their voices were literally *heard*; authors resident in London often performed their own work, and others heard their words read by the likes of Lamming, Brathwaite, and Naipaul. "Caribbean Voices" was much more hospitable in those formative days than any metropolitan publisher to the accurate representation of West Indian speech, and an entire generation's experience of listening to the programme must be regarded as an important impetus behind the regional interest in orality and performance poetry after Independence.[8]

Unquestionably, selection for these broadcasts was a tonic for the writers, whether they regarded it as validation by the standards of the tradition, or more simply as a moment of glory. One's work was heard by one's friends, and it is worth noting that the BBC paid at the impressive rate of one guinea per minute.[9] This is approval and dissemination that cannot be gainsaid, and it was generally the only available approval, given the lack of any forum for poetry outside the newspapers and a few magazines of sometimes a very local and ephemeral nature (think of Roach's early work: how many frayed copies of *The Teachers' Herald* currently survive? How many will last even another decade?)

With the reading of a set of ten poems by Harold Telemaque in 1947 the programme began the practice of occasionally featuring a single author in relative depth. The event coincided with the publication of *Burnt Bush*, a volume in which 35 of Telemaque's poems appeared along with 26 by A. M. Clarke. It is worth noting that "Caribbean Voices" appears to have broadcast only a single poem by Clarke; the implied judgment is consistent with the virtual exclusion of Clarke's work from later West Indian anthologies – even from Sander's collection of Trinidadian literature during Clarke's heyday, the 1930s. Telemaque, on the other hand, was a frequent and highly regarded contributor to the program through 1953, the year of his second volume (*Scarlet*).[10] It was presumably Telemaque (or perhaps Lamming) who first brought Roach's work to the attention of the BBC. In 1949, the year of Roach's debut, Derek Walcott also appeared for the first time, with six poems (his book *25 Poems* had appeared in a private printing the previous year; there was a second edition in 1949). Walcott was a precocious nineteen at the time. The grouping of Walcott's poems is as oddly assorted and uneven as Roach's debut set, but there are two major poems, "As John to Patmos" and "A City's Death by Fire", and the first of them is a claim-staking manifesto which we will shortly need to consider in connection with Roach's corresponding inaugural statement, "Invocation".

Roach's work continued to appear frequently throughout the early 1950s. During 1953, for example, ten of his poems were presented in five different programs, and he was by this time offering very provocative material. We will consider these later poems in detail in the following chapter, but such compositions as "Haitian Trilogy" (with its passages in creole), "The Legend of Daaga", "In Mango Shade", "Despite Ancestral Rape", and "Caribbean Coronation Verse" (a poem addressed directly to the newly crowned Elizabeth II) are individually among the most politically engaged poems to be broadcast, and taken as a group they provide a very plausible basis for Roach's early reputation as the "blackest" of West Indian poets, and one of the angriest. It is noteworthy in this connection that the two most overtly political poets of that era are all but absent from the "Caribbean Voices" programme. George Campbell's epoch-making book *First Poems* was reviewed in 1946, but apart from a reading of the famous poem "Holy" in 1948, his work was not heard again until 1958, and it was only in that atmosphere of dismantling the colonial service in the face of federation that a single poem of Martin Carter's – "University of Hunger" – was broadcast. Roach's poetic style was richer than Campbell's and more accessible than Carter's, but the work of both poets would have played effectively on the radio. Unlike Roach, both Campbell and Carter were intimately associated with political movements in their respective countries, but it seems unlikely that the programme's editors would have been skittish about such associations.

In the late 1950s, when considerably less poetry was being broadcast on "Caribbean Voices" than formerly, Edward Brathwaite came to dominate the program both as a reader and as an author. It is indicative of Roach's visibility as a poet, and of his reputation (at least at the BBC) that in 1955, when nine of Brathwaite's poems were broadcast, Roach was represented by seven. Surprisingly, no new work by Roach was included after 1955. That might seem a reflection of the taste of the new editor, V. S. Naipaul, but Naipaul's remarks after the broadcast of individual poems of Roach's are always positive, even in cases where we would not expect the poems to be to Naipaul's taste. Faced for example with two poems, one in dialect and the other a fairly fierce account of the rape of the Amerindians, he saw in them "the strength and simplicity of the writer who has absolute command of his medium"; the dialect poem "The Ballad of Canga", he further judged was "extraordinarily effective, and the matter well supports the manner".[11]

Roach's work first appeared outside Trinidad and Tobago on Aug. 21, 1949, when a set of five poems were broadcast together: "Invocation", "March Trades", "Shallow Underground", "Token", and "The Old Man". Describing the author as "my friend E. M. Roach of Scarborough", Telemaque personally read the group of five poems, which he called "really promising".[12] Though we cannot be certain whether Roach, or Telemaque, or someone else was primarily responsible for the specific selection for broadcast, we do know that none of these particular poems had been published anywhere before, and it is apparent that they constitute a very self-consciously designed debut. Taken together, the poems demonstrate skill in several forms and in several registers of diction. These poems are never private or (with the possible exception of "Shallow Underground") elliptical in expression. On the other hand, Roach resists the temptation to appear exotic. While distinctively West Indian detail is evident in all but "Token", it is never merely ornamental, but bound up with the generation and subsequent development of Roach's themes. All of these poems make sense, if not their richest sense, to readers entirely unfamiliar with the Caribbean. Reading them closely, as a group, offers considerable insight into the portrait of himself as a poet that Roach wished to project.

*

"Invocation" is a self-consciously inaugural poem, conceived in terms of making and taking possession of a space for his art, and assuring its productivity and value. The poem begins as a prayer for the redemption of the speaker, not particularly as a poet but simply as a man – a Caribbean man with a history of slavery. Indeed, history appears at once, literally inscribed on the body of the speaker: he bears the whip-weals of slavery and so harbours the hate they engender. His "knotted hands" signify both the deformation caused by slave labour and the sinister power of such a heritage to incapacitate future productive work. In the first two stanzas he calls upon the sun, moon, and stars to transform his impaired soul, heart, hands, and eyes. More immediate than these celestial powers, the perceivable *agent* of transformation is represented in stanza III as simply the passage of time. These first three stanzas, with their strongly correlative verse and effective rhetorical climax could conceivably stand as a complete poem.[13] As a whole, they constitute a prayer to reclaim the ground of his soul, by relieving the burden of a bitter history and offering some promise of a better fate. The poet envisions himself enfolded in a fertile and apparently *ornamental* garden (a true Eden; no farm or homestead here), created and maintained by the work of time: the years, the flowing winds, the streaming waters.

The fourth and final stanza then moves forward to redeploy in more compressed form all the elements of the foregoing rhetorical structure – the invocation of a transforming power, the naming of the object to be transformed, the combined agency of years, winds, waters – in order to speak not of the man but of his *verse*. This is not simply a second related subject, but a redefinition of the first; the progress of the poetic argument is not so much "my soul *and* also my verse" but something more like "my soul – *I mean*, my verse." In the course of the poem both are envisioned as plots of ground; both are "marshes" to be reclaimed, one transformed into a "garden", the other into "fair acres":

> O Muse, O Goddess, turn my turbid verse
> From sour marshes . . .
> Into fair acres where the pouis bloom . . .
> Where willow fingers reap from the wind's lyres
> Rich fluent rhythms
> That shall nourish these and other years. (FR 52)

The years, winds, and waters recur together in this closing stanza, but the waters have become metaphorical in response to the change of subject from man to verse. Instead of literal waters we have "rich *fluent* rhythms" which are described as "nourishing" and are produced by willow trees – trees doubly associated with water: botanically (since they tend to grow beside streams) and literarily, via the familiar Biblical image of willows beside the rivers of Babylon.

The word "willow" presents the one interpretive crux in the poem. Many readers will take the willow as an entirely literary object, and find it hard to ignore that familiar set of associations with exile, oppression, grief and song, even though the familiar image seems to be brought into the poem bereft of those traditional allusions. But Roach probably has in mind not the Biblical tree (a poplar most likely), nor the weeping willow most North American readers are likely to visualize, but instead a tree very common throughout the Caribbean, the casuarina. These tall, almost feathery evergreens are frequently grown in rows along beaches or property lines as windbreaks – the tree is also known in some localities as whistling pine, a name which adds to the confusion but aptly describes its characteristic sound and appearance.[14] So while not exactly disruptive, the exilic imagery is perhaps unavoidably present without being at all engaged in the poem's business. Instead Roach uses his casuarina/willows to carry out a reversal of the typically Romantic image of the Aeolian harp or wind-harp (an image which as we will see reappears in important connections throughout his work). In this instance the willow is not a passive lyre that the wind plays (as we might expect); instead the willow's fingers play rhythms on the lyres of the wind. In the poem's complex economy, it is these rhythms that the willows reap from the wind that will nourish the plot – his work – year after year.

This poem itself, though free of rhyme and regular metrical form, is characterized by "rich rhythms", both on the metrical scale of the individual line and on the larger scale of the poem's overarching rhetorical structure of parallel invocations (to sun, stars, moon, and muse). I have mentioned already the functional resemblance of "Invocation" to Derek Walcott's "John to Patmos", which was broadcast only a few months earlier. The parallel extends beyond the subject matter to the high diction that both poets seem to have felt as appropriate to mark the occasion of a poetic debut. But where Walcott's model is Dylan Thomas, for Roach a version of Milton is the powerful sponsor. Milton's influence is apparent at such significant junctures as the very opening ("Sun of my day make dry, / Make dry the dark green swamps") and the sharply inverted syntax of the climactic third stanza ("Me, let the circling years"). The odd adjectival use of a noun as in "*legend* hair" (or "Circe lure" in "Shallow Underground" and "wizard laughter" in "Token") is surely also Miltonic. But Roach's Milton recalls the self-consciously recuperated Milton of the 18th century, the remote source of true poetic energy to which Collins and Gray and the early Blake sought access. In Roach's case it is colonial marginality as well as the bulk of Edwardian and late Victorian poetry that seem to cut him off from that power. So in this poem Roach's syntax moves toward the sinuous, but within that frame the flatness of the adjectives is chronic, especially in the many lines constructed on the classic (and classicizing) 18th century model: adjective + noun + adjective + noun. This is patent in "The flowing winds, the streaming waters," or "With equal freedoms and with common love," and the pattern even infects lines which merely *seem* to have that structure, because of a corresponding reliance on two-word units of sense standing out in the grammatical underbrush, as in these two neighbouring lines:

Into *fair acres* where the *pouis bloom*
As *lavish-golden* as your *legend hair*.

I dwell on the poetic pedigree of "Invocation" in order to open up a question to which we will find Roach frequently returns, both implicitly in his practice and explicitly in his criticism: how – and where – will he find models for a poetic diction that can communicate the kind of things he has to say to the audience he intends to reach? Formulating the question in that way also introduces the matter of audience, of the social dimension of the poem, to this discussion of "Invocation". Again comparison with "As John to Patmos" is revealing. For all his later reputation as a "humanist" and confessional poet, for all his recurrent anxiety about the issue as his career unfolds, Walcott in this early poem declares his decision to remain at home and swears to the people of the place that he will be their poet. There is no such point made in "Invocation". In spite of the vision of "equal freedoms and common love", there is no hint of a community or even of other people in this poem; it is focused on a solitary figure who is ambiguously – polysemously – the soul, a poet, and a man of the land, and who seems to share the world only with the elements and the cosmos. Strangely, apart from the prayer "unbend my knotted hands" there is no suggestion that this man will do any work or otherwise contribute to the reclamation; he anticipates living in a garden, and the only reaping in the poem is done by the willows which inhabit, after all, not the speaker's actual surroundings but rather the "fair acres" which *metaphorically* signify his verse. Not too much should be made of this, considering the importance of labour throughout Roach's work, but it draws attention to a matter with which Roach is clearly preoccupied in the poems of this period: the problematic relationship between a poet's vocation and his community.

*

The second item in the broadcast, "March Trades", is a poem of natural description *moralisé*, drawing conclusions that touch upon history, politics, and personal character from a consideration of the seasonal Caribbean experience of the strong winds of March. It begins grandly:

Earth leans the arctic
Once more to the sun
As the fond lover
After anger's done
Returns unto the loved one. (FR 53)

In the temperate zones, spring comes in (as we say) like a lamb, and the poem can speak of it as an infant, as a baby "being born". In the tropics, however, the coming of the same season instead "wakes" sleeping lions – the trade winds, natural forces already in their prime (the trade winds in this poem have adult manes). Roach begins – as he often does throughout his career – by envisioning how the rock of island or continent squares off to resist "the savagery of wind and sea".[15]

The opening of the central stanza, especially to the extent that it is merely descriptive, is the poem's weakest part. The revelation that when clouds are shredded by the wind, "fluffs . . . scud like . . . puffs" doesn't get us very far; similarly the compounded inversions of lines 24-26 seem an unprofitable stylistic investment: "Are riven from the boughs / leaves ochreous / of cedar, plum and shrub". In a different kind of poem the fleeting possibility that "ochreous of" functions by analogy to "redolent of" might be a coup, but in this instance, having sorted out the sense to produce "ochreous leaves of cedar, plum and shrub are riven from the bough," few readers will feel the game was worth the candle. Is the wind supposed to have dishevelled even the lines? As the stanza proceeds, however, its language becomes sharper and more controlled, and at the same time the inherent attitude toward the winds becomes distinctly more positive. After all the shredding and fretting, after mango and immortelle are stripped of their blooms, there are indications that this violence is part of the process of renewal. The winds shear the blooms from the mango trees, we are told,

> As they shear the fire from Immortelles
> To startle the dark wood,
> As they shear sheath from bud
> And seed from shattered pod.

These lines suggest that the bud *must* be unsheathed in order to bloom; the pod *must* be shattered to free the seeds that propagate the parent. The image of the immortelle as wood stripped of its fire is thus particularly remarkable. It is obviously an image of deprivation, disfigurement, even loss of spirit, but at the same time, by drawing attention to the blooms as metaphorically a "fire", it is also an image of rescue and salvation – wood *with* its fire isn't going to last very long. It is as if without the shearing of the blooms the wood itself would be consumed by them (we will see that Roach often makes use of the symbolic implications of trees like the immortelle and poui that flower on bare wood, and sprout leaves only after the blooms fall).

The final stanza moves us from the bud in its sheath and the seed in its pod to the West Indian in his house (which is also by implicit synecdoche his island, and by explicit simile his ship):

Close eastern windows
While the high wind blows
Too wildly in the eaves
And curtains fill like sails
And the rooms fret like cabins
Of gale gripped galleons.

This stanza goes on to draw the poem's conclusions: it moves from description to exhortation, from indicative to imperative verbs that essentially repeat the same advice adduced earlier from observation of nature: "close eastern windows"; "make all ship-shape"; "let all be girt . . . to take the buffet". But it is not at all a matter of hiding from the weather (whether natural, historical, or political).[16] The turn at the close of stanza II prepares us to interpret this correctly: a tight ship is what makes the bold adventure possible; you resist the buffet *in order to* prosper in it (a persistent principle throughout the corpus). For bud and seed resistance is futile in the short run, but an essential act (even in its futility) in the long run. The poet's island can resist the "savagery", as we know from stanza I; his house, his homestead – his ship, as that house moves through history – must be like the island and like the ships of the past to negotiate the weather of the present (this was 1949, when talk of self-government, federation, and independence filled the air, and the great migration to England was about to begin).

"March Trades" is technically the most interesting of the poems in Roach's first BBC broadcast; by its use of rhyme as a kind of structural pointing it anticipates an important feature of his later practice. Here the five lines of the opening sentence mark out an evident ABCBB pattern of rhyme words: arctic / sun / lover / done / one. The next clause comprises two lines ending "zone / born," while the following clause ends both the entire sentence and the 12th line with the word "ocean" – distant in reading time, but close enough in sound to the repeated "B" rhyme (done / one) to convey a sense of closure. Except for "sand" and "island" near the end, there is no further rhyme in the first stanza, which comes to an end with a third long sentence stopped not by rhyme but by the poem's longest and most resounding line so far, its first full blank verse line: "sturdier than savagery of wind and sea". Stanzas II and III each end with a bundle of rhymes or near-rhymes: stanza II closes with the sequence quoted above (wood / bud / pod) and stanza III brings home the moral of the poem like this:

> Let all be girt
> In sinew, heart and spirit
> To take the buffet
> And to prosper in it.

This use of incrementally increasing rhyme as means of structural articulation and progressive closure is something Roach investigates frequently; we will see it next in "Oh, No More Now".

The poem's most striking use of rhyme occurs in the very prominent passage on history in the third and final section. In the course of drawing the poem's moral these lines appear:

> Make all ship-shape
> In stubborn Colon's simple way,
> In the black slave-traders way,
> In buccaneer and pirate way,
> In the sturdy sea tramp's way;
> Make all ship-shape.

Roach sets this off from the rest of the stanza as a sort of flight of imagination and rhetoric by several prominent devices: the parallelism of the prepositional phrases, the sweep of the time frame through several centuries (especially in contrast to the vast but cyclical and a-historical time of the seasons which otherwise dominates the poem), and the gesture of repeating a line ("Make all ship-shape") in order to signify a return to "normal" discourse in the poem. These four successive lines end with the word "way" for rhetorical reasons, and so chime without constituting "rhyme" in the usual sense – the repetition functions as a kind of suspension, a marking of time behind the solo flight. But it is noteworthy that the long "a" vowel sound of "way," so common in rhyming poetry in English, does not occur at the end of any other line in the poem; indeed, only one other line ends in any vowel at all – interestingly enough, the final line of stanza one, already noted for its closural force on other grounds.[17] Whether intuitive or calculated, these effects demonstrate Roach's considerable technical skill.

In spite of its many imperative verbs, evident even in these brief quotations, and in spite of its eagerness to give advice, this poem, like its predecessor, has setting but no people. The poem goes out of its way to avoid pronouns, and apart from one reference to "our ever glittering torrid centre", there is no basis upon which to decide whether it is addressed to the poet himself, some "us", or a "you". Like the ambiguity about the figure of the poet/farmer, the absence or deliberate obscuring of such pronominal discrimination is characteristic of Roach's poetry even as late as "At Guaracara Park". Repeatedly the poems range freely, offering insights formulated in such a way that they apply to the human spirit in the abstract, to the idiosyncratic self of this particular poet, to a specific peasant community, or to an idealized folk.

*

The next poem, "Shallow Underground", is the most populous in the series, though the human figures appear only in long shot. It takes place on the evening of the full moon, when the moon rises just as the sun sets, and the heart of the poem is a correspondingly stark contrast between a happy crowd of lovers and children dancing on the green in the twilight, "their precious ignorance / buoyed by innocence" (FR 55), and a solitary buried skull, presumably the skull of a slave, for whom the full moon never brought any hope of romance, or any hope "that the dragging feet / should be given to dancing". This poem actually begins with a smoke screen that obscures the scene, presumably throughout. The idea is underscored by the momentary obscurity of the opening lines' harshly inverted syntax:

> Makes a long soft screen
> Across dusk's graying green
> Somebody's blue bush smoke.

Even the emphatically placed indefinite pronoun ("somebody's") adds to the effect. To begin in smoke invites disaster, and the invitation is unfortunately accepted; even the form is bedevilled by obscurity.[18] Roach's quatrains of iambic trimeter are appropriate for the sort of poem he has in mind, but the effect is weakened by his further commitment to rhyming resolutely in couplets. Because the poem is serious and the rhyming is so exposed in this form, several approximations that result in awkward accents (e.g. rose/gorgeous; skull/hopeful), along with two instances (stanzas III and IX) where there simply is no rhyme, come across as lapses of resolution. A reader is even less likely to tolerate forced or defective rhyme in a poem where it is clear the poet is quite willing to forego rhyme entirely on occasion. As a whole, the poem's formal constraints lead to trouble, as the meaning and syntax often have to lurch for the sake of a rhyme.

In particular this leaves the *balance* of the poem's various elements quite unclear; for several stanzas the poem seems to be casting about for an approach to its central conception.

Be that as it may, the vision of the dead slave underlying the pastoral is a powerful one; it might be an insight out of the anti-slavery poems of Blake or Cowper, and the gothic element here also recalls some of Blake's very early poems. But having established this contrast to be at once historically commonplace and somehow uncanny, like that between the sun and the full moon, the poem is not very clear about what we readers are to do with it. It is after all only a guess that the skull belonged to a black slave; without the drums and our knowledge that the poem comes from the Caribbean (for which the only internal evidence is the phrase "bush smoke"), other relationships than race and class might just as well present themselves. Again thinking of Blake, for example, the skull might plausibly belong to one of those repressed and now resentful souls whose voices of experience – however problematic in themselves – haunt the margins of the world of innocence. Some such view is actually supported by the poem's unlikely but undeniable reference at one point (lines 21-28) to both the most famous sentence in Gray's "Ode on a Distant Prospect of Eton College" and that statement's context. In the sixth and seventh stanzas, just before the first mention of the buried skull, Roach is writing of the "halcyon weather" of those whose "hope and love and light / Is not engulfed of night", whose "precious ignorance [is] buoyed by innocence". Gray's too familiar lines – "where ignorance is bliss, 'tis folly to be wise" – mark the point in that poem which corresponds closely to the situation here, but viewed from a perspective more sympathetic to the ignorant innocents. It is possible to imagine the skull as pathetically forgotten, or as a permanently unresolved accusation, or as an imminent threat of deserved consequences. In contrast to the imagery of poems like the "Haitian Trilogy" or "Carib and Arawak", the wronged skull here seems unlikely to sprout or flower – no life comes from its death. That it is only a fragment, a skull rather than a buried body (such as in "The Old Man"), emphasizes its incapacity to act as well as its extreme deracination from identity, from history. That observation might help to narrow the interpretive possibilities, but what seems crucial – and undecidable – is the skull's relation to the dancers: is this the relic of an ancestor, or of an ancestor's victim? We know almost as little about these dancers as about the skull. Several different attitudes toward them are invited by the poem, but the relative value of the alternatives is indeterminate, making it difficult to know how we should finally be feeling about them. In practice, the problem of the dancers (and to a lesser extent of the identity of the skull) is unfortunately resolved not by anything the poem provides but by the individual reader's unreflective predisposition: for example, some will spontaneously envision the dancers as white, a family of planters, and an interpretation follows easily; others will spontaneously see them as black, with quite different but equally convincing interpretive consequences.

The closing stanza adds yet another element to the obscure confrontation, emphasizing with ominous effect that the slave did not merely lack an opportunity for dancing (and so for "hope and love and light"), but positively had to suppress a powerful impulse to dance:

> Even though the dark wood
> And the hopeless blood
> Shuddered to the thrums
> Of the uttering drums.

The "dark wood" first mentioned here is pointedly *not* in the same open green where the happy crowd is dancing, but the text offers no more than that. The dark wood could be a realm of maroonage, of a remembered or mythical "Africa", or of purely psychic atavism. There is even the possibility that the drums are real; that the poem's somewhat belated disclosure of the skull beneath the ground here leads to the almost-*too*-late disclosure of another entire community of dancers, hitherto eclipsed, screened from view, as the skull was. But while any interpretation of the poem may find itself investing heavily in such speculations to round out the reading, the meagre textual support quickly turns interpretation into the composition of a new poem. Having brought all these hypotheses into play, I feel duty bound to produce some satisfying resolution. But the poetic problem in "Shallow Underground" is that it offers a voltage gap without a spark: the antithetical happy crowd and unhappy skull are presented to us, the drums begin to sound – and the curtain falls; nothing comes of the tension, and though we are given plenty to play with, we are not given enough to extrapolate confidently.

In "Invocation" the word "willow" is a kind of fork in the road of the text: hardly any reader would consider the term ambiguous, but some will understand the term in its local sense and others in its conventionalized literary sense, and as a result those readers' poems will differ. West Indian writers have grown accustomed to anticipating this consequence of the fact that they routinely address multiple audiences.

In "Shallow Underground", however, there are several such forks in the text, with substantially greater consequences for understanding, and in each case the choices hinge not on differences between Caribbean and metropolitan nomenclature but on something all but independent of one's knowledge. In this case, choices reveal what we might call the *political* predisposition of the reader – insisting that the term include not only various ideological prejudices but also the reader's accumulated experience with and habituated response to certain scenarios, literary conventions, and symbols. It can hardly have been Roach's intention, but, to the extent that "Shallow Underground" presents merely the dancers, the skull, and the offstage drums, this is less a poem than a Rorschach to elicit secrets from the reader – to dig out the skulls under *that* ground.

*

In spite of its weaknesses, there is much to discuss in "Shallow Underground"; the same cannot be said of "Token", little more than a freehand sketch for a poem. The subject is love, but love here is a matter between the poet and sublimely elemental nature – the beloved is entirely absent even as a memory, let alone as an agent. He is much more in love with being in love than with any living thing, and he is most in love with telling his love to the winds, the stars, the earth, the rocks, the trees, the waves "all one by one" (that list recalls the series of cosmic entities addressed in "Invocation"). Several other features are also familiar: the numerous imperative verbs, the absence of human society, and the strong impulse to address nature with one's individual business. Not surprisingly, this is the only one of the five broadcast poems with no historical dimension. Even more than in "Invocation", Roach here employs the high – almost aureate – diction which he seems to associate with the theme of heroic solitude; we will soon hear that diction mature as he finds other, more successful ways to articulate his sense of being isolated in the universe, and of not knowing whether to regard himself therefore as *rara avis* or a strange bird.

*

The series ends with "The Old Man", a clear and compelling poem that matches the force of "March Trades". It is one of only two poems in the group in which Roach commits himself to a regular stanzaic structure, but by comparison "Shallow Underground" seems more an art-ballad, calling to mind revivals of the traditional form by the Romantics, or even by a modern poet like Hardy. "The Old Man" deploys a naive but forceful diction which Roach uses only occasionally (in "Ballad of Canga", for example); it recalls the studied plainness of Ian MacDonald, and something like it appears among others of his West Indian contemporaries when they take up folk subjects. The opening, especially, is deceptively folksy and ingratiating:

> The old man is as old,
> As old as kingdom come,
> So old, his days drum
> Muddled in his head,
> His sight blurs in the sun. (FR 58)

This is the first of three stanzas that describe the old man (incidentally establishing the poem's pattern of repeating the end of the first line of each stanza at the start of the second line: "The old man is as old, / As old . . . ," "The old man is as gray, / As gray . . ." etc.); the account of his appearance leads up to a formulation of his significance as witness to and embodiment of "our century of salvation": "He is our history's / sagest contemplation".

From that base the fourth stanza makes a leap into complex metaphor:

> The old man is a scroll,
> A scroll on which I see
> My strong ancestral tree
> With roots of iron tapped
> To thirsty shale and rock.

The doubleness of the metaphor (scroll *and* tree) is curious, as is the unexpectedly personalized interpretation: *I* see *my* tree. The image of the vigorous plant rooted in rock is the most persistent single image in Roach's corpus; in the present instance that metaphor alone – the man as tree – would seem to make the poem's point adequately, especially since the final image is of a tree growing from this man's grave. Yet the interposed metaphor of the scroll brings several things with it. For one, there is of course a Biblical aura to the image. While the poet can somehow see the inscribed tree, the statement that the man has "sealed our century of salvation" seems to suggest that the scroll is sealed, a closed book, and so a reminder of the sealed scrolls of prophecy – and of history – that haunt both Testaments. In addition, the layers of such a rolled-up scroll, the pages of the book laid one on another, and the years of the century which the old man has "seen and set and sealed" one by one – all these images introduce the idea of sedimentation, of history as eventful and layered (indeed, the tree's seasonal growth rings would do the same, but Roach nowhere uses that image). This is a more fully articulated version of the notion of the buried past sketched in "Shallow Underground". Eventually the old man is buried in his own proper layer of earth; he becomes part of history, as earlier he had witnessed and recorded it.

Before the revered ancestral figure can be laid to rest, however, Roach introduces a calculated and explicit breaking of both form and tone. The fifth stanza insists fiercely on a turn away from the old man and the imagery associated with him. Grammatical disjunctions are enacted by both the opening "But" and the shift of verb mood established by the first four of seven imperatives that charge the second half of the poem. There is a disjunction of imagery (he has been a scroll, but now we "turn the *page*") and a disruption of form (the pattern of repeating phrases noted above, which persisted through four stanzas, is brought to a halt by the intrusion of the word "Break" just at the point where another repetition is expected). Most compelling is a disjunction of affect: the poem has been positively devout in praising the old man as embodying and enclosing history (he has "set and sealed" the century), but suddenly that enclosure is seen in a negative light ("break from history's *limit*"):

> *But turn, turn* the page,
> *Break* from history's limit,
> *Adventure* like Colon
> Within the earth's full circuit
> Upon an opening ocean
> After the present stars,
> The bright inviting stars
> Gleaming where they stand
> Over wave and island,
> Wizard to the spirit. (FR 58) [my emphasis][19]

The man who contains history is seen as contained by it, and the alternative image, of Columbus adventuring "within the earth's full circuit", is so energetic that it mimetically bursts the bounds of the stanza, which goes on at double length, ten lines instead of five, to express the elation of "adventure". Interestingly, the sense of the passage is essentially complete by the end of the normal limit of a five-line stanza; the additional five lines are a strung-out prepositional phrase, whose length has the further effect of emphasizing that adventuring is a response to the "inviting stars" which are "wizard to the spirit".

In "March Trades", too, it is the mention of Columbus that precipitates the disruption of form. This requires some attention. In both poems Roach plainly urges appropriation of the adventurer's character and sense of self, of limitless capacity; he seems to be saying the history of slavery and domination should not foreclose heroic aspiration – let the colonized become in their turn Colons. This image of Columbus as adventurer Roach had first voiced in "Discovery". Yet to invoke it here is to propose a role model quite different from the one who has served as the eponymous hero of "The Old Man". The old man has seen the passage of history, the changes in a remarkable "century of salvation" (say 1838-1938, from Emancipation to the roots of the Independence movements). But now he is bedded down in that history, and the poet insists on leaving him there, living a new life, envisioning ourselves (or perhaps only himself – as usual in Roach this distinction is difficult to make) not as the passive contemplator, but as the swashbuckler. In contrast to the man rooted in and nourishing his soil (an image that for Roach in this poem and many others carries enormous weight), the poet here fights to imagine and gain access to a completely different kind of mythic and indeed ancestral figure. The struggle (against Roach's own inclinations and pieties) is evident in the rhetorical and structural breaks required to make room for Colon. In "March Trades", for example, the image of the adventurous seafarer is domesticated by an accompanying conceit of the West Indian island as a boat, sailing bravely into its post-colonial future. But in this poem Roach faces the problematic relation of the adventurer to history. He cannot carry the baggage of his history except in the most reduced form, a few household gods or perhaps nothing more than the confidence distilled out of his sense of self and heritage. It is possible to be both preserver and maker of history (Walcott sees Aeneas in this light),[20] but for Roach the appeal of adventure is itself always a matter of intense isolation – on the sea, under the stars – and its rewards are almost inaccessibly private. Yet in this group of poems at least, the alternative, the possession of one's piece of land, is also presented as a strangely private act. There are those references to "*our* century", "*our* history", and the old man is compared to "kingdom come" and to Jericho, proverbially the oldest city in the world; but, as we by now expect, there is no community in this poem for man to belong to – no kingdom, no city, not even a village or family.

In this poem, for the first time, Roach addresses what will remain for him a fundamental and poetically productive conflict, that between the lives represented by the old man and by Colon, between the appeal of rootedness and the appeal of solitary flight. We will soon see how he engages in this conflict by manipulating the fields of images respectively associated with the horns of his dilemma: the flowering rock images and those of soaring birds. For the present, the conflict is only acknowledged, not negotiated. At the end of the poem the old man is in his beautiful grave, a sanctifying presence in the land. In a manner of speaking, of course, no reader who has followed the advice of the poem will get to its last stanza; having turned away, we leave behind not only the man but the land itself, and thus also the linear plot of *history*, living instead in the perpetual present of the open ocean, a theatre of action beyond "history's limit". In this vision, time stops even in the heavens, which are described as if they were immobile: "the *present* stars . . . *stand* over wave and island". Yet, at least rhetorically, limit remains; Roach is careful in his choice of the word "circuit" – the wider horizon is still a boundary – and he underscores the point by rhyming it with "limit". At its valedictory end the poem returns to the old man in his setting and does not go off the edge of the world with Columbus:

> Leave to the worn old man
> The hour which time has given him,
> Grow myrtle on his grave
> In sad kind memory of him,
> Let the threnoding willow
> Keep a tall legend of him.

With this final stanza that lengthens to six lines, alternate lines rhyming very effectively on repetitions of the word "him" in unstressed position, the poem ends memorializing the old man, but also burying him (unstressing him), turning away from him to a different sort of future. He will live in legend, while his grave is marked with myrtle and "threnoding willow" – the willow which, as in "Invocation", plays on the wind the music of the man's "tall legend". At the same time, this elegiac conclusion looks ahead to Roach's most widely known poem, "Homestead", where the old man in question is the poet's own father. As an ambivalent whole, however, "The Old Man" anticipates Roach's much later, indeed final, articulations of his relation to history. Apart from the unevenness of the verse and the relatively narrow range of reference, this could almost be a poem from the 1970s, when it is himself he sees as an old man, and specifically as an old man of a gone time.

*

Since the interrelationships of these poems are indicated in the foregoing discussion, and since generalizations based on so small a sample would be of limited usefulness, I will defer consideration of the BBC poems as a group until the end of the following chapter, where they can be analyzed in conjunction with the poems Roach was publishing in *Bim* during the same short period.

CHAPTER 3 – GOING PUBLIC II: *BIM*

Harold Telemaque had first introduced Roach's poems on the BBC by saying that, "They breathe the true atmosphere of my beloved Tobago, the Arcadia of the Caribbean."[1] Encountering that remark after such close attention to the texts of the poems, it is hard to resist the impulse to look back through them again, in search of the specifically Tobagonian touches we must have missed. Whatever Telemaque was responding to among the unpopulated, elemental landscapes and abstract emotions of those poems seems irretrievable. But the atmosphere of Tobago is much more apparent in the poems to which we now turn, those published in *Bim* during 1949-1950.

The venerable Barbadian literary magazine *Bim* had its inauspicious origins in the Young Men's Progressive Club. In 1938 the club began publishing a small magazine, *YMPC Journal*, that offered light creative writing, topical comment, and club news.[2] Thus it was comparable in tone and content to the weekly literary page of the *Trinidad Guardian* of the same era. This *Journal* continued to appear until 1942, when two members, E. L. Cozier and W. Therold Barnes, enlisted the aid of Frank Collymore to help them produce a more ambitious publication. From this collaboration *Bim* was born, its first issue appearing in December of that year, perhaps because Christmas was already the traditional time in the West Indies for literary supplements. In the early days, *Bim*, like its predecessor, was buoyant and frivolous, full of quizzes, nonsense verse, and anecdotal fillers. In 1946 a small sampler of poems by a dozen West Indian writers was introduced like this: "We've put all the poems together, so that they may be the more easily skipped."[3] In short the early *Bim* was a modest magazine very much of and for Barbados. It is with the tenth issue in 1949 that *Bim* comes of age as an explicitly *West Indian* journal. Its cover is unique in listing contributors by country (for this reason Baugh calls it "a historic document"),[4] and the representation is impressive: Lamming and five others from Trinidad, Gloria Escoffery and A. L. Hendriks from Jamaica, Derek Walcott and Harry Simmons from St. Lucia, A. J. Seymour from British Guiana, as well as a dozen Barbadians. *Bim* #11, in which Roach makes his first appearance, included the work of seventeen poets from seven West Indian territories, and #12 carried its regional mandate to its fullest extent by including pieces on the art and literature of the French Caribbean.

In the years before Independence, *Bim* was certainly the place to be seen, and in conjunction with "Caribbean Voices", it established Roach's reputation. Between 1949 and 1962 he published 32 poems in *Bim*; only three issues during those years do not include at least one poem of his. The raw numbers are a revelation: when Roach appeared in *Bim* for the last time, in #34, he had published more poems there than any single poet except Collymore himself, whose total (a whopping 63) reflects his many short comic verses. Otherwise, Brathwaite by that time had published 25 poems, Walcott 23, and the now unregarded Phyllis Inniss 18. Even as late as 1972, the date of *Bim*'s cumulative index, only four poets had yet met or surpassed Roach's total: Collymore of course, and Brathwaite (43), and two Jamaicans: Mervyn Morris (45) and A. L. Hendriks (32). Not Walcott (27), and not Ian MacDonald (24).[5] Judging from *Bim*, Roach in 1962 had a well-established position as one of the three or four finest poets in the region – a position which in 1972, even after ten years of silence, was hardly overshadowed.

*

Roach's long relationship with *Bim* began in December 1949 not so much with a debut as with a preview. Two of his poems ("Oh, No More Now" and "Stranger, Beware") appear in a mini-anthology of poems collectively identified as "Work in Progress". The poems are by various hands including Walcott, Raymond Barrow, and Geoffrey Drayton. Several pieces from this group (including "Oh, No More Now") were later presented together on the "Caribbean Voices" programme (May 21, 1950). These two poems are distinctly different in style from the BBC set broadcast just a few months earlier, in August. Their style is more lyrical, with a lighter texture and more fluent pulse. Both are love poems, and the subject they share – fidelity, and a faithless lover on another island – suggests they draw on Roach's personal experience. Even so, there is nothing remotely confessional about the poems; as usual in Roach's work, actual personal experience is an impetus to art but rarely its subject matter. Still, the notion that these poems aim for universality must be tempered by the unemphatically but distinctly Eastern Caribbean setting they share, indicated by the casuarina trees and the general topography.

Whether the decision is Roach's or an editor's, it is notable that someone decided these should be his first poems in *Bim*. They are poems that illustrate competence and familiarity with the tradition, rather than the kind of idiosyncrasy and boldness of gesture that characterize the first BBC poems. Perhaps because they were to be presented as part of a mixed group, these particular poems do not come across as the introduction of a new voice; in fact both are written in a way that makes the appropriation of a traditional voice part of the exercise. Though the manner is very different, Roach, like the young Ezra Pound, seems to be finding personae for intimate experience via archaic or self-consciously "poetic" diction and form. To choose a parallel closer to home, these sound not unlike Walcott's poems of the same period. Both share an inclination to classicize either with respect to the Greek or the British tradition, and even the specific theme of erotic jealousy. Given the nature of the West Indian audience for poetry, it may be the case that virtually anyone who read these poems in *Bim* would already have heard Roach's work on the BBC, but it is worth asking, if only hypothetically, what impression of Roach would be left on readers who first encountered him through these poems? The objective they exemplify is quite conservative: the successful transformation of personal experience in a West Indian setting into an accessible poem that would not seem out of place in the British literary tradition. Beyond that, they convey not so much a personality or a voice as an aspiration to technical assurance, or at least a sensitive response to the technical challenge which is also a face of the received tradition.

In "Stranger, Beware", by far the lesser of these two love poems, the betrayed poet addresses a warning to his lover's new man. In the poem's most interesting and sustained passage, he urges the new lover to ask her to count out all the hoarded days of her past for him, coin by coin, with this objective in mind:

> If on a coin you see an image
> Black as Tartar, sad as Caesar's,
> Give it back unto the giver.
> What is Caesar's leave for Caesar. (FR 61)

Caesar's coin is of course an image out of the New Testament, but the conceit (in conjunction with an aggrieved but threatening tone) seems also to recall the conclusion of Wyatt's famous sonnet describing a similar though not identical situation: "Who so list her hunt (I put him out of doubt) / As well as I may spend his time in vain. . . . / There is written her fair neck round about: / "*Noli me tangere*, for Caesar's I am."[6] Roach's poem continues beyond this idea, however, vamping on light, conventional imagery from the erotic tradition, which often seems to be selected more for the sake of a rhyme than for any other reason:

> And his love does brood like mountains
> All around her and within her,
> And his love does flow like fountains.

Gianetti finds the repetition of lines from stanza to stanza "recognisably West Indian in manner", taking on "a peculiarly West Indian tone of challenge", but the actual line in question – "lightly turn and fondly ask her" – seems to belie this interpretation.[7] In fact several other lines are repeated in the poem (often with variations, as in the lines just cited), and the repetitions frequently occur across stanza breaks with evidently formal intentions. For North Americans, unfortunately, this way of repeating phrases, coupled with this particular meter, interposes the considerable distraction of Longfellow's "Hiawatha" between the reader and any appreciation of Roach's poem.

"Oh, No More Now" is the lament of a patient but increasingly hopeless lover. The argument of the poem is straightforward: out of his grief he fancifully poses questions to Penelope, whose waiting for Ulysses was rewarded, but the response comes, in the form of further questions, not from legendary Penelope but from a nearby stand of casuarinas. The poem is immediately striking for its technical self-consciousness, its subtle attention to rhyme and mimetic form. The opening stanza of the poem counterpoints an unusually clear pattern of rhyme (ABACDD) against an eccentric metrical scheme that only gradually become the basis for an insistent metrical norm of double dactyls in the two middle stanzas. The poem's arrival at this rhythm constitutes a witty allusion to Homeric verse, since it occurs in a stanza which explicitly treats an Homeric subject.

Stanza II begins seemingly without rhyme, but there is distinct formal play in progress:

> Fond queen of Ithaca
> What were you waiting for?
> Did your love's greenness
> Petrify yet green

In hope for Ulysses?
Did the black arrow sing
The triumphs of sweet spring
To your blood returning?[8] (FR 60)

The word "queen" links aurally with "greenness" and "green," while incidentally the trick of associating "Ulysses" by eye-rhyme and final position with "greenness" symbolically unites the hero with his wife. This reunion, the story of which is the subject of the stanza, is further celebrated with the triplet of rhyme that ornaments the third rhetorical question (with its strongly implied positive reply). The game is carried further in stanza IV:

Lucky Penelope,
Luckier far than I
Who by my green warm sea,
Wait ever hopelessly,
Ever more hopelessly.

Here absolutely regular dactyls provide the background against which the poet takes two distinct but very close rhyme-sounds (*Penelope* and *I)*, and nudges them together with *-ly*, a perfect rhyme with one but a traditionally accepted rhyme with the other. Repeating "hopelessly" then has the effect of reinforcing this sonic resolution into monorhyme across five lines. While the form by these devices moves toward an impression of harmonious union (enlarging its scope from couplet to triplet to illusory quintuplet), the *sense* of the poem moves out of the enchanted realm of myth to the hopeless lover on the shore in the present – it is no accident that the upbeat effect of the monorhyme is undercut by the very word that makes it possible: "hopelessly". We come out of that very artificial realm of Penelope into a conclusion that seems to avoid rhyme.

From the very start the poem's issues are being worked out in terms of a pattern of imagery recurrent in Roach:

Oh, no more now
Ascends the heart
like the green bough;
No more commands the sun
The rhythm of the blood
Like singing sap in wood.

The loving heart is a green bough, the blood is its sap, responding to the commands of the sun, which here represents the force and the object of love (in other poems it is youth, ambition, aspiration, all manner of passionate striving; in "March Trades", the sun appears only briefly but, as here, it is imagined as a nourishing lover). In the absence of love – in the absence of his love – the poet's heart is no longer like a green bough; so he questions Penelope, envisioned as a green bough; and then the green boughs of the casuarinas address him, with corresponding questions. Both versions of the poem insist on highlighting the word "green", as I have just done; the *Bim* version, especially, repeats the word in every stanza except the last, where the metaphorical bough is replaced by actual ones.

Less central – in fact rather distracting in this poem – is imagery of rock that for Roach is routinely antithetical to images of green growth. The antithesis is important here. While the apparently conciliatory image of the rock that flowers is ubiquitous in Roach's work, it is *always* paradoxical, an imaginatively achieved reconciliation of opposites: for water or flowers or any life to spring from rock is never anything but miraculous. In this poem, what comes closest to that oppositional usage is the shift by which the heart is no longer like a bough, but like a sea-eroded rock (a change which incidentally reverses the symbolic valence of water; the rock is not nourished into growth by water, but reduced, worn down by it). Roach's strong impulse to harmonize these images lies behind the wishful notion that Penelope's love might somehow "petrify" and yet remain green (a possibility only imaginable in this realm of mythical romance). In this connection it is illuminating that Roach's revisions for the final stanza all affect adjectives, a strong indication he was taking pains to coordinate and control the various images in play.

The musical virtuosity of the central section obscures the fact that the poem's questions remain the same, and remain unanswered: How is it possible to remain green, passionate and vital in the suspense of hopeless waiting? Can love be kept alive during separation? Can the return of the beloved truly resuscitate love? The final stanza, as it takes up these questions, in its turn certainly makes a conclusive, if melancholy, *sound*: the voice here is that of the casuarinas lined up along the shore, we may assume, like the grieving wives of sailors in some story out of Ovid. The wind in those green boughs reiterates the questions of the central section: "does the flower come to the withered stem?" Attending to the adjective, one's answer must be "No." But that answer will be less confident for any reader of Roach's contemporaneous poems, full as they are of references to pouis and immortelles, varieties of tropical trees that bloom on bare wood. There is further reason for uncertainty when the poem in its final lines asks the question again in terms we have not been prepared for: "Does the prayer begin / at the prayer's amen?" The question is peculiar, and this new imagery of prayer seems much more equivocal. In the most trivial sense, of course, the answer is again "No." But prayers are addressed to some power; they stand in the same relation to that power as Roach's bough to its sun. And the fact is that the *answers* to prayer come only after the amen; it is precisely then (in the imagery of the poem), that a prayer bears fruit.

Analysis routinely magnifies obstacles that trouble no actual reader's passage through the text. Roach probably does not intend to leave this question quite so open; but he *has* chosen to end with an open question, and he emphasizes the openness by providing a source for the question (the whispering casuarinas) which might be taken in the spirit of Romanticism as absolutely authoritative (the voice of nature itself), but might also be taken as delusional – nothing but the wind in the trees as heard by an overwrought lover. These features of the conclusion might even be drawn upon in the interests of accurate psychological representation: through them Roach conveys the lover's unwillingness to abandon the hope he knows he no longer feels. The conduct of this poem also makes it clear that Roach is the sort of poet who thinks by way of metaphors, rather than the kind who uses figurative language to buttress and ornament his completed thought.

*

The five substantial poems Roach published in the next two issues of *Bim* are very different in style and subject from those two love poems which I have characterized as a "preview". Among the five, the first group of three constitutes a focused, mature, and very explicit statement of lifelong themes, very public by the standards of the time and the medium. The companion poems in the following issue – "Transition" and "Frigate Bird Passing" – clearly carry forward the same statement. All of them reveal Roach strenuously engaged with working out the logic of his central metaphors.

"The Flowering Rock", "Beyond", and "Death Does Not", printed together in *Bim* #12 (June 1950), assert extraordinary poetic authority. Even their placement is significant. They are the first thing in the issue, immediately after the brief introduction; evidently the editors saw this as an important debut, and it provides perspective on that valuation that the same issue includes "Shadow Suite", an ambitious sequence of poems, and the first publication by Edward Brathwaite, countryman and friend of the editors, scholarship student, and some 15 years younger than Roach. The decision to place Brathwaite's as the final poem in the issue, almost at the end, and Roach at the outset deserves some comment here. These three poems are more self-conscious, more programmatic poems than "Shadow Suite"; given Brathwaite's patent imitation of Eliot, Roach's poems may well have appeared less derivative at the time. They also establish securely an area of imagery and theme that will be central throughout the career, and show Roach writing from the heart of his imaginative landscape. None of these poems is so explicitly inaugural as "Invocation", but behind the thematic claim-staking there is also an assertion of characteristic voice, of a characteristic posture toward the world (and toward the tradition of poetry in English), and of a conception of what a poet is/ should be in (and for) the Caribbean.

The image of the flowering rock appears literally at the centre of the poem of that name, but we approach it through several ideas that become seminal for Roach. The poem begins at noon and ends at daybreak; the sun throughout is understood to be the source of energy and fertility, though the point is not dwelt upon. What the sun presides over at the start is an idyllic life in tune with nature: in the shade the village girls "cradle" their infants in song; in our valley "the stream water croons / Cool rhythms among stones" (FR 65). The imagery adds a specific implication to the idyll: music (and so by extension poetry) is the natural product of natural human processes. The mother's song corresponds to the music of a running stream and "our singing sighs like zephyrs". The idea is commonplace enough, but in context it seems a response to the notion – or to the anxiety – that poetry has no place in so unsophisticated a setting as this poet's homeland. The second stanza, still dominated by musical analogies, adds a new dimension by asserting that there is pain and hardship even in Arcadia – though the hardship also seems romanticized when expressed in such self-consciously artful terms as these: "Our voices bear the tracery of tears, / The burden of their cadence". Still, the music of the pastoral has modulated from something like Steven Foster to the blues.

In the midst of these musical metaphors, Roach introduces an image of a different order – "A froth of laughter / Tops our sea of sorrows" – which first draws attention to itself by its difference and, as an expression of the principle that indomitable vitality comes out on top against all odds, soon turns out to be a preparation for the central flowering rock image, which follows in the next stanza: "Oh, from gaunt rock / As white as sanctity / The lily blooms". The lily's assertion of life and beauty is triumphant, holy, "too pure for fragrance". Its relation to the rock from which it emerges is described in terms that are almost alchemical: it is "the distilled stone", "essence of darkness" – not the epitome of darkness or stoneness, but its always antithetical essence or attar, the gold from its lead. And the "gaunt rock" it springs from is not some particular stone in the village but (as we've seen in other poems already) the island itself, to which the poet and these villagers belong. The adjective "gaunt" carries a great deal of weight here, after all; it is no common way to describe a rock, and the one place Roach's readers are likely to have encountered the two words together is in John of Gaunt's famous encomium to island nationhood in *Richard II* (2.1).

Against the background of those associations, Roach draws his inference:

> This is our symbol –
> Beauty famous in the slum;
> The hungry boy who
> Tomorrow shall become
> The country's hero;
> The black loam bears him,
> He breeds recurrent
> In our fertile womb.

The lily thus comes at the end of a series of potential symbols suggested by the immediate environment, such as the streams and the froth on the surf. It is settled upon as the best symbol of what the people are like, but then the individual human instances of the case are taken themselves as symbols, as warrants that this does happen and will continue to. The lily is a symbol that speaks "us" to ourselves; the beauty and the boy can speak us to others, to outsiders, to "the world". Especially the boy, Roach implies, because he embodies not just the physical beauty of the flower, but its accomplishment in the face of adversity.

There is a further implication here that the hero is not a rare or unexpected miracle, but "recurrent", a persistent product of these conditions, or of these resourceful people who take the buffet and prosper in it. Such faith depends on a significant shift in the conception of the matrix of the image, which without fanfare has changed from "gaunt rock" to the "black loam" of "our fertile womb" (even this change could be suggested or at least reinforced by the details of Gaunt's speech, which envisions its island both as rock battered by the sea and as "this teeming womb of royal kings"). Flowering out of black loam is an image related to that of the flowering rock, but with quite different valences. Less an image of the inhospitable place than of its people, it emphasizes their energy and creativity, the strengths stored up in the accumulated sediment of black generations, layered with ancestors like the buried old man or his fragmentary, uneasily dormant antecedent, the skull in "Shallow Underground". A few years later these two closely related images converge on a third, the "black rock of Africa", with its important implications for Roach.

Some aspects of this poem, especially in the "black loam" stanza, suggest that Roach may have been reading (or hearing on the BBC) contemporaneous Jamaican poetry, at least that of George Campbell. On the subject of West Indian affiliations, it is worth mentioning that the image of valiant or unexpected growth out of a stone is one that becomes important for Brathwaite in the early sixties, just at a time when, as we know from his essays, he was reading and thinking about Roach; Brathwaite's use never looks like borrowing, and there are many independent reasons for his choice, but the affinity is interesting – both poets invest considerable idealism in the image. Coincidentally, Roach's next lines here grow out of a technique which also becomes very common in Brathwaite, though Roach in this instance makes the device mimetic of its subject:

> The distilled stone,
> The still *voice* of the skeleton.

Just as the rock splits to make way for the lily, here the second line is a kind of sonic expansion of the first, to make way for the intrusion, the flowering, of the word "voice", which appears on the page to emerge from a fracture between "distill" and "stone" to stand between the echoes of those words in "still" and "skeleton". Ultimately of course the saxifragant voice, which is evident though somehow "still", is that of the poet, and the poem ends by including the poet – along with his "darling" – in the central conception of this people as the flower of their earth. As day breaks, Roach writes, "our souls *like sunflowers* /Turn toward the dawning" – toward the sun which several poems ("Oh, No More", "March Trades", "Beyond") condition us to regard as a nourishing lover. But speaking of lovers, that "darling" deserves comment. The closing stanza retrospectively and quite surprisingly offers to frame the poem as something the poet is telling his "darling". If this is an *aubade*, images like the lily, the stone, and the fertile womb have to be reconsidered as elements in some very eloquent pillow talk. Whether or not that narrower approach to the poem is appealing, the presence of an added frame is quite unusual in itself, and the fact that the frame sketches an intimate scene between two lovers is unique in Roach at this point: setting aside the jilted lover's monologue in "Stranger Beware", it is the closest thing to an actual conversation in all of the poems this chapter considers.

*

All of the poems published in *Bim* during 1949-50 demonstrate a concentration of effort, a centripetal focus on developing a pattern of closely related images; yet at the same there is extreme disjunction between two diverse manners of diction and tone. Most of these poems are written in regular forms, developing closely related material in a self-consciously plain diction, with very limited figuration. It often feels as if Roach is working toward a monosyllabic ideal, and that is most apparent in the first and last poems of this particular set: "Flowering Rock" has only eight words of three syllables and none longer;[9] while in "Death Does Not", only five words (*arithmetic*, *gracefully*, *remember*, *precipice*, and *oblivion*) are more than two syllables long. Between these two chaste, structured poems comes "Beyond", an unrhymed, rhapsodic torrent of a poem, with extremely opulent diction dominated at its highest pitch by verbal nouns ("darer", "plunger") and by compound participial adjectives: "wind-driven", "light-throated", "sun-carolling". There are eighteen present participles in only thirty-one lines, and their presence contributes to an air of manic dynamism that suggests Whitman or D. H. Lawrence. The overall effect, however, is perhaps more like an English translation of some Sophoclean tragic chorus; the poem's tendency to break into unabashed dactyls (a by-product of the participles) contributes to this invocation of classical epic or choric ode.

In contrast to its extravagant language, the poem presents a sparse visionary landscape awash with sunlight (mentioned once in every stanza), and otherwise pared down to the essentials: sea, horizon, mountains and, somewhere below, the drudging peasants. Yet even this scene is almost immediately overpassed: the poet urges his subject, a being addressed as "singing man" (we will consider his identity in a moment), to soar like an eagle beyond the horizon, and then, beyond even the imaginable horizons past the one we see, into another realm altogether, the "horizonless and glorious landscapes of the soul". While he flies he sings, and Roach seems to want to suggest that for such a being flying is singing, not just metaphorically but as if song were the actual sound produced by his passage through the world. In stanza III the song is unexpectedly described in terms of what it is *unlike*:

> Not as stark men upon a drowning deck
> Or on a berserk salient doomed;
> Not as wind-driven wingers crying,
> Nor lowing as lost ones from flocks;
> Not as the hermit in his cold cell chaunting –
> Not these, not these, but the light-throated,
> Sun-carolling of the joyous defiant,
> The darer in air, the plunger in waters. (FR 71)

The effect of that passage is to emphasize several differences between this eagle-like flier and the rest of the human and animal worlds. Other creatures make ugly, craven, or ineffectual sounds as a consequence of their response to their situations. They suffer and grieve when they find themselves alone, in dire straits, at the mercy of brutal nature; by contrast, the singing man relishes isolation and his unmediated contact with the elements. Roach has some very fine distinctions in mind here; his singer is not distinguished merely from the masses, but from men who might reasonably be regarded as heroic in their own right. The men on the sinking ship and even more those on the "berserk salient" are characters we would be inclined to see as heroic, even if defeated; the atmosphere the poem itself has already created will predispose a reader to envision the sailors and climbers as adventurers – men who have enthusiastically put themselves in this position – rather than as hapless merchants, immigrants, or retirees on vacation. In fact, even in the language of "Death Does Not", the poem which literally shares the page with "Beyond", these men would seem to be numbered among "the last, the best, the rare", since that group explicitly includes those who "stand at the precipice at the end of the race". Similarly the hermit chaunting in voluntary isolation does not seem especially unlike the solitary soaring singer. The overall effect of these lines is clear, but in them Roach seems to be postulating crucial differences which we are left to discover for ourselves without much help from the text.

For practical purposes, the discrimination of heroisms is rendered moot by the next stanza, which presents a much plainer contrast between the singing man and a group of benighted folks rooting around in their cabbage beds. As he flies overhead, his song falls upon them like sunlight and like rain (sunlight itself is metaphorically fluid here, "flooding" and "pouring"). The effect on the hearers is ambiguous. They turn to its sunlight from grubbing roots, but it makes them "remember their youth, their glory gone in the midden of years, their spear heads rusting" and the singer is actually urged by the poet to "wake them to pain, to laughter and to loveliness again".

Precisely because the singing man is characterized by detachment, even obliviousness, what is problematic in "Beyond" are the relationships that structure the poem: those between the singer and other sorts of heroes, between the singer and the peasants, and between the singer and the poet. As for the last of those, there can be no doubt that this singer is one of Roach's radical idealizations of himself as a poet; to urge on the singer so hyperbolically is to encourage himself. The mechanism of the poem is literally ecstatic – Roach imagines and addresses the "singing man" with such passion that he becomes him. It is thus notable that, as the poem concludes, it compromises the singer's isolation:

> Go on, O singing man!
> There are the eagles the great-winged before you
> Reigning in sunlight, the hawks and the swallows:
> O join them soaring beyond and beyond
> Over limitless landscapes!

There is certainly an implicit hierarchy in the sequential mention of eagles, and hawks, and then swallows, and the unexpected appearance of this ranked crowd seems calculated to make the point that something very much like the idealized experience of the singing man is accessible to poets of varying talents or opportunities. Perhaps Roach makes this concession in a moment of self-doubt, but it recalls the hierarchy sketched in "Stair of Song".

Once Roach removes his subject from everything human and then projects himself into that high-flying singer, it is apparent that the poet's own relationship to the poem's drudging peasants is envisioned as problematic. This is a far cry from the bucolic scenes of poems like "The Flowering Rock". Roach goes out of his way to make these peasants antithetical to the singer, insisting on their association with darkness rather than light, the earth rather than the sky, and insisting further that this earth is not the peasant's romanticized partner in fertility, but something almost repellent, a matter of cabbages, tubers, and middens. These are peasants out of Millet. The singer is not in any sense one of these people; he is another breed altogether. As a figure for the poet, he embodies poetry solely as a matter of vision, self-conception, or personality rather than labour or social function. This singer is overheard only, as migratory birds are ("Your cadenzas . . . shall strain dark cataracted eyes from cabbage beds"). He is a feature of the landscape, a mythic presence heard by but removed from society. He has no part in the life over which he passes. His very "song" is a reflex or a consequence of his passage, not a form of communication; yet it is somehow so inherently nourishing and transforming that its effect is felt even at a great distance and independent of any intention.

In "Beyond", Roach is exploring an extreme perspective on his relation as a poet to the people he comes from, and indeed at this time still lives among. As I have already hinted, this exploration is carried on in the very next poem. While "Death Does Not" first presents itself as even more regular in form and more comfortably rhyming than "The Flowering Rock", this poem actually pursues the same issues that underlie the gorgeous noise of "Beyond", but in an entirely different tonality, much more meditative and – indeed – practical. The many imperatives and the images of soaring birds remain, but the language is almost gnomic:

> Set winds in motion or
> Take wing in winds; soar
> Like the lean hawk; . . .
> How you hang gracefully
> Under the dazzling sky
> Some gazer's eye will mirror,
> Some lover will remember. . . .
> Stand at the precipice
> At the end of the race;
> Pose and leave pictures there,
> The last, the best, the rare;
> And like fearless diver
> Leap into the air;
> Plunge graceful as a swan
> Into oblivion. (FR 69)

Though these lines now seem prophetic of Roach's own death a quarter century later, in their original context they assert the faith – an almost desperate faith – that a certain way of *living* leaves permanent traces in the world, and that this simply happens, involuntarily. One leaps or soars, and the world cannot help but take the impression. As usual, the target of these imperatives is ambiguous; Roach presumably urges the comfort of this stoical ideal upon any self-aware individual who reads him, in particular upon any aspiring poet, and even more specifically, perhaps, upon any poet trying to work in an unresponsive West Indian society.

Most of this poem is concerned only with the self, and the private comfort that one "leaves pictures", one is remembered by *some* gazer, *some* lover. The indefinite modifiers underscore the severe egoism of the poem. The stanza between those just quoted, however, bears the seeds of another thought, though it is probably not one that actually surfaces when this poem is read in isolation:

> O, with the seer's rod, knock
> Upon the native rock;
> Call forth its limpid fountain,
> Or, in contempt of pain,
> Sculpture a form of faith
> From the stone's dull death;
> Make of that totem pole
> A symbol of our soul.

Here in the centre of the poem, otherwise so single-minded that the two stanzas quoted earlier are virtually interchangeable, both imagery and subject change substantially, though there is not a ripple in the surface of the rhetorical texture to draw attention to the change. For the duration of this one stanza we are in the realm of "flowering rock" imagery, which rarely appears in the same poems as Roach's images of soaring birds. It is as if that recurrent image has become so compelling it cannot be keep out of the poem.

The use of the "seer's rod" to draw water from the rock evokes Moses in the wilderness, forcing the rock to give up its nourishment, its fecundity – that leap into air. But within the economy of the poem that attribution of a seer's rod argues that for once the veil of ambiguity is drawn aside; the only person Roach can plausibly be exhorting here is himself. Indeed, this whole confrontation with "the native rock" – the island and its hard soil – is much more locally specific than the rest of the poem. But the passage continues. "Or", he says (and the alternative is surprising), "sculpture a form of faith from the stone's dull death", and elevate that form, which he describes as a "totem pole", into a symbol. The implication seems to be that if visionary power cannot make the rock give up its life-force, as it were, voluntarily, the alternative is to *impose* on the refractory rock the form of the totem, which is ultimately a variant of the same recurrent icon. There is again a suggestion of hierarchy here, of *degrees* of power. The fully empowered seer can make the rock "flower" to produce our symbol; lesser imaginative force, mediated through physical labour, can shape the rock itself into such a symbol – an artifactual rather than a natural one, but no less eloquent and evidently for Roach not likely to express anything significantly different.[10]

This maverick stanza poses two important dilemmas which, though inert in this poem, will require Roach's attention throughout his career. First, the image of sculpting the rock introduces a notion of programmatic labour that seems foreign to the celebration of self-justifying "grace" in the rest of the poem; the aesthetic issues raised by the contrast are far-reaching, and we will take them up in Chapter 9. The second dilemma is posed in the poem's allusion to Moses, who strikes the rock not for art but for life, and not only for himself but for the sake of a tribe. Both the fountain and the totem pole are things normally produced to nourish others, either physically or spiritually, and there is no particular motivation for the addressee of the poem to do these specific things for himself – nothing suggests that he's personally in either literal or metaphorical need of a drink or a totem pole. This issue is left hanging in the air here; the poet may be concerned about it (he writes that the totem will be a symbol of "*our* soul"), but this particular poem is not. We have not, of course, heard the last of it.

*

Taken together, those three debut poems ("The Flowering Rock", "Beyond", "Death Does Not") provide a remarkably dense statement of what will persist as the central concerns and images of Roach's poetry. A pair of poems appearing in the following issue of *Bim* (#13) enrich that statement further, first because they stand in an intentionally dialogical relationship with one another, and secondly because in both of them Roach is consciously exploring possible connections between the contrary groups of images which in "Death Does Not" were almost absent-mindedly juxtaposed. Thus the first of these poems, "Frigate Bird Passing", shares many details with its companion poem "Transition", but the proportions are different in a way that transforms the outcome. Like "Beyond", which it resembles but surpasses, "Frigate Bird" is a poem committed to the male ego at its most heroic, free ranging, and overreaching:

> Consider here that great hawk arrowing
> The rare air, crashing opposing cloud,

His eye needling horizons, iron wing,
Untiring heart, his blood a fountain singing;
For perch upon this sea-ringed rock
Consider his contempt. (FR 74)

This is the first of three stanzas which envision the bird with something like stunned admiration. A spate of rhetorical questions in the second stanza recalls Blake's "Tyger", or more likely Blake's own model for that technique in *Job*, and the passage is also touched a bit by Hopkins: "Then O from there he beat the buoyant wing". The inhuman frigate bird is full of neutral brutality. His solitude is complete, his independence nearly so ("he dips wing only to eagles"). As he flies on, he dreams, he "shrills his epics to the risen sun" – his self-absorption is too eventful to have need of contact with anything but prey. Yet the forbidding sight of him cannot help but invite meditation that explores our relation to the bird – our distance from it and its life – and more extensively the bird's imagined interiority; its attitudes and behaviours. Roach seems to want to make us aware of the tension between the unapproachably alien nature of the bird which he means to celebrate and the routine, almost irresistible poetic invitation to "reach" it and read it as a representation of something we are or can be: "Up there beyond our grounded blood and bone / Only our dreams can reach him, / Only the pinioned spirit check his course". The bird is plainly impervious to the questions our curiosity prompts us to ask about it, and indeed to describe us eager questioners in terms of "grounded blood and bone" makes us sound dangerously like prey.

This poem undertakes a remarkable critique of the kind of imaginative projection by which the poet in "Beyond" glibly appropriates the singing man for himself. Here the frigate bird staunchly resists appropriation and asserts, simply by being what he is, his inapproachable otherness. Roach even makes a point of emphasizing that the bird rejects not only us, but our little "sea-ringed rock" as well. A nice touch, since there's a twist to it: his contempt for the island reflects the *inhabitants'* sense (and it is often Roach's too) that the place is incapable of sustaining the heroic or offering it room to survive. The implication is that we project our anxieties at least as prodigally as what "Transition" calls our "dreams"; Roach seems intrigued by the idea that this self-contempt is articulated by means of the very same imaginative projection which serves such a different purpose in "Beyond".

It is to achieve this poem's more trenchant purposes, I think, that Roach stresses how this bird comes from elsewhere (" . . . veering east he grew into our view"), from somewhere unknown ("Where last did he touch ground?") – it is not, like the singing man, his own poetic creation. Insisting on that point makes it possible to see the depth of Roach's self-scrutiny in this work. Thus in a phrase like "his blood [is] a fountain singing" we recognize that Roach has endowed the frigate bird with his highest marks of value; but the poem forces us to recognize too that to put one's mark (even if it is only one's rhetorical mark) on the bird is necessarily an act of appropriation and assimilation – as even to say "*my* God" involves an oddly proprietary gesture. Likewise it seems reasonable to assume that here, as in "Beyond", Roach's own dreams of escape and accomplishment are figured in this language of violent opposition and natural superiority, of frank incommensurability with the ordinary world. But if we truly accept the proposition that we are trying to talk about an actual bird, and not a poet's confection to keep a drowsy reader awake, then two uncomfortable questions arise which sound very much like the kinds of questions Roach repeatedly asked of himself: first, what does it mean to wish to be remote and contemptuous, and secondly, what does it mean to idolize something which meets your gaze with superiority and contempt? Either question might initiate years of therapy, but the second is particularly intriguing as a reflection of the psychopathology of colonialism.

It may seem that I am pressing this point inordinately, but there is further evidence that Roach is in effect deconstructing the sort of lyric he is engaged in writing with exactly the same motives as a deconstructive critic: to uncover the repressions in the text, to work out dilemmas that were beginning to surface in the system of his most central images. "Frigate Bird Passing" is the kind of lyric which resulted when the old emblem poem passed through the hands of the Romantics. The Renaissance emblem books took a picture, usually a woodcut, appended a poem explicating the picture, and added as well a pithy saying as a sort of caption. When Roach inherits the sub-genre, the object of attention is more often something in nature rather than a work of art, and the caption has been replaced by a tendency for the poem to adduce a moral (in the loosest sense of the term). I have been pursuing the consequences of Roach's experimental insistence that his frigate bird is actual and not literary; something interesting also happens at the point in the poem where we would expect the emblematic subject to be moralized upon.

After four stanzas of descriptive consideration of the frigate bird, ending with the line "He shrills his epics to the risen sun", the poem seems to be downshifting to such a conclusion. The new stanza begins like this: "And as I dream my lover in the noon". The "as" sounds like a temporal conjunction, and this first instance of the first person singular pronoun seems to signal the transition to a humanizing conclusion in which some lesson will be drawn from the contemplation of this bird (say, "As I dream my lover in the noon / I'm glad I don't have to fly around all the time and eat carrion"). But the easy transition to a familiar domesticity is a trick; in fact this passage turns out to be not a return to the world of the speaker, but instead a turn away from it, into a simile (the initial "as" is not in fact temporal) that merely *refers* to that world.[11] The poem remains in the alien realm of the frigate bird, a real bird observed, and problematically held up for our consideration as a symbol. Instead, however, we find ourselves reminded that the bird here is emphatically Other; the poetic trick with "as" is a way of emphasizing that we cannot easily make contact with this creature. The poem thus engages none of the dialectical interplay which seems to be functioning in "Beyond" – an interplay most familiar from Shelley's "Ode to the West Wind", where (as in this poem of Roach's) the conception of the poet's relation to a high-flying spirit hovers between "bethou me" (make me you) and "be thou me" (make yourself me). When we read the extended double simile correctly, its unexpected point is that the frigate bird is so alien even the first step toward empathy is daunting:

> as I dream my lover in the noon
> Divinely kind and soft and warm at dusk,
> Or as the holiest picture paradise
> Clear at death's distance, island of their God,
> So in the inner mirror of his eye he sees
> The dazzle of his white Andean perch,
> The cruel ice-rind of the wintry pole.

Human love, which seemed to be where the poem was leading, is not actually *in* the poem at all, except as something dreamt about by a character inside a simile. In this highly metaphorical poem it is in fact the only simile, a state of affairs which emphasizes its enclosed unreality and probably also contributes to our initial inclination to misread "as". The point of the comparison is simply that the bird likes his perch, but the message we readers receive is that one would have to be able to feel the same attachment toward ice-rind as one feels toward one's lover, or toward the idea of heaven, in order to *begin* to enter the consciousness of this creature. The poem then ends without drawing any conclusions whatever (we will be considering the details of the ending momentarily, in connection with "Transition").

Though the tone is calmer and more thoughtful, the opening lines of "Transition" are full of thematic and even verbal echoes of "Frigate Bird" (I have emphasized below the common terms and phrases; "arrower" here corresponding to "arrowing" in "Frigate Bird"):

> Watching my wisp of smoke
> I know where *our dreams* go,
> I know how *spirit* builds
> Pylon and pyramid
> *Needling* receding heaven;
> How soul the *arrower*,
> Burster of *horizons*,
> Goes out like *hawk* and *eagle*. (FR 72)

What bursts horizons and needles heaven here (like a hawk), is "spirit", "our dreams", all the restlessness of human striving that keeps bursting out in these poems, and the stanza ends with an observation which is virtually a resolution: "I go where my dreams go". But this poem is called "Transition" because it now becomes quite a different poem, explicitly *rejecting* the open horizons of the hawk with his flying dreams and answering the contrary call of blood, of community and its dependencies. To make the point, the resolution is twice revised: first to "I go where my blood goes" and then to "I go where my love goes". Even the traditional gendering of these two contrary attitudes (restlessness and domesticity) is brought into play. The solitary pylons and birds are stereotypically male; the community of blood stereotypically female. But the second stanza manages a deft transition of its own, wherein waking to the new day is seen in terms that reverse the usual: it is "man slipping in from sleep / As from another journey / Into the inn of day," and the inversion underscores the realignment of the poem's sympathies from the ranging male to the enclosed security regarded as female. So the surrounding sea here is female and protecting, the island is "my mother island", the village is protectively "huddled", and its women are "deep-bosomed". The entire second half of the poem celebrates an idealized image of the village in which relations between the sexes, between generations, and between humanity and nature are harmonious.

The little wisp of smoke that inspires the grandiose phallic Babel-building of the opening – pylon and pyramid, arrow and needle, the macho accomplishments of pipe-dreams – dissipates with the coming of daylight. That imagery is actually superseded twice over in the course of the poem. When the light of day first returns, the imagination's pylon is replaced by a more modest natural equivalent: a "green hill's tower" that "stands against the sky", but does not pierce it. The implications of that particular correction are echoed in a marked contrast between this poem and "Frigate Bird". Both poems mention vocal responses to the sunrise. In "Frigate Bird" the poet fantasizes that the bird "shrills his epics to the risen sun" (with the implication that the poet does the same); in "Transition" what sunrise induces is "Bird-talk, cock-crow, dog-bark" – more modest, less self-serving, but also more real. The noisy animals and the green hill exist; the pylon and (by implication) the epics do not.

The phallic imagery is trumped even more compellingly when the poem ends with the truest realization of those dreams in the village's more literal and finally more consequential issue: the children underfoot. The initial "wisp of smoke" (leading to insubstantial and grandiose dreams of male assertion) yields finally an image visually similar but much more substantial and productive:

> children scamper barefoot.
> Ah, there the heart-gold goes
> Slender as a young palm,
> Comelier than Sheba
> Golden in young sun.

The poem begins in smoke and night to end with the light of the "young sun". This "young palm", another plant bursting up in Roach's familiar way, constitutes a living, natural pylon that puts the fantastical one to shame. That this pylon is a young girl – not male at all – confirms the poem's successful transmutation of its initial terms. It may be significant, too, that none of the children is presented as the poet's own (a claim of ownership might have been construed as carrying on the competitive male dream of potency in a more covert way). Instead the children are implicitly "ours", the product and future of the village as a whole, like the children in such other poems as "The Flowering Rock" and even "Shallow Underground". "Transition" ends with a gratifying vision of community and continuity, a world where "blood pulses into blood; / Kinsman hallos kinsman; / Deep-bosomed women gossip / From dooryard into dooryard". Looking back at "Frigate Bird Passing" from this vantage point challenges that poem's harsh bravado. The tricky simile near the end of "Frigate Bird" can look like a frustrated attempt to make the move which

"Transition" successfully accomplishes, the move away from emblematical creature of dreams to cozy village reality. The contrast between the endings of these poems too is stark, and thought provoking. This is the last we hear of the frigate bird:

> He flies and dreams.
> His hard sure instinct beams him on
> While steep beneath him sleeps the green sea death
> That shall immobilise his viking wing.

These lines wear their tragic mask well, and "viking" (in context it sounds almost like a participle) marks the poem's attitude (or at least, the poem's reading of the bird's attitude) as self-consciously heroic and uncompromising. But "Transition" draws attention to the fact that this story ends with no mate, no procreation, no accomplishment but those unheard epics; only a final plunge into the oblivion of the sea whose greenness is quite different from that of the green hill's tower beneath which "Grand, green fields of corn / Preach of splendid harvests".

I have been reading "Transition" as a rejection of the outlook represented in "Frigate Bird" and in its own initial stanza. The forward momentum of the poem, along with the disproportionate balance between the first stanza and the rest, argue for such a reading. An alternative deserves mention: it might also be possible to regard the poem as an attempt by Roach to reconcile his contrary impulses. He has been expressing them both freely in contemporaneous, even literally simultaneous poems, and may here be essaying a kind of armistice – along that line the poem's evident distinction between the characteristics of day-thoughts and of night-thoughts might be pressed to bear more weight.

*

Before concluding, we should note briefly Roach's *second* broadcast on BBC (May 21, 1950). Three poems were presented, all of them dominated by variations on the "flowering rock" imagery: "The Flowering Rock" and "Oh, No More Now", both of which we have already examined, and along with them "February", a companion poem to "March Trades". The early stanzas of this poem, in which immortelle, poui, and mango bloom and shed their blooms in the wind, take over details and even entire lines from "March Trades". But, shaped into quatrains with very casual rhyme and slant-rhyme throughout, this is much less ambitious in craft and in imaginative scope, and where "March Trades" is muscular, this is charming, bucolic, a relaxed and fluent poem depicting (like "Transition") a harmonious and amorous world. Even the winds themselves (raging lions in "March Trades") here laugh and caress the inhabitants of the island with the hands of a lover.

All those various trees, lightly personified in the poem, turn out to be manifestations of a larger personified presence:

> Life lolling underground,
> Hearing news of spring
> Leaps in the floral blood,
> Breaks out in beauty dancing. (FR 63)

In this case, for once, the flowers that burst forth into bloom are literal and not symbolic. What emerges from underground is simply the force of life itself, not a haunting history or a guilty secret as in "Shallow Underground" or "Carib and Arawak", and it meets with none of the hostility, frustration or discouragement that so often oppose the symbolic flowerings in Roach's work. The atmosphere here is positive, even redemptive.[12] Consistent with that atmosphere, "February" differs most, and most significantly, from "March Trades" in its attention to the fellowship of the village, grounded on the intimacy between the peasants and their "lovers" the trade winds: the winds love us; we love the month of their coming, and the earth we nurture and are nurtured by. This is most apparent in the closing stanzas:

> The trade winds blow, and we
> In our year long sunny season
> As proper farmers tend
> Each one his given garden.
>
> The green rains come, and we
> Out of our nurtured earth
> With hoe and hope and courage
> shall charm high harvest forth.

As those lines indicate, Roach makes frequent use of the first person plural throughout this poem, and it is remarkable that he so unproblematically includes himself among the idealized peasantry as a working member (rather than as spokesman or shaman). True, Roach specifies that each farmer is tending his own "given garden", and one might argue that something could be made of that (perhaps it is a small, compulsive gesture of individuality?). But "February" is undoubtedly the sunniest and most genial poem of all those considered in this chapter.

*

As a result of surveying the dozen or so poems of Roach's international debut, a number of general observations can be made about the salient features of his verse and about the issues that most seem to concern him at this point in his career. It is clear from his imagery and diction that Roach has been reading widely and fairly predictably, with particular attention to Shakespeare, Milton, the high Romantics, and Yeats. As noted earlier, there are (to my ear, at least) unexpected affinities with the reviving lyric of the late eighteenth century, particularly Gray, Collins, Cowper, and Blake. It is difficult to know what books Roach had available at this time but, with the exception of Blake, those poets were fairly well represented in a text as ubiquitous as Palgrave's *The Golden Treasury*. In the case of Blake, Roach's work recalls early poems not frequently anthologized. But the enthusiasm of Yeats for Blake's less familiar poems might be a factor here; Yeats's edition of Blake – which became available in the widely distributed Modern Library series in 1928 – might plausibly have reached Tobago. The apparent affinity may in any case be more situational that filial, a reflection of coincidentally parallel anxieties about belatedness and remoteness from the wellsprings of English poetry.

There is considerable variety of poetic forms in this group, which ranges from free verse to fairly rigorous quatrains. Just about half of these poems are composed in regular stanzas, ranging in length from four lines ("Shallow Underground", "Stranger Beware", "February") to ten ("Transition"). Regular lineation in these poems does not necessarily correspond with regularity in either rhythm or rhyming. As we have seen, Roach regards rhyme as a formal resource in its own right, not simply as a way of articulating stanzaic shapes; he is certainly interested in the effects of various degrees of imperfect rhyme. Of the poems that could be described as "free verse", "Beyond" and "Frigate Bird Passing" stand apart from all the other poems of 1949-50 for their unique style, characterized by sublime diction, heavily participial syntax, and strong rhythmic pulse. The correspondingly strong resemblance between these poems in theme and imagery makes it clear that Roach associates this distinctive style with quite specific subjects and even specific positions, at odds with those maintained (or proposed) in others of these poems. Free verse and a reach for the sublime also distinguish "Invocation" from the other poems of its set, but in that case Roach employs very different *means*, in particular a highly determined rhetorical structure. The form of "Token" is also loose enough to be called "free", but Roach includes a scattering of rhymes, as if he felt a need to provide an impression of shapeliness. Rather like "Invocation", "Oh, No More Now" foregrounds rhythm as it loosens form, and it adds the pointing of some structurally significant rhyme. The thoughtful interplay of form, rhythm, and rhyme distinguishes this poem and "March Trades" as the most innovative and detailed formal experiments among the poems of this period. It is apparent that Roach has a parsimonious attitude toward the resources of craft, a frame of mind equally patent in his characteristic economy of imagery and even of vocabulary.

The first five BBC poems also have a peculiar formal tic in common. Except for the generally negligible "Token", all of them include some sort of turn or break or intrusion into the argument about two-thirds of the way through: there is the shift of subject from man to verse in "Invocation"; the unforeseen discovery of the "unhappy skull" in "Shallow Underground"; the pair of passages about Columbus that interrupt both "March Trades" and "The Old Man". In three of those instances – "Invocation", "March Trades", and "The Old Man" – we have seen that there is a corresponding disruption of formal expectations. Curiously, the *Bim* group, by contrast, presents virtually no trace of such formal breaks and strains. The difference seems entirely accidental, but the details are worth spelling out briefly. Several of these *Bim* poems have instead a singleness of purpose that expresses itself in a seamless surface: "Beyond", "Stranger Beware", "The Flowering Rock". The oddly handled simile in "Frigate Bird" (and its cousin in "February") might recall the kind of thing that happens so often in the BBC group, especially given their particular point of entry into the structure of their poems, but in neither case is there any mimetic disruption of form. The *Odyssey* reference in "Oh No More Now" and the fountain/totem stanza in "Death Does Not" contrast with their immediate contexts, but neither involves a structural turn. Nothing is trying to break out of the bounds of these poems, as Columbus for example – the fabled adventurer embodying a very concrete version of the sublime, overreaching "hawk" image – certainly is. In the poems of this group, unlike the BBC poems, nothing along the way affects the expected outcome, except in the special case of "Transition", where some sort of change is of course announced by the title. Particularly if we read that poem, in the spirit of its title, as a progression and not as the expression of a dilemma, it must be said to unfold in a very untroubled way. The conversion the poem depicts is certainly substantial, but it is presented as entirely natural, something brought on simply by the coming of daylight – a dramatic enough event (though not so described in the poem), but hardly disruptive.

As he would be the first to admit, and indeed to boast, Roach comes to poetry with something like a work ethic, which is certainly evident in his handling of formal matters. It also lies behind his compulsion to work out the complexities of a handful of symbols which are for him the most charged and vital; thus his habit of writing paired poems that rework the same ideas along different lines, some of which will be discarded or at least not brought forward. Ingenious imagery is not the focus of his attention. If anything, he seems much more interested in his sound; "March Trades" for example is a particularly vivid poem, but it possesses a vividness of sound more than of visual image, and Roach does not seem especially eager to generate striking phrases. He is a thoughtful, not a witty, poet; he himself might say, a peasant and not a courtier.

With very few exceptions, such as the scroll of "The Old Man" and the sailing-ship similes in "March Trades", or incidental images like the mirror of "Stranger Beware", the "shutters of the soul" and the "vats of grief" in "Beyond", almost all the imagery in these poems is drawn from nature. The point hardly requires illustration. Apart from nature imagery, the only other significant family of figures is musical, and for the most part they are applied to nature, as is the case with the "rhapsody" and "nocturne" in "Transition", and with the poui blossoms described as trumpet-notes in "February". For the most part, Roach's musical imagery is associated with themes of the peasant's intimate relationship with nature. Melodious streams and the song of the wind in the trees assert humanity's persistence as a part of nature. As "The Flowering Rock" makes conveniently clear, such music occurs in both "major" and "minor" tonalities: there is music of harmonious pastoral but there is also the cadence of tears. In addition to the music of village life, however, there is the very different music of poems like "Beyond" and "Frigate Bird Passing" – the compulsive self-expression of the solitary bard/bird. This music is epic rather than pastoral, and its very different field of associations is correlated with the distinctive form and diction of these poems. Despite such differences, Roach's musical imagery consistently enhances his insistence that the production of poetry is part of nature.

Roach's predominant nature imagery is so constrained in its range and so assiduously explored that it makes sense to speak of a "grammar" of his metaphors. Deep in the structure is an ideal, the image of a tree unproblematically growing out of fertile soil into the sunlight, with no hint of resistance or opposition. The conception of blood as the sap of life rising toward the sun ("Oh, No More Now") is a kind of shorthand form of this ideal, and at a greater metaphorical distance it underlies such images as life's leap in floral blood ("February"), or the fountain of singing blood in "Frigate Bird". But for the most part what appears in the poems is an array of intonations, deformations, and displacements of that ideal image. These poems generate two clusters of imagery concerning different kinds of trees, both strongly positive in their implications: the willows / casuarinas and the pouis / immortelles. The willows grow out of soil securely possessed either through longstanding ancestral claims ("The Old Man", and probably also "Shallow Underground") or through an act of reclamation ("Invocation"). They are associated with the trade winds, but this is a relationship of interaction rather than of resistance: together the wind and the trees produce harmonious music. Pouis and immortelles, though also associated productively with winds ("March Trades") are especially important because their botanical nature legitimizes the idea of life blossoming from apparently barren wood. These images of flowering wood approximate Roach's central symbol of the flowering rock, an image that can be described as the realization of that original ideal tree within the less-than-ideal contingencies of the actual Caribbean.

The complexities of the flowering rock image are being explored in nearly all of the *Bim* poems, but among the group of poems for BBC it is less frequent. It appears explicitly only in the picture of the strong ancestral tree springing from thirsty rock which is inscribed on the metaphorical scroll in "The Old Man". In this instance the force of the image is softened, however, since it is succeeded by the depiction of the willows that literally sprout from his grave, with no hint of difficulty or opposition. "Token" oddly enough offers one passage which, in retrospect at least, seems a vast projection of the essential elements of the flowering rock imagery. But the scale is so large that the image loses most of its force:

In the dawn's grandeur
Now transfigured stand
Out of tartarean night
To utter to the sun. (FR 57)

Of the BBC poems, "March Trades" seems to mark the most significant moment in Roach's development of this imagery. Here the rock of the physical island stoically resists the savagery of wind and waves, and in the end of the poem this is interpreted as a lesson that the *human* aspect of the island – the island as homestead, as ship the islanders ride into the future – likewise will prosper if it takes the buffet. The middle stanza illustrates the principle of prospering through the buffet with branches stripped bare of their leaves and flowers, as part of a natural cycle; but even though the trees referred to would allow the inference, the idea that blossoms appear on apparently lifeless wood is not in play in this poem, and that notion of life springing paradoxically from death is essential to the images of the "flowering rock" group. The elements are here; but the obsessive image has perhaps not yet been formulated.

There is no need to recapitulate here the elaboration of this imagery in the *Bim* poems, both on its own terms and in such variants as fountains and pylons; we have already seen how central a concern it is there. But it is important to note the two very different valences of the particular matrix the flower springs from. These are spelled out, appropriately enough, in the poem entitled "The Flowering Rock": the "black loam", recognizable as the layered earth of "The Old Man" and related poems, here signifies a positive attitude toward origins without sacrificing any awareness of hardship or obstacles overcome. As a source, the loam is symbolically equivalent to the village, its life, and its people, as nurturing grounds for the emergent individual. If, on the other hand, what the flower springs from is "rock", the implications of lifelessness and sterility emphasize the improbability of such flowering, and (even worse) the likelihood of tragic consequences should it actually manage to occur (as we know from the gospel parable, a seed may sprout on rock, but it cannot survive there).

What the gaunt rock lacks as an image, in contrast to the loam, is of course the implication of a specific history and point of origin. The rock is simply a given, an isolated node of endurance. As we've seen, many of these poems treat the image of "the rock against the elements" in its own right, and not solely as an element of the flowering rock figure (e.g. "March Trades", "Oh, No More Now"). To some extent the isolated rock battered by wind and sea is for Roach a starker version of the tree resisting the wind, and in conceptual terms (though probably not in its actual origins) the "flowering rock" imagery itself can be described as constituting a reconciliation of the "rock" and "tree" clusters.

The beleaguered rock serves in these poems as a symbol not only of the self, but of Roach's own island and of Africa-in-the-Caribbean. Yet (in spite of the successful marketing of pet rocks once and crystals now), it is not an image that evokes much sympathy, and Roach has hit upon what might be called a more *inhabitable* image with many of the same implications in his eagles and frigate birds. Like the "rock" (as endurers of buffet), and in contrast to the "flower" whose miraculous origin is crucial as an encouragement to faith, these birds pointedly have no discernible origins. Perhaps that freedom from history, as much as their evident freedom from the things of the earth, is what makes them such attractive objects of our aspiration (and of Roach's own). Remarkably, the BBC group includes no heroic birds; "March Trades" and "The Old Man" treat some of the same principles – adventuring versus snug home-life – that would appear in the hawk and eagle poems, but in completely different terms. In the *Bim* poems, however, Roach investigates this image of the soaring bird with more subtlety than any other: it is unashamedly celebrated in "Beyond", yet "Frigate Bird" incorporates (I have argued) a critique of its appeal, and "Transition" seems to enact a rejection of all that it stands for.

The terms of that rejection underscore the fact that Roach's favoured images of rocks, plants, and birds are deployed in two contrasting imaginative worlds: a "green world" of farms and villages, and a barren landscape of elemental nature. In keeping with their inaugural function, all of the BBC poems except "Token" are intensely territorial and constructive: one reclaims the swamp associated with slavery; another makes the island-home shipshape to prosper; in the other two, the buried remains of ancestral figures establish rights of possession. The claim is only adumbrated in "Shallow Underground"; because the skull is unacknowledged or even quite unknown, the moment of recognition and its potential outcome remain in doubt. But "The Old Man" recognizes and sanctifies the link to the past: he is the scroll on which the rootedness of the present is inscribed and authorized – the deed to the land. The growing willows at the gravesite are the enduring sign of the man's life, of the respect he inspires, and of his beneficent influence; if we can assume that the existence of some sort of community is implied in the text, he is the guarantor of that community's continuity and of its right to the place. If anything, these poems are more interested in entitlement than in the specific nature of the ground in question. The land is imagined at a level of generality that renders a garden, a working farm, or a virgin landscape indistinguishable.

In the *Bim* poems (taking the affiliated "February" along with them) Roach imagines his settings much more explicitly. These poems are dominated by farms and shady dooryards, the peasants' nurtured plots. Perhaps because that is the context, the village in these poems is a natural rather than historical entity, a womb of cyclical rhythms. There is almost no sense of the ancestral, of human history as eventful articulation of those cycles. Only "Flowering Rock", with its black loam and its tears, acknowledges even symbolically the particulars of Caribbean history. On the other hand, the poems in both groups that strive for the epical and sublime are characterized by an elemental and frankly inhuman setting, comprised of little besides the sun, moon, stars, and sea. The contrast is powerful and intentional; explicitly opposed to the imagery of the village is the very unearthly – earth-denying – imagery of the hawk poems. In the context of extreme idealizations of the solitary, these poems routinely present the realm of peasant life as an object of great condescension: there is the "contempt [for] this sea-ringed rock" and this "grounded blood and bone" in "Frigate", and the very unflattering view of the working peasants in "Beyond". But again we must note the contrasting rejection of both this attitude and its associated landscape in "Transition", which explicitly turns away from the solitary ideal to celebrate the community and its continuum.

The complex friction generated both within and between "Frigate Bird" and "Transition" expresses most plainly the fundamentally political questions that Roach has begun to grapple with. It is convenient to formulate these as questions about his relationship *as a poet* to his physical place, and about his relationship *as a poet* to his people; but while such clarity of formulation is helpful, we need to bear in mind that it is achieved at the expense of overspecificity and a certain amount of anachronism. At this early stage both terms of both questions were problematic for Roach; in other words, there are really three issues: the relationship to place, the relationship to people, and the delineation of the human subject(s) whose relationships they are. Indeed, in these poems the identity of the subject is so regularly unfocussed that the manoeuvre comes to seem intentional, a technique by which each poem can be made simultaneously pertinent to the case of the individual in the abstract, to the case of the peasant member of a village community, and to the case of aspiring poet as such. Roach's chronic refusal to distinguish "I" from "we" suggests that the technique may indeed be intentional, but the poems gain this multiple resonance at considerable cost. The many imperatives, for example, cannot help but lose some of their force when they must be read as addressed to himself, to his compatriots, *and* to every reader. More significantly for the development of Roach's work, this manoeuvre makes it difficult to confront or even recognize the problem of the poet's relationship to his people, since he is already effortlessly one with them by fiat, in the warm embrace of this ambiguity.

The issue here is of course not Roach's personal relationships to place and people, but his developing figuration, his idealization, of those relationships in the poetry. On that basis, the relationship to place is perhaps easiest to consider, since Roach has not yet taken it very far. I have referred to territoriality as a theme of the BBC poems; but Roach in various ways stops short of representing his own relationship to that territoriality. "Shallow Underground" is symptomatic. Here the poet's voice speaks with great specificity about the scene as if he were present, but part of the difficulty in interpreting the poem is that we cannot make out where the speaker *stands*, even in the most literal sense. In "Invocation" the poet presents himself as motivated by a need to reclaim a piece of ground. There is a hint of the idea of reclaiming the country from the heritage of slavery, and clearly the poet has a sense that the practice of his art must have something to do with the actual historicized place, but those urgencies are deferred. Instead the emphasis is on the plot as a metaphor of the poet's soul, and of the verse he will make. The space in question is (in Keats's phrase) "a vale of soulmaking" rather than a physical place. There is a similar hesitation to claim the ground, or to state the terms on which it will be claimed, even in "The Old Man". The ancestor's own relation to the land is clear, but the poet's is not. Without resolution, the text proposes both to embrace the ancestor and to leave him behind, and the same contrary impulses characterize the poet's attitude toward the space the ancestral presence defines as home: it is described as idyllic and Arcadian, yet the text literally bursts with desire to escape its spell.

Roach's indecisiveness in the face of the contrary appeals of rootedness and of "adventuring" is figured more dramatically and perhaps more self-consciously in the antithetical worlds depicted in the *Bim* poems: the world of the bird who is forever on the wing, and the world of the peaceful village. Each has its attractions, and these poems variously explore corresponding positions for the poet (or the self): as a bird who sings amid vast spaces, or as a lily flowering from refractory soil in the midst of the village. The selection of images is an aesthetic matter, but the underlying issues are vital and urgent. Roach's repeated deferral of the distinction between "I" and "we" is relevant here, and it serves as a reminder that he was not alone in his preoccupation. Brathwaite, in an important early essay written just a few years after these poems ("Sir Galahad and the Islands", 1957), sees it as endemic to the writers of the region: "the desire (even the need) to migrate is at the heart of West Indian sensibility: whether that migration is in fact or by metaphor."[13] Even among those who (like Roach) remained in the Caribbean during the great migration of the 1950s, he recognized a form of metaphorical exile in the tendency to withdraw into "brilliant loneliness".

The wording of that phrase highlights the link between physical isolation and *social* alienation. Roach's early work repeatedly depicts human aspiration and accomplishment as a matter of thriving in the face of natural forces. Yet in these poems (apart from "February") this accomplishment is invariably conceived as individual, even solitary. Poems like "Invocation" and "Token" frankly set the poet alone against the powers of nature, and other people intrude on the BBC poems so rarely as to seem positively excluded. Even in "March Trades", when Roach imagines an island nation holding out against the prevailing weather, he characteristically resorts to the monolithic image of a battered rock, subsuming and effacing any human presences. By contrast, the poems in *Bim* all acknowledge the presence of human society, and by so doing problematize their own representations of the poet; Roach here seems prepared to address the question which that acknowledgement immediately raises: how does the poet fit in? Envisioning the role of a West Indian poet in a West Indian society remains a daunting project even now; Brathwaite, who has most successfully realized such a role in his own life, could not have done so if he had not left the "plurally fragmented world" of the Caribbean to spend years in the "cultural wholeness" of a rural West Africa community.[14] Roach's own lifelong concern with the question of the poet's function begins with these poems, with their recognition of the gap that opens up between his images of the poet (as a kind of personality), and his images of that same individual as one of the peasant farmers.

This chapter ends the story of Roach's poetic debut with much talk of isolation, yet the story itself ends just at the moment of his acceptance as one of the major poets contributing to the ongoing discourse of West Indian letters. Hereafter he is not measured against his fellow countrymen – Clarke, Telemaque, Herbert – but against the best of the region. It is the moment of his successful initiation into a community, but it is a "community" in a somewhat rarefied sense. This community existed in London, on the airwaves, and in the hyperspace of "the West Indies"; there was no village – rural, or global, or electronic – but rather a fellowship of self-styled exiles. Such a paradoxical sort of belonging persists at the heart of Roach's career, as we will see beginning in the next three chapters, which turn to the poems of Roach's most productive decade. In these poems he is actively engaged with the issues identified in the preceding pages: in sorting out the implications of his central images, and in studying the essential questions identified here – the relationships to place and people, and the definition of the figural subject engaged in those relationships.

CHAPTER 4 — THE HOMESTEAD: INTIMATE POEMS

The previous chapter began with Telemaque's observation that Roach's poems breathe the true atmosphere of Tobago, and ended with attention to the themes of isolation and community. Yet on the basis of the poems themselves a pressing question presents itself for consideration: where is Eric Roach of Tobago in these poems – the particular man at home in his immediate social and physical surroundings? The texts we have considered thus far reveal almost nothing, and in fact virtually all of Roach's total output before 1970 is marked by a powerful suppression of the personal. Many of Roach's poems, of course, might draw on or reflect his own experiences – among the poems already discussed "Stranger Beware" is an obvious example of this likelihood. But Roach's aspiration is to produce lyrics that have the wide currency of proverb or folksong, rather than confessional immediacy. Even more than the associated emotions, the initial experiences are filtered and heightened on their way to poetry. Roach is no Lowell, sharing with us every taxi ride and clogged sink. In this he differs not only from Walcott, but from many others among his younger West Indian contemporaries: such poets as Mervyn Morris, Dennis Scott, Lorna Goodison, Anson Gonzales, Victor Questel, and Mark McWatt all write frequently of domestic matters, of home, family, neighbours. In doing so, they participate in the familiar post-colonial project of putting the place and its people into art as vividly and explicitly as possible, an impulse, almost ethnographic in nature, which dominates Caribbean fiction but certainly affects poetry as well. Roach undertakes a parallel project of cultural work, but by different means.

Roach published nearly fifty different poems from 1951 through 1962, mostly in *Bim*. To understand their manifest suppression of the personal and its motives, it will be best to look at the handful of poems from that array which *do* present themselves as in some way autobiographical – a few poems either about or explicitly addressed to friends, and a group of poems about his parents. Even in these instances the suppression is under way; revised versions of several of them were published, and in every case, as we shall see, the later versions are *less* intimate than the earlier. It is quite remarkable what we cannot know about Roach from his poems: there is no reference to anything like his occupation or place of residence. Even his marriage in 1952 passes without comment in the poems, and in fact there is no indication that he has a wife, or a child (until his last published poem in 1973), or a sibling.[1] Of course it is probable that, with independent biographical information, some actual people could be identified behind figures in his poems. But apart from one late essay, "Growing Up in Tobago", and some brief biographical notations for anthologies, Roach himself has predictably left very little information about his own life.

The fullest account we have of any young poet's coming of age on a small island in the West Indies derives from Walcott's *Another Life*, and some of his essays.[2] For readers who know them, Walcott's anecdotes and his reflections on them can be of some help in forming an impression of Roach's early years. But Walcott grew up in a relatively urban and sophisticated climate; an ambience of *musicales*, recitations, and amateur theatricals defined his parents' somewhat beleaguered artistic circle. Roach had nothing of the kind in Tobago. His immediate culture included lively verbal arts, of course. While it is not directly pertinent to Roach's work, Roger Abrahams provides an excellent account of the diversity of language arts practised in several villages of the Eastern Caribbean, and some of his fieldwork was done not far from Roach's village in western Tobago.[3] Rhapsodic improvisation was prized, and the speechifying often travestied a "high style" that derived from the diction of the local church, the local school, and perhaps the radio (Roach himself remembers a village orator of his youth, especially valued for his "random flowery phrases").[4] But substantial social and conceptual barriers separated the "man of words" and associated phenomena from the exalted "Poetry" of the classroom and the library. What was preserved in printed books was not recognized as in any way like what went on in the village.

If there was no educated circle in Roach's rural Tobago, his family situation was not especially congenial either to the nurturing of literary talent. He describes his mother as "barely literate", a reader of no book but the Bible, and his father as "taciturn and spare of speech".[5] In those conditions, where does his interest in – or even his knowledge of – literature come from? What sustains it in the earliest days? He answers: "My individual luck was that I loved to read."[6] His development as a writer thus begins when he was sent to the new high school (just founded in 1925) six miles away in Scarborough. As Roach describes it, he studied math, Latin, French, Spanish, English literature, History, Geography, and the New Testament. Almost fifty years after the event he writes, "passages of English poetry rolled off my tongue. I strutted about like Naphthali mouthing that European rubbish"![7] The final phrase reflects Roach's attitudes of the 1970s, among them self-denigration – the memory of a love affair with poetry has become embittered. But the passage is typically ambivalent; he cannot resist displaying Naphthali, one of the many strange fruits of his education.

Roach's lifelong relationship with books begins in the experience of the charged world of childhood reading, and, most likely, in the experience of that world as a *refuge*. As the poem "Mother and Son" suggests, his immersion in books is analogous to the more common Caribbean mode of escape into a more satisfying world through immersion in the Bible (his mother's approach, which he puzzles over as either parallel or antithetical to his own). Writing, too, provides access to another life, but even more than reading, it can offer an escape into one's own, *owned* world – a world where one shapes the landscape and controls the weather. The striking exclusion of both individuals and society from so many of Roach's mature poems owes something to this aspect of writing as a private preserve, *hortus conclusus*. There are many indications that Roach preferred to regard the space of writing as a kind of paddock, a secluded exercise ground, more than as an arena of public competition. His wide reading certainly taught him his craft, but (to make a rough distinction) his engagement was rather with poems than with poets. With very few exceptions (we have already encountered "Anacaona" and "The Tragedy"), none of Roach's poems engage in a sustained dialogue with other specific texts, or with the characteristic personae of other poets. Very likely because of the poet's remoteness from the central tradition, his work displays none of the revisionary dialogue between texts which Harold Bloom has so extensively investigated – has indeed asserted to be the matrix of English literature since Milton.[8] Searching out "influences" in Roach's poetry, one finds allusions generally limited to words and phrases picked up in his reading. For example, Lloyd Brown discerns the influence of "Ode to the West Wind" on the passage in "March Trades" about "leaves ochreous".[9] Yet the advice in that poem is something like "batten down the hatches" – quite at odds with the ecstatic empathies of Shelley, and yet not poised as antithesis or revision of that precursor. In fact the *theme* of the "Ode" does appear in Roach with some frequency, but it appears in the poems of soaring birds, where there is no such clear allusive signal of the Shelleyan context. Though there are frequent casual echoes of standard anthology pieces (as when Ernest Dowson's "wine and roses" makes a cameo appearance in "To My Mother"), the referentiality of his work is never dense and rarely sustained. What he learns from other writers is unusual words, phrases that are evocative but not conspicuous, and good ideas about rhyme or rhythm. Even his dependency on Yeats is not quite the apprenticeship it seems; it sometimes looks as if he allied himself with Yeats as the traveller in North Africa hires a guide – not out of a need for guidance, but to deter the solicitations of other guides.

The allusive field of Roach's poetry remains sparse during the 1950s. There are occasional references to Homer's epics, and to such episodes from classical mythology as the stories of Jason, Hercules, Atalanta, and Actaeon. It is a reflection of Roach's very earthbound sensibility that those are all human characters; he mentions no classical gods except Venus\Aphrodite, who appears several times. Roach has an easy familiarity with the Bible ("I left my mother speechless with my word knowledge of the gospels as we had to learn whole passages by heart").[10] Even so, his allusions to it are generally brief rather than sustained, and require no particular comment here.

Nature continues to be the primary source of Roach's imagery, and he continues to prefer elemental or symbolic landscape to sharply observed pictorial detail. References to music continue, but Roach has a habit of taking up musical terms which are actually the names of specific forms – such as *canzone*, *canzonet*, *rondeau*, and *villanelle* – and using them as little more than generalized synonyms for "song". The practice suggests that Roach was not above seeking inspiration in a thesaurus; it is certainly true that the *only* citation given in OED for "aphonous," which Roach uses in several poems, is *Roget's Thesaurus*. Only one composer is mentioned in these poems, and it is *not* Beethoven, as one might guess, but rather strangely, Chopin.

Roach refers to a few specific paintings (Botticelli's Venus, Rembrandt's wife, Goya's duchess), to several painters, and to the act of painting as analogous to his own art. He never travelled to Europe, and probably saw few paintings of any quality in person. Instead he would have relied (like Walcott) on reproductions in books. Apart from the reference to Botticelli, evoked in a very specific context, Roach's taste is consistent, even narrow: he favours the extreme, texturally almost coarse work of Gauguin,

Goya, Rembrandt and Van Gogh. These are painters noted for their treatment of unusual subjects, and for sometimes unflattering frankness; they combine what Roach might have regarded as "peasant" virtues with sublimity. And they are all, ironically, painters whose work for the most part does not reproduce very well – especially by the techniques of printing before 1950.

Very few poets are mentioned by name, and most of the mentions are concentrated in three poems: in "New Year Poem for Cecil Herbert", in "Poem (Pray That the Poem out of Nowhere Come)", and in "She Never Dies". The pantheon is revealing of Roach's taste (it corresponds to his taste in visual art), but not especially of his practice. There is first of all Homer, whose high status for Roach we considered in Chapter 1, and then the most "manly" and unruly poets of the English Renaissance: Marlowe, Shakespeare, Donne, and Milton. The Romantics are represented by Keats, Shelley, and Byron (who has the dubious honour to be addressed along with Shelley as "you fornicators, you lovers and abductors of women"). Among the moderns only Yeats is mentioned, and his presence is of course pervasive in the poems. There are occasional traces of moderns like C. Day Lewis and W. H. Auden, and the absence of T. S. Eliot remains conspicuous – conspicuous because of Eliot's international status in the 1950s, but even more so because of his formative influence on other West Indian poets of the period.

As for the West Indian poets, I spoke at the end of the last chapter about Roach's contacts with that community; yet despite close personal connections, especially with Telemaque, Herbert, Collymore and Lamming, to each of whom he addressed a poem, Roach's *work* is rarely if ever engaged in dialogue with theirs. These and other poets in the region read and encouraged one another, but there was no network of intertextuality, probably because until after Independence there was virtually no network of professional activity. As late as 1973, it marked a turning point when Walcott in *Another Life* conspicuously quoted the Jamaican poet George Campbell. Their isolation, and perhaps along with it the fragility of their identity as artists, is thrown into high relief by the comfort West Indian writers found in the *illusory* conversation which the BBC staged in its broadcasts, through the juxtaposition of texts from different authors and islands.

The origins of Roach's stylistic parsimony are no doubt complex. Though we should not rule out the possibility of defensive measures taken against the danger of literary colonization, its deepest roots are certainly in his personality, and in the process of coming to terms with the very concrete limitations of his literary culture. In response to such limitations, some writers become acute observers of provincial nature or manners – Jane Austens or Edward Thomases. For Roach, however, the fundamental gesture of self-definition is a visionary transumption of the closed round of life and work, of personal biography. If it is safe to assume that Roach begins, in some sense, with an escape into art, then his work can be seen as the ongoing negotiation of that escape in a way that has very positive political implications. He means to fashion himself into a representative poet, and to fashion his immediate place and people into a visionary but recognizable place, "the West Indies", of which that poet can be the voice. The protagonist/speaker of these poems, with few exceptions, is thus not Roach of Tobago but "the West Indian poet". In spite of Telemaque's comment, Roach does not want to be a poet of Tobago, but of the archipelago. The chief impediment to such an ambition, of course, is the West Indies itself – themselves. It is only a slight exaggeration to say that the Federation was stymied because there is no central place to build a capital, and the topographical fact that the West Indies is *all* margin, a fractured rim around nothing, frustrates even imaginative efforts to take a stand on it as a cultural or political site. That problem discloses another facet of Roach's fascination with soaring bird/bards who never perch anywhere and so can be the voices of the whole area they patrol. As that imagery implies, Roach in his poetry is nearly a man without a life; a man engaged in a single-minded effort to transform himself (and people like him, if there are any) into a symbol. One strand of his work is a continuing study of images that can represent the talented individual isolated in a pared-down environment. It is by first coming to terms with the figure of the poet-isolato that he can proceed to address the place of that functionary (if there is a function for poets) in the community. The community is in these poems an idealized or rudimentary version of the village – before the 1970s he rarely considers any urban or more complexly political environment.

At the same time, however, Roach is obviously engaged in mythologizing the village – or more precisely, the peasantry. Roach is not a poet of concrete particulars. He rarely identifies specific settings for his poems ("Grafton Bay" is one exception). As he avers in poems like "Invocation" and "Poets and Painters", his "plot", his "nurtured field", is his own soul or the West Indian soul, and not some Patmos, not the specificity of Tobago. Similarly, as will become apparent in this chapter, he is disinclined to identify specific people. But it will also become apparent that much of his work is devoted to shaping for the peasantry the same sort of representative figure he seeks for the poet – and for himself. The ambiguity about the human subject in many of his poems, which we had reason to note above, sometimes blurs the line between these two projects: to find his own place as a writer in his immediate world, and to serve that world by articulating for its inhabitants the place they do or could occupy in the larger world. Both of these are on his mind; they are similar; and indeed for him to segregate them too sharply would be to acknowledge too fully an alienation he is trying to overcome. This makes for some confusion, but it is also fortuitous. As a consequence of this situation, even his most extreme solipsism tends to be presented in a way that makes it accessible as a study of something much larger and finally more resonant, more useful. This is one of the indications that he is a profoundly "Federalist" poet, a poet of the shared landscape as of the shared identity and history, who functions typically and by preference at the level of archipelago. It will become clear that he elides the details of his life in his poems not simply out of reticence, but out of a sense of mission, in response to a felt need for a representative voice of the place and people.

At some point – or perhaps only in some instances – he moves further along this line and writes poems for *others* to speak; writes political work in that particular sense, which might even be described as a kind of second-order "folk" poetry, insofar as it is designed for circulation and use. This is the force of the wish he expressed to Lamming: "Oh for your oratory for the stricken dumb" ("Letter to Lamming"); to put words in their mouths that not only fit their mouths, but fit the circumstances of their lives. The curbing of autobiography and confessional, the writing as representative man, perhaps has this as its goal; and a text so oriented will in fact not look too different from a text aspiring to a place in the international tradition. He is aiming for a very particular sort of "universality"; to write poems that suit not only the *eyes* of the timeless arbiters of taste he hoped were watching over his shoulder, but also the *mouths* of actual West Indian people – words that West Indians can find themselves speaking, positions in which they feel comfortable. Indeed, for Roach the poem that enables its readers to speak certain words from certain stances seems to offer a way of defining the West Indian. When the poem fits, wear it – clothes make the man.

That effort to give the West Indian a place and a voice is a frequent topic in indigenous criticism, often carried forward in terms of the metaphor of finding or building a house.[11] Roach is primarily a poet of open air and public space, but as it happens the first and last poems of the group before us are ostensibly about houses; indeed, in a passage we will return to at the end of this chapter, Roach once described "Homestead" as "a hut deliberately but not very artfully constructed to shelter my nakedness".[12] That poem, however, is more concerned with land than with a house, which is mentioned only glancingly in its second line, and "The Old House", though exceptional in its attention to interior space, is about a house which is not his own. Even though the idea is not central in either instance, both of these poems begin with a house standing up against the buffet of the wind, and in so doing they recall "March Trades", a poem primarily about weather and "adventure" on the open ocean which paradoxically includes one of Roach's rare interiors: a house that feels like a ship's cabin.

*

A desolate "wind-moaning" house stands amid "neglected lawns" at the beginning of the first version of "The Old House" (1951), "remembering her treasures" – that is, the family that once dwelt within.[13] As usual in Roach's domestic scenes, there is a mother softly crooning her cradlesong, and as usual the representation is not especially pictorial, but otherwise the evocation of the remembered family is unusually vivid:

> I, a boy, a stranger walked through their doors,
> Found the house gracious and lovely,
> Found them brown, rose-mouthed and comely,
> Dark-haired and curly, and was joyous among them.
> Here with beautiful innocence we laughed our green laughter
> Buoyant as birdsong in the woods of our youth.[14]

There is something of Hardy in the estrangements here; a family circle now sadly broken by death, and one that, for that matter, even unbroken, was never his own. This was a family he only visited, though there may be a vague sense in the poem that these visits were for him escapes to another life. Yet of the few poems that could be called remotely autobiographical, only this one is explicitly so. Even the love poems are veiled, generalized; there are no revealing details. "The Old House" is unique in the degree of its openness about his relationships, his actual story; none of his earlier verse comes close, and there will not be another poem that names names as this one does for over twenty years. This is his most legibly personal poem until "Verse in August". Perhaps to call it "legible" is misleading. Events in the life of a family are alluded to rather than presented, written about in a sort of shorthand that assumes familiarity, so that the underlying scenario is in some doubt for most readers of the poem.

The father of the family has died, and since his death "his gray widow nods in town among a rude generation", leaving the house abandoned. The central stanzas of the poem grieve for her, for a daughter, now dead, who played the piano, and for what seems to be another daughter, ill and now perhaps also dead. There is also a son named Michael, the poet's boyhood friend, to whom this poem is addressed.

Unaccustomed to making such disclosures, Roach has not succeeded in telling us what we need to know about these relationships, but it is likely that he regarded this text as a draft of a poem. As the quoted passage illustrates, the form is irregular and even rather lax, while its gestures at structure are tentative: mentions of the sun and the moon both at the beginning and near the end of the poem, and similarly an attempt to frame grief between remembered and present laughter. That framing unfortunately produces rapid, unprepared modulations of emotional tonality, and as a result the rationalization of the ending gives particular trouble. After about forty lines of grieving, the poem takes an improbable emotional turn for the better: "But, for you and I, Michael, / The careless, cloud-laurelled jongleurs of life, / . . . What are tears? What are tears?" The poem then ends very strangely indeed, with an affirmation of friendship and poetry that seems more enforced than truly achieved: the poet is in Michael's "ruinous house", writing "the canzones of our blood" in the grime of the windowpanes; a carrion crow perched on his shoulder (!) scratches out the words, at which the poet says "I laugh, re-echoing your laughter were you here".

Roach had not previously faced the peculiar technical problems involved in writing *accessible* confessional poetry, and his realization of the effort required to master them may have been one factor (in addition to temperament) that put him off writing poems of this sort. It is revealing in this connection that a character called "Michael", who seems to be based on the same actual person, appears in Roach's story "The Cricketers" (BBC broadcast, Nov. 6, 1955); in any case "Growing Up in Tobago" establishes that several other details in that story are directly from life: the name of the cricket team (Select), the characterization of the team captain with his lament of "water in me eye", and the partisan umpire Angus.[15] This contemporaneous willingness to use life experience directly in *fiction* reinforces the impression that Roach programmatically excluded it from his poetry as part of his conception of the function of poetry. Not until the valedictory "Verse in August" do such personal memories surface again, and there (incidentally) this same Angus is one of only two people mentioned by name. All this suggests that we should regard this version of "The Old House" as an abandoned, rather than a failed, project.

The nature of Roach's subsequent revision of the poem supports such a judgment. When broadcast four years later on the BBC, "The Old House" was recast in regular four-line stanzas, and systematically depersonalized. The description of the widow is a case in point:

> La mère seems deathless in her age,
> Green in her decrepitude,
> Laughing from the skeleton,
> Rattling the dead bones of her years. (FR 78)

The expression *la mère* might be heard as affectionate creole, but the context is so literary ("decrepitude" has Yeats's name written all over it) that it may just as well seem a piece of arch poetic diction. Like much of the work Roach revised in this period, these lines are among many in the poem that seem somewhat contaminated by the imagery of "The Flowering Rock". The revision goes on to reach its conclusion with no old house, no Michael, no carrion crow. Instead, though the title is unchanged, it has become frankly a poem about poetry, in Roach's most Yeatsian symbolic mode. It invests heavily in a confidence that the lost household can live again in the ever-green structures of the poem:

> And I who nourish a rose tree
> With blood from vein and artery
> Drop down at the rose's root
> And give my heart that it may flower.
>
> That they may live a poem's age
> In the green house a poet builds.
> O may they know, who told my youth
> To dance and sing, I tell their death.

Roach remained true to these lines. The duty to memorialize the dead dominates his poetry – but, as these same lines illustrate, it is not their individuality that he memorializes.

*

After "The Old House", we need to consider three rather ceremonial poems written for women of the Herbert family, and then the poems about Roach's mother and father. "Birth (for Judith Herbert)" (*Bim* 15, Dec., 1951, 181) celebrates a joyous occasion, the birth of a daughter. A revision was subsequently broadcast under the title "Cradlesong, for Judith" (BBC March 14, 1954). The two poems are quite similar in form and argument; they differ mostly in rearrangements of short phrases. The newborn child bursts on the scene as "a flame ascending in the passive air, / Beauty rose-opening, a birth taking bone" ("Birth"). The birth of the child induces the birth of the poem, which emerges "As from the womb to your morning of being" and embraces the child in its protective spell: "The magic of songcraft circles your cradle". This imagery is obviously constructed out of elements reminiscent of "The Flowering Rock," but here those elements are shaped into something very different. In these poems Roach exploits the imagery's inherent grace, rather than its conceptual content.

In stark contrast to the poems for Judith Herbert, however, "The White Coffin (for Jean Herbert)" (1954) tells a death out of order, the death of a child. Despite Roach's relationship with the Herberts, this poem is not addressed to the family really, and indeed is not consoling; there is a kind of brutality here which recurs virtually whenever he writes about his intimates. It makes one wonder how his friends responded to these poems. Perhaps this is one reason why he wrote so rarely for or about living individuals: too much *saeva indignatio*. But there is more to it than that; this trait surfaces most shockingly in the poems about his mother, and it tends to make a disturbing appearance in Roach's poems about other women as well. We will have to look at it more closely when we take up those poems in the following chapter.

This present poem almost immediately looks outward from its occasion and seems to imagine for itself an audience not of friends who knew the parents of this dead child, but of people quite remote from the event, people who might reasonably be comfortable with the poem's initial sentiment: "the commonplace recurs, it's a child's turn" (FR 110). No act of consolation, this poem is rather an outcry at how the occasion bares the failure of adult faith: not only in the hypocrisy of the preacher ("the wicked man . . . faith long denied him"), but in the whole assembly:

> Oh, all our youth, the hope and the heaven
> Are gone into graves deeper than this girl's,
> Blacker than her mother's mourning,
> Our faiths died in man's worst famine.

The poem ends with a problematic redemptive vision (but what redemptive vision is not problematic?):

Shall she dance
In Eden? This coffin would flower;
The dead would break their bones for bread
And offer their blood for our faiths
And light the world with their candle of Christ,
For they know our night, our famine and fear
As we crouch under the volcanic sun.

The floating subjunctive syntax of the closing lines embodies something uncanny, a fierce blending of despair, imaginative power, and something like rage at grace withheld. There is a missing step on this stairway to heaven, an elided "if that were true . . ." on which the realization of everything contingent on that "would" depends. The apocalyptic details invite our elation as fit conclusion to this poem of grief, but that effect is overshadowed by the poet's evident distress at the ease with which he can imagine a redemption he cannot believe in. The poem voices a reproach: If there were saints, and they knew our condition, they would do *anything* to help us; yet here we are. Many of Roach's poems are concerned with achieving various kinds of immortalities; this one is about the lack of faith out of which that craving comes.

*

We turn now to the poems about Roach's immediate family – that is to say, about his parents, since no other relations appear in them, no children, grandparents, siblings, uncles. He published only two poems that are certainly about his own mother. Appearing six years apart, "To My Mother" and "Mother and Son" share many common elements. Both celebrate the mother's strength, and both end by turning attention to her relation to her son's poetic vocation. Yet they remain distinct poems with different objectives, and (as the changed title indicates) the second increases its distance from its subject by shifting to the third person. We will consider them first, and then take up the poems explicitly about his father, the first of which, "Poets and Painters", is in many respects a preliminary sketch for the second, "Homestead". "Homestead" however exists in three very different forms, and one important feature of the revisions is a *progressive* effacement of the personal, as his own father becomes an "un-named" peasant farmer. In other words, the poems about both his parents, like the only other truly intimate poem of this period, "The Old House", are all revised in a way that decreases their already limited intimacy.

Among all these poems, the most personal is "To My Mother", broadcast in 1955 and then published in *Kyk-over-al* (1957), the first of several occasions when it was printed as a companion-poem to "Homestead". Considering that the poem is addressed directly to his own mother, the opening may seem to offer *very* cold comfort:

It is not long, not many days are left
Of the dead sun, nights of the crumbled moon;
Not far to go. (FR 123)

But as the argument continues in this rather pre-emptive vein, we recognize the rhetorical progression characteristic of many of Roach's more or less occasional poems: a movement away from initial direct address, through meditation, to hortatory imperatives. In this instance, the imperative is disguised as an axiomatic declaration: "And it is nothing, . . . the old . . . welcome the earth's suction / and the bone's extinction into rock". But the statement has the usual imperative force; his mother's opinion on the matter is not solicited.

At the centre of the poem is a compelling portrait of his mother, depicted with the uncompromising frankness of a Rembrandt. Above all, he envisions her as peasant farmer and self-sufficient householder, controlling with her own labour the entire natural process from planting to product: "Hoeing the growing, reaping the ripe corn; / Kneading and thumping the thick dough for bread". This bread returns in the guise of a metaphor to conclude the poem, but the central description is dominated, like so many of Roach's poems, by a metaphorical tree. He writes:

I found you strong and tough as guava scrub, . . .
And now you're bowed, bent over to the ground;
An old gnarled tree, all her boughs drooped
Upon the cross of death, you crawl up
Your broken stairs like Golgotha, and dead bones
Clutch at your dying bones........[16]

This is another of those passages that make one wonder if Roach's mother ever saw these poems; it is instructive to contrast it with the opening lines of "Tree" (1952), an earlier poem which might in fact also have been inspired by his mother, though it does not present itself in those terms:

Her flowers are gone and all her boughs
Are arching with maturing fruit;
She chants magnificats to sun,
Proclaims her worth in motherhood,

Proclaims perpetual fruitfulness of earth,
Serves me for symbol. (FR 86)

The effect is almost antithetical to that in "To My Mother" – much more positive, perhaps, precisely because the mother-figure here is *not* drawn from life, and is idealized into a symbol of the poet's own productivity, which is described in male terms ("I stand up siring my song") though the tree which symbolizes it is described as female. In the later poem the boughs that were arching with fruit are bending down toward death, and the poet's response manifests the blunt stoicism that Roach would have recognized in Yeats's *Last Poems*, but hardly had to learn there: "I do not mourn, but all my love / Praise life's revival through the eternal year. / I see death broken at each seed's rebirth."

These vast cycles of "the eternal year" recall the much more modest cycle of growing corn for bread, and that homely activity provides the symbol the poem ends on:

Oh, time's run past the time your hands made bread
To this decrepitude; but in the stream
Of time I watch the stone, the image
Of my mother making bread my boyhood long,
Mossed by the crusty memories of bread.
O may my art grow whole as her hands' craft.

Some unexpected complexities of expression here deserve attention. The basic idea of an affinity between the mother's work and the son's is first touched upon in a very early poem, "New Loaves". Now the point of the affinity is clearer: the material of poetry, like dough or clay, has to be worked into shape and then baked, fired, fixed in a "permanent" form. But in the course of these lines an additional metaphor comes into play: the stone persisting against the buffet of the stream of time. What persists for the poet through the streaming years is the fixed memory of his mother making bread. But what does it mean that the remembered image is "mossed" with multiple memories of bread itself? Perhaps what Roach saw could be gained by the complication is the idea that, while the memory of his mother's craft persists independently, it is also accessible every time he breaks through the crust of a new loaf. Such an idea has the added effect, through metaphor, of domesticating the craft of poetry; making it no less familiar, but also no less miraculous, than the mother's daily bread.[17]

That passage however has the additional effect of removing the still-living mother to a great distance: she becomes a remembered image, fading with time, distanced in metaphor, and further obscured by being "mossed" with another, different image. The reader will also have noticed that shift from "your" to "her" in the course of two of the stanzas from "To My Mother" quoted above, as if the sentences themselves could not resist the urge to increase the distance between the poet and his subject. These almost involuntary gestures, recoiling from intimacy, pave the way for the next poem, "Mother and Son" (1961), which is cast entirely in the third person; it constitutes the same sort of depersonalizing revision that Roach undertook for "The Old House". On the other hand, such elements of premature eulogy as mark "To My Mother" are entirely absent from "Mother and Son". The shadow of death falls only patchily on this poem's praise of the mother, which is expressed particularly through associating her with the earth, with clay and stone, as well as with the analogous dough. She is "stone-strong yet pliant as her clay"; "Her humble rectitude was a rock / outcropping of the stubborn land" (FR 146). Inverting the perspective of the flowering rock imagery, he writes that she sowed her son "barefoot like a tree" so he would be nourished by "the patient clay, the solemn courage of the stone".

Drawing his strength from that clay and stone and homemade bread, what he grew into was a poet, and as in "To My Mother", the concluding lines of this poem take up the mother's role in that development. In the earlier poem her own craft is presented as an inspiration to him; here however the relationship is very different, because the diet in question is intellectual. All her learning, and all her lessons for him, come from one book, her Bible. It is her *voicing* of the Bible that inspires his devotion to language, but his devotion is to secular poetry and not to the sacred word. She is then distressed to find herself the cause of this misdevotion, while he presents himself so defensively that he seems to want to appear a helpless victim:

> Hearing her speak the speech of prophets,
> Tell memoried psalm and miracle
>
> He entered a dry womb of words,
> A Merlin's maze he cannot leave,
> That gives salt grief to her old age.
> He sees her stubborn dying eyes
> Weep for him crossed upon his rhyme.

It is a passage of rare – and wrenching – intimacy, this acknowledgement of an impasse that in a way outlasts them both. He has no access to faith like hers, but he finally has no sure faith in words either. To describe it as "a dry womb of words" in the context of a poem about his mother paints a very grim picture of his vocation, and the self-laceration continues in the contrast between what the poem earlier called her "sweet dream" of revelation and his "Merlin's maze," or indeed between her Biblical prophets and his heathen wizard.

There is an inherent contrast too between speech and writing which needs to be spelled out here because it will prove to be highly pertinent to Roach's theorizing about literature in the 1970s. The poem tells us that her "speech" inspires him to write, with a strong implication that, precisely because for him that one Book is not a matter of prophetic speech, but of scholarship, his own words will lack magic, lack imaginative power. I quoted earlier a statement that seemed like a boast: "I left my mother speechless with my word knowledge of the gospels." But we can now see that his emphasis would have been on the phrase "word knowledge"; that is, on the *contrast* between what the gospels were for him and for his mother. And we can see, too, the hollow triumph in the word "speechless". However deluded, naive, or ignorant, she could speak with the tongues of prophets, and in his prose memoir written more than a decade later he seems to make a point of savagely demystifying that power (which after all he aspires to, and fears he cannot attain) by describing not her speech, but her reading: "Every night, with the slow mumbling and finger tracing of the barely literate, she read the black family bible. . . . She thumbed it through from Genesis to Revelation though only her God alone knows what she could make of that mass of material whose full meaning I began to grasp much later on from the writings of biblical scholars and theologians."[18] This visualization of his mother replaces the assurance of inspired speech with timidity and hesitation, with "mumbling"; it transforms her experience of the Bible into a kind of maze, like his own. The passage continues with the complex false modesty of a man with a chip on his shoulder. The whole manoeuvre of the memoir, at once self-serving and anguished, only elaborates what is expressed in this remarkable poem. In "To My Mother", his mother is a tree with its boughs "drooped upon the cross of death"; in this poem he is the one "crossed upon his rhyme". Each of them sees the other as crucified; only one of them regards that as a path to redemption.

*

In "Mother and Son", the mother represents an *alternative* course of life which the poet must constantly confront. His father, however, was already dead when Roach began to write poems about him, and his appearances in the poetry are always powerfully idealized. He represents something for the son to measure up to, a challenging but *un*problematic model. The first poem involving Roach's father is "Poets and Painters", broadcast in 1950. The poem's objective is to mobilize West Indian "poets and painters, thinkers, strugglers". They are called upon in an opening apostrophe that summons up Yeats's "Under Ben Bulben" as a kind of sustaining context for this poem.[19] The imperatives addressed to them in the conclusion recall those of "Invocation", broadcast the previous year, though these express a political rather than a personal agenda: the landscape, too generalized to be Tobago, bespeaks Roach's support of Federation:

> Tear barriers down, efface the frontiers,
> Water the barren plainlands, drain the marshes;
> Plough deep in the drought season;
> Rich harvests ripen upon nurtured acres;
> Cool courage shall confound old griefs and fears. (FR 70)

Obviously, this poem is not *about* Roach's father; but he appears at the heart of the poem, between the opening apostrophe and the closing exordium, to stand as an emblematic example, and thereby provide the poem's motivating force:

> My father the strong man
> Could set his stamp upon
> The sterile fields of clay or stone;
> With mattock, hoe and spade, the good couth tools
> He wrote his will upon such stubborn earth
> And charmed sweet harvests forth.
> Are we lesser pioneers than he?

Roach often insists that the essential model for the productive West Indian is the man who works the soil; here his own father, in the role of solitary peasant, is presented as the model not for himself but for the addressees of this poem. The challenge, "Are we lesser pioneers than he?" is meant to stir the poets and strugglers to action. The particular images introduced in these lines will be developed more extensively in "Homestead" (that may be why this poem was published only once, much later and rather obscurely). Here the father shapes the fields into his own image, to his own desire and need, and the statement that he thereby "wrote his will" upon the earth does double service: it means that he imposed his will, but also that the fields constitute his legacy, his heritage. There is then the further implication that the fields are a kind of document, "signed and sealed" (in the words of "The Old Man"); at the same time the mild magic of "charmed sweet harvests forth" suggests even etymologically that the fields are a "poetic" text, a *carmen*, which he created and bequeathed.

The argument is also nudged toward its imperative conclusion by a bit of dramatic staging:

> Midnight is struck
> And on my eastern hill as pale as mist
> The waning moon swims in a sea of mist.
> The death within us dies; grief's phoenix sire
> Is fagged to ashes in redeeming fire,
> And dawn is eager for the thundering wing.

The poem is conceived as being spoken in the dark before the dawn, but that commonplace political imagery takes on additional power from the notion (already established) that the fields are a legacy; this is thus the time when the phoenix sire is consumed and the new sun/son is imminent. The father's exemplary relationship with the land, in combination with the natural magic of the poem's passage through midnight to imminent dawn, explains why the imperatives are couched entirely in agricultural terms, even though the passage is certainly *about* nothing but art. The lines describe farming (on a large, communal, scale in fact, even though the peasant invoked is solitary) but they refer to the total intellectual productivity in the islands, the nurturing of that harvest in the predawn of nationhood.

While "strugglers" often work in concert, and "painters" sometimes do, "poets" and "thinkers" do not; the ticklish matter of how to make their individual labours serve a common good – so urgent a question in West Indian intellectual circles – is not really confronted here, but it is at least represented in a deft equivocation about how isolated peasants might carry on corporate farming. In this respect "Poets and Painters" resembles the exactly contemporaneous poem "February", and the slightly later "Men" (1952) and "Corn" (1955), each of which presents a similar community of solitary farmers.

"Homestead" is Roach's most widely disseminated and probably his best-known poem. The poem was published seven times during his lifetime, and the various texts are far from identical. Three significantly different versions of the poem must be distinguished. One, published in *Kyk-over-al* in 1957, is a maverick version unlike any other, which I will refer to as [B]. The main textual tradition originates earlier, with a version published in *Caribbean Quarterly* in 1952 [A]; that is the version published in the *Collected Poems* and it is the primary text under discussion here. A revision of the [A] text in *Tamarack Review* (1960) introduces a few changes of detail – single adjectives modified and the like – but it need not detain us, since all of these changes are incorporated in the text published in *The Sun's Eye* in 1968, which in addition is so substantially changed in the final two stanzas as to constitute a new version of the poem [C]. Since the immediate historical context impinges significantly on [C], my treatment of that poem is deferred to a later chapter. The other publications can be disregarded; all of them duplicate one of the versions just mentioned, in some cases introducing obvious errors.

Roach begins with a consideration of nature that gradually leads to consideration of a human figure:

> Seven splendid cedars break the trades
> From the thin gables of my house,
> Seven towers of song when the trades rage
> Through their rich green season foliage.
> But weathers veer, the drought returns,
> The sun burns emerald to ochre . . .
> Then they are tragic stands of sticks . . .
> And north beyond them lie the fields
> Which one man laboured his life's days[.] (FR 79)

It is because the trees are now bare that the poet can see his father's fields, but their apparent lifelessness also turns his thoughts to the dead man. These trees play a more prominent role in Roach's other versions of "Homestead" [B and C]; in this text they reappear only in a brief simile: "His ghost's as tall as the tall trees". Instead the focus in [A] is squarely on the peasant and his relation to the land. Critical attention to this poem has, understandably, also concentrated on this figure of the peasant.[20] He is a man of the soil, and the associations with bread and clay recur here, as in all the poems about his parents. Roach repeats from "Poets and Painters" the idea that the peasant imposes his will, his image on the land, but adds a new sense of the personal *price* of that legacy: "one man wearying his bone / shaped [the fields] as monuments in stone." Similarly the poem emphasizes how close to the earth the peasant is; even before he dies into it, his labour "drags him daily into earth".

In the face of that death, the poem is preoccupied with establishing the father's continuing presence on and in the land he worked. Its operative terms are: *recall*, *return*, *reclaim* and *remain*. The poem accomplishes his return; or rather, that of his ghost, "tall as the trees", which returns as naturally as the foliage returns to its place on the barren branch; as the poem goes on to say, he and his kind have just the sort of immortality that the foliage of the cedars has – they are "perpetual, . . . unkillable as the earth's grass". That very grass recognizes and acknowledges this fellow creature as "the spirit of the place", but the poet still wants to take some responsibility for the return, and to claim some credit for the power of his verse: "In the fervour of my song; ...... / I hold him firm upon the fields / in many homely images", just as the man once imposed himself upon them while he lived.[21] In the context of that claim we can note a deft touch: as in any classical georgic, this peasant is also remembered for his skill at weather forecasting: "he read day's event from the dawn / And saw the quality of morning / In the sunset mask of evening". This facet of his closeness to nature is treated as a sort of naive augury, and like the word "charms" in "Poets and Painters" it reveals the glint of a power that might give hereditary authority to the prophetical gestures of this poem by his son.

The father's apotheosis into spirit is completed once he stands securely perpetual in his particular fields; the poem then universalizes him by a sleight of syntax that makes the "one man" into many:

> *A* slave-man's son, a peasant one,
> Paysan, paisano, *any common*
> Man about earth's fields, world over,
> In the cotton corn and clover
> Who *are* unsung but who remain
> Perpetual. [my emphasis]22

We have come to "Homestead" by way of "Poets and Painters", and so I have been speaking as if the identification of the peasant as the poet's own father were unequivocal. That such is the case in this poem is hinted at by the earlier phrase "left me heritage" but it is hardly emphasized; without the explicit corroboration of "Poets and Painters" it would be easy to understand the central figure of this poem to be a neighbour, sympathetically observed in the Wordsworthian manner, and a number of critics have done so. In [B] as we shall see the appropriateness of the identification is even less sure; the whole matter recalls something discussed at the end of Chapter 3: the ambiguous identity of the human subject (himself, his compatriots, his common or uncommon reader) in many of Roach's poems. In any case, this present passage completes the metamorphosis of the father-figure into a myth without human attachments, diffusing him into the worldwide peasantry he represents, so that the final praise (which harks back to "The Old Man") is for the group, not the individual:

> And from their graves within their graves,
> They nourish arteries of earth
> And give her substance, give her worth.

That roundly conclusive note is followed by envoi of imperatives, the moral to be drawn from this exemplum:

> O sons, O strong ones from their loins,
> Boldly inherit the rich earth
> Though you keep their homespun traces
> Or run in splendid gilded races.
> O poets, painters, thinkers turn
> Again and take new craft from old
> Worth and wisdom on the wold.
> O cornerstones of the crazed world,
> O nourishers of earth's best blood
> Reclaim the weary dying good.

This final stanza has a grand sound, and (even more than in "Poets and Painters") the relationship to "Under Ben Bulben" is patent in its rhyme, form, and diction. Yet its intentions are not entirely clear; it is not surprising that the end of the poem is the part Roach kept rewriting over the years. Some rough spots go almost unnoticed: the gilding of the fourth line seems excessive, and in the same neighbourhood the syntax is a bit wishful – Roach seems very much to want "though" to mean "whether." But beyond that some quite crucial elements of the stanza seem only provisionally explicable. Certainly three different groups are being addressed: first, the (literal or figurative) sons of the unsung common men, who are being asked in effect to *maintain* their contact with the earth; then the artists and thinkers, who are asked to *return* to peasant values from which they have presumably grown remote; and finally – strangely – a group that must be the common men themselves. No other parties to this poem can reasonably be referred to as "cornerstones" of the world or "nourishers of earth's best blood", yet their appearance at the end of this list is so peculiar that I suspect many readers unreflectively assume that the peasants cannot be meant here, and take the whole stanza as addressed to the sons, in defiance of what the text actually says. It is no help that the eloquent final line can be read in several different ways, all of them resonant, none of them very satisfying as to sense: it really can't mean "reclaim those of the weary who are dying good," though it may seem to say that. No arrangement of commas can make "good" securely the noun it seems to need to be, and whether "good" refers to good people, the good old days, or homespun values, nothing in the poem has prepared us to see any of them as weary or dying. Here Roach may be resolving a worry he feels, which has not actually made its way into this poem.[23] Only the poem's solitary question, its one moment of irrupting anger, hints at what might be on his mind:

> Is labour lovely for a man
> That drags him daily into earth,
> Returns no fragrance of him forth?

The poem as it stands, however, goes on to assure us that the earth returns not his fragrance but something surely better, his ghost, his continuing presence as *genius loci*; and further, that his labour will indeed have meaning, if only the sons and poets do what this poem urges them to do.

The [B] text of "Homestead" (*Kyk-over-al* 22 (1957), 52-53) is of interest to us here primarily for certain differences in the conception of the poem's objectives. In addition, there are a few passages whose treatment clarifies their meaning in other versions of the poem. This version of the poem has more modest ambitions than [A]; as it says of itself, it is a straightforward epitaph, written "in his own blood of hope and faith", offering assurance of the man's abiding presence and of the meaningfulness of his life. If [A] is largely about the earth (the word "earth" and its close cognates [earthy, earthier] occur ten times in that poem), [B] is about vegetation. There are only three instances of "earth" cognates, and the image of a stone monument built up at the cost of bone is absent; instead the emphasis is on cedars, woodland, plants, grain, and grass. The pattern established in the opening stanza – the trees first green, then bare – implicitly invokes the cycle of seasons, which remains in the background as a potential closural device throughout the poem. The [A] text, which begins virtually the same way, might easily enough have returned to the trees; the sons called upon at the end might reasonably be described as new growth on the old stock or some such thing – but the fact is that no such idea is operative in [A]. In [B] Roach exploits that potential of his opening gambit; this poem begins and ends with the trees, and steadily prepares for that conclusion as the argument progresses. Thus stanza I ends with the trees bare, but stanza II ends with the following lines (which incidentally clarify the corresponding, but more compressed, lines in [A]):

> This heavy drudgery for a man
> But plants his spirit in the earth
> That blooms no fragrance of his worth.

No fragrance may come from his planted spirit, but there is the expectation (even if frustrated) that it ought to, and in fact the lines do not necessarily say that the plant failed to bloom. Stanza III ends more hopefully still: "He harvested his faith in grain". Following this upward trajectory, the poem as a whole ends on its most positive note; in the final lines the soul of the peasant turns out to be the force that drives the forest to flourish:

> Whose temperate and patient soul
> The heavy loam of human earth
> Feeds woods of wisdom, art and faith.

In the two passages just quoted this version of "Homestead" is much closer than any other to the realm of "flowering rock" imagery, and indeed to specific details of the poem, "The Flowering Rock". The word "soul" above looks almost like a misprint for "soil"; we are surely meant to hear the substitution and the close relationship it implies. As he does somewhat less explicitly in the corresponding lines of [A], Roach is writing again about the "black loam" celebrated in "The Flowering Rock," the accumulated experience of the peasantry and the fruits of human creativity it produces. And it is at least worth recalling that the same poem includes a lily which *does* bloom without fragrance. As the grammatically singular word "soul" indicates, [B] focuses more narrowly on the individual farmer. At the same time, there is an implicit vision of village life in the closing lines, and the vision is organic and cyclical: the peasantry endures, while each individual comes and goes, emerging from and then enriching the "human earth".

"Homestead" [B] thus ends with a brief glimpse of the generations to come, but in contrast to [A] there is no hint of augury here, on the part of either the peasant or the poet, and correspondingly there is no final exhortation – none of [A]'s anxiety about the "crazed world", none of that social urgency. There is no sense either of the power of poetry, as comparison with [A] makes clear. The poet's avowal in [A] – "In the fervour of my song / I hold him firm upon the fields / In many homely images" – suggests that personal memories about the man (homely images) are given permanence by the poet's creative power (the fervour of song holds him firm); nature recognizes him as the spirit of the place, but it is human art that enables other humans to see him there. In [B] the corresponding lines have very different implications. Roach writes rather flatly that, after the peasant's death, "he is present in the fields / In natural holy images". There is no reference to song or fervour, no poet's work, no creation of a myth for the community. Indeed, the juxtaposition of "natural" and "holy" calls to mind an illuminating context, the "natural supernaturalism" which M. H. Abrams led scholars to find at the heart of the project of Romanticism and especially of Wordsworth.[24] The phrase amply characterizes the atmosphere of this, Roach's most Wordsworthian poem.

One other difference deserves comment. Absolutely nothing in [B] suggests that the peasant is the poet's father. On the contrary, he is said to be "an un-named, unknown slaveman's son", and we are told that he "left his sons an heritage", where [A] says "left *me* heritage". More than in any other version of the poem, Roach here suppresses the relationship in order to portray a representative man. This is not the Homeric glorification, however brief, of quirky individuals, as often in Ian MacDonald and Walcott, but rather (as in Brathwaite) the transumption of personal experience into the mythic, into a form available to be put on by each reader. This is one way that, for all the differences of texture and scale in the work, his poetic *project* resembles that of Brathwaite in *The Arrivants*: the personal as staging area for the representative or even the mythic. In "Homestead" Roach "contributes" his own father to the common good, mythologizing him into wider accessibility as an ancestral, paternal, figure, not just someone's anecdotal parent. A similar move is made in the less successful poem "Corn" (1955), where Roach's attachment to his own roots is presented at two removes. The centre of the poem introduces Roach's surrogate, "the peasant boy" nurtured by this place's "simple culture" and "natural love". The following sentence then speaks of someone "drawn / by the tether of his blood / back to the corn-womb of his folk / where his father's bones are rock". Most readers would expect this to be a statement about Roach, under the guise of the peasant boy; but the actual subject of the sentence is "wandering Ulysses" – yet another substitution, very surprising, not entirely appropriate (the father of Ulysses was alive when he returned to Ithaca), and quite unprepared for by anything in the poem. These are instances of Roach's effort to write poems that are masks any Caribbean man would be comfortable putting on. They are masks, of course, in the usual Caribbean sense: not disguises, but public, even theatrical, instruments of definition, amplification, self-knowledge. Here Roach aims to create a poem that any West Indian can speak, with his own particular exemplary peasant in mind, and the poetic magic will still work to root and vitalize that particular speaker. "Homestead" successfully accomplishes that aim. Since its publication, the poem has functioned for the West Indian imagination in very much the same way as the transformation of the peasant Makak into myth, into a familiar guardian spirit, at the end of Walcott's masquerade play, *Dream on Monkey Mountain*.

*

It is surprising, then, that when Roach himself comments on "Homestead" he describes it not as a mask, projecting its act of possession from the stage of history, but as a "hut": "My whole history is my immediate family, and dimly seen behind the parents, the generations of heavy slave folk trampled into the clay where the sweet cane prospered in our bitter sweat. The poem, 'Homestead', is an artifice of pride: a hut deliberately but not very artfully constructed to shelter my nakedness."[25] To see a poem of such successfully public speech as an act of private enclosure is no paradox, of course; that statement might fairly stand as the definition of a certain kind of lyric. But Roach was writing those lines during a period of deep discouragement, when the chronic West Indian estrangement from the "dimly seen" generations only deepened the acute isolation he felt in his own immediate surroundings. Roach, building his hut of poetry, is self-consciously unaccommodated man devising for himself a history and a future and the sure title to a domesticated space.

What is striking about Roach in that frame of mind is the absence of what might be called the genealogical impulse: he undertakes no collecting of ancestors, relatives, family stories, such as we find in dozens of books by authors in something like his position. As he conceives it, a hut built by Eric Roach is not chock-a-block with mementos, but spartan to the point of sublimity – the rhetorical opulence of "Homestead" notwithstanding.

The terms in which he would phrase his function are not fashionable at the moment: he would probably speak of "purifying the language of the tribe", or rather of purifying the tribe's representation of itself and its place. His objective might be described as a refinement of experience to the abstract and essential, or a reduction to its common denominator (to choose language with opposed political valences). Perhaps he could be said to give back to his people an expression of their experience, language, and aspiration improved by his labour, as the land is improved by theirs. Thus, for example, he chooses not to write about his father, or his experience of his father, but about that aspect of his father which is accessible and meaningful to a certain set of people, West Indians. In fact, their disposition to respond to what he presents might be regarded as a *defining* sign of their common cause. It might almost (if not quite) be said that this emotional response is a litmus test for the West Indian; that "Homestead" and others poems like it – the texts Roach aspired to create – function as shibboleths for West Indians. But if so, these are shibboleths not in the usual exclusionary sense of that term, but by virtue of bringing them together around the expression of what makes them who they are. Roach's poems make manifest for West Indian readers not who they are individually, but what they are precisely insofar as they are West Indians: the expression of a certain kind of person in a certain kind of place with a certain kind of history and expectation from the future.

It is quite revealing – about Roach himself and about his society – that no mythic family is conjured up in these poems (the exception, "The Old House", proves the rule, with its already-disintegrated family). No poem presents his father and mother together; the poem of the father includes no mention of a wife, and that of the mother no mention of a husband. The parents themselves have no antecedents, relatives, or friends in the poems. Roach's autobiographical essay emphasizes the father's sociability, his cricket and his cronies;[26] all that is distinctly absent from the poems, and the contrast establishes that the rigid discipline of the poems on this matter is intentional. Each parent is transformed individually into a poetic figure, and this is the case, at least in part, because their isolation, their (enforced) self-sufficiency, is an essential part of their experience, one of the parts that makes them material for myth. Isolation is a part of the experience of the poem's *readers* that needs to be provided for in the representation.

The parents' isolation is physical as well as social: In contrast to the cozy domesticity depicted in "The Old House" (which, remember, is *lost*) Roach's own parents are always situated in the fields or the dooryard (like so many of his villagers), and not in an interior space. Each of the poetic figures derived from his parents is thus radically unaccommodated: seemingly houseless, unattached, without personal history. Their defining accommodation is to the land, and in the case of the mother also to the Bible. These few terms are the materials with which each of them defines an inhabitable cosmos, a sustaining order – a hut or a homestead.

In Roach's poems about his parents they are treated not only separately but differently. Some of the differences can be ascribed to gender stereotypes, or to the fact that only his mother was alive at the time he was writing these poems. To make a rough distinction in the terms generated by earlier poems, Roach aligns his father with the values associated with the solitary striver, his mother with those of the village. Poetry transforms the father into an idealized symbolic figure, while it produces for his mother an uncompromising life-portrait. On the other hand, his father in the poems is only a generalized model for the conduct of life; his mother is acknowledged as the source of his own specific vocation. At least according to "Mother and Son", however, she is its uncomprehending source; she all but repudiates what she has herself inspired. Not mythologized like the father, she is the living, still problematic parent, an ambivalent opponent of his ambitions. For Roach, each parent thus becomes the locus of a specific anxiety. His mother embodies a faith he does not share, and stands to question the value of any secular poetry at all. His father constitutes a legend of *true* productivity, an example of stolid endurance against which the poet constantly measures his own intangible, unrewarding, but equally unavoidable, work of nourishing. And as there are anxieties about his mother's naiveté, there are also anxieties about the apparent insignificance of the father's life and work (which the poems so elaborately act against), and these only amplify Roach's anxiety about the value of his own work. The "Merlin's maze" in which he finds himself suffers by comparison *both* with the monumentally inscribed "will" of the father's achievement *and* with his mother's "sweet dream" of religious faith.

It is not his alone, this problem that the ambition to speak of and for the people comes a-cropper in one's own dooryard, among uncomprehending or dismissive relatives. But Roach's legitimate identification with the peasantry exceeds that of most other West Indian writers, and for that reason the problem is a fundamental one, exerting pressure on the whole course of his work. The handling of his "immediate family" in these few poems seems to demonstrate that Roach turns himself, his place and his people into poetry only by turning away from all that as overt subject-matter. The programmatic suppression of the personal which this chapter documents is partly motivated by reticence, a reflection of the hard-won privacies of village life, and partly a way to negotiate the debt he has incurred, the obligation to use his talent for the people who give it to him, and from whom that very talent alienates him. But, as we have seen, there is a sublimation as well as a suppression; his life, as Yeats would say, "serves him for symbol". There may be no West Indian family depicted in these poems, but Roach's solitaries are all assays at tracing the lineaments of what Brathwaite calls "Caribbean man in space and time".[27] The gallery of representative figures Roach creates following the lead of "Homestead" will be the subject of the next chapter.

Chapter 5 —
Figures in the Caribbean Landscape

Roach tinkered with "Homestead" for nearly two decades (from before 1952 until publication of the [C] version in 1968). The shifting text of that poem is the imaginative space in which Roach undertakes the transumption of his actual father to autochthonous hero, to a persistently present ancestral spirit, an *egungun* or a *loa* (both terms Roach himself uses, though not in this connection). One reason why success in the construction of "Homestead" was crucial is that, in some sense at least, the transformation of his father into an available communal hero through the power of poetry entailed demonstration at the same time of successful transformation of his own contingent marginal self into a poet whose ability to "soar", whose successful meeting of the universal standards for poets, paradoxically authorized his claim to be poet of a specific community. This was plainly a central project for Roach during a very productive period (some thirty poems appeared between 1952-1955), and many other poems bear some relationship to the means or objectives of "Homestead". This is most patent in a group of poems in which Roach assembles a pantheon of local heroes to accompany his central *genius loci*, the peasant/father figure initially developed in "Homestead" and such cognate works as "Poets and Painters" and "Men". Regional critics quickly recognized the distinctive power of these poems; thus far, only his overtly political poems from the era of the Federation have attracted greater critical attention.

During the late 1940s Roach had produced some examples ("She", "Dancer") of the nationalist icon, a genre that was being produced throughout the region in response to political developments. Though motivated on quite different grounds, the underlying male ancestral figure also provides Roach with a way out of the confines of that limiting genre, and because of it Roach's poems of the 1950s are quite different from contemporaneous celebrations of Caribbean manhood along the lines of Archie Lindo's "Bronze" or Sherlock's "Jamaican Fisherman". The energy of such poems was visual and even erotic. Roach offers something much stronger, denser, and sometimes angrier in the poems we will consider next: "Haitian Trilogy" (1953), "The Fighters" (1953), "Legend of Daaga" (1953), "Ballad of Canga" (1955), and the later "For A. A. Cipriani" (1959).

It may surprise many casual readers of Roach to discover that during the second half of the decade (1955-61) he produced at least as many poems *about women* which have passed virtually unnoticed. This work does not simply carry on the nationalistic "pin-up" tradition into the 1950s; like the poems with male figures, Roach's poems of women take a distinctive path (or two) of their own. But when we turn to these poems later in this chapter it will be apparent that they cannot adequately be characterized as companion poems to those of the male pantheon. We have observed the great divergence in attitude and even diction that separates the mother-poems from the father-poems; an analogous disjunction separates the poems to be considered here. If male poems of the 1950s develop and explore the gestures of "Homestead", the agenda of the female poems is quite different. There are goddesses, but they are out of Robert Graves, not Greece, and several of these poems are problematic along lines we saw adumbrated by some of the poems about women discussed in the previous chapter.

All of these poems, in any case, whether male or female in subject, exemplify the great seriousness of Roach's mature poetic enterprise. The single exception of "Canga" draws attention to the fact that there is almost never a touch of satire or comedy in his poems. There is fine comedy to be found in Roach's stories and plays. By contrast, the poems are sometimes almost dour. Not without reason. The poems we will be concentrating on in the first half of this chapter embrace a diverse assortment of male figures: victims, defiant revolutionaries, boxers, an obeahman, a mainstream politician – they are slaves, freedmen, 'postcolonials'. Yet everyone he writes about in these poems is dead by the end if not from the start, and many are presented to us as martyrs: Toussaint, Daaga, the North American fighters, Cipriani (a martyr not literally, but via simile: "he's as indestructible as legend, as a martyr's funeral pyre"), and even in a way Canga Brown. The word "grief" echoes through the poems of the 1950s, usually with reference to the trauma of colonial history. In these poems Roach pays increasing attention to the

Americas and their history of colonization. In addition to writing about historical events like the betrayal of Anacaona (in the 1955 revision of his earlier poem) and the revolt of Daaga, Roach makes an effort – sometimes an overstrenuous effort – to include features of Caribbean culture. Examples include the creole passages of his Haitian poems and the catalogue of folkways displayed in the course of "I am the Archipelago". Not surprisingly, both race and colour assert themselves as factors in these poems. Unlike the farmer of "Homestead", these male figures are not universalized. They are emphatically black heroes; in all of them race is an explicit issue, and they are heroic rather than specifically ancestral or paternal figures. The central characters in all but one poem (the relatively late "Cipriani") are black, and in all but one ("The Fighters") West Indian – and both of these exceptions are calculated and thematized. Thus the male poems reveal their affinities with the "black prince" stereotype of much pre-independence poetry, common to Négritude, *Afro-cubanismo*, and even the Harlem Renaissance. Some of the poems about women similarly emphasize blackness and nobility. They speak of the "dark moon-goddess" ("A Reed for My Rime"), or "the black rose" ("Lady by the Sea"), and employ the almost obligatory comparisons to Sheba ("She Never Dies") and Nefrete ("Doggerel for Adolescence"). In other cases, however, Roach follows the widespread Caribbean habit of envisioning idealized women as creole hybrids: consider the "clay-brown woman" of "The Curse of Her Beauty", or the "rust-brown hair" of the woman in "The Picture". The true ground of Roach's work is in any case not race but quite literally the ground. His representative figures are always rooted in specifically Caribbean soil, and in these poems the heroic figures are repeatedly associated with rock: Daaga's stone, Christophe's "stone tower", Toussaint's stone dungeon, Cipriani's statue (bronze perhaps, but "a colour of clay"), the pile of stones at the opening of "The Fighters" and the rock of Africa near that poem's end. Like the peasant of "Homestead", these are all buried ancestors whose presence continues, or should continue, to be felt.

In his search for figures emblematic of the Caribbean landscape Roach looks to Haiti as the most dramatic instance of Caribbean experience; he looks even to North America, in "The Fighters". Roach's new attention extends not only to the African heritage in the Americas, but to continental Africa itself, both as an historical and as a contemporary entity. Africa appears explicitly in most of the male poems of this era (its relative rarity in the poems of women reflects the emphasis there on Caribbean *mulatez*).

It needs to be borne in mind, however, that for most pre-Independence West Indians in the 1950s (the exceptions are progressives like C. L. R. James and George Padmore), "Africa" evoked eastern and southern Africa, rather than their own ancestral lands along the West African coast. This was not merely because of the routine suppression of African roots in colonial education; in the early 1950s the daily news was of apartheid in South Africa and the Mau Mau in Kenya [1952-56] – an emphasis reflected in such literary works as Walcott's "A Far Cry from Africa" (1956) and Vic Reid's novel *The Leopard* (1958). So too in Roach, apart from some allusions to ancient Egypt which are really Biblical in origin, the references in this period are to assegais and kraals, to Jomo Kenyatta and Daniel Malan. West Indian attention and awareness only shifts decisively to West Africa during the 1960s via Nkrumah, the independence of African states, and the Black Power Movement.

POEMS OF MEN

These issues are apparent in a group of undeveloped poems, broadcast together as "Haitian Trilogy" (1953). During the early 1950s, both Roach and Walcott were leaders among West Indian writers occupied with the problem of how to identify and *value* Caribbean heroes, and both in that process took up the refractory material of the Haitian Revolution.[1] For all its horrors, this was the one secure instance of historical agency in the region. As Walcott puts it, in writing about his own motivation: "There was only one noble ruin in the archipelago: Christophe's massive citadel at La Ferriere. It was the summit of the slave's emergence from bondage. Even if the slave had surrendered one Egyptian darkness for another, that darkness was his will."[2] The end of World War II had ushered in a period of pan-Caribbean stirrings. West Indian periodicals were beginning to notice the arts and literature of the non-Anglophone Caribbean, and in addition to the BBC broadcast of Walcott's play *Henri Christophe*, which Roach most likely heard, there was the ground-breaking historical work of Trinidadians C. L. R. James (*The Black Jacobins*, 1938) and Eric Williams (*Capitalism and Slavery,* 1944) which Roach surely knew.

In this context the contrast between Roach's Haitian heroes and Walcott's in *Henri Christophe* is revealing: Walcott presents them through Jacobean models of language and characterization, as larger-than-life dramatic figures, somewhat removed (by his archaizing style) from immediate Caribbean experience. Walcott was pre-empting for Caribbean literature what was at that moment (thanks to T. S. Eliot) the most recently recuperated (and thus highly valued) theatrical tradition, the most privileged model of the ambiguously heroic: "the Jacobean style, its cynical, aristocratic flourish came naturally to this first play – the corruption of slaves into tyrants."[3] Walcott speaks of this material as a *subject* fit for the highest metropolitan style. He understands the behaviour of the Haitian leaders in traditional European terms as tragic hubris or Marlovian overreaching. For Roach the Haitian leaders were indigenous – almost natural – phenomena, to be understood in terms of remote African roots and influences; Roach was taking possession of these heroes, their ambiguity, even their psychopathology, as inherently Caribbean and deriving from the mixture of elements that make up the Caribbean.

These three poems were never published in any form during Roach's lifetime; they were meant for broadcast rather than print, and their sketchiness of execution is clear in the occasional prolixities that never would have survived revision (e.g. "They raged like tigers, ravening through rabid frenzied hate" in "Black Kings"). Neither revised nor quarried for other work, they stand as experiments not pursued. In them Roach seems to be exploring his complex responses to these uncertainly heroic figures; but where his mixed or dialectical feelings about the prizefighters in "The Fighters" proved abundantly productive, these poems as we have them are more like worksheets. This is especially true of the second ("Black Kings") and third ("A Tear for Toussaint"), which treat the Revolution in primarily historical terms.[4] We can see how Roach generated idea and images, but there is no sorting out of the material here. Thus "Black Kings" looks like a poem at odds with itself. On the one hand, Roach develops an almost elegiac sense that the "maddened men" of the Haitian revolution are buried and gone; their passion, "that terrible antiphony they drummed" is now "quieted dust, ashes in memory".[5] Yet Roach appears also intrigued with the implications of the *contrary* idea that neither the victims nor the "tiger" who murdered them (that is, Henri Christophe) can truly rest in the "green, innominate" earth; as in "Carib and Arawak" and elsewhere, Roach envisions historical rage and violence as forcing their way into the present: "Night's dark rage is rolled / With loa and loud god, / With blood in bloody earth, / Springing rose petals forth" (FR 92). It is difficult to decide how Roach intended this poem to conclude: Was he gesturing toward the idea (much more clearly expressed in "Legend of Daaga") that the Caribbean landscape is saturated with traumatic history? Or is there, along very different lines, some suggestion that the carnage is redeemed and discharged either by nature, or by transformation into the aesthetic?

Whatever Roach's intention, there is a more personal meditation going on behind the scenes of this poem. The poem's most explicit stanza describes how Henri Christophe "up-hurled his passionate spirit" in the form of the citadel, built "to crown the clouded mountain / Where only the staggering frigate / And eagle dare attain".[6] This account recalls vividly the opening of "Transition", in which "spirit builds pylon and pyramid needling receding heaven" and the soul "goes out like hawk and eagle". I argued earlier that Roach in "Transition" is trying to reconcile (or choose between) contrary conceptions of the poet's role. Here in "Black Kings" Roach seems to be considering in *historicized* terms those same problematic implications of his own devotion to "soarers" as ideal images for the poet, or for "Caribbean man" generally. In this present case, however, the imagery of soarers brings the figure of the poet into uncomfortably close proximity to the realm of leaders pathologically disconnected from their people.

The first of the three poems, "Black Gods," is by far the most rewarding of the group; there is drama and visionary scope lacking in the others, perhaps because here Roach is approaching his concerns from a different angle. The subject matter is mythological rather than historical; the poem is about a transported African god, not an indigenous Caribbean ancestor, and there are no "heroes" in it (as there are in the other two poems), no individualized human figures at all. Instead of a character arising out of Caribbean land and history like Christophe or Toussaint the poem is about the serpent god Damballa, who comes from elsewhere to make himself at home there. Damballa Wedo (or Ouedo, in the French spelling – the word functions as a sort of surname for a family of deities) is an important god with a dense array of attributes, but for our purposes it is adequate to note that in Dahomey he is a relatively remote sky god associated with thunderstorms and usually represented as snake coiled around or in a tree.[7]

Roach in this poem creates a myth, according to which Damballa followed the slaves from Dahomey to the Americas, devouring those jettisoned ("living and dead") in the course of the Middle Passage. In the New World, after he "crawled like seaweed" onto the shore, Damballa finds the same cock and goat that were sacrificed to feed him at home in Dahomey, so he's happy:

> Cock waking crowed at dawn,
> The serpent laughed,

Goats bleated noons
He darted his forked tongue
Tasting blood in the familiar voices. (FR 90)[8]

This is an unflattering, even rather sinister, view of the god; one need only contrast Brathwaite's conception in *Islands*, according to which the African deities travelled along *with* the slaves, and now share with their worshippers the scars of deracination.[9] It is a peculiar point of departure for a poem primarily concerned with the god's role in the Haitian Revolution, and that peculiarity will deepen as the poem proceeds. But first, human voices are heard. The second set of two stanzas (out of six altogether) enacts a vodun ritual of blood sacrifice. Breaking in upon the otherwise highly symbolic narrative, this dramatization presents a confusion of live voices from which we have to piece together a fragmented, shadowed, account of what is happening in the dark. Several West Indian poets of this era were experimenting with ways of representing ritual in verse – Sherlock's "Pocomania" (1943), Shake Keane's "Shaker Funeral" (1950), Owen Campbell's "Shango Drums" (1954) – and this episode of Roach's poem participates in that larger enterprise. With phrases Roach presumably culled out of some book on vodun, the people call upon Ogun as god of iron and so of swords (it is uncertain whether Roach would have been aware of the notion that Damballa does not speak, and Ogun acts as interpreter for him).[10] The almost haphazard appeals to various gods (there are 18 exclamation points in 16 lines) provide local colour around the central petition:

Ogun Feraille! You come?
Pound drum! Pound drum!
Ouedo! You see this shame?
Ogun! Give sword! Give sword!
We give you blood!

These are not merely the restless natives of the stereotype. Roach intensifies the atmosphere of questioning to encompass the people's real fear of abandonment by the god:

What Ouedo say?
The serpent gone?
We go die in shame?
Dahomey dead?

Supported by the devious play of sound that links "Ouedo say", "We go die", and "Dahomey", the tone of this passage has become exasperated, reproachful, even challenging. References at this point to the early Haitian rebels Boukman (who started the revolt in 1791) and Makandal (a precursor whose attempt failed in 1758) reinforce the tonal shift, establishing a revolutionary atmosphere and context for the remainder of the poem.[11] The final two stanzas shift back from the human scale to the divine, depicting the revolution as the stormy anger of the gods, brought down upon colonial Haiti in response to the prayers heard in the preceding stanzas. Damballa is virtually transformed by historical exigency:

> The serpent darted rage,
> Hate changed his skin,
> Blood blinded him.
> The serpent crowed in the red fires
> Of the cane acres,
> Through the crescending drums.

"Black Gods" is a shapely poem, but obscure in the implications of its shape. The turns of the plot are very elliptical; it is difficult to trace the sequence of events these symbolic statements are meant to indicate, and the mechanisms by which the divine and human planes interact are not made clear. Why does Roach frame the revolution in Damballa's story? Does he intend to convey the idea that human history is contained within and neutralized by the divine, by metaphysics; that the throes of revolution amount to no more than a brief irritation for the immortals? Such comfort seems wasted on an Anglophone audience for whom, after all, the Haitian Revolution does not mean very much. The main problem is clear: what is Damballa to Roach, and what does the poet mean the god to be for his readers? Upon the answers to those questions depends our understanding both of the motivation in the poem, and of the meaning of its conclusion. We will have to confront these questions again in a larger framework, since we will encounter Damballa again, both by name and in the guise of a serpent, in some of Roach's very last poems. For the moment it is enough to see what can be said on the basis of this poem alone. Damballa's taste for blood is a constant; there is peace when he is "sure of satiety". He seems virtually defined here by his need for a reliable supply of sacrificial victims. If this is his essence, it must also be the site of his motivations. We are informed that during the Middle Passage and also (*for that reason*, the poems seems to hint) during the Revolution his diet was human; yet there is absolutely no sense that he takes advantage of unrest among the human community to feast on stronger meat, though such an account would seem plausible if proposed. His satiety certainly transcends any specific political considerations, and there is no indication that the revolution produces a scarcity of chickens and goats. What then stirs him to "hate"? It would make sense that it is hate among his human devotees which compels the serpent to change his skin; but Roach states unambiguously that anger and rage are felt by the god himself.

After the revolution, a season of peace (and independence) follows; the selection of details Roach chooses to include in the final lines is intriguing:

> Dahomey conquered;
> The green land drinks peace.
> Da sleeps in Eden round the tree of life.
> The cock and goat again his sacrifice.

Pride of place in the very last line is reserved for an assurance that the sacrificial blood is again animal rather than human; Damballa's satiety apparently *is* the keynote of the poem. Haiti has become a Dahomean Eden, with the serpent sleeping placidly there around the tree of life – but the terms "Eden" and "the tree of life" compel us to regard the outcome in Biblical terms, according to which Damballa can only be identified with Satan. The consequence of this identification for the poem as a whole is powerful but unclear. As a result the tonality of the ending, particularly its affect, remains ambiguous (we've noted a similar ambiguity in "Black Kings", and in some earlier poems, such as "Shallow Underground" and even "Transition"). Were it not for the sardonic edge Roach gives to these lines, this could pass for some missionary's contemptuous poem about heathen gods. But the nature of the ambiguity here reinforces a peculiarity in the relations between the titles of two of these poems and their contents. To emphasize via the prominence of the title that Damballa is a *black* god and Christophe a *black* king communicates an irony that comes very close to the hypothetical missionary's reproach: 'look, this is what black gods are like' (this is recognizably the same play of irony that I noted at the outset in the phrase "black Yeats"). The most obvious difference between Roach and the missionary, of course, is his "proprietary candour", his unruffled confidence that he speaks as a critical *insider*. "Black Gods" may be something of an unpolished draft, but Roach addresses this matter of the ambivalence of self-consciously black pride (and black anger) under oppressive conditions once again, with great subtlety and sophistication, in "The Fighters".

*

"The Fighters" (1953) is a complex and important poem, much commented on early, though strangely not reprinted.[12] Its structural and tonal affinities with "Homestead" are evident but not obtrusive. Following a format Roach often employed, the poem moves from two opening stanzas through two concerned with specific mythologized figures to another two of concluding exhortation. In the process it passes through a familiar sequence that can be traced by the shifting pronouns: "we" (the community), "they" (the exemplary figures), and finally "I" (the community's poet) exhorting an implied "you" (the artists). The poem opens with an image not encountered before in the corpus,[13] according to which an accumulating heap of stones – social congeries rather than a true society – represents the origins of West Indian society in slavery:

> We were thrown down upon our blood and bone,
> Stone heaped on broken stone in alien acres
> Of these western shires. (FR 106)

Each deracinated African, reduced to his minimal, anonymous self, his blood and bone, is a stone shattered by the trauma of Middle Passage; as history unfolds, "fresh" unseasoned stones land on those already broken. And the solidarity is unmistakable: this is us; we are those Africans. Sonic echoes in these lines draw attention to a link between the phrases "blood and bone" and "broken stone." Reading the poem in the context of Roach's previous work, a conceptual link can be discerned underlying the audible one – both are incipient "flowering rock" material: blood of life springing from seemingly inert bone, stone broken by some flow or flower. This will eventually turn out to be very much a flowering rock poem, though with a new anger. At this moment in the opening of the poem these images carry no such value, but the incipience is underscored by another glance at the idea in the immediately following lines:

> all our inheritance
> Was man's first heart, its springing blood,
> Its ever springing hope; . . .
> O our poor heart that sprung griefs to green rhythms.

By the repetitions of "springing" and "sprung" Roach insists that there is vitality and hope to be found among those stones broken by Middle

Passage and slavery. But this poem will emphasize aggressiveness rather than exuberance, and the theme of springing up is modulated in the first words of the second stanza, "men grow tall through fighting" – words which restate Roach's perennial theme about West Indians prospering in the buffet of their circumstances. The poem is about fighting into life, as the flower fights its way into light and air. And that draws attention to the most immediately striking feature of the poem: the fact that its heroic fighters are not West Indian but African-American: the boxers Peter Jackson, Joe Louis, Sam Langford, and Jack Johnson.

The discovery that African-American fighters are to be the focus of attention retrospectively widens the scope of the poem's opening, widens the scope of the poem's *concern*. The fact that Roach chooses them as his models rather than the likely alternatives tells us something about his frame of mind at the time. These are self-consciously black men functioning in an arena of racial politics. They are not the humble, strong peasants of the "Homestead" poems, nor does Roach here write about the entirely indigenous stick fighters of Trinidad and Tobago, whose pride, strength, and individuality within the domestic confines of the community's *gayelle* are celebrated more or less contemporaneously by Ian MacDonald in "The Stick Fighters".[14] Nor does he turn to cricket, where the forces of colonialism and race certainly come into play – recall "To Learie", where Constantine's achievements on a British cricket pitch are meant to be mirrored by Roach's own performance within the confines of a Miltonic sonnet. Instead this poem aims to make contact with Africa (in stanza V), but it does so by way of a kind of detour through America; if the way to Caribbean identity was "through Africa", as C. L. R. James famously prophesied,[15] this poem at least hypothesizes that the way to Africa might lie through America, where the racial confrontation is more direct, as the milieu of boxing, hand to hand, indicates.

At the halfway mark, then, this poem appears to be about race, and pride in African heritage, a celebration of black heroes' victories against prejudice and oppression. The boxers are deracinated Africa "prospering in the buffet"; with anger, hope, and pride they attack the "wall" which constitutes the barrier of race.[16] But the poem has already started to take an unexpected turn. In the two central stanzas devoted to the boxers, it becomes increasingly puzzling that the fighter-figures are not more positive models. Peter Jackson is called "princely and gentle", and Sam Langford "was the one true negro gentleman" who stood for "chivalry", but Jackson ends in self-mockery, and once a term like "chivalry" is in play, there's something sinister about "Joe the tiger [Joe Louis] . . . stealthy and silent, stalking the arena". Jackson and Langford get half a stanza each, but a full stanza at the heart of the poem is devoted to Jack Johnson – the first black heavyweight champion (1910), who had died in 1946 – and there is no trace of pride, hope, or chivalry here:

> Jack Johnson stood, with vengeance the black stone
> Gripped in his fists. Too angry for his race
> Great fame defamed him. He killed with contumely.

Repeatedly the story is of black fighters' pride becoming embittered in victory. It is the achievement of fame within the confines of the ring that "brewed tragic ferment". The fighters are pointedly compared to Samson – a figure of strength and tragic pride, one who quite literally pulled down the walls, but with minatory consequences.

One of the poem's earliest readers, George Lamming, offers a fine analysis of the complexities here, when he writes that in the second stanza Roach "denotes two stages of action, two orders of anger":

> The first is born of hope, aimed at the wall that sets up a barricade between man and his freedom. The second stage of anger and action is generated by that 'fanatic pride' [that is, the *oppressor*'s pride] which ignores man's hope and strives to rebuild that wall 'where it is worn and cracked and crumbled.' It is the wickedness of this intention that contaminates the original anger, child of hope and a sword in the defence of freedom. From now on, victories are soured by bitterness: 'And bitter in their pride struck out *again*, / Till fame brewed tragic ferment in their blood.'[17]

Lamming then goes on to speak of the poem's pivotal fifth stanza: "If there is much to admire in the personal dramas of these heroes, there is also much that demands an opposite emotion. Roach faces this squarely in [stanza V]; in doing so, he initiates a fine dialectic of feeling, a harmony of conflicts that open the way to a possible resolution" (40). This stanza begins with the poem's only instance of the word "I" ("my" also appears only once, at the start of the final stanza):

> I claim their strength and their affranchised pride,
> Reopening stubbornly the dead well
> Of history of our wretched race that fell
> Through utter hell to man's last degradation.

Claiming an authority based on his participation in the fighters' strength and pride (notably he does not mention anger), the poet intervenes, and does the poet's work of seeing beneath the surface. It may be appropriate to imagine another stone barrier, a wall or lid, that must be breached to open the well and work down (that is, back in time) past the immediate situation of the fighters, past the repressed trauma of Middle Passage – that Medusa so petrifying to the historical imagination – until finally the excavation finds water. As Lamming notes, once the poet stakes his claim and undertakes his work, "the rhythm changes pace; the repetition of 'deep' is a grave and considered prologue to the ceremonial evocation of water issuing from and retaining the essential purity of the 'black rock of Africa'" (40):

> Deep down in the deep seam the water's clear
> And clean from the black rock of Africa.
> There are bards there and craftsmen, heroes, kings,
> And dark ecstatic dancers throng the kraals.[18]

Here at the bottom of the well is a rock which Roach imagines as *living*, not sedimented or buried. In the conception of this black rock, several of Roach's most familiar images converge. One is the rock battered by the sea, which serves in these poems as a symbol not only of the self, but of Roach's own island and of Africa-in-the-Caribbean. Another is of course the ubiquitous "flowering rock" image, the sterile or inhospitable stone from which water or plant so miraculously springs. Closely related to the flowering rock, but with somewhat different valences, is the image of flowering out of black loam. Less an image of the inhospitable place than of its people, it emphasizes their energy and creativity, the strengths stored up in the accumulated sediment of black generations, layered with ancestors like the buried old man in the poem of that name or his fragmentary, uneasily dormant antecedent, the skull in "Shallow Underground". The deep well in this poem functions as a kind of telescope, providing a vision of a *whole* society of accomplishment in Africa. Roach presents this Africa not as a primitive past one is forced to acknowledge, but rather as an original ground of freedom and self-realization. Lamming expresses this in historical terms: "Freedom, it seems, is the original ground; slavery, a brutal but temporary defeat" (39).

In the course of "The Fighters", Roach thus executes an elaborate feint by which boxing is initially cause for pride, but then pales (and tarnishes) by comparison with the social (and psychological) *fullness* apparent in an unblinkered view of life in the kraals – an arena of accomplishment not narrowed by race, oppression, or single-minded anger. As an image, the kraal corresponds to the "heroic square" of the boxing ring, but shows up its paucity, its narrow confinement, and exposes it as a space opened by the oppressor for display of subjugated strengths and skills (comparison with the "battle royal" in the first chapter of Ellison's *Invisible Man* [1952] would not be out of place). Thus Roach mentions "heroes and kings" in his two lines about the kraals, but rather surprisingly no warriors. In the terms which the poem ultimately achieves, what corresponds there to the activity of the fighters is *dance* – exuberant physical expression that is *not* oppositional.

A subtle sequence thus has lead from the poem's initial suggestion – the sonic association of "blood and bone" with "broken stone" – to an apparent fulfilment of that hint in the fighters who prosper through fighting, and then beyond that in the dialectical move that brings us to the rock of Africa from which the truly clear water springs. This effect of "seeding" imagery for later use in the poem is repeated with another detail: the image of Jack Johnson, "with vengeance the black stone / gripped in his fist", is morphologically the seed that flowers into the poem's climactic image of "the black rock of Africa". The association established between "vengeance" and "the black stone" predisposes us to read "the black rock of Africa" in the same way, as literally the *source*, the fount, of vengeance. Roach's dialectic requires our full acceptance of the fighters' role so that it can be subsequently superseded. But when the poem completes its dialectical movement., it shows that to use the black rock of Africa as a weapon will in the end not be right The poem eventually reveals that this capacity for violence is only one of many creative resources apparent in the kraals, even though in this fallen world of the colonies it may be the only functional one, as the available arenas are so limited. "The Fighters" finally valorizes not the jab-in-the-face raid deep into enemy territory, but the full life of the undisturbed kraal, in which such a raid is only an incident elsewhere, a foray recounted.

The poem might have ended with its glimpse of the kraals, but the image is perhaps too nostalgic, too backward-looking, for Roach's purposes, and in any case his habit of closing with an exhortation is deeply ingrained. So, instead, he characteristically projects the force of remembered Africa into the future:

> O come my spirit from the rancorous dark
> Into the bounty of the human air.
> Painter, sculptor, poet in whom the seed
> Takes leaf and the leaf greens and flowers like fire,

Speak for the old slave hosts; speak out for us
Who are their heirs, griefs molten from their loins.
Persist to sheer perfection in the work
Like those who pit their perfect and tough sinew
Against arrogance and hate; art, intellect
May scale the granite wall or tear it down.

The vision in the crucial first two lines of that passage is very compressed. The implication is that the spirit, the water, can come up *through* the deep well of history which constitutes the "rancorous dark" of slavery and colonialism (the dark which the boxers still inhabit) *into* the "human air" of a time beyond all that. Put another way, the spirit comes up and flourishes in the open air having been nourished in its passage by the "black loam" of the Caribbean – the fertile humus which centuries of rancour has made (as it were) out of those broken stones with which the poem began. Against the background of that vision, artists are urged to perform a double task: to give voice to "the old slave hosts" and to do so for the sake of those who are their heirs in the present. Through art, they should transform the private, ingrown bitterness borne by such individuals as the fighters into something public and healthy, effectually communal – like the envisioned world of the kraal. Artists are called upon to imitate the *talents* of the boxers in order to move beyond their limited accomplishments. It is now time for art and intellect to overcome the wall built of fear and "fanatic pride" which the fighters exhausted their strength in attacking. The substitution of artists for fighters is the most explicit evidence of the poem's "dialectic of feeling", but the crux of that dialectic is really the multivalence of the term "pride" – a very shifty term in this poem, as it is in "Haitian Trilogy" and also (if somewhat less problematically) in "The Legend of Daaga", to which we will shortly turn.

First, however, it will be useful to look at a poem which, though written much later, amounts to something like a sequel to or re-make of "The Fighters". Roach published "At Guaracara Park" in 1970, together with the first version of "City Centre '70"; that is, at the last moment when he felt capable of anything like optimism. "At Guaracara Park" celebrates the poet's last unproblematically heroic figure, even though the poem displays marked affinities of detail to "The Fighters", where the heroes are not by any means unproblematic. It appears that what enabled Roach to write so positive a poem so late in the game was the nature of its particular occasion. According to Paula Burnett, this poem was written in anticipation of the appearance of the Kenyan sprinter, Keino, at the Southern Games of 1971.[19] Africa, of course, plays a prominent role in Roach's poems of the 1950s that celebrate male figures; it is easy to imagine that for Roach the coming of a celebrated and accomplished East African would in some sense bring the world of the kraals to Trinidad, making it possible for once to actually taste that water "clear and clean from the black rock". Roach as usual takes great liberties with his African details, combining Zulu terminology ("impies of assegais") with the West African milieu of Middle Passage and Ogun. As he readily admits in "Senghor Visiting", an unpublished poem from the mid-1960s about the visit of another famous African, he regards Africa as a "monolith", in contrast to the West Indian "tapestry... in rainbow hues" (FR 191). For him, a visit from Africa is above all an occasion for nostalgia: "Your presence is our past".

There is a characteristically West Indian gesture of appropriation in that statement, a habit of locating Africa securely in the West Indian past and not in the world of the present, and that gesture points to what *is* problematic in the poem "At Guaracara Park": not the heroism of the runner, but his identity. The poem may be *about* Keino (as Burnett seems to suggest), but it makes more coherent and resonant sense if it is about a West Indian runner. The poem opens by attempting to catch the runner's motion in a blur of present participles with no finite verb: "the bronze god running; beauty hurtling" (FR 150). The argument of the next two stanzas is straightforward – "speed was survival there . . . and speed and stamina were the warrior's pride". It is important to note, however, that the verbs are in the past tense. The "hero" being described in this part of the poem seems to be not the runner in Trinidad, but a figure *behind* the runner. The runner is being linked not to present-day Africa, but to an idealized African past, virtually identical to that invoked in "The Fighters". Just as in "The Fighters" (and other poems), Roach is delving back into the "well" behind a present event or scene. The poem enacts the process of plumbing such a "well", back through the degradations of slavery to the world of the kraals, so as to recognize "Ogun's aura" (and not transitory secular fame) as the present force behind (and in) the runner. The runner can boast the achievements he does because (in the terminology of "The Fighters") the stream still flows; without that spring of pride his oppressive circumstances would reduce him to nothing:

> the blood of the fierce gods we lost,
> the pantheon of the kraals made him immortal
> or he would have been a scarecrow in the canes.

Though an expression like "Ogun's aura" is about as close as Roach ever comes to the language of spirit-possession, this assertion of the enduring ancestral presence in contemporary West Indians is strikingly similar in conception to Brathwaite's account of his discovery of "Ogun's aura" in his own carpenter-uncle (there is no question of "influence" here, but Brathwaite's poem "Ogun" appeared almost simultaneously, first in 1968 and then in *Bim*, where Roach would probably have read it, in 1969).

Whether he is to be identified with Keino, or with an imagined West Indian runner,[20] the "lithe hero" whose exploits are described in the past tense is associated with African animals, African warriors, and African gods. In an intriguing manoeuvre, Roach makes a point of representing him as both predator and prey – leopard and antelope – and situating him in a society of warriors who "tore tigerish through the brush and raided \ and bounced back upon the kraals". That vignette looks back to the idea in "The Fighters" that the warrior ethic of the undisturbed kraals is a matter of forays, not of constant enraged fighting for dignity and even life itself. Roach is also diplomatically vague about *what* gets raided by the warriors; consciously or not he seems to be trying to solve one of the problems that arose in "The Fighters" by imagining a 'no-fault' victory. This explains the force of the poem's most remarkable phrase, "their cradling war", which attracts attention not only because of its central location in the text, but also because the resemblance between the sounds "cradling" and "kraal" invites us to hear the phrase as the defining feature of that society. This conception of Africa then extends to the scene at Guaracara Park. The stadium constitutes another arena of contention, like the *gayelle* or the boxing ring, but in this instance the poem conveys no sense that the runner is involved in any sort of competition. This mode of presentation traces back as far as "To Learie", in which Constantine seems to be alone on the cricket pitch. As Roach envisions these scenes, the athlete performs in solitary splendour in the presence of a crowd that responds with love. It requires no great effort to recognize such scenes as projected resolutions of the dilemma which had troubled Roach since "Beyond", that of the reconciling the poet's nature as solitary soarer with his social function for the community.

*

It is difficult to imagine why "Legend of Daaga" (1953), which like the roughhewn Haitian trilogy appeared only on BBC radio, was never published; this is a balanced and powerful poem, with none of Roach's occasional unevenness or insecurity of diction. At the centre of the poem is an elliptical narration of Daaga's revolt, unsuccessful flight, and execution. The actual events can be summarized thus: on the night of June 16/17, 1837, a Yoruba called Daaga led a mutiny of members of the First West Indian Regiment at the barracks in St. Joseph, Trinidad, and set off to walk back to Africa. By his own account, Daaga (a.k.a. Donald Stewart) had been a chief, warring on neighbours and selling captives to slavers until by treachery one slaver took him too. The trade was no longer legal in 1837, and the ship was seized by the British. Daaga, along with others similarly captured, was "freed" and immediately pressed into military service. This regiment consisted of slaves captured directly from slave-ships; they had been taken to Grenada and Dominica to fight alongside British troops there, and afterward garrisoned at St Joseph. The mutiny led to a week of fighting and forty deaths, until the rebellion was put down, and Daaga with two others was executed on the 16th of August.[21]

The details of the story suggest that Roach might have been attracted to Daaga as another highly equivocal representative of heroic resistance, like the Haitian leaders or the American boxers. The events took place *after* emancipation, and the "hero" was himself a slave trader, though an African prince. Surprisingly, Roach's poem embodies no sense of these complexities, and it seems probable that he knew only an inaccurate account of the events I have just summarized. Unlike the other poems I have just been discussing, this one romanticizes Daaga as an African king tragically enslaved (as elsewhere, Roach employs an inappropriately *East* African decor of assegais and kraals), and envisions him (mistakenly) as working in the canefields. We should not assume, however, that cultural politics moves Roach to play fast and loose with the facts of the matter. One of the points of the poem is that stories like this go unrecorded, and we should probably take the word of the text when it suggests that the poet knew only what he was told by a "laughing man" at the site in St. Joseph – by a local informant passing on the local version, idealized through oral transmission. The central stanzas, then, provide an admiring account of Daaga and his tragedy, which begins like this: "I summoned that dead hero from time's shade \ and blessed his savage pride that could not let \ him slave down the tall years when kraal and kingship \ waited him" (FR 103; Ramchand emends this to "awaited"). As in "The Fighters", underlying memories of a coherent African community motivate the action. The savagery of Daaga's pride, his "spirit", and his "courage" constitute the keynotes of the characterization, clearly linking this figure to Roach's conceptions of Christophe and the boxers. Daaga is described as a "wild bull" leading the herd eastward toward "freedom" in "their Africa". The attempt fails, but the final fusillade is noble: in "their fatal square of men and guns", drums roll at high noon, and the firing of the guns is described as a salute to Daaga's "contemptuous heart".

The real meat of the poem, however, is its figuration around the bare event. The abrupt opening has the characteristic assurance of Roach at his best:

> The stone preserves the taste of the spent blood.
> Child, innocent of history, bystander,
> Unaware of the unwritten hieroglyph,
> Uncarer, foreigner, ignorant of grief here,
> The waves' despair, the threnody of streams,
> Listen one moment to the rock-breaker,
> The recreator, the reteller of legend.

The abruptness derives from the indefiniteness of those initial definite articles: "the stone, . . . the spent blood" – what stone? what blood? That implied response from the reader accounts for the mild, almost weary reproach of the next lines. The literary model at this point is of course the *siste, viator* of gravestone inscription, but the characterization of the *viator* figure is unusually full and unflattering: even the word "innocent" is darkened by juxtaposition with Roach's description of the auditor as immature ("child"), ignorant, unaware, uncaring, alien. The poem addresses a "bystander" – not the traditional "passer-by" with a past and a future of his own, but someone not part of the action. This auditor is disengaged, unmoved (in both senses) by history, unfamiliar with the nature of the place where the stone stands ("grief, . . . the wave's despair, the threnody of streams" – each of those phrases summoning up a recurrent motif in Roach's poetry). This stone commemorates one instance of that grief. It records the particular bit of history it witnessed and was marked by; Daaga's blood on or in the stone makes it a hieroglyph. Between the stone and the bystander comes the poet – a poet conceived not just as a reader of the inscribed rock of history, but as saxifrage, breaking open that stone. History, the "legend" of Daaga, will not flower from this rock without the active intervention of the poet.

This sense of the poet's obligation to intervene, to bring legend to the attention of community and "bystanders" alike, is stronger than in earlier poems, and I will return in a moment to how the role of the poet is defined in this poem. But closely related to this intervention is the unusual move of the second stanza. The gist of the first stanza would seem to lead *directly* to the business of narration in the third: 'listen to me; Hearing of Daaga from a laughing man I summoned that dead hero.' But instead the imperative of the opening ("listen one moment") precipitates a whole stanza of imperatives directed at the auditor:

> Stand anywhere you are on any street,
> Hill, or field or in your quiet house,
> And question the fossil inhabitant
> Of gone time upon your storied place,
> The aphonous bone, history's abiding witness;
> Lean ear into the murmuring fountain
> Of felled blood, meter the scalding anguish.

The more active role which this poem imagines for the poet is matched by a more active role for readers, who are charged not just to listen to the poet of tribal memory, but to learn to hear for themselves the history buried in the place. Against the cliché of Caribbean historylessness, and even against the spirit of Walcott's remark that "we have not wholly sunk into our own landscapes, . . . our bodies make only light, unlasting impressions on our earth",[22] Roach emphasizes that word "*anywhere*"; to the reader he says: your own particular place in the West Indies, wherever it is, is already deeply historied, inhabited, haunted. The "fatal square" where Daaga dies bears a close resemblance to the boxing ring in "The Fighters" and to the Trinidadian stick fighters' *gayelle*. These are spaces of action or contention, of *agon*, that render more legible the agony inscribed in all West Indian spaces. Thus, to listen even to this unmarked stone is to hear a murmuring fountain of felled blood. Roach suggests here and elsewhere that there are many such all over the landscape, waiting to be heard. Putting the anguish into meter may be the specific task of the poet, but all West Indians – perhaps all Americans – need to attend to the murmuring blood in their quiet houses. This poem is focused on the figure of Daaga, but it is also a poem of place, insisting on the rich heritage, legacy, and "legend" embedded in even the least promising features of the landscape.

This poem maintains that it is the task of the poet above all to be attentive witness and active recounter; the imperative ("resurrect the legend") that opens the final stanza is still addressed to the bystander, but it is enacted by the poet:

Oh, resurrect the legend from the soil
And see his courage statued in the sunlight
And feel his spirit solider than granite.
I stand to say he's fed my hungry love
And given a stature to my hollow clay.
In the song's womb the hero is reborn,
The slave-bones dance to freedom's singing drum.

There are pointed echoes of earlier poems in these climactic lines. The phrase "legend from the soil" obviously looks to Roach's poems of buried ancestors who "flower" from the loam of history in various forms. The relation between the "black column" of Daaga's pride and "the song's womb" recalls the collocation in "For Freedom" of a phallic "shaft of light" with the womb from which the island-nation will be born, and the similarly gendered contrast between the pylon and the village which Roach developed for different purposes in "Transition". Using this imagery Roach works out an elaborate reciprocity in the relation between the poet and his hero: the poet's "hollow clay", initially associated with the receptive womb of song, is fed by the indomitable solidity of Daaga's spirit, and consequently the poet is able to stand *because* Daaga stood – yet it is the poet's stature which finally makes possible the hero's rebirth in the consciousness of the present. The overall movement of the poem is thus from the initial stone, featureless and aphonous, to a final "statue" – the articulate form a poet's work can give to Daaga's spirit. The final line makes the same point in different terms: it is the poet's *free* drum that brings Daaga's spirit to life again, that makes his bones dance.

*

After "Daaga", the "Ballad of Canga", first published in *Caribbean Quarterly* (1955), illustrates in its small way Karl Marx's remark (in *The Eighteenth Brumaire of Louis Bonaparte*) that all great personages and events appear in history twice; first as tragedy and then as farce. This poem is pure wish fulfilment, a blithe fantasy version of "The Fighters" and "The Legend of Daaga". It is a rare example in Roach's work of public verse overtly aspiring to the currency of folksong; it is also one of his most popular poems, broadcast on the BBC and printed four times during his lifetime – once accompanied by a translation into Taki-taki, the creole of Surinam.[23] The cultural background here is for once specifically West African, and unusually consistent: in Roach's poem Canga is an Ashanti obeah man, brought as a slave to the Caribbean. Whipped for not working in the canefields, he uses his magic to throw all the pain off onto the white mistress. Incorrigible, he's chased off the plantation into the bush, but he calls upon Damballa for magical food and drink. He turns himself into a soucouyant (the Eastern Caribbean equivalent of a vampire) for revenge against the master and his cattle. The devil comes for him but Canga's magic defeats him; when God Himself comes to get him, Canga's arrogant cheekiness ("Look, if I going up or down [i.e., whether you're sending me to heaven or hell], \ Lord, call me Mister Brown") moves Him beyond rage to olympian laughter, and in the end the Lord pulls up a big chair for Canga in heaven (FR 119).

Part of the poem's appeal is its form, a slapdash ballad quatrain that sounds almost improvised, as in this account of the soucouyant episode:

> He suck the white man blood
> Till his flesh come dry.
> Only three days later
> The man lay down and die.

The choice of diction is a major factor in achieving the effect of folk poetry. Michael Hughes asserts that "Some of his [Roach's] earlier poetry was written in a moderated dialect."[24] But this seems an overstatement; there is really only "Canga" and the imitation Haitian dialect of the central voodoo passages of the unpublished poem "Black Gods". This is the only poem in which Roach uses dialect as the medium of the narrative itself and not solely for the (direct or indirect) speech of a character. Intentionally or not, the poem reflects the contemporaneous achievement of precisely that goal, on the scale of an entire book, in the first novels of Vic Reid (1949), Sam Selvon (1952), and George Lamming (1953). Only twice in the poem do we hear Canga's words – but even that is a rarity for Roach, whose heroic figures are usually silent. The two instances reinforce each other. The first occurs when, in response to an overseer (presumably), the hero speaks of himself in third person: "work is not for Canga". Superficially he speaks as the stereotypical lazy native, but the proper label for Canga here is "signifying monkey"[25]; his usage appropriates and exploits that stereotype in a manoeuvre corresponding to the negative dialectic of Négritude. The second instance is Canga's response to God, who has addressed him (in this descending sequence) as "Canga Brown", "Ba Canga" [ba = brother], "Canga", and finally "Sinner". When Canga replies, "Lord, call me Mister Brown", the issue is again self-definition, distinction, naming, though expressed under cover of the hoary trope of the slave's impudence.

As even my brief plot summary illustrates, this is a poem of satisfyingly successful resistance, building on powers of magic or authority brought as heritage from Africa. The theme is implicit even in the opening lines of the poem, which envision Canga "stilted on his legend \ Taller than a tall man, \ Living beyond his end". Canga appears as a Moko Jumbie stilt dancer, a combative figure familiar enough from carnival not only in Trinidad but elsewhere in the Americas; but Maureen Warner Lewis has pointed out a specific association between "Moko" and vengeance which enriches the image.[26] The poem is further associated with carnival by its vaunting "Midnight-Robber" style, about which there will be more to say in the next chapter (we encountered this style first in "He Plucked a Burning Stylus", and as in that instance the boasting in "Canga" is curiously deflected – it is in the third person, not the first).

"Canga" constitutes a pugnacious and comical affiliate of "The Old Man" and all the ancestral poems (note the tell-tale word "legend" here, recurrent in those poems). The poem asserts a history of power and confidence, even cockiness – though cockiness with a strong metaphysical backup, figured here as the magic of obeah and the divine patronage of Damballa. The notion that Canga's assurance draws on ancestral African resources is reinforced by the notable *absence* of any reference to sexual exploits, which are typically a feature of the broad boasting style (in fact, the white mistress of Canga's plantation is the *only* woman mentioned in this group of poems). Beneath the bravado by which he copes with his oppression, Canga is still one of Roach's heroic solitaries, a kind of "soarer".

*

One other hero is celebrated, four years after "Canga", in "For A. A. Cipriani" (1959). The poem bears the recognizable characteristics associated with the progeny of "Homestead", but it comes quite late, standing chronologically apart from the rest of this group, so there has been some evolution of these characteristics. For example, the poem depicts a male figure in the landscape, but Cipriani's setting is a social and urban landscape, rather than rural nature. Further, it was written after most of the poems on the theme of West Indian federation (which we will be examining later), and the values of the poem are those of the federation poems. It is Roach's first poem about an actual politician, and so stands at the cusp of his post-federation poems, several of which are about specific politicians, though the tone of those poems is dark while this is positive.

First a word about the poem's subject. A. A. Cipriani, from a family of Trinidadian planters of Corsican heritage, had been radicalized (like many of his countrymen) by the experience of military service during World War I. After the war he worked his way up from the rank and file of the Soldiers and Sailors Union to the presidency of the Trinidad Workingmen's Association (in 1924). Cipriani strengthened the ties of TWA to the British Labour Party, an alliance reflected in the renaming of the organization as the Trinidad Labour Party in 1934. He rose to recognition as a labour leader, but at the same time his power-base was the black middle class. McDonald argues that, in the skewed political polarities of the era, Cipriani's European background paradoxically made him "a neutral ethnic type".[27] Trinidad was a Crown Colony, and under the constraints of colonial administration, the exercise of anything like home rule was effectively limited to the arena of *municipal* politics in Port of Spain. In that arena Cipriani flourished; he was elected to the Legislative Council in 1925 and served as mayor eight times between 1925 and 1941 (he died in 1945).

Roach's opening lines call Cipriani "a poet of humanity" (though the word "poet" does not bear much more than rhetorical weight here), and the final line calls him a saint: "He spent himself with a saint's humility" (FR 136). Cipriani was indeed highly regarded in Trinidad, and the particular appeal for Roach is suggested by Cipriani's political slogan: "Agitate, Educate, Confederate."[28] The climax of the poem speaks with appropriate vagueness about Cipriani's "rare gift, the love of man", but it is clear earlier in the poem that Roach is praising Cipriani primarily for his dedication to the ideals of federation, conceived as the political dimension of a multicultural society: "His catholic love embraced barefoot Africa, \ Indentured India, China and Syria. \ He preached race, caste and colour meaningless." These are ideals that arise naturally for someone with a personal history like Cipriani's, and flourish more urgently amid the social conditions of Trinidad than in such homogeneously black islands as Barbados or Roach's own Tobago. We will learn more about the development of Roach's federation politics in the following chapter; we have already seen, however, that such multicultural principles are *not* voiced in Roach's poems of the early fifties. Those poems focus almost exclusively on the black peasantry and their African roots, and even when there are celebrations of "hybrid" Caribbean beauty, the interest is purely aesthetic or erotic; there are no visions of a creole society.

This poem is not precisely about Cipriani; its subject is a representation of the man, a statue erected in his memory in Port of Spain. Of course, even though the erection of the statue is the occasion, the poem could have developed as a reflection on, even a dialogue with, the spirit of the man himself. Roach insists instead upon a curious deflection, establishing the indirectness of his contact with Cipriani with the oddly-placed modesty of the opening lines and then alluding to it throughout:

> And may the poet speak his epitaph
> Who was so far removed from poetry[?] . . .
> I saw him only once; I was a boy;
> . . . I recorded nothing but his image,
> And have no phrase or fancy of his I may praise.

The poet is here again presented as a producer of epitaphs, as the one who gives voice to "aphonous stone" or "legend" (as we by now have come to expect, that charged word makes its appearance in the poem: "he's as indestructible as legend"). The poem makes a point of its status as an epitaph, a memorial text to accompany a memorial statue which would be not much more than aphonous bronze without the poet. As for Cipriani, he is now bones "cool in their tomb of history", and in the context of Roach's poems their coolness contrasts tellingly with the "hot", unquiet graves of the many Caribbean figures who die with unfinished business in poems like "Black Kings", "Carib and Arawak", "Shallow Underground". It may not be fanciful to suggest a relation between this detail of the quiet grave and the theme of federation: federation as a political instrument for the *resolution* of all that causes those dead to be restless and unsatisfied.

The resonant final stanza makes effective use of the rhetorical device of a kind of muted rhyme on the unaccented monosyllable "him" (a device Roach has used before to conclude another elegy, "The Old Man"):

> Let him reign in bronze or what they've cast him
> Like or unlike him, in the city that loves him.
> If he's a colour of clay it will content him.

More significant, however, is the reference to "clay". This is not a neutral descriptive term for Roach; he uses it repeatedly to connote the sedimented matrix of the peasantry, the "black loam" of "The Flowering Rock".[29] In this instance the term clinches the praise of Cipriani's political reach – this brown man, this creole, "a squat tan man in khaki", who is so closely linked to the "clay", the black loam of the people. In writing the poem, Roach responded to a specific occasion (as so often) and the poem reflects on – and reflects – not only his federation politics but also his thoughts about the social function of the poet. I have mentioned already the oddity of Roach's description of Cipriani as a "poet" though "far removed from poetry". What the usage may point to, though the text does not say so, is Roach's inclination to regard poets and politicians as standing in analogous relations to the community. Cipriani is praised for his genuine intimacy with the people he represented, an intimacy achieved even though he was not actually of them, and sustained, even though he necessarily had to move in other circles than theirs in order to be of use. One senses that this intimacy, transposed into an attribute of poets, is at least as important to Roach as Cipriani's federalism.

*

It is a convenient commonplace of post-colonial criticism that literary representations of "natives" and other subaltern figures mature through a sequence in which the subaltern is first observed (talked about), then addressed (talked to), and finally allowed to speak. The third term of the commonplace does not apply very aptly to the case of Roach. A peasant by birth, writing about the peasantry, his interest in peasant language as a medium for *his* poetry was desultory at best (whatever he thought of it as a medium generally), and in the poems we have been examining throughout this chapter hardly anyone speaks: we hear the anonymous voices of the vodun congregation, two statements from Canga, and an indirect reference to one fighter's "coarse jeering word", but no word from Cipriani (the poet remembers hearing him speak, but not what he said), or Daaga (most ironically, in the light of a contemporary account of his trial, which makes a point of noting that, "his voice is the most remarkable we ever remember to have heard, being of astonishing depth and power"[30]). Roach's concern is not with voice but with what he calls "legend". The term occasionally means nothing more than personal history, a defining anecdote, or myth, but Roach's *sense* of the term is better conveyed by "presence", "abiding spirit", something in the air that derives from the individual but is now not necessarily reducible to anything so articulate as a personalized story. The task of poetry is to make people aware of, attentive to, these presences: to be inspired by the cry of a soaring bird ("Beyond"), to sense the presence of a father in his splendid cedars ("Homestead"), to recognize the seas as the folktale of our grief ("Lady by the Sea"). All the male figures in the poems we have been examining are dead and gone. They cannot speak. So the rare term "aphonous" turns out to be more than a trinket from the poet's magpie hoard. It denotes his sense of what the record of history is like, and what a poet needs to do about it. In a variety of forms, these poems represent "history's abiding witness" as "aphonous" – speechless without the midwifery of poets, whose duty it therefore is to "spell an epitaph on the marble-stone of time" ("Men"). As is fairly explicit in "The Fighters", this poet conceives himself as speaking *of* the heroic figures *to* the living community (it is that final link in the transaction that Roach repeatedly acknowledged in his habit of closing poems with exhortations). It is again a measure of Roach's sense of affinity that he feels so comfortable speaking for the people, though there will later be moments (especially as he begins to lose faith in the existence of that community) when he expresses considerable anxiety about placing himself in this exposed position. These poems about male figures come from a period of confidence, and that confidence is reflected not least in Roach's productivity. We now turn, however, to poems about women, written during equally productive years, in which the basis of the poet's relation to his subjects is not very well described by the term "affinity."

POEMS OF WOMEN

There is a first group of poems published from 1953 through 1955 which seem to praise women and which certainly mystify them. The group includes both versions of "Pray that the Poem . . ." (1953 and 1957), the two related poems for Maeve Elliot (both 1954), "Doggerel for Adolescence" (1955), and "Legend of Anacaona" (1955). These coincide chronologically with the male figure poems, though what they do is quite different. A few years later, in the period around 1960 – a difficult period for Roach personally – he seems to concentrate on the subject; most of the new poems published in the years 1959 through 1962 are about women. The result is a group of strange and unsettling poems which often devalue women. Chief among these are: "Mother and Son" (1961; already considered in Chapter 4), "She Never Dies" (1959), "The Picture" (1960), "The Old Woman" (1960), and "The Curse of Her Beauty" (1961).

Early on, Roach had written nationalist pin-up poems about women, and it is not difficult to imagine the adjustments of depth and seriousness that might have lead him to write poems about women (in such roles as market women, freehold-farmers, even revolutionaries) closely analogous to "Homestead" and "Legend of Daaga". But Roach did not write those poems. "Legend of Anacaona" is the nearest thing to an example of what we might have expected: a poem celebrating a female hero among those that celebrate males. "Anacaona" certainly resists the mannerisms of the nationalist pin-up genre (an index of this: Roach's refusal to frame his heroine in the usual abundance of tropical flora). But despite her status as *cacica*, a political and cultural leader, for Roach Anacaona is not a female counterpart to Daaga or Christophe. She is depicted as a victim, rather than a hero, and while there is a trace of the association with rock so typical of his poems about male figures, the equivalent for Anacaona is something less: loose flat stones, not set in the earth, but broken and indeed lost. Yet with this exception, the poems about women simply do not form part of the same project as the poems of male figures. Roach's male heroes have real or legendary histories behind them, but, apart from Anacaona, there is no anecdotal or legendary basis for the women in his poems. Even poems that appear to be about specific women ("Doggerel", "The Old Woman" and "The Curse of Her Beauty") do not identify them. Indeed, except for Anacaona, these women have no *names*, not even arbitrary ones. These women are faceless, or have the faces of so many archetypes imposed upon them that they in effect have none. We have seen hints of this sharp disjunction in Roach's practice already in the differences between the poems about his father and those about his mother, but the treatment of women in his poems bears more looking into.

Perhaps we can best orient ourselves by harking back to the first version of "The Old House" (1951), with its highly asymmetrical treatment of the parents. The husband is already dead, but within the poem he is described as still "mellow and ripe", while the living widow is one of several aging woman (including Roach's own mother) whom he treats with a stoicism bordering on brutality:

> Measuring miserly days in town,
> Measuring her drams of tears for the lover
> Cheated away into the lap of the clay.[31]

This is entirely characteristic. Roach's male figures (good or bad) are idealized; it would be very awkward to try to use that term to describe what happens to women in these poems. Besides the anonymous crooning mothers of the dooryards who appear in the backgrounds of several poems, Roach's women tend to be either victims or victimizers. Through the poems winds a trail of sacrificed, lost women, most prominent among them the old women, the widows, the various spinsters (in "The Old Woman" and "Notes for a New Poem") who have aged with a vengeance. Across a great imaginative divide are the "goddesses", ageless "eternal beauties" who persist through the centuries; they are the closest female equivalents to the father figure in "Homestead", but the nature of their immortality is quite different. Roach either under- or over-values these goddesses extravagantly – they are madonnas or whores. Similarly, he never addresses or even seems aware of the discrepancy between his two recurrent premises: women never age; women age ruinously.

Men are treated as the germs of new myths for the Caribbean; women are subsumed under existing mythological figures, almost always from the European tradition. The relationship to nature also differs. In poems about men Roach's project is ancestral: the claim to the land, and a guarantee of nourishment by it, with an emphasis on the succession of generations. As for the poems about women, "flowering rock" imagery abounds in the first group, from 1953-55; in the later group, women are much less definitely situated in nature – with the intriguing exception of "The Curse of Her Beauty", where the woman's apparent rootedness is illusory, an obsessive hallucination imposed on a hapless lover by something like witchcraft. What we do find in the poems about women are links not to the land but to the sea and the moon. In deploying these ancient associations, Roach's emphasis is not usually on traditional fickleness or cyclic essence, but contrarily on an enigmatic eternity. Even the posture of the poet is different in these poems. In the absence of the easy affinity that Roach evidently feels toward his male subjects, the poet's responsibility to give voice to the legend modulates into a compulsion – often conceived quite darkly – for which the women themselves are somehow made responsible.

Something urgent and personal certainly underlies Roach's treatment of women in his poems. The previous chapter offered ample evidence of the measures Roach took to keep his actual experience and relationships out of his published work, but we saw also, in the case of "The Old House", that Roach is sometimes more revealing in work not offered for publication. The same is true in the present case. There is a very early and brutal indication of Roach's attitude in these lines from an unpublished poem, which Ramchand dates sometime before 1950: "Girl, goddess, bitch, \ I've . . . loved and hated you \ From boyhood, and still \ My manhood's poled upon your will" (FR 173). A story called "The Carpenter" is exactly contemporary with the first group of poems we are about to consider, and will prove to be relevant to their undertaking. One passage deserves to be quoted here, however, to the extent that it seems to offer a glimpse of autobiographical detail. As the title character approaches the house of a woman who welcomes him, he remembers, "the dead unburied period of his life he spent in the army and the rotten core of it, the wild-horse woman who threw and trampled him in the mud."[32] The argument of this book is limited to how Roach represented himself in his published work, and his reticence on personal matters is an integral part of that self-fashioning, so I will leave the biographical sleuthing to other inquirers. But certainly these two quotations from unpublished sources suggest that there *are* personal reasons why in Roach's poems women are depicted not as exemplary models, but as persistent forces to be reckoned with in the world – in some sense, as *opponents*. Even so, we need to treat the suggestion with caution; the antithetical relationship at the heart of "Mother and Son", for example, can hardly be explained as fallout from an unhappy love-affair.

*

The relation of the first group of poems about women (1953-55) to the pin-up tradition is overt. "Poem (Pray that the Poem out of Nowhere Come)" (*Bim* 19, Dec., 1953, 179) was substantially revised for republication in 1957 as "Poem (Pray that the Poem Come Out of the Dark)" (*Kyk-over-al* 22, 54-55). In both cases it presents itself as a virtual meditation on the genre of the pin-up poem – a poem about the writing of a poem like "She".[33] Call it a meta-pin-up. Though the rhetoric remains high throughout, a paraphrase of the main business of both versions is straightforward: 'Praise her mulatto beauty. Born from the union of a "viking" and a dark island woman, this beauty puts to shame any statue of Venus.' This central compliment is framed in both versions by opening and closing passages of about six lines each, in which the meditation on genre takes place. We will return to these passages in the context of a general discussion of Roach's aesthetics in Chapter 9.

Entirely consistent with the emphasis in "She" upon "the commingling of our blood", the key phrase at the heart of the framed compliment of "Pray That the Poem . . ." is the description of its object as "her whole and hybrid beauty":

> Praise out of heart her whole and hybrid beauty
> Now that her bone stands up among upstanding
> Beauty of boughs blossoming flame and flames
> Leaping and falling in fields, on hearths, in hearts
> Tender and kind in their first uttering love;
> Praise her great rose among the season's roses. ("Dark")

Roach's depiction of her as a rose among roses, a blossoming flame among blossoms and flames, owes something to the generic convention according to which the exotic beauty is posed amid tropical decor, as in

W. Adolphe Roberts' "The Maroon Girl" and other exemplars. But even in "She", which explicitly presents its subject in the conventional way ("she's beauty set in a rare frame of beauty"), the relation between frame and framed is already blurred a little by metaphor: she herself is "fruit and flower" of history. In the present poem her integration with her surroundings is even more profound, and it is reinforced by the ecstatic style, which emphasizes process, rather than static image, envisioning her very much as an expression of the place, like the fountain from its rock, or flowers from loam. We can confirm, incidentally, that Roach was indeed self-conscious about this issue of framing from the aforementioned short story, "The Carpenter". The story's female protagonist is framed in the traditional way – "Her house stood back from the road in a grove of fruit trees . . . : breadfruit, orange, mango, chennep, pear, coconut, custard apple vied with each other, close and thickly-leafed" – but Roach in this instance is setting up a structural contrast with the male hero, the village carpenter, who "thought of himself as a stone in the stream, below the surface of life that moved about him; he was the submerged dead rock; he was the stranger within the village, watching it, unmoved, indifferent".[34] These antithetical images recapitulate the terms of "Transition": the isolated (male) "soarer" who takes the buffet versus the nurturing (female) enclosure of the village.

I bring up this story because Roach includes the same dilemma (the choice between ideals: social integration or free agency) in both versions of this poem, but situates it elsewhere, with more subtle consequences. Here the opposition is staged not in the relationship between two contrasting characters but at the point of the beauty's *origins*. Her father is a viking – an historically bizarre idea, but in Roach's usage the word is indelibly charged with the fierce isolation of the bird\bard in "Frigate Bird Passing" (the word may have had peculiar resonances for a West Indian poet named Eric). The father's "adventurer" gene fuses with the "dark flame" of the dancing island woman:

> the intemperate sun . . .
> Kindled wild torrid passion in his heart
> For dark desire whirling through her drums:
> She is their seed, the passion and the dark. ("Dark")[35]

The result is a child who, for the purposes of this poem at least, resolves the dilemma in her own person. In this figure of the dancer, Roach combines his praise for the hybridity of her beauty with an insistence on its vitality, its living changingness. There is a corresponding insistence on motion here, though it is not effectual or "heroic" motion – not the kind of motion associated with the viking (or for that matter with the boxers in "The Fighters"). Instead the "adventurer" heritage is subsumed under the natural flowering exuberance of dance. Dancers are, of course, a stock-in-trade of the pin-up genre, but to understand Roach's objective in this poem we should recall that dance (envisioned in a very different mode) is his image for the activity of the idealized community of the kraals in "The Fighters" – the world at peace where heroic action is not needed.

While my first quotation from "Pray That the Poem . . . " insists on one sort of specificity (Praise her *now*), that passage also makes it clear that Roach is concerned here with an emblematic rather than a particular woman, and I have been speaking of her as an emblematically West Indian woman (again, consistent with the project of "She": "She is Caribbean . . ."). But at the climax of the compliment something unexpected happens. Roach writes:

> She is the dancer in dreams, the grace in the tides,
> The flower of foam that gleamed at Paphos, goddess,
> Goddess, eternally woman, legend and living. ("Dark")

In these lines, her Caribbean specificity is abandoned; in the course of asserting that her beauty is alive and thus far superior to any statue or fixed ideal, Roach transforms his woman into a universalized "Venus", with exclusively European attachments (as is apparent in the list of her gifted lovers). He says quite plainly that she is the true Aphrodite – the actual divinity, a woman eternally reborn and loved. The *mulata* is lost in a European *ewig Weibliche*, yet there is simply no sense in the poem that hyperbolic praise has led to a conceptual difficulty. Perhaps the difficulty slips by because the poem so successfully negotiates other paradoxes: that inherent in the poem's theme (a beauty at once "whole and hybrid"); that implicit in the phrase "legend and living" (terms often opposed in Roach's usage); and that embodied in the differences between the two parents. But this difficulty with universals recurs in Roach's poems about women, and even the very specific problem of the relation between Aphrodite and island beauty arises again in the pair of poems to which we turn next.[36]

*

Roach wrote two poems dedicated to Maeve Elliot: "A Reed for My Rime", broadcast on the BBC (March 14, 1954), and "Lady by the Sea", (*Bim* 21, Dec., 1954, 14-15). The two texts appeared almost simultaneously and share substantial material – each is in seven stanzas (though a page break in the transcript makes this not absolutely certain for "Reed"), and the first stanza of "Lady" is identical to that of "Reed" (a single "and" has been deleted). However, they develop in very different ways and so really do constitute different poems.

Whereas "Pray that the Poem . . ." is an encomium framed by considerations of poetry, "A Reed for my Rime" is an encomium temporarily disrupted. The poem sets out from its subject's proximity to and intimacy with the sea. But almost at once the poem's attention shifts to the tragic past; what the lady hears "continually" is the sea's "grief and rage".[37] A series of observations about ways in which the sea is *within* her provides the crucial pivot: the second stanza then begins, "O, she [i.e. the sea] is in *us*" (emphasis added). After that shift of focus from the single lady to "us", the main body of "Reed" is a trenchant meditation on Middle Passage and the sea-change it constituted for the people who became West Indians. The governing trope here is that Caribbean people are the firstborn children of the sea, but that the process of their birth was the traumatic passage of the slave trade, as a result of which they are foundlings, abandoned not only by their mother the sea, but by their gods as well. "Reed"'s two stanzas on the sea (II and III) are compressed into one (II) in "Lady". Then "Reed"'s next stanza (IV) on the experience of Middle Passage corresponds closely with "Lady"'s next stanza (III), with only a few revisions along the way. It is at this point that the poems diverge substantially. The stanza recalling Middle Passage in "Reed" leads into two stanzas on the poet's reaction to the grim condition he shares with his people; this section of "Reed" develops rhapsodically in response to the rapid movement of the poet's feelings rather than according to any predetermined shape (such as "Lady"'s refrains, formal balance, sharper focus). This passage uncovers a familiar dilemma born of the poet's conflicting emotions: "I fly this scene of my resentment \ To wander alien, footloose, rootless, \ . . . yet I swarm with a fierce love for us \ the continentals broken up on islands". How reconcile his devotion to West Indian people with his conviction (encountered repeatedly throughout this chapter) that the Caribbean is a tragic landscape saturated with grief? The emotional dilemma converges on an equally familiar vocational one: is the poet a rootless soarer, or a functioning member of an actual community?

Once the poet's lamentation ends, "Reed" becomes again encomiastic, but now with a practical objective: it evokes the lady's beauty as an instrument of redemption by which several of the poem's problems are addressed. Thus the dilemmas that have stymied the poet are circumvented (if not precisely resolved) by the lady's beauty, which shows him the way to a subject other than grief. The people's rage over slavery and colonial oppression, which the poet so strenuously shares, and which he has just vented in the intervening stanzas, is the real source of the "grief and rage" initially attributed to the sea in the second line of the entire poem. The birth of a beautiful West Indian woman resolves the "folktale of our grief" by providing it with a happy ending:

> . . . you walk in the sun,
> A dark moon-goddess ravishing the day,
> And hates and fears are fathoms drowned
> Beneath your wave you lovely of the land.

With her gesture, she brings redemption from that grief and rage, and the manifestation of her beauty resolves another matter as well. The problem of history, as this poem poses it, is the problem of how to build any future on the devastation of the region's past: "What faiths shall we feel,\ What rose bloom from the trodden stone of our hearts?" The poem's conclusion answers *those* questions by recapitulating the manoeuvre that led into the meditation on the Middle Passage. Once again there is a crucial shift of pronouns, as "you" is generalized to "we" for the poem's final point. With a nod toward the argument of "The Flowering Rock", Roach leads us through a sort of aesthetic syllogism: "The lily sparks the drought"; "you walk in the sun"; "We had been taller once [that is, before the indignities of slavery] . . . \ But never lovelier [now that we are in the Caribbean and not Africa]." The lady's Caribbean beauty makes peace with the very history that produced it, by presenting *prima facie* evidence that West Indians are not shattered Africans – no longer "continentals broken up" – but something new and different. Though the point is not made explicitly, "A Reed for My Rime" seems to end by taking the lady's beauty as a sign that the folktale of grief is over, and a new story has begun.

Let me return to the point where the two poems diverge, that is, just after the stanzas on the Middle Passage, because at that point "Lady by the Sea" takes a decidedly more positive turn than its sibling-poem. It does not shift into self-pity or even introspection; there is no first person singular pronoun (as we have seen several times already, this elimination of the first person singular is typical of Roach's revisions). As a result, the closing stanzas of "Lady" are quite different, concerned with such communal issues as the future of "the people" and the social role of a (depersonalized) poet. Broadly speaking, “Lady” turns out to be a poem about West Indian federation. Something should be said here, however, about “Lady” to the extent that it is a poem about a woman. Like all of the foregoing poems, “Lady by the Sea” alludes to Aphrodite, the goddess born of the sea, the *haunting* beauty, “the eternal woman who walks within men’s dreams” (FR 112). As we have seen, she is developed most elaborately in the two versions of “Pray that the Poem . . .”, and in “Reed” she again makes an appearance in connection with the birth of West Indians as a new breed. Actually the word “Aphrodite” occurs twice in “Reed”. The second instance is a cryptic reference to Aphrodite’s voice at the very end of the poem, which has the effect of again making it difficult to tell whether Roach is envisioning beauty in the Caribbean as just another manifestation of the old Aphrodite, or as something *sui generis*. By contrast, the first instance is carefully delimited: “. . . we were firstborn of her, not beautifully \ Though[,] as Botticelli dreamed of Aphrodite”. Here the distance between West Indian reality and classical ideal is preserved: birth from the sea, as West Indians actually experienced it, was *not* beautiful, and the beauty of the myth is itself circumscribed by Roach’s emphasis on its fictionality (“as Botticelli dreamed”). “Lady” is even more circumspect than “Reed”. Aphrodite is not named at all, and is referred to only as “Beauty . . . tragic and lovely as her mother the sea.” This is a particularly appropriate phrase for specifically Caribbean beauty, distinct from the classical ideal, because born out of the sea of a traumatic history (“flower and fruit of ruthless traffic” as Roach puts it in “She”). To the limited extent that “Lady” overtly compliments its dedicatee, it does so by associating her not with Aphrodite but with the sublimity of her immediate surroundings:

> Look, beauty burns:
> Scape and flower delight the child and stranger;
> The cloud swims in the wind, wind in the light;
> The sea around us, the dark womb of earth,
> Eternity is fluid, constant, terrible
> And splendid beyond all feeling;
> And you, our lady, looking on the sea,
> The black rose our blood bears out of its fortitude,
> Century after century. (FR 113)

It is a good index of the difference between the objectives of “Reed” and of this poem that the last three lines of that quotation, which constitute the only direct compliment in all of "Lady", stand in such uncertain syntactical relation with the rest of the passage.

Since "Lady by the Sea" circumvents the problem posed by the invocation of Aphrodite, we should look ahead a bit, to note that the association of ideas which she represents will be found recapitulated under the aegis of a different myth in the words of the dancer which conclude "The World on Islands" (1962):

> . . . I am the phoenix Eve,
> The mingled wine of the world's grapes;
> I am the supple rhythm of the seas[.]

Here the dancer is presented not as Aphrodite but as the "phoenix Eve" of a new Eden, whom Roach endows with an affinity for the sea. This metaphor more successfully represents the elusive concept of an *eternal* female ideal for a *new* mixed race ("mingled wine"), since it has the advantage of being both double and oxymoronic: she is Eve and phoenix, at once without precedent and eternally renewed. As a solution, this notion of the "phoenix Eve" is analogous to Walcott's famous trope of the "new Adam", which effectively addresses similar problems of cultural continuity and disjunction.[38]

There is some slippage in the analogy, however. For Roach, it appears, there can be a new Adam, but there is always the same Eve; while his archetypal man fathers real or metaphorical progeny, his woman is eternally or recurrently only herself. A look at a relatively minor poem makes this contrast sharp. As its modest title signals, "Doggerel for Adolescence" (1955) has no pretensions; it really is a pin-up poem plain and simple. It takes as its point of departure a trivial incident – the poet himself waving to a young girl as she passes in the street – and throughout the poem the adolescent girl is thoroughly objectified, not a person but the occasion of the poet's excitement. There is no nationalistic subtext, and the only hint that this might be a poem celebrating specifically black or brown beauty is very indirect: a rhetorical question that implies a comparison with the "clay complexion" of Nefrete (FR 125). The delight the poet feels at the unexpected encounter with beauty is expressed through several stanzas in which he leaves her behind to play among his own familiar repertory of images (the word "doggerel" in the title seems to apply not to the verse but the informality of the argument). Roach concludes with an avuncular prayer for the girl's future – in the background of the whole poem is the structure and sentiment of Yeats's "A Prayer for My Daughter" or

"Among School Children". Among Roach's own poems "Doggerel"'s affinities are with "Cradlesong" and "Birth", which also make much of the gap in age between the poet and his subject. So the line "You'll know the irony of noon" here evokes a morning \ noon \ evening trope related to that employed in "Cradlesong" and "Birth", and a common tone – that of Prospero moralizing to Miranda – is shared by all three.

I've taken a moment to glance at this simple poem because Roach's handling of his female subject here is entirely consistent with what we have seen in the more substantial poems under discussion in this section. The girl is a proud dancer, a "bud of beauty bursting on the old rose tree", and she quickly becomes a symbolic figure (even the term "legend" makes a perfunctory appearance). Though Roach's prayer expresses concern about her personal future, he at the same time effaces her individuality with characteristic ease: she is "Awakening Eve, each goddess young; \ . . . all men's greener dreams". In its relative directness of expression, "Doggerel" makes Roach's practice especially clear. In the poems about men, the emphasis is on something like fellowship constituting a far-flung community in the present; the father-figure in "Homestead" is linked to "*any* common man . . . world over", not to Adam or Apollo. A woman, on the other hand, is an instance of "Woman", of Venus or Eve. Roach's poetry is adept at bringing dead men back to life, but even at its most celebratory it tends to praise living women by replacing them with manageable and imaginary stereotypes.

*

Taking a leap from 1955 to 1959, which corresponds exactly to the gap between the poems "Canga" and "Cipriani", we encounter "She Never Dies", the first of the group of harsher poems about women clustered around 1960. As the title itself indicates, this too is a poem on the subject of the eternal woman, and it reiterates many features from the poems of the mid-50s, but the tone colour is much darker, and the poem (like those that follow) enunciates an attitude toward women akin to what, in the register of race rather than gender, Ramchand has called "terrified consciousness".[39] Roach's attitudes (and more narrowly, his statements) about women are not strikingly different from those of his male contemporaries in the Caribbean. Nevertheless, occasional disturbances on the surface of the poems indicate he is *working* on something here, or vaguely aware that there is work to be done. Apropos of the heuristic parallel with "terrified consciousness", Lamming's praise for Roach's forthright handling of the theme of *race* in "The Fighters" can be useful here in an unexpected way. Lamming sets up his discussion of Roach's success by talking first about another, even earlier poem on the subject of African ancestry, Vera Bell's "Ancestor on the Auction Block" (1948).[40] For Lamming, Bell's poem, despite its considerable audacity, has the characteristics of a transitional work: "an uncertainty of tone, an ambiguity of vision, and the psychological timidity that restrains the intellect and inhibits the imagination as it prepares itself for some positive act of cultural commitment" (36). This characterization, along with Lamming's sense of the "inauthenticity" and "embarrassment" that ensue when a poet has the courage to take on a subject which then proves too daunting, seems to me to stand as an almost clairvoyant account of the nature of Roach's poems about women – troubled poems written from a *transitional* moment in the process of making contact with an objectified or fetishized Other.

Such disturbances are evident at once on the surface of "She Never Dies". The gist of the argument sounds like a restatement of the themes of "Pray that the Poem . . .":

> [Homer] sang, and every poet sings
> Because her image maddens every heart,
> Although the best and worst of her's
> In a cloud, mysterious as a dream. (FR 135)

Once again Roach speaks of Woman, a singular entity, transcendent and eternal. The cumulative effect of the poem's imagery is to present her as a changeable moon, veiled in a cloud, but exerting a powerful influence on the earth – which is to say, on men. Roach has written in these terms before, but now the inscrutability of women is on the way to becoming a source of distress and hostility. In the earlier poems she inspires "kings and priests and poets"; here (though the point is lightly made) she "maddens" them. Most of this poem, in fact, is about those whom love has maddened. Abelard, Shelley, Byron, Keats, Solomon, Tristan, Antony[41] – the list is quite similar to those in the two versions of "Pray that the Poem . . . ", but in those instances the woman's power over men is presented as mysterious and charming rather than sinister. In defiance of its title, "She Never Dies" is a poem full of *men*, men ruined by women. The force to which they are subjected is as irresistible as planetary motion: "The living man must love. \ He turns his cycle, \ His eyes intently on his satellite". Through the ages, woman's power over the tides of male emotion has often been written about as an inevitability to be accepted with chagrin and even humour; Roach expresses instead a resentful embarrassment at how easily men are made lunatics for love. The following passage is particularly illustrative. The three lines about himself and his Sheba could come from a conventional love poem, but in juxtaposition with the preceding lines about Keats they take on a nasty edge:

> I think about you, Keats
> Dying and staring on one silly woman
> As I at my full moon
> More dark and passionate
> Than Solomon's.

The image of the dark moon, mysterious but positive in the Maeve Elliot poems and some others, is now in the process of being demonized. The cumulative effect of the poem is to make us less sure whether the fact that "she never dies" is entirely a good thing.

The immortality of the goddess is again at issue in "The Picture" (1960). Very much like "Pray that the Poem . . . ", this poem begins with the poet's anxiety about his art. He wishes that he were Rembrandt, capable of immortalizing an unidentified woman's mobile beauty by effectively capturing it on paper. Roach's admiration is unabashed, and as the poem approaches its midpoint it appears to be engaged in the same business as H. A. Vaughan's familiar poem "Revelation", asserting black Caribbean beauty in the face of Eurocentric aesthetic standards. Vaughan writes, " . . . let them see / What loveliness escapes the schools, / . . . and be the perfect answer to those fools / Who always prate of Greece and Rome, / . . . but keep tight lips / For burnished beauty nearer home."[42] Roach similarly intervenes between the woman and "them":

> I would take care to show her in her world
> That scorns and envies and outlaws her worth,
> The freedom she must live, the gaiety she is,
> The whole earth's love and pity she possesses. (FR 140)

Indeed, this theme is reiterated in the final stanza, where Roach asserts the "worth" of the "legends" of women; the enduring accounts of their beauty which poets and artists have created stand as a positive testament of faith. This evidence that passion survives through the vicissitudes of time "warms history's sodden heart":

> Time cannot burn the lovely legends down;
> Their golden flame warms history's sodden heart.
> Why, all that love and pity had Isolde,
> And such a beauty had the Magdalen.

The reader's recognition of the relationship between this conclusion and the opening is ensured by the repetition of the phrase "love and pity". But these virtues, which had been attributed to the woman who is Roach's subject in line 12, are now associated with Isolde (and Magdalen). That manoeuvre raises two issues. First, the final resort to European analogues seems to undercut the thrust of the rest of the poem in almost precisely the same way that the intrusion of a Naiad troubled "A Lover Speaks", or that of Aphrodite affected "Pray That the Poem . . ." The move perhaps makes more sense here, to the extent that this is a poem about aspiring to the art of a European painter. Rembrandt painted many women possessed of love, pity, and beauty who might have been mentioned to make this point; why mention these two in particular? Neither Isolde nor Magdalen is an unproblematic figure, and their inclusion seems to require explanation.

These issues would probably not even arise into the reader's consciousness were it not for a kind of convulsive tic that bursts out in the central stanza of the poem, enacting an entirely unmotivated betrayal of the female subject by the artist:

> I should take care to name the picture 'Harlot',
> Lest those who come, not knowing, but enraptured
> By the wild beauty and the goddess gesture
> Should say she was the duchess of my heart.[43]

The word "Harlot" comes as a violent shock, and though the next stanza appears to be offered by way of clarification, it is not very helpful:

> It would not be the first time nor the last
> The truth were wronged nor the lie hidden in
> The line or colour; the man must love the model,
> Or the work comes stillborn from the soul.

After these two stanzas the poem goes on as if nothing untoward has happened, and the eight lines of text just quoted do not make it easy to understand either the motivation for the abusive spasm or its function in a poem that will go on to assert that "the man must love the model". It is difficult to sort out the relationship between a "wronged truth" and a "hidden lie" as they relate to the matter of titling the picture. If the poet's admiration for the woman and her "goddess gesture" is real, as it seems to be, why does he feel compelled to slander her – to wrong that truth – in order to protect himself? Yet it is not even clear whether he fears the assumption of a mistaken link between them, or the discovery of a true one. If the closing lines of the passage mean not 'paint what you love' but 'love whatever you paint', then perhaps the whole passage expresses the poet's resentment at this condition of his art; "The Picture" would then take a place beside "She Never Dies" among the poems in which Roach writes of love as an unhappy, even ruinous, necessity – the kind of relationship one has with an Isolde. Like "She Never Dies", this poem presents woman "in a cloud", but in this instance the cloud is generated not by the mystique of woman but by the poet, apparently in order to obscure the truth of his own emotions – even from himself.

Like "The Picture" and several of the poems we are considering in this section, "The Curse of Her Beauty" (1961) seems to be about the depiction and immortalizing of a woman. In this case it is a woman whom "Legend, . . . \ Has fixed . . . in the frame \ Of the siren coast" (FR 145). But the kind of brutality introduced into "The Picture" by the word "harlot" colours the whole of "Curse". This is in fact another poem about betrayal, but in this case the poet is the one betrayed, and the main turn of the poem at the end of the middle stanza makes overt something that has been lurking behind several of the poems we have been considering: "He thought her a goddess \ Till he knew her a whore." Again like "The Picture", brutality erupts into the poem only after quite a different mood has been established. While the manner of the poem is thoroughly Roach's own, the technique of the opening – especially the studied absence of a verb – suggests a familiarity with American Modernism:

> Wind-harried, tough
> And twisted trees,
> Burnt black by bitter
> Sea spray flying
> From the barrier rock;
> That clay-brown woman
> Slim as saplings,
> Old as ocean,
> Young as mornings.

The juxtaposition of tough, twisted trees and lissome woman appears at first to establish a sharp difference, as if this were a kind of prolix Imagist work. The woman is *contrasted* with the harsh setting, and the use of the word "saplings" evokes (especially for regular readers of Roach) the realm of flowering rock imagery: this appears to be another instance of beauty flourishing in the inhospitable setting, making its surroundings bearable and even beautiful. Up to a point that is the case; Roach writes that he once "saw beauty walk on the wind and the sea to him on the rock" and as a result, "love tinted that shore," colouring the landscape with her beauty.

Now, however, betrayal in its turn has "tinted that shore". The setting in which he met the goddess who turned out to be a whore is transformed along with his perception of her. Let me quote in full the passage which I edited somewhat misleadingly at the start of the previous paragraph:

> Legend, deceiving as she is,
> Has fixed her in the frame
> Of the siren coast,
> The wind-harried day,
> The stained, tortured trees
> Where the curse of her beauty
> Branded his heart.

As in so many earlier poems, this is yet another Caribbean site marked by tragic events, by "legend"; but the event here is private rather than communal, and the extent of marking reaches a saturation point, approaching a pathological extreme of the pathetic fallacy. This carries a step further the implication in "The Picture" that the cloud of unknowing that veils the woman is in fact generated by the man. Here a kind of spell, an obsessive hallucination, interposes itself between the hapless lover and the external world – he is another man maddened by "woman". The entire landscape appears to project her image, so that even the coast, taking on her attributes, is called "the siren coast". In his eyes the coast has become, like this woman, like Homer's Sirenes – like all women, it seems – a seductive attraction that turns out to be a treacherous monster. Even "legend" itself, Roach's standard term for the persistence of the past in the landscape, turns out to be implicated in the treachery – now that it has made the very topography resemble the woman who betrayed him, he considers it as "deceiving as she is". The gnarled trees of the opening lines, which originally seem to establish her sapling beauty by contrast, now seem framing-images wholly consistent with her true nature, and in an inspired touch, Roach adds a small human figure to the depiction of this accursed landscape:

> The corpse of his love,
> A fragment of heart-wreck
> Still knocks on those rocks.

Since I am using this poem to illustrate the negative pole of the fate of women in Roach's work, it may be useful to note the extent to which this is written as a kind of "Homestead" *manqué*. Both poems start with the trees that bespeak an individual, and end by fixing that individual in the landscape in a way that achieves for him or her a kind of immortality. "Him or her", however, is not a phrase that comes very easily to any discussion of Roach. The peasant farmer of "Homestead" remains an individual even when he is associated with others like him all over the world and through the ages; the same is not true of Roach's women. This poem begins by speaking of "that clay-brown woman", and the demonstrative pronoun says it is plainly about a specific if unidentified person; but this specification is quickly counterbalanced (or contradicted) in Roach's characteristic way by the almost immediate treatment of her as archetypal: "old as ocean, young as mornings". Women achieve a different sort of immortality than men in Roach's poems, and it is rarely site-specific; "The Curse of Her Beauty" is an exception. The most highly regarded male figures are honoured as individualized spirits of the place, because they are rooted in the loam of the community's history, and their presence in the landscape is always regarded as a form of blessing; but in this case the woman haunts, and her presence is a curse. Roach presents her not as a person with attributes or accomplishments but as a malignant being with *effects*. To the extent that all of the poems in this series are about Roach's "eternal goddess" figure, we cannot fail to notice the void at the centre of their "descriptions" of her: these poems about women are preoccupied with *men*, while few if any women appear in the poems about men.

TWO AGED FIGURES

Roach has provided us with two poems, published just a few months apart, which together can effectively conclude this discussion of his male versus his female figures. "The Old Woman" (1960) and "He Juggles Images" (1961) are both reflections on old age with its memories of lost love and youth; with their shared emphasis on bodily decrepitude both poems are far from the world of Roach's heroic figures. The diction and manner of these poems are quite different from one another, however, and different in ways significant for the issues of this chapter.

"The Old Woman" begins by introducing its subject, "the twice-widowed woman," a figure related to "The Old House" in particular, and to other poems invoking spinster sisters and widows (FR 141). A second stanza then poses the poem's central question: what does she dream, what does she remember, watch for, take any interest in? The rhythm of the opening lines – "As gray as time, \ As wrinkled as faith" – looks back to the pattern that dominated "The Old Man" (1949), but it is not sustained. Instead, Roach establishes a very strong rhythmic pulse, grounded on variations on this norm: (- / - - /). This is above all the characteristic metrical pattern of the apostrophes or invocations that begin each of the stanzas after the posing of the poem's questions; that is, the phrases "O pitiless God", O pitiless time", "O pitiless world". In effect, the pattern of those crucial phrases – naming the powers that have brought the woman to her present state – *determines* the pulse of the poem. Perhaps, too, we are to hear this insistent rhythm as the pulse in her veins, keeping her alive while it mocks her weakness. There is a disillusionment beyond consolation in "The Old Woman", an exhausted fury, which will dominate the poems of Roach's last decade. With a bitter pathos, this poem harps on shame, regret, remorse – Roach is unrelenting. Time brings remorse whether our lives are sacred or profane: "The mother of Christ \ moans at *her* cross" (emphasis added); yet the pagan goddess of love similarly "curses her ruin". Great differences like these that finally make no difference seem to haunt Roach's perception in the late poems, as in the following lines from another work of 1960, "Notes for a New Poem":

> My *barren* pear tree keeps her leaves
> And seems as prim and passionless
> As spinsters, . . .
> My *fruitful* pear tree's shed her leaves
> But bears a pitiful poor score
> Of a ping-pong-ballish sort of fruit
> Blistered by the burning weather. (FR 137; emphasis added)

These lines deepen the impression left by "The Old Woman": no life can be looked back on with pleasure or satisfaction. And after remorse comes oblivion: the widow is presented as *un*remembered and locked away for good ("no one remembers her \ in her coffin of age"). Significantly, the term "legend", by which Roach rescues so many losses elsewhere, makes no appearance in this poem.

Throughout this poem there is no fertile soil, only dust and dryness, unwaveringly asserted in the final lines: "In her dusty rooms \ She makes friends with the dust". The vital imagery of boughs and Trade winds does make an appearance, but the imagery is negated, one might almost say renounced; now it recalls only the drooping boughs of the aging mother in “To My Mother”. There is a whiff of palinode here, as one of Roach’s signature images, that of thriving under the buffet of the Trades, is reduced to this: “dry boughs [that] no more tremble to Trades of desire”. Likewise the aspiring dreams of “Transition” and related poems seem to have come to nothing in the poem’s concluding vision of vacancy:

> Oh, she sits lonely,
> Wistfully watching
> Sky, cloud, and landscape,
> Hearing the knell of the sea
> Tolling her on.

This is the poem’s despairing answer to the question, “what does she dream?” Here the kind of elemental landscape by which Roach strove for sublimity in such poems as “Invocation” and “He Plucked a Burning Stylus” reappears, but emptied of meaning or persuasive force. The passage has a special poignancy when read in the light of a parallel moment in “Lady by the Sea”. There too a woman looks out at the sea, and Roach makes use of brilliant visual effects (recalling the earlier poem “Colour”) to describe what she sees:

> The cloud swims in the wind, wind in the light;
> The sea around us, the dark womb of earth,
> Eternity is fluid, constant, terrible
> And splendid beyond all feeling.

Such emotionally charged vision has been emptied of all affect in the closing lines of “The Old Woman”. There is nothing “splendid” in that flat line, “sky, cloud, and landscape”. In the spirit of palinode that haunts the later poems, “The Old Woman” seems a calculated recantation of its predecessors.

All this is in the starkest possible contrast to the many poems of ancestral male figures (the “Homestead” group, “Shallow Underground”, and “The Old Man”). In those poems the buried male figures become literally part of the landscape, and Roach repeatedly depicts them as flourishing into legend out of that loam. Roach’s male figures (during the 1950s at least) are not surrendered to remorse, dust, and oblivion. The treatment of the old man in “He Juggles Images” is consistent with that practice. He is described as self-aware, knowing, full of feeling. The images he juggles are images of death and images of sexual desire – images charged with enormous emotional power, the force of which he clearly still feels strongly. These features of his character contrast sharply with the old woman's general physical and mental lassitude. In the very first lines of the poem Roach endows him with a capacity for irony:

> He sees with blurred and dying eyes,
> *Without* regret, *without* remorse,
> With irony his own demise. (FR 143; emphasis added)

This opening passage thus positively and explicitly inverts the emphasis on regret, shame, and self-pity in "The Old Woman". The old man is curious about his fate, he questions it, he remains *interested*. None of that is true of the widow. The issue here is the poet's capacity for empathy. "The Old Woman" is about a forgotten widow, and then in a wider perspective about "us" – about the human condition; but "He Juggles Images" seems always on the verge of revealing that its true subject is "me", the poet. Roach is very much at home in this poem. Though hardly an old man at the time he composed it, he is committed to communicating by every means possible the liveliness of the man he writes about. When for example the topic shifts from thoughts of death to thoughts of lust a lovely thing happens to the verse, which settles for the duration into the kind of jaunty, scandalous iambic tetrameter couplets which come from Blake by way of Yeats:

> The carnal eye's delighted in
> The frenzy of original sin,
> Grins as the seed in its wet sack
> Hollows the prim virgin's back.

One point being made in "He Juggles Images" is anticipated in the following lines from "The White Coffin" (1954): "Oh, we are old, our hopes are grayed . . . \ Yet our eyes mirror beauty \ And our bodies feel the shudder of begetting" (FR 110). I quote the passage, however, not for the thematic correspondence but for the further confirmation it provides that Roach identifies readily with the old man, and imputes to him attributes he hopes will be his own, while when he invents an old woman she is almost devoid of affect – she is entirely *observed*, not inhabited by his consciousness, and comes across as unthinking, unreflective (consider how little seems to be on the old woman's mind, as the poem presents her). For all the compassion and furious grief honourably expended on the widow, she remains an alien being.

The difference between "The Old Woman" and "He Juggles Images" only epitomizes an aspect of Roach's work which this chapter has extensively illustrated. But if the poet cannot be said to have triumphantly overcome these asymmetries of gender in his poems, it *can* be said that he grew more aware of them toward the end of his life, and was not complaisant about the realization. As we will see in the next chapter, the poems of the 1970s express profound disenchantment with the male figures of his pantheon and their ilk – disenchantment even with the terms by which he had defined their heroism. On the other hand, one of his very last poems, among those left neatly on his desk the day of his suicide to be read as final statements, grapples candidly with his treatment of women. At nearly four pages, "I Say it Was the Women" is among Roach's very few long poems, all of them pivotal works: "Caribbean Calypso", "Verse in August" (the last poem he published), and the longest of all, "Littering Earth's Centre", another of the very last poems. In "I Say it Was the Women" Roach leaves a dense and scrupulous testament, with much attention to ambivalence and conflict ("I dream of your grave faces,\ . . . and in the dream I listen, I approve, \ but in the bitter day I turn aside").[44] At the end of the poem's struggle comes a final statement of position:

> I die maintaining this:
> it was the women who restored us. . . .
> I know the end's not chaos,
> that you have shaped an end, a destiny
> and we shall grow
> though we ourselves,
> ashamed of our own shames, . . .
> would silence you. (FR 199)

This poem is certainly healthier about its ambivalences than "Girl, Goddess, Bitch". Ramchand praises its courage ("For a man of his age and his generation this was a hard poem to write, one that bruised even the unthinkingly chauvinist mind"), and goes so far as to regard it as evidence that Roach "was still moving on, beyond the narrow limits of the so-called radicals with their manly rhetoric."[45] Symptomatically, however, even here "you" refers to the women, and "us" to the men – there is still a presumption of opposition, and it is still the men who in Roach's mind define the community. Roach's sense of community, and of his relation as a poet to that community, will be the focus of the following chapters, which turn to his overtly political poems. As we shall see, the scope of these poems is vast. Roach's aspiration both as a poet and as a West Indian reaches a zenith in the poems explicitly concerned with political and cultural federation. But if Roach's treatment of women constitutes an inherent flaw in the structure of his imagined community, much of the damage sustained by that structure was inflicted upon it by external forces, and subsequent chapters must also come to terms with the bitter disillusionment which impelled the poems of the last decade of Roach's life.

Chapter 6 — Poetry and Politics I: Federation

Chapter 4 concentrated on the poems which arose out of Roach's immediate circle of parents, family, and intimate friends; Chapter 5 broadened the focus to consider the poems of individual Caribbean heroes and mythologized women. Now Chapter 6 takes up a series of poems in which Roach envisions the peasantry as a collective (usually identified with the "village") and concurrently meditates upon the nature of the West Indian poet's relation to that community. To speak of such a broadening of focus is purely an expository convenience; I don't mean to suggest that this locution corresponds to some progressive evolution in Roach's work. All three of these chapters are occupied primarily with the poems of the 1950s, Roach's most productive decade, and there are poems even before 1950 that come under each of these three rough categories of subject-matter. Of the three, the matter of the village is somewhat the latecomer, emerging full-blown in several important poems of 1950. However, the village becomes increasingly prominent during the 1950s and very early 1960s not only because Roach was thinking about his relationship to his own village but also in response to the pressure of external events – above all, the formulation and inauguration of the Federation of the West Indies.

The years after World War II saw the gradual dissolution of the British Empire; in that context the idea of federating the small states of the Anglophone Caribbean into a single political unit within the Commonwealth presented itself as a plausible course of action. For West Indians themselves, what chiefly suggested the viability of such a federation was the perception that it would constitute not just a political convenience but a true cultural unity: "the cricket-playing Caribbean" (a strategy of definition even more accurate than one on the basis of shared language). Building upon earlier conceptions of the Caribbean as an American archipelago of city-states, West Indian intellectuals saw federation as an opportunity to stabilize political and economic common cause on a foundation of cultural homogeneity. The notion was accepted in principle by West Indian leaders meeting at Montego Bay in 1947. In 1956, after a series of studies and committee recommendations, London began the process of establishing a single federal government for most of its Caribbean colonies, and the Federation was inaugurated on April 22, 1958.

Roach himself was an enthusiastic supporter of federation.[1] The increasing momentum toward that goal during the 1950s stimulated him to think about his role as a poet, and his relation to village, island, and larger entities on the scale of Federation and Commonwealth – to think about the stages on which he aspired to perform, and the results he wanted his poetry to achieve. Indeed, the issues that arise in virtually every one of the poems to be treated in this chapter can be characterized as archipelagic issues: literal political federation, cultural homogeneity, the relation of the individual village to a collective peasantry spread throughout the region, the relation of Eric Roach to his own peasantry, and the relation of his disembodied voice to the dispersed Caribbean audience.

The early 1950s also brought a massive post-war migration of black West Indians to Britain. Economically motivated, this "colonization in reverse" initiated a new diaspora, at odds with the centripetal impulses of federation. It drained off not only surplus labour, but many of the most promising writers, among them Sam Selvon, Wilson Harris, V. S. Naipaul, and George Lamming. Roach, newly married in 1952, must certainly have been tempted by the vision of opportunity abroad which was luring away so many of his countrymen. Though he never left home, the poems of the mid-1950s frequently grapple with the possibility of migration.

This chapter examines how these more political poems approach the problem of defining the poet's own place against the backdrop of such contrary forces. Proceeding in roughly chronological sequence, it begins with a group of poems from the early 1950s which in various ways depict the collective: "Something Seen" (1952), "Letter to Lamming in England" (1952), and "Despite Ancestral Rape" (1953). These poems of the peasant community complement the poems discussed in the preceding chapter, which were concerned with individualized figures. Just as those poems had as their subtext the development of an heroic vision of the *poet* (as ancestral figure, or as soaring voice), so too these poems about the community are accompanied by others during the same period which are primarily concerned with the relation of the West Indian poet to his village. In such poems as "Tree" (1952), "Hawk Heart" (1955), "I Walk

Abroad" (1953) and "In Mango Shade" (1953), Roach is thinking about his own actual community, and more broadly about the rural peasantry which for him remained the germ of West Indian society.

Those poems of the early 1950s, increasingly animated by Roach's political ideals and his expectation of their imminent realization, are followed by a group of poems which set the high-water mark of Roach's career, the three federation poems of 1957-58: "Love Overgrows a Rock", "I am the Archipelago", and "Fugue for Federation". These are among the best known of Roach's poems, and they constitute the moment of his greatest assurance about who he is, whereof he speaks, to whom, and for whom. These poems (along with "Lady by the Sea" from 1954) incorporate his most confident view of himself and his role; the view is stated against some odds, certainly, even in these poems, but these are the poems in which he clearly envisioned his social support and function – the reconciliation of the "soaring" adventurer with the dooryard community from which he springs. These poems thus continue the process of *self*-figuration, the creation of a persona for the poet who is not only an observer or exhorter but also a "figure" in his own right, a participant in society who fits among such exemplary men as his poems describe. In these poems Roach is working hard at reconciling that self-indulgent, self-gratifying view of success, election, and fame with a more responsible figuration of the poet as the voice of the island(s). Several of these poems are attempts to conceive how the poet responds to, addresses, and speaks for the community, and what his speaking might accomplish. Roach is still developing images of the poet as soaring bird/bard, as swashbuckling adventurer (thus Columbus makes his presence felt in several of these poems). These images, however, are now being elaborated through association, on the one hand, with the international medium of the airwaves, and, on the other hand, with the highly localized diction of the Trinidadian Midnight Robber.

Such images of the poet certainly affect how Roach envisions the community for which he speaks. I have been using the term "village", but in the course of the 1950s that often yields place to something more topographical than social: the individual island envisioned as a hill or hillock in the sea, what Roach calls an "eyot". The terminological shift does not signify a withdrawal from politics; in the mid-1950s "eyot" is the term of choice even in poems profoundly engaged with West Indian society, such as "Lady by the Sea", "Fugue for Federation", "Love Overgrows a Rock", "I am the Archipelago", "I Walk Abroad", "Caribbean Coronation Verse", and "In Mango Shade". Yet this conception of the "eyot" harks back to Roach's earlier use of the word "eyrie" for the remote and isolated perch from which the bird/bard soars. To situate the poet in elemental nature sets aside both wider human concerns (the "village") and the local specificity of Tobago. Both of those manoeuvres become more significant when he is writing in support of federation. Just as the specific peasant farmer in "Homestead" quietly becomes representative of "any common man", the setting of most of the poetry is not really Tobago but "any West Indian island". By the same token, Roach treats his village as a regional archetype, rather than a particular dot on the map.

Two themes then will dominate this chapter: Roach's efforts at defining the nature of his community (village, island, or region), and his formulation of the poet's responsibility to that community. Roach variously envisioned a poet's strength as deriving from his people, from his specific geographical place, or from a generalized "West Indian" place – an imaginary origin for the poet which his own work invents. At the same time he felt strongly the need for a West Indian poet to be incorporated into something larger, be it the Federation of the West Indies, the international radio audience, or the tradition of English literature. In the course of developing these themes a moral imperative emerges: the poet's obligation not only to depict the predicament of that community, but to depict it *to some purpose*.

MY DARLING VILLAGE

Roach's poems of 1950 ("February", "The Flowering Rock", "Transition") are all grounded in a consistent vision of the "huddled village" where the men are "proper farmers", while the women are mothers, nursing and gossiping in a "village dooryard" under "homestead trees". The vision is idyllic in "February" and "Transition", where a timeless charmed circle, a simple home-place, constitutes all the world one could need. There were other poets with a similar interest in the peasantry in the early 1950s, all of them (like Roach) working to progress beyond the aesthetic of the picture postcard and the nationalistic poster. St. Lucian Derek Walcott's poetic drama, "The Sea at Dauphin", may be the most widely known example, but readers of West Indian poetry are familiar also with a variety of approaches to village life during this period, variously inflected – with romantic nationalism in Telemaque, with political idealism in George Campbell of Jamaica, with almost Homeric nobility in Trinidadian Ian

MacDonald.[2] Roach, however, was much closer to the experience of peasant life than most West Indian poets, and presumably for that reason his poems are not ethnographic but visceral; not poems of the discovery – or recuperation – of the peasantry, but articulations of peasant experience and aspiration "from within". Roach's right to say 'we' is never in doubt.

Lloyd W. Brown writes insightfully about "Roach's dual perception of the peasant as victim and hero" but his further claim that this perception is "enriched by a penetrating self-awareness with respect to his dual role as sympathizer and outsider" requires qualification.[3] Brown's reading of "Homestead" as an outsider's effort seems to forget that what distinguished Roach from other poets of his generation was his roots in the village. Roach's friend Cecil Herbert, for example, who grew up in Belmont and attended Queens Royal College, had impeccable credentials as a man of the city, and almost predictably his poem "Lines Written on a Train" expresses the alienation he feels from cane workers viewed through the window of a moving train. At the core of the poem is an instance of the mystification of peasant authenticity that bedevils the poetry of West Indians with middle-class backgrounds: "through the peasants' hearts – though they seem as callous as stone – some river runs which soothes their hurts, while willy-nilly hearts like mine . . . ").[4] By contrast, Roach, who grew up rural and poor, was confident (and quite unselfconscious) about his status as an insider. His perspective is always that of the villager. The best indicator of this is inadvertent: Roach increasingly laments the marginalization of villages that are subsequently abandoned by their young people, but there is no trace in his work of the other side of that coin, a mainstay of West Indian literature in all genres written by city-dwellers, at least since de Lisser's novel *Jane* in 1913: the exploitable domestic worker newly-arrived from the country. Only in his last years was he driven to regard himself as increasingly isolated from his village and its dispersed people, and he blamed this on *external* forces (the pain of this isolation comes to be voiced in such late poems as "Poem for this Day" and "Piarco").

As early as "The Flowering Rock", Roach can make room in the idyll for sorrow and heartbreak, even for the word "slum". But there is no anger in these poems of 1950, and no shadow of history; the word "hope" is a keynote, usually underwritten by the agricultural rhythms of recurrent harvests. There had been a political dimension to Roach's poetry even in the 1930s, so we can assume that the extreme simplicity of this initial vision is intentional, not innocent. He is working to establish a sort of reference point which is not merely an abstract common denominator. This is particularly clear in "Transition", where (as we have seen) the satisfying image of the village is a goal gradually arrived at. "Men" summarizes the overall argument of "Transition": "Blood will wander where / It must but return home / To the heart's villages" (FR 83). For Roach the village is not conceived as a point of origin (not a reproduction of either the annihilated world of Anacaona or the African kraals idealized in "The Fighters"), but as the isolated radical of island experience. It is not Adamic origin but space of refreshment; not Eden but Beulah-land. And indeed this vision is soon politicized – though the word "hope" persists in "Letter to Lamming" and "Tree", the poems of 1952 pay much more attention to the burden of history, to the implications of social change, and to the future.

In the previous chapter we noted that the themes of Africa, of colour, and of colonial grief entered the poems around 1953 – coinciding, that is, with the coronation of Elizabeth II and her much publicized tour of the Commonwealth (but also with the suspension by the British of the new Guyanese constitution). Symptomatically, the words "tragedy" and "tragic" come to prominence in the poems of the early 1950s,[5] but the quantum leap in the political charge of the poetry is most overtly signified by the sudden and insistent appearance of the word "nigger" in "Tree" (1952), twice in "Something Seen" (1952), and in "In Mango Shade" (1953). The most prominent and provocative instance is in the poem addressed directly to Queen Elizabeth, "Caribbean Coronation Verse" (1953): "now my nigger voice from the slave islands / Proclaims her majesty in Shakespeare's tongue / To queen a commonwealth of flowering freedoms". Those are among the poems to which we now turn.

*

In 1952, the same year as the first version of "Homestead", Roach published what amounts to its demonic twin, "Something Seen". This too is an evocation of black peasant labour waiting to be memorialized in a poem, but it takes quite a different path, crossing the hard-won pride of poems like "Homestead" and "The Flowering Rock" with the rage of "The Fighters". The result is Roach's most unappeasably angry poem before 1970. After an introductory stanza establishes the premise of the poem ("some image out of childhood comes to mind . . . that was not understood"), the first image seems to prepare a celebratory mood:

> A scene I saw today uproots the past
> That lay bone-quiet in its grave of years:

Three women hoeing on a hillside field,
A green and terraced acre of potatoes,
An emerald page in the mid-morning sun
On which the past lay printed like a poem. (FR 88)

The past that comes to mind is a noble vision of "the strong men whom I honoured as a boy", but this vision returns to the poet burdened with what he has learned in the intervening years about what he once saw: the labourers were indeed worthy of his admiration, but "neither they nor I on that day knew / Them deeply cheated of their drudgery's worth".[6] The original vision of men who "challenged iron labour with tough bone", now darkened by experience, is further exacerbated when Roach conjoins it with a separate memory: "Join this sad image to a word I heard / Out of a mouth worth blooding with a blow:/ 'Teach niggers Latin to lose good cheap labour?'"[7] This impulse to physical violence is controlled (or frustrated) as the speaker pursues the consequences of what he knows:

Nor beauty, worth, nor human wealth can flower
In this antinomy of seasons, this
Deliberate cleavage of the island climate:
Roll by and laugh in your luxurious car
While I, feet cracked and charred in sunburnt dust
Spit angrily behind you and curse out.

As in "The Fighters", the violent anger in this poem is something the poet himself regards as bad, though he sympathetically traces its emergence, and even shares it. That much is clear from the explicitly racial terms in which he voices his own hostility: faced with "the greed and the wolf cunning of the unscrupulous skin", the speaker curses in order "to curdle up the pink and white complexion". Cursing white folks is generally alien to the objectives of Roach's poems; he would have regarded learning to curse as the attribute of a still-gullible Caliban, easy prey for the next round of masters. Indeed, he later sharply criticized the work of younger poets like Bongo Jerry who seemed to be about that business.[8] But this is an unusually confrontational poem, so agitated about both class and race that it arrives at a view of the future that is apocalyptic rather than federationist, and racially polarized rather than multicultural:

A bitter fruit will ripen on our tree
Poor minds left in deliberate neglect
Like soil untended, choke with vulgar weeds

Of kindling anger hate and wild revenge,
Will snarl and roar for justice and reprisal
Till blood dries rabid on the emerald leaf.

The apparently bucolic image of a poem on a page with which "Something Seen" began now looks very different in the light of oppression and exploitation. The sight of peasant labour now calls to mind not an emerald poem on a page, but a sinister transmutation of that image into another – blood on an emerald leaf. Even so, Roach makes it clear that this is not an outcome to be desired (i.e., not a *revolutionary* outcome), but rather the predictable fruit of such criminally negligent husbandry. It is in such a context that "reprisal" as an objective is set on equal footing with "justice", and the motivating forces are characterized unfavourably as "anger, hate and wild revenge" (the judgmental force of "vulgar" in this context should not be underestimated).

The stanza just quoted anticipates effects in the poems of the 1970s when it introduces a new twist on Roach's fundamental "flowering rock" imagery: the possibility of unhealthy growth. This is the first poem to acknowledge that the fruit can be bitter, the flowering can be weeds. For the sake of its eschatological connotations, Roach often uses the scriptural term "tares", and (with or without that specific term) the idea appears in several poems of the 1950s.[9] Unlike the present poem, these usually employ the crop of tares as an image for a discouraging setback that will eventually be overcome. "Reed for My Rime", for example, looks back to a time when, "the seeds of our blood were wasted as tares", but ends with the beauty of "rock-growth flowers", while "In Mango Shade" spells out more explicitly Roach's faith that, though the first crop amount to tares (specifically vetch and black-thorn), after will come the bounty of "lovely corn". The nature of the modulation is clearest in "Fugue for Federation" a few years later. The final image of the poem is of burgeoning hope, but earlier, at a point where we might expect an insistence on the beauty that springs from the black loam of the peasantry, Roach takes a different tack. He writes instead that "the Slave Trade's buried / but its eternal tares of scorn / breed in our barren soul, / batten on the black, despised blood" (FR 130). In "Something Seen" a very similar sense of the crop of tares underlies Roach's description of the "animal existence" of slavery days as "buried in our ground" by emancipation, and at once grotesquely "resurrected" in the new form of "ill-paid large-tasked labour". This passage takes on even greater force when viewed against the background of

Roach's previous work. As in some of the very late poems, here his anger turns back destructively upon himself; this sardonic trope of resurrection parodies the familiar image of the fertile black loam, and so also makes self-lacerating mockery of the faith he usually invests in that image. On the surface, the poem seems to follow the hopeful trajectory of "Reed" and "Mango". Having already written that beauty and worth cannot flower in this "sunburnt dust", Roach ends the poem with a description of freedom couched in the hopeful language of the flowering rock, of "some law or force of life" that makes growth possible in the most inhospitable soil: "Freedom is not a word; is not the loss of bondage but the stature, the growth of the free spirit from the dust." On its own terms, this statement has a fine, axiomatic force, seeming itself to flourish out of the bitter text of its poem. But in the context of this poem "freedom" *is* just a word. No path is traced from this rousing statement to its realization in actuality.

"Something Seen" succinctly lays out the main themes of the present chapter: the relation of the speaker to his people (how far is he from them?, how effective for them?), the nature of his representation of the people, and the objectives of that representation. The poem's treatment of these themes, however, is very dark. What the poem describes is the condition of the peasantry, rather than the nature of the village. The peasants are seen out in the fields, not at home, so that the setting underscores their alienation from their devalued labour, and the need, which this particular poem does not address, to find a way to a community. Here the ethos of the peasant and the village is already being undermined, by the persistent heritage of slavery as well as by new forces of urbanization and development. The village is polarized against an exploitative world that now intrudes upon it and denies it roots, just as slavery once did. In this instance Roach sees no path beyond that impasse (there is certainly no trace of federationist thinking here), and indeed it is notable that in "Something Seen" history goes back no further than slavery; there is no Africa in the background, no remembered kraal, no clear spring flowing from Guinea, such as offer a solution of sorts for "The Fighters".

"Something Seen" also inscribes a position for the speaker in actual politicized social life: the authorial "I" here is one of the peasants, a man experiencing a crucial *prise de conscience*. He is not, however, presented as a simple surrogate for the community; his representativeness is qualified. There is first the historical distance from the remembered labourers of the speaker's youth, and later the alienness of the passing car, which limits and demeans the observed life, and by its passage makes the speaker aware of how his world looks from that car. This is the view of powerful others, imposed upon his consciousness, not offered for his adoption. Memory makes him a witness to the community's experience, but it is also worth noting that in this text he is *not* a poet or an artist. That posture emphasizes his frustration. Within the fictive space of the poem, the speaker is not equipped to speak for the community, to articulate, encourage, or mobilize. Thus his rage is helpless. The poem depicts a rude awakening and a certain resoluteness for the speaker, but the awakening of the labourers themselves is deferred to the future. The speaker responds with an anger which I earlier called "unappeasable" because, while he can foresee the consequences of the current situation, in this poem he can offer no hope, because he can offer no course of action more effectual than cursing in the dust left by a departing car. It is an index of Roach's frustration that he represents this as a confrontation to which the antagonist seems entirely oblivious – whoever is laughing in the car does not see the cursing peasant. The peasant is left alone with his anger.

That failure of hope is most important to the poem, and exposes a problem Roach will continue to worry about. Though "Something Seen" achieves a purely formal closure by returning at the end to the language of its opening, its content poses the open question that hangs over many of Roach's poems: what, for a poet specifically, does the step from consciousness to action entail? Beyond mere description (even when it includes expression of the satisfaction or regret or rage that it inspires), what can or should the poem accomplish? This last is most pressing: How can a poem function as a political gesture; what constitutes action for a poet?

What can a poet do? Roach was haunted as much by that question as by the tragic situation of his people. Poems like "Something Seen" express his frustration and even despair, yet at the same time other poems demonstrate confidence in the poet's effectiveness. One need only contrast this stymied poem directly with the redemption of thankless labour undertaken in such poems as "Homestead" and "Men". Many other poems try out answers to the question. Some of these offer merely rhetorical comfort, and a reading of the poems in sequence generates no sense that Roach gradually refined a single satisfying answer over time. We do not find a linear progression toward a solution; rather, the nature of the solution changes with the nature of the problem perceived, and the context within which it is seen to be situated. There are indications, however, that as the dream of federation came closer to realization, Roach was thinking deeply about his social (and political) responsibilities as a poet, and so began to write in more concrete terms. We will now look at some of the answers he considered for the fundamental question: what can be done about the "empty tragedy" of West Indian life?

That phrase "empty tragedy" comes from "At Grafton Bay" (1954), a rarity among Roach's poems both for having a specifically identified setting (a beach near Plymouth), and for being about fishermen. It originates in the poet's experience of watching fishermen haul in their nets – a common enough sight in Tobago. Yet this is his only poem about fishermen, and what the fishermen do is twice referred to as "reaping", as if the poet could not resist assimilating them to the farmers who are his usual subject (FR 114). The first two stanzas contrast sharply with the remaining two. The poem begins (in stanza I) with a moralized landscape: the wind tosses the arching fronds of the seaside palm trees, and the coconuts they bear are figured here as chalices of bread and wine, a "eucharist for all" – this is a kind of manna, sustenance ready to hand. The second stanza invites us to regard this providential world as an enormous poem, "the lyric of each wheeling world, the epic of the universe", which can be heard when the sounds of wind and water blend with the "whisper of growth and cloud's soft drifting". Having established this sublimely harmonious landscape, the poem turns in the final two stanzas to the men who inhabit the scene, and abruptly the world ceases to be Edenic. These fishermen are busy *labouring* for sustenance, and like fallen Adam their fate is to work and die. Roach began with a scene devoid of human presence, and the fishermen are cut down almost as soon as they appear, returning us to an elemental landscape, but one with very different intonation. As in "Something Seen", new human awareness casts profound shadows on the symbolic "poem" which both of these texts initially take the world to be:

> Death scythes down the sinewed reapers;
> Lo, they fall to earthen bins,
> To the bitter shark-tooth burial;
> Their dole of labour, hunger, pity
> Stumbles on empty tragedy;
> The ceaseless, ruthless, sullen sea
> Snarls at their rock of destiny.

The sacramental imagery in "At Grafton Bay" might provide the material for some final redemptive gesture along orthodox Christian lines. But Roach frustrates that expectation when he replaces the initial image of wind tossing foliage by another, that of the "ruthless, sullen" sea battering a rock – a very different take on the "epic of the universe". His insistence on the emptiness of the tragedy, depicted entirely in terms of elemental nature, leaves no room for the interventions of religious faith. The progression of the poem is very much like that of "Something Seen", though the circumstances and issues are quite different: in both cases the scene is made tragic by increased awareness, but neither poem offers the means to move beyond that discouragement. St. Peter's Day (June 29) is celebrated in Roach's Plymouth (and elsewhere) as a fisherman's fete, a blessing of boats. If the poem is associated with that festival, as seems likely, it may hinge on an antithetical trope of refusing to bless, a rejection of the conventional gestures of faith out of a furious helplessness. We have seen a very similar response to death in "The White Coffin" (published in the same year), with its open hostility to the preacher and its strangely conditional conclusion. In spite of the explicitness of its occasion, and the likelihood that the author was actually present at the event this poem meditates upon, "At Grafton Bay" suggests by its trope of unblessing that these fishermen vanish from the scene not for lack of a priest but for lack of a poet to immortalize them. But what can a poet do?

It seems to have been easiest for Roach to imagine that the poet could redeem himself; indeed that poetry could redeem him. Although it was published after some more subtle approaches to the problem, "Hawk Heart" (1955), because it cobbles together features of some of Roach's other poems, can illustrate very clearly his simplest manoeuvre for redeeming "empty tragedy". Here, as in a poem like "Invocation", blessing seems to work. Almost at once Roach here recapitulates the ending of "Grafton Bay" (which had been published in the preceding issue of the same magazine): "Lo, all the generations downed, / Mould-coffined, mute as stone, / Barren as sand" (FR 121). After this recognition, however, Roach asserts that there is a group which somehow escapes this fate:

> Only our rarest dance, flower,
> Sing . . .
> The hawk's heart and the hawk's rage
> Possess them; they whirl up
> In powerful spirals from their roots.

The trump cards here are still those of five years earlier: the image of the soaring hawk from "Beyond" is conflated with that of the flower springing from its roots ("The Flowering Rock"), in order to repeat the claim of "Death Does Not" that the tragedy of death is not empty for everyone. By these means Roach clears a space for a fairly predictable prayer (a direct descendant of "Invocation") that he may be included among those "rarest":

> Oh, may the sun burn open cages
> Of my being, heal my halt hope,
> Hawk my desire past horizoning islands
> To cry world over wisdom's words,
> A tempest to the spirit, beating
> Rank darkness back.

The specific terms of this conclusion show affinities with poems written later than those just mentioned, such as "Letter to Lamming" and "I Walk Abroad"; the emphasis on soaring "*past* islands . . to cry *world over*" incidentally reflects Roach's increasingly clear ambition to be a world-poet *from* this island, rather than an exile, or an island poet for his own place alone. But the grandiose promise of public service is unfocussed, and the poem's resolution is a decidedly selfish one. This is all too apparent in the narrowing progression of the poem's pronouns: '*they* die; some of *us* flower, I hope *I* beat rank darkness back'. In "Something Seen" and "Grafton Bay" the fate of the multitude enlightens only the speaker, and similarly here only the speaker's own neck is saved by the verse.

The condition lamented in "Grafton Bay" and "Hawk Heart" is human mortality, rather than historicized Caribbean experience; even "Something Seen" is not actually a depiction of a village, but of the situation of its people. Though he lived in the intimacy of villages during most of his early career, there is no sign of that *particularity* in the poems; particulars are always already made representative (exactly as Roach does with his family and friends). This is true even of "Despite Ancestral Rape" (1953), though it includes Roach's most vivid portrayal of a peasant community:

> Our village grips the hill,
> Clings rickety to rock and laps the sea,
> Whose salt breath blacks bare boards, . . .
> We creak and groan when the trades gale;
> We know that hurricanes will grind
> And sweep us to the angered sea; . . .
> Feeling the sun-glance livid in our veins,
> We live in his insistence,

Though our issue is sun-clothed
And our spare earth but barely blunts our hunger. . .
We scotch the rock for foothold and foundation,
We furrow slopes and terrace rasher steeps. (FR 94)[10]

This is the village seen from within, and Roach moves beyond even his own earlier representations; his praise here is not for crooning mothers in shady dooryards (imagery aimed at bolstering self-esteem) but for the force of peasant life and peasant will in the midst of apparent fragility. The result is compelling in a way few West Indian poets could match. It is also *different* from what other poets were doing. For example, many Caribbean poets are preoccupied with the act of naming (so crucial to both Walcott and Brathwaite), and with the poetry of place-names, which animates the work of poets as diverse as A. J. Seymour and Lorna Goodison. Yet this preoccupation is quite alien to Roach, who plainly regards himself not as visualizing or describing the peasantry, but as one of their own speaking for them. Similarly Roach does not participate in the drive of West Indian poets toward increasing dramatization, which originates in the writers' discomfort with depicting the folk as mute objects of curiosity. Confident that he speaks for and from the village, Roach feels no obligation to provide his people dramatic (that is, *distanced*) speech.

Accurate representation of peasant life (something about which Roach felt little or no anxiety, as a poet) is thus not the real focus of "Despite Ancestral Rape". The poem depicts the village's marginality and poverty, but the mood is positive and forward-looking. From the start Roach sets aside the story of suffering and rape that created these conditions by containing the traumatic past syntactically within the grammatical capsule of the opening prepositional phrase: "*despite* ancestral rape" This poem redeems the situation of the peasant from "empty tragedy" by applying the tropes through which Roach earlier envisioned personal redemption:

Far out our cockle boats insult Atlantic;
We dare, we know we dare the uncertain ocean
As we coerce the earth
And hazard with hard time for richer futures.

We hazard, for the sun incenses,
The stars excite our hopes,
Incite imaginations, and the moon
Compels like tides our ignorant blood[.]

What gives the tragedy meaning in this case is a remarkable conceptualization of the village as a *collective* adventurer. The unusual word "cockle" echoes Roach's very enthusiastic account of Columbus' "three cockle ships" in the early poem "Discovery" (1938). The sequences "ocean, earth, time" and "sun, stars, moon" in the passage are identical to the sequences that shape "Invocation" – a poem about radically solitary adventuring. Even more pointed is the relation to the language of "March Trades", with its conception of the island as a ship that prospers by taking the buffet of the wind. The present poem carries forward those predecessors; here Caribbean nature itself makes adventurers of the peasantry, but they constitute an adventuring collective, not a miscellany of solitary heroes. Roach's concluding imperative insists that the resolution of "empty tragedy" must be communal:

> We must ascend the rainbow road
> And ride like frigates the adventurous trades,
> Or die, or die.

The telling comparison to frigates (both birds and ships) evokes the bird/bard kotched on his perch in "Frigate Bird" and "Beyond". The effect is to represent the village as a whole by an image previously associated only with the individual in radical isolation from the community. Roach may be testing whether the heroic language he had developed for individual achievement can convincingly be applied to the village; the manoeuvre certainly also offers a new way to reassert the social integration of the poet. Roach's postulation of a communal adventurer is ingenious, not least because of its inherent federalism, developed more explicitly in "Fugue for Federation"; yet the idea remains conceptually cloudy (if each of "us" is a frigate-bird, what sort of community is that?). Moreover, certain valences of the adventurer make the image problematic. In poems such as "Transition", Roach is straightforward about the inherently conflicting ideals of adventurers and communities. He wants to distinguish "good" adventurers like his Columbus and his recurrent "viking" from bad adventurers like John Hawkins and Don Fernando (in "Anacaona"). A *basis* for that willed distinction unfortunately does not appear in the poems. The phallic adventurer remains difficult to distinguish from the invasive rapist; the peasantry constitutes the black loam from which the heroic flowers, but also a matriarchal womb subject to violation by "heroes". This particular poem chooses *not* to concern itself with past "ancestral rape", but its own language reintroduces the theme of violation: adventurers "insult" the ocean and "coerce" the earth, and this poem praises them for it.

Poems considered in Chapters 4 and 5 abundantly demonstrate the individual quest for heroes (or heroic self-image) as Roach's response to empty tragedy – his attempt to find meaning in it. That is very much a poet's aspiration, grounded on the aspiration of ambitious individuals. But what aspiration is possible for a West Indian village? When Roach describes his island communities as "cockle ships" going forward together, he imputes to the village the same *agency*, the same power to act, that characterizes his heroic individuals. These poems cannot actually provide power. Even in his wildest dreams Roach cannot have imagined his villagers saying to one another, "'ascend the rainbow road'? – of course, why didn't we think of that?" What poets can do is provide the vision which can inspire the *will* to act.

The figure of the adventurer has another inconvenient valence: it is associated not only with rape but with escape. The bird/bard soars away from human habitation. How can such escapees function as spirits of the place? For himself, Roach is mulling the question how to be an "adventurer" and yet stay productively at home. Whether the West Indian poet can be a functioning part of his community is one issue; another, increasingly urgent in the 1950s, is whether to leave altogether, joining with many members of the community in emigrating to England. "Despite Ancestral Rape" broaches this subject as it grapples with the poet's relation to his community and its "empty tragedy". Only one brief line in "Despite Ancestral Rape" (1953) hints at the pressure to migrate: "[We] stand on hilltops hungering to horizons". By 1955, however, when he revises that poem to produce "For the Peasant People", Roach expands the statement considerably in the final stanza, where migration offers escape – at a price – from claustrophobic island society: "Winds call the young away . . . But where they go they take them, \ Theirs forever more".[11] Roach works through this complex of issues in three poems of 1952-53: "Letter to Lamming in England", "I Walk Abroad" and "In Mango Shade".

STAYING AT HOME

In "Letter to Lamming in England" (1952), Roach presents his most thoughtful meditation on the problem of "empty tragedy". The poem is prompted by the emigration of one of the promising young poets of the period, George Lamming, and it addresses the problem by expanding the field of reference to take in the possibility of migration. In the early 1950s West Indian migration to Britain was at its height, and for Roach personally that course of action may have seemed more appealing, or more urgent, from the midst of the responsibilities he had just taken on with his marriage.

In those circumstances Roach ("older", "cooler", "more content") sees Lamming as the dashing young poet who has "jumped for England". Roach employs his recurrent symbols of poetic success, and the usual ambivalence is in play: Lamming is the lonely seagull, the kestrel, the free-flying "soarer", but at the same time his roots are tapped into the hard soil of the Caribbean and his song is "water wizard from these rocks" (FR 82). Lamming is not a role model, of course; Roach, the elder poet, is for the most part *giving* advice. But there are further inflections to the relationship. Roach is expressing a wish for a *compadre*, for solidarity in a solitary business (this is most overt in the seventh stanza). He is also envisioning Lamming as a more impetuous alter ego. The ambivalent symbolism and the multivalence of the relationship point to a likely motivation for the poem: defining what Lamming can do helps Roach define what he himself can do. Yet the poem is not framed as a meditation on the case of Lamming. Instead the central statement is addressed to Lamming personally, and is already complex. It can be reduced to something like this: "excuse me for wishing you'd want to come home; remember anyway where you come from." The apologetic imperatives are noteworthy ("Forgive the thought divining you unhappy . . . Forgive the dream that drags you back to islands"); Roach apologizes for his wishes even before he states them. One reason for the manoeuvre is obvious enough: the wishes mask an envy of Lamming's freedom and a reproach that he has fled his responsibilities (the reproach is occasionally audible, as in "you have thrown [your island] to the sea and jumped for England"). But the odd apology also suggests that Roach is already reflecting critically on his own wishes, along something like these lines: "*why* do I want him back? What do I want him to do here that he can't do over in England? What do I want him to do that I myself can't do here?"

The poem's reflection on their relationship and on what Roach can learn or deduce from the case of Lamming is most concerned with their common ground: the state of poetry in West Indies, and folk life as its subject. When Roach asks to be forgiven for "desiring your genius home again / Among the immortelles and poincianas", the lines may seem to idealize poetry, evoking an image of the poetic genius as a pin-up amid tropical flora – George Lamming as the Maroon Girl. In fact, however, the appeal to Lamming as a poet is premised upon a social vision. I have cut off the turn made in that sentence about immortelles and poincianas, which immediately moves on to something less idyllic:

> Among the immortelles and poincianas
> Dropping red pathos on our naked graves;
> Among our peasants barefoot as their cattle[.]

It is in that same spirit that stanzas III, IV, and VI depict the social reality of indigence which now affects both the rural village and the urban ghetto. The words "naked", "bare" and "hunger" echo through these stanzas; they are hardly calculated to lure Lamming back, except to the extent that they might instill a sense of obligation, of dues to be paid.

This is not the only portrayal of the peasantry in "Letter to Lamming", however. We have seen that to accomplish the objectives of this poem Roach brings together multiple valences of the image of poet, of this particular relationship, and of his own wishes, so it should not be surprising that there are also several different sorts of representations of folk-life here. Stanza V for example glimpses behind those grim pictures to discern the psychopathology of the colonial condition. This vision will be developed further in "The Fighters" and most extensively in "I am the Archipelago"; for the present Lamming's conscience seems to be the target of Roach's frustrated anger at "ranting politicians" and at the heritage of cane-slavery, miscegenation and colour-prejudice. Roach even suggests that the exile cannot escape these negative aspects of home, when he says that he imagines Lamming in England as "unhappy", "hungry", "aliened by pure prohibited complexion".

After those trenchant views and some almost despairing questions, the final stanza unexpectedly presents a frank idealization as Roach's prayer for Lamming:

> Remember cadences of island patois,
> Old men goatskin drumming,
> Young men's tin percussion,[12]
> The sun's rose ruddy in our blood,
> The wine excitement of our island women.

It is certainly strange that this rosy picture comes *after* the exposition of rudely realistic detail that had brushed aside the idyll of the poet among the flowers. But it is not thoughtless or inadvertent. Stanza VI speculates whether Lamming is haunted by classic Caribbean images of overworked grandmothers, hungry children, and "hunger dancing / to reiterated rhythms drumming blood". In a pointed redemption of the specific details of those "classic images" of empty tragedy, the memory in the final stanza emphasizes robust vitality: the generational extremes of grandmothers and feeble schoolchildren are replaced with young men and women in their sexual prime, and old men who are still beating their drums. Moreover, this conjunction of sun, drumming, dancing, wine, and island women recurs in a frankly celebratory scene at the end of "World on Islands" and even "Verse in August" includes a diffuse version of it, a lost world that survives only in the memory of an old man. In "August", the village has become a nourishing memory for an *individual*; in "Letter to Lamming", however, this exhortation to remember is not merely private. George Lamming in particular is asked to remember *because* of the proven power of his oratory, his home-grown voice which is "water wizard from these rocks". He is asked to remember as a means to achieve something as a poet.

The poems ends with the psychologically nourishing vision of an edenic village that recalls the idealized kraals of "The Fighters", but it has also presented a politically motivating vision of hunger and "empty tragedy". There does not seem to be a dialectical relationship between these visions in this poem; neither replaces or transforms the other (as happens for example in "Transition"). The multivalence of an ongoing thought process is characteristic of "Letter to Lamming", Roach's ruminative confession ("forgive . . . forgive") to his alter ego. This poem about what Roach himself should do, as poet of this place and people, is couched in terms of oblique suggestions about what Lamming should do.

The clutch of questions near the end express frustrations presumed to be shared:

> Why were we born under the star of rhyme
> Among a displaced people lost on islands
> Where all time past is knotted in time present?

The sense of obstructed moral obligation, which Roach feels and here projects onto his fellow-poet he also projected onto another friend, Cecil Herbert, at about the same time. "New Year Poem for Cecil Herbert" (1953) twice asks its crucial question: "Did ever season murder song?" – is it conceivable that the Caribbean climate or setting makes poetry impossible? In response Roach urges Herbert (and incidentally himself) to write for this reason: "To be silent in our silent air / Is suicide; we're given speech." Who can speak, must. So poets have an obligation to speak;

but in what sense can their speech succeed? For Lamming, Roach spells the problem out thus:

> Here we are architects with no tradition,
> Are hapless builders upon no foundation;
> No skilled surveyors mark our forward road.
> Can we speed through a score of centuries gone,
> Leap from the sheer escarpment of our time
> And mount like eagles proud-winged among eagles?

With no tradition, nothing to build on, is it possible for talent and courage to carry us up among the "eagles" of the literary tradition? That question veils extraordinary ambition and extraordinary anxieties. It must have been a great relief and encouragement to Roach that he could at least ask it in the plural, sharing with Lamming the burden of responsibility, the uncertainty about means, the lack of resources. Here at least the leap from the escarpment is not overtly suicidal, as it is in "Death Does Not". But Lamming's "leap" was his "jump for England". To some extent, this poem presents Lamming as having deserted the region (as it turned out, he also abandoned the genre of poetry – so did Cecil Herbert).[13] Lamming's example thus forces Roach again (as in "Beyond") to face the problem of connecting the poetic eyrie to the poet's eyot, and he continues to aim for the most precarious solution: neither escape into the realms of art, nor local political engagement. In the climactic appeal of the poem ("oh for your oratory for the stricken dumb") Roach is pointedly not saying "let the subaltern speak"; this is a wish that the poet could speak *for* the victims of "empty tragedy" as eloquently (that is, as effectually) as Lamming does.

It is in the spirit of this solution that Roach reminds Lamming he is a "man of islands", and urges him to keep his work rooted in its origins, even after his "leap". At the same time, Lamming's experience in England legitimizes Roach's solution in an unexpectedly practical way. At first glance the opening of "Letter to Lamming" is just another instance of a familiar image, the disembodied voice of the soaring bird whose song inspires the people on the ground:

> . . . beyond my gaze,
> I hear only your seasonal voice,
> A lonely seagull's, crying on Atlantic.

But how does Roach hear his alter ego? This poem is in fact about listening to Lamming's voice broadcast across the Atlantic via BBC radio.[14] That premise is not emphasized, but it is unmistakable, and it clarifies for the first time an important feature of Roach's recurrent soaring man imagery. Taken at face value, the bird/bard is a Shelleyan image for the poet. In Roach's work, this image seems to come out of nowhere, suddenly dominating the poems of 1950 ("Beyond", "Transition", "Frigate Bird Passing"). But "Letter to Lamming" shows us where it comes from; those poems were published about a year after Roach first heard his own poetry broadcast on the BBC (in August, 1949). From the start, the Shelleyan metaphor of the soarer describes not a romantic fancy but an electronic *reality* that can transcend placedness without abandoning it, making it possible for a poet to be everywhere and *some*where, to speak from the smallest eyot to the world at large, with the uncannily domestic intimacy characteristic of radio – a voice right here among us, and yet not.

Benedict Anderson has pointed out the importance of radio for the cultivation of nationalism in many colonial settings.[15] In the West Indian case, a federation of non-contiguous island states would not have been feasible without the radio. For Roach the federationist, there is a political dimension to the image of the poet that radio makes possible (and Shelley, too, managed to promote these same seemingly refractory conceptions of the poet, as transcendental soarer and as "unacknowledged legislator"). Soaring out of the village via the airwaves makes it possible for the poet to be heard in all the villages, and to that extent gives him a politically meaningful power to gather all the islands while remaining on his "private hillock" ("Love Overgrows a Rock"). Many of the poems to be considered in the rest of this chapter present evidence that Roach's advocacy of federation was bound up with his faith that through technologies of radio and print he could genuinely speak from his own island to a much wider audience.

Roach's effort to reconcile his own confinement to his eyot with the broad horizon of his aspirations was galvanized by the fact of Lamming's migration and success in England. To concede that migration means freedom seems to imply that the eyot is indeed a prison; Roach wants to reject that view. In that context the possibility of becoming a voice on the airwaves must have appeared to offer a powerful reconciliation, a way for the poet, at least, to be both squarely *here* and at the same time everywhere. As we have seen, his effort to redeem the conditions of Caribbean life was never merely personal, and it is one facet of his desire for federation that he regarded the expanded horizon of a federated West Indies as a better solution for all the region's inhabitants than abandonment through migration. Federation made it possible to become part of something larger than the eyot without emigrating. At the end of the twentieth century, Caribbean people occupy complex post-national social systems that encompass the entire North Atlantic Basin, but in the 1950s that extraordinary consequence of migration was unforeseeable. For Roach's generation, migration could seem solitary, desperate, and irrevocable – a desertion, rather than the first step in a kind of reverse colonization.

Roach's personal ambivalence about migration is stated most plainly in a poem of 1954, "A Reed for my Rime": "I fly this scene of my resentment / . . . But yet I swarm with a fierce love for us / The continentals broken up on islands".[16] The contrary terms of that ambivalence are first pursued in two poems of 1953 ("I Walk Abroad" and "In Mango Shade") which look as if they had been conceived as twins. Even the decor of the two poems is coordinated; in contrast to the shadeless sun and proud possession of "I Walk Abroad", "In Mango Shade" is set in dooryard shadow, and depicts a poet unhappy on his island. These poems might be described as exploring the terms "eyrie" and "eyot" as alternative intonations of his isolation: is he the soaring solitary eagle or the poet isolated in the village? Do the technology of radio and the infrastructure of a Federation make it possible for a poet to function without leaving his little eyot? The choice might have been clearer if Roach saw himself as "the poet of Tobago", so it is worth reiterating that he never imagined himself in that role. He wants to speak from a place in the Caribbean, but he is not a poet of the minute particulars of this place; rather, he wants to be a visionary of a powerfully imagined place, the "West Indies".

"I Walk Abroad" (1953) is characterized by two remarkable slippages. The first occurs almost at once. The poem begins by enacting possession of and identification with the island: "This is my own" (FR 96). But this is not a specific piece of land, and the real emphasis of the poem is on defining the possessor, not the possessed: "This is I". The writer defines himself by establishing his rightful possession of a place in space and time rather than in concrete geography: "I walk abroad in my fierce July noon / Desiring no shade". As so often in the poems (like "Invocation") where Roach is intent on assuring himself of his vocation, this home place is defined primarily in elemental terms: hilltop, sun and sea. This is a "West Indian" space, not Tobago specifically. Roach creates the impression of greater-than-usual detail, with the relatively intimate reference to "my garden", and the links to immediate, more domestic, nature: "I join my voice to the frog-throat in the pond, / to cricket shrill and bird cry in the wood". But as usual the setting is not recognizably specific. In the pond, the garden, the woods, animals are heard (but not seen), and again as in other poems of this kind there is no human presence except himself – this is not at all a social space.

In this poem the poet situates himself securely in the Caribbean, and in so doing acknowledges history. His skin and hair are "African", "continental", but Roach's point here, as in "A Reed for my Rime", is his West Indian *difference* from Africa. Caribbean identity is established by forgetting Africa, and the poem's statement of that principle is also couched in purely topographical, not social, terms: "I have forgot the depths and dreams of rivers / in a long endless land". He is a changed man; "the sea tides in my blood" as it never would have done in Africa. Roach powerfully reverses the more familiar image of "Africa in the blood" when he states that his African features are superficial; *beneath* them "I take Caribbean nature, . . . the skull assumes the infinite variety, shapes and moods of islands."[17] The act of cutting himself off from the main, of severing the umbilical link to mother Africa, is boldly asserted, and with that decision to put down his bucket where he is, to define himself in terms of this small island which is his own, the poem seems to be ending with an almost contractual act of writerly possession of this West Indian place:

> I sign upon my hills;
> The pen slips down the slopes,
> The ink streams out and stains the native sea.

The conclusiveness of this climactic statement has been carefully prepared. It is the third in a series of parallel constructions about poetic expression that began with "I join my voice to the frog-throat" and "I sign my name upon the papyrus / Of plantain leaves broad in my garden." One might even take "the ink streams out" as an image for the dissemination of his work. But the verbs are disturbing, literally unstable in their implications – "slips", "streams", "stains" – and the very next line takes an unexpected and unprepared turn: "Who holds me to these accidental rocks?"[18] The entire project of the poem seems to be undone by this question, as if the poet's resolve has been deflected by a mere image: the ink streaming away from the hillock leads him to envision himself streaming away. As a result of this second slippage (set off by the very word "slips"), a poem about possessing, and being possessed by, his eyot becomes, at almost the last moment, Roach's most explicit consideration of migration:

If I go out as I came in, across Atlantic,
Become adventurer, world will know me
Feeling my footsteps on the latitudes,
Clocking my cadence down the long meridians.[19]

This final move is a surprise: a radically different speculation that seems to come out of nowhere, entertaining the thought that to leave here and enter upon the stage of the world would lead to fame specifically *as a poet* (that much is clear from the imagery of cadence and footsteps). This puts an unexpected spin on the title: initially "I Walk Abroad" had seemed to mean "out in the sun"; but at the end we're contemplating another sort of "abroad", another *scale* of abroad. The ground has shifted beneath those apparently definitive statements: "This is my own . . . This is I".

If "I Walk Abroad" ends distracted by an appealing alternative, "In Mango Shade" almost deserves to be *entitled* "vacillation and resolution". In an obvious reversal of the opening of its companion poem ("I walk abroad . . . desiring no shade"), this one begins in the shade, with the poet brooding on the foolishness of wasting his days at home. The generally parallel sequence of *sounds* in lines 1 and 2 emphasizes a sardonic link between "eyot" and "idiot": "rotting on my eyot in Atlantic, / Reckoning, idiot, the running tides" (FR 101; but Ramchand has "rotting in"). The only journey undertaken in this poem is imaginary, "a trek of dreams", but the text makes significant progress from self-pity in the shade of reverie to resolutions and encouragements. While resisting the urge to "walk abroad", Roach actively struggles toward a private peace, a sense of worth, and also toward a sense of positively belonging to the place where he is.

Roach's trek is only sketchily traced in the poem. In his "dream" he returns to West Africa, but not to dwell there (this is consistent with the "forgetting" of Africa in "I Walk Abroad"). He begins there only in order to retrace the Middle Passage back to the Caribbean. Africa at the historical moment of enslavement is "a midday in history" when events and emotions, however painful, had a shadowless clarity. But as the journey continues through years of plantation slavery and colonialism, shadows lengthen, anger is bottled and sours, intensity goes stale, art diminished, and truth "out of tune". After traversing four of the poem's seven stanzas, the trek seems to end in a twilit present where "nothing is plain".

In the face of that grim progression the poem then takes an upward turn: "I say to my heart: Be gay, be gay. Weep not . . . Do not despair". This sounds dangerously easy, the sort of thing Roach might have corrected if he had ever published the poem. But some of what is said in the concluding stanzas is of more interest than the rather irresponsible rhetoric that frames it. Much of the poem's conclusion is intensely introspective. Roach's choice of images contributes to an impression that we are listening to an articulate member of the peasantry (as in fact we are), and the poem is not about adventuring, nor even about the village, but about rootedness in the earth itself:

> Be anonymous, be
> The pliant clay in the soil's breast; be
> The dough of the bread of life and death.

Images of clay and dough are particularly prominent in Roach's poems about his parents, but here he identifies himself with the material, rather than with the worker who shapes it, anticipating by more than a decade his own description of "the generations of heavy slave folk trampled into the clay where the sweet cane prospered in our bitter sweat."[20] As the passage continues it draws upon other images with special resonance for Roach:

> keep love's light alive
> In the private heart; in the spirit's tower the beacon;
> Beneath the bone, behind the old rock face
> Pray for the grace of the fountain aching from stone.

The fountain bursting from rock and the spirit's tower are recurrent images for the most private wellsprings of the poet's identity and sense of self. These passages depict a stoical poet coming to very private terms with the world, while love remains hidden in the heart, grace beneath the bone.

Such advice to himself is only part of the poem's business, however. "In Mango Shade" is addressed outward to others as well, and the transition is managed by way of a calculated sequence of pronouns (I say "calculated" because grammatical constructions that avoid pronouns seem unusually common in this poem, e.g. in the second stanza). Roach starts with a self-absorbed "I" dreaming under a mango tree, then he addresses his own heart as "you", and the second-person pronoun imperceptibly shifts so that it might apply either to himself, his heart, or his audience with the words "do not despair wanderer \ on island landscapes, perpetual exile, \ leaser of history's goodwill, sharecropper, squatter \ on feudal acres". The focus on the solitary poet widens to take in a paradoxical community of solitaries when he addresses his audience in these terms, making plausible the convivial "we/our" of the final stanza.

Those phrases characterize West Indians as deracinated, moving lightly over the earth even in their own islands; the poem as a whole counteracts that impression in two ways. First, it emphasizes the soil, in imagery that recalls "The Flowering Rock". West Indians are rooted in the black loam of their heritage ("our feet are deep in slave-despairing ground"). That soil "is fed from good spring waters of the human spirit", waters that here, as in "The Fighters", flow ultimately from Africa, and eventually bring forth fertile crops. Less explicitly, the poem also argues for the role of art in connecting West Indians with their place and their history. In this, too, the poem progresses from negative to positive. In the Caribbean the drums of Africa, once capable of summoning gods, are said to have degenerated into "the frippery of carnival", and the speaker's own poems seem to be ranked even lower when they are characterized as "rhyming rondeaus" and "a foreign cansonet". At the poem's central nadir the grim conclusion is drawn: "art is gone back to heaven or gone to ground". In the final stanza, however, the long trek from Africa which had been a merely dream at the start takes on greater substance – an aesthetic substance. It is a "taled trek", a "legend". Throughout his work Roach always associates the term "legend" with the unspoken histories poets exist to articulate, and here for the first time he introduces another term by which to describe the relation of art to history: "pray to preserve the centuries we slaved / A sacred arras of ancestral story". We will see that this "arras", usually under the name "tapestry", becomes very prominent in the poems of the 1960s and 1970s, as Roach comes to distinguish its implications from those of "legend".

FEDERATION POEMS

"In Mango Shade" is not a polished poem, but when taken in conjunction with "I Walk Abroad" it illuminates how Roach was thinking about his vocation under pressure of the need to choose between federation and migration. He chose to stay at home; by so doing he effectively committed himself to write about the desirability and implications of a Federation of the West Indies. "Lady by the Sea" (1954), the revision of "Reed for My Rime", was first published in *Bim* alongside "Grafton Bay". It is the first of the poems that speaks unequivocally about federation. In its bare outline, the overall progression of argument in "Lady by the Sea" is similar to that in "Hawk Heart", and can be paraphrased thus: "our situation is tragic; we have a few great ones; may I be one of them." However, "Lady" adds a richer historical dimension to its account of the "empty tragedy", and this provides a foundation broad enough to sustain the multilayered solution Roach envisions in this poem – a solution suited not only to the private aspirations of the poet but also to the aspirations he attributes to the people.

Veering away from praise for the lady of the title, the middle section of the poem contextualizes the plight of the peasantry within the story of Middle Passage and its consequences. This is a compressed version of the corresponding section of "Reed for My Rime"; the most significant change is the virtual elimination here of the poet's ambivalence toward his place (the earlier version had said "I fly this scene of my resentment"). The story is no less harrowing, but instead of "acute hurting love like a disease" ("Reed"), Roach now writes about "these parishes our hearts hold now / With love green as the landscape, / Peopling the archipelago with hope" (FR 112). Though history is imagined as "writing down our stress and anger", it is also "nursing tomorrow's foetus". This image of the future about to be born from the womb of history is a variant of the poem's dominant image of flowering blood (most centrally, the lady is figured as "the black rose our blood bears out of its fortitude"). It is only in the final stanza, however, that Roach links this directly to the political vision with which the poem concludes. "Blood grows and blooms", he writes, summarizing the accumulated imagery, and then he draws his inferences:

> One hand may disinter
> All the folkfaces stationed in the stone;
> One mind may knead the nation's
> Till each island eat one large philosophy;
> One poet's dream may join the people's
> And rejoin the wind and sun and sea,
> Flowering and fruiting like a tree
> Century after century.

The phrase "one large philosophy" plainly refers to the idea of federation, and to call it also the *people's* dream is to insist that it is not an imposition on the region from outside, but an assertion of common cause on the stage of world politics by those who have suffered this history and these physical conditions. The unpredictable path from praise of the "lady" to this conclusion is finessed by rhetorical means, and not only through the association of images I have just mentioned. The refrain ("century after century") at end of the second, the fifth, and this final (seventh) stanza contributes an impression of inevitability, while the cumulative parallelism of "one hand may . . . one mind may . . . one poet's dream may" works to similar rhetorical effect, closing in on the role of poet himself. The image of a sculptor exhuming faces from stone recalls the emphasis in "Daaga" on the poet's responsibility to the "aphonous stone" of the ancestral past, and here it leads to a description of the poet's work as bread with which to feed the whole region – a diet of consensus. Roach presumably intends us to hear the paradoxical pun on "knead" (he later spells it out explicitly in "Caribbean Calypso"): The poet "kneads" bread to nourish the people from whom he himself, in turn, "needs" nourishment. Two instances of a particular grammatical ambiguity in the following lines seem to acknowledge the same reciprocity of agency. "Nation's" and "people's" are written as possessive, but the context makes it likely that both are *heard* as plurals. The text says for example that the poet's dream may join the already-formed dream of the people; but aurally suggests that the poet's dream can bring the various peoples together into a cultural federation. This ambiguity thus expresses both the poet's contribution in bringing the people together, and the personal advantage for him of reintegration with society and with nature.

The poem goes further, by appending a second verb ("rejoin") just where the rhetorical trajectory of the poem had seemed complete. Roach wants to assert here not only the poet's unanimity with the people, but also the reintegration of poet and people with the elemental landscape in which they *all* grow. The very end of the poem imagines a new racination after the deracination of Middle Passage and colonialism; that is what will make it possible for the dream of the poet, now identical to that of the people, and in harmony with place and climate, to flourish "like a tree". The language of these final lines, underscored by unusually heavy rhyming (sea/tree/century), looks back especially to a corresponding integration of poet, commonality, and nature that was hoped for in the following lines from Roach's inaugural "Invocation": "Me, let the circling years, / the flowing winds, the streaming waters, / and the patient earth enfold and bless . . . with common love" (FR 52). Yet the closest relative of "Lady by the Sea" is of course "A Reed for my Rime", and when the two poems are compared it seems clear that the final lines of "Lady by the Sea" indicate a fundamental rethinking of this most solitary and self-pitying passage from "A Reed for my Rime":

> I am wrecked on the soul's shores,
> Washed by our tragic memory of tears

Till in my singing, heart, hand, harp
Are grief with the willow's grief,
With the river's continuity of sorrow.

Even more can be said about the decision which excluded these lines. Considering the explicit reference to the exilic psalm "By the rivers of Babylon", to delete this passage is to make a point of excising all reference to migration from the later poem. Reaffirming a commitment to the region, "Lady by the Sea" makes it clear that the substrate of nature, like that of history, is essential to Roach's vision of human success in the Caribbean (we will return to this point in Chapter 8).

*

In 1957-58, contemporaneous with the institution of the new central government, Roach published three major poems in support of federation. Each approaches the subject from a different angle and each develops in a distinctive style. "Love Overgrows a Rock" (1957) argues that federation can relieve the oppressiveness of small-island societies; its style looks back to "Invocation", "Beyond", and "Transition". "I am the Archipelago" (1957) invokes federation as a way to heal and exorcise the history of slavery; its style derives from the Marlovian sublime of "He plucked a burning stylus" and "Tree". "Fugue for Federation" (1958), a public, even ceremonial poem with affinities to "March Trades" and "Caribbean Coronation Verse", develops an analogy between the voyages of Columbus and the political adventure upon which the islands were then about to embark.

"Love Overgrows a Rock" begins with one of Roach's elemental landscapes:

Only the foreground's green;
Waves break the middle distance,
And to horizon the Atlantic's spread
Bright, blue and empty as the sky. (FR 127)

The encircling reef over which the waves break, though not even named in these lines, is the crucial feature of the scene. Separating the blue of open ocean from the shallow coastal waters, the reef is here a boundary that nothing passes. Though the "horizons of our love" extend even beyond the Atlantic, the reef's protective custody imprisons the psyche and defeats aspiration: "My eyot jails the heart, / And every dream is drowned in the shore water." This topography entails a claustrophobic, deforming culture:

Too narrow room pressed down
My years to stunted scrub,
Blunted my sister's beauty
And my friend's grave force[.]

Acknowledging the constraint of horizons which poems like "Beyond" had tried manfully to ignore, Roach envisions no flowering tree, but "stunted scrub", pot-bound by "too narrow room". That view is, of course, only the beginning of the poem, not its end. The objective of "Love Overgrows a Rock" is to urge the wider horizon of a Federation as an antidote to the claustrophobic scale of islands, and in fact the argument is even more pointed; it is specifically an argument that federation is preferable to *migration* as a response to island life. If one's island is too small to contain love, rather than leave it, let larger love (that is, the idealism of federation) bring together the islands it has outgrown into a larger entity, with greater scope for action and achievement. By migrating to England, Roach writes, "We turn Columbus' blunder back / . . . We explore the hostile and exploding zones" – but the move is still a blunder. In the interests of a larger unity, Roach temporarily separates himself from the "we" who migrate: "the drunken hawk's blood of / the poet" streams through "climates *of the mind*," not through the merely geographical "zones" that "we" rootless West Indians explore. As he insists in "The Fighters" and "I am the Archipelago", West Indians must be moved by intellect, by "the mind", rather than by the pressure of circumstance, and what intellect dictates is clear. The poet's concluding exhortation, in this case, is to "disdain the sea" (insofar as the sea is the space of migration, the space by which the West Indians are isolated from one another), and instead to "gather the islands' hills", not within their individual barrier reefs, but in the capacious encircling net of the Federation.

The poet's momentary alienation from a people bent on migration is purely strategic. We hear the solitary voice of the bird/bard from his private hillock/eyot, but at once perceive that he is in the act of joining a cry already in progress; that his voice is part of a chorus of opinion. "Join" here has the same integrative force that we saw in the case of "join . . . rejoin" at the end of "Lady by the Sea". The poet's solitary voice is invoked as a catalyst for community. In the spirit of federation, the register of Roach's voice here is both distinctive and intentionally representative. Even though "Love Overgrows a Rock" includes a semblance of autobiographical detail in the account of how "too narrow room" stunted the speaker's years, blunted his sister's beauty and his friend's force, these references are treated as representations of a typical life, on no particular island. The poem warrants their "human truth", but not their autobiographical truth.

"Love Overgrows a Rock" refers in passing to Columbus's "blunder", but "Fugue for Federation" is a poem preoccupied with Columbus, and it treats him very positively indeed, praising him specifically for his courage in adventuring *beyond* "breed, bounds, creed". Roach valued that transgressive impulse very highly in 1958; it was the force that could break through the individual barrier reefs to a wider West Indian community. Perhaps for that reason, Roach imagines Columbus as transgressive not only in his deeds but in his nature, describing this hero who "joins two worlds, two ages" as if he were himself already a Caribbean creole ("Jew or Gentile, Spaniard or Portuguese").[21] As in "Discovery" twenty years earlier, Roach distances Columbus from the consequences of his adventuring (to write that "Hell followed him" downplays any causal relation between the adventure of discovery and its aftermath). The explorer is held up as a model to be emulated, and in that spirit the crucial trope of the poem is a similitude between Columbus's ships and the islands of the West Indies:

> Men's ideals advance, leap
> Over seas, league islands
> Small as his caravels . . .
> So now they sail, set sail
> To destinations of the heart's desire.

In this poem the islands are not described as "eyots", with that term's negative connotations of confinement and pressure; instead they are figured as adventuring "caravels". The conception looks back to "March Trades" with its episode of "adventuring", and its exhortation to "keep all ship-shape" on each buffeted island. This time however it is linked to the Federation, that "league" of islands which reproduces Columbus's little convoy of cockle ships, and which makes it possible to move beyond individual island loyalties and identities, breaching the reefs that encircle each eyot, so as to bring isolated worlds together.

This trope of the islands as caravels explains the title "Fugue for Federation". Roach's use of musical terminology is often imprecise at best, but certainly the word "fugue" has for him implications of grandeur and ceremony, and in the sense that the word denotes a structure in which voices follow one another in imitation, then the fugue of the poem is certainly the relation between Columbus's voyages and that of the island-caravels (technically a relation of subject and answer, if Roach knew that much about fugues). In this case the fugal answer (the Federation's own voyage of self-discovery) is redemptive of Columbus's original voyage, recapitulating it in a way that leads to different destinations, a different "development" (in musical terms), and so a different resolution. The physical and moral centre of the poem is thus the series of questions asked in stanza four:

> What sailed he seeking? Did he
> Discover it upon this windy
> Tide-knocked shoal of islands? . . .
> Did the gross sun bawl lying
> Rhetorics to greedy huntsmen
> of a golden myth?

Formally, this is the motif shared by fugal subject and fugal answer. The question "what was Columbus seeking?" is "answered" by another: "what are the islands seeking in their twentieth-century 'adventuring'"? The poem's response is clear: the Federation sails to destinations of the heart's desire, to "sovereignties of Freedom". "Sovereignties of Freedom" is a deeply paradoxical term, but by implying that the Federation can provide means for at least taking control of the limitations on one's freedom, it seems to constitute a response to the doubts raised about "Freedom" at the end of "Something Seen", where Roach insists that "Freedom" is not just a word, yet still refers to it in the final line as a dream. But "Fugue" is a ceremonial poem, and perhaps for that reason Roach's exhortations are not very specific. Indeed, though the poem is, strictly speaking, written in the first person singular, the poet is remarkably unobtrusive. "Me" and "my" occur only in the second stanza, when Roach begins to recount the "Hell" that followed Columbus into the Caribbean. In one case, the referent of the pronoun is transhistorical, not personal: "Frey Bartolomo [de las Casas] / Fetched me from the Congo". In the other, "Look, my black fingers pencil / his memory", it draws attention to the poet's presence in the text as its producer. The expression "my black fingers", however, is a decidedly more diplomatic version of the phrase "my nigger voice" used in a similarly ceremonial poem ("Caribbean Coronation Verse") – doubly so, in fact: note, in addition to the shift from "nigger" to a more polite racial signifier, the shift in medium from orality to writing. Throughout the poem Roach directs attention away from himself and toward Columbus as an heroic antecedent for the islands of the contemporary

Caribbean ("his courage is their compass"). Apart from that "Look", there is only one other imperative in the poem: "Through storms and doldrums / grow, go forward islands". That brief closing exhortation to federate merely rephrases the call to follow the example of Columbus.

The view of Columbus in "Fugue" – forthrightly positive when we might expect ambivalence – has the effect of drawing attention to a peculiar cluster of ambivalences elsewhere in the poem. I referred earlier to the questions in stanza four as the moral centre of the poem. Some of those questions invite reflection on the admirable purposefulness of Columbus, but the last of them ("Did the gross sun bawl lying rhetorics to greedy huntsmen") draws attention to the Spanish hunger for gold, and that theme, a kind of counter-melody to the subject of this fugue, is especially prominent in the poem's account of how variously the nations of the Caribbean react to the idea of federation:

> Nations and islands, angry
> Or lazing under flaming sun, swear
> Harshly or dream languidly
> Of good and gold-faced Demos
> Coming careless as breeding,
> Or bright and imminent as dawn.

There is something unsettling about the interweaving of "or" and "and" in those lines. This is a ceremonial rather than a ruminative poem, and it may seem strange to cloud the celebration of imminent self-government with this acknowledgement of disagreement – especially when federation is envisioned in the form of a placid, benevolent Demos. To call Demos "gold-faced" certainly associates this eponymous god with the rising sun of a new day (Roach had invoked this familiar political imagery in "For Freedom"). But the value of gold has already been compromised in the second stanza of this poem by association with the process of extracting sugar from cane on the plantations. Now the relationship between the "flaming sun" and the myth of "gold-faced Demos" two lines away reproduces that in the previous stanza between the "gross sun" and the myth of El Dorado – a juxtaposition with sinister implications. Why would Roach want to suggest that the myth of gold-faced Demos constitutes an objective for the island nations analogous to the myth of El Dorado for those "greedy huntsmen", the conquistadors? This seems to subvert the poem's careful insulation of Columbus from the consequences of his voyages. Yet the description of Demos as gold-*faced* (rather than golden) further reinforces the analogy with "El Dorado", since that term actually refers to a man not made of gold, but merely gilded, painted with gold. This disturbing passage turned out to be prophetic. A few years later it would indeed be Demos, in the form of a popular referendum in Jamaica, that dismantled the Federation, and Roach's faith that he spoke for the peasantry was shattered when he discovered how differently they expressed themselves when given a political voice of their own.

Before that catastrophe, however, Roach published a famous poem which embodies the extent of his identification with the peasantry, the scope of his anger, his hopes for the Federation, and the highest register of his poetic voice, confidently speaking for the region. If "Homestead" is the reference point behind many poems of the 1950s, their culmination is "I am the Archipelago". It was first published in a *Kyk-over-al* anthology on the eve of federation, and was printed five times during Roach's lifetime, making it his most widely-disseminated poem after "Homestead".[22] The reason for its popularity has been aptly expressed by Ramchand: "In the English-speaking Caribbean, is there anyone who had written as passionately about slavery and its devastations before 'I am the Archipelago' hit our colonised eardrums?"[23] It is charming that Ramchand thinks of the poem as *heard* (actually this was never broadcast), but readers of this book will realize that the answer to his question is of course, yes, Eric Roach himself had so written. The central concern of "I am the Archipelago" is one that has dominated the poems discussed in this chapter: the "empty tragedy" of West Indian experience, and the poet's task of envisioning ways to make that tragedy meaningful. How can poetry come to terms with the heritage of Middle Passage and slavery that has buffeted these islands and continues to contaminate them with the "disnomia" of colour frozen into custom?

We are now in a position to see where "I am the Archipelago" comes from. The account of the Middle Passage here recalls similar treatments in "Reed for My Rime", "Lady by the Sea", and "In Mango Shade"; the rudiments of it can be found as early as "She". So too the deformation of the West Indian family has been touched upon in earlier poems, such as "Something Seen" and "Letter to Lamming". In "Homestead" and many other poems, Roach envisions the peasant as struggling with nature – with weather, soil, and sea. In "Archipelago" the same hard life is interpreted entirely in economic and social terms: the site of thankless labour is not the land, but specifically the plantation and the grinding "imperial wheels". Building on forerunner-poems such as "Something Seen", "The

Fighters", and "Letter to Lamming", this is Roach's fullest account of the psychopathology of the colonial condition, consistent in several respects with Fanon's account in *Black Skin, White Masks* (which was not available in English until 1967).

Despite the stark portrayal of "hate's dominion", however, the real business of this poem is to seek a way *out* of it. Roach's answer to "hate's dominion" is the Federation, that other dominion into which "hope would mould" the archipelago. The image of the broken and brutalized West Indian is powerful:

> I cower in the island of my skin,
> The hot unhappy jungle of my spirit
> Broken by my haunting foe my fear. (FR 129)

But that is not the end of the poem. Those lines recall the depiction of black rage in "The Fighters", and it is indeed to that text that Roach turns for the strategy by which he moves this poem beyond rage. As in "The Fighters", Roach here specifically calls upon the intellect to "outrun time" – the relationship to that earlier poem is underlined by Roach's conception here of intellect as an athlete, a runner "challenging Atalanta". Now he has in mind not only the cultural work of artists and writers, emphasized in the closing exhortations of so many poems, but also the particular value of the West Indian Federation as a dominion of hope, grounded in intellect and ideals, to supersede the dominion of hate. The precise meaning of the last four lines is difficult to sort out with confidence:

> O drummers, fall to silence in my blood
> You thrum against the moon; break up the rhetoric
> Of these poems I must speak. O seas,
> O Trades, drive wrath from destinations.

The not-quite-parallel construction of these final exhortations makes them ambiguous, particularly with respect to the drummers. One plausible paraphrase: Roach is urging the drummers to get out of his blood and into his poems.[24] In other words, the drummers, symbolizing the African heritage, are asked to stop pointlessly generating "voodoo passion" and ineffectual rage (the "tragic ferment" mentioned in "The Fighters"), and instead to contribute spiritual vitality (by breaking up mere rhetoric) to poetry that is urgent ("these poems I must speak") and potentially much more productive. If wrath can be silenced in the blood, it can also be driven from "destinations", that is, from the new "place" which is the Federation (there is an analogous usage, “destinations of the heart’s desire”, in “Fugue for Federation”). Despite the local ambiguities, the larger context makes it reasonably clear that the poem ends with an *exorcism* of wrath, achieved through intellect and art.

As noted, “Archipelago” shares its line of argument with earlier poems, especially “The Fighters”, yet it offers no new program for the resolution of “empty tragedy”.[25] What is different and striking about “Archipelago” is the nature of the “I” it constitutes through its language, and the impact of imminent federation on its argument. Consider first the voice. The speaking subject of the poem is defined for us by his condition, and especially by his remarkable *sound*:

> I am the archipelago hope
> Would mould into dominion; each hot green island
> Buffeted, broken by the press of tides
> And all the tales come mocking me
> Out of the slave plantations where I grubbed
> Yam and cane.

There have been many occasions to observe Roach’s characteristic shiftiness about pronouns, often exploited to suggest the poet’s rich and easy interaction with the peasants about whom he writes. This poem is resolutely – even loudly – in the first person singular, and to a very hasty reader might seem autobiographical (“my sister sired without love or law”). But this speaker is not an individual. He is explicitly the archipelago, a trans-national entity (“I am . . . each green island”), yet he is also a trans-historical person, encompassing the slave on the West Indian plantation, and exploited black labourers “in Congo, Kenya, in free, unfree America.” His position in the world is initially constituted through a demoralizing look at the outcome of colonial history – “My language, history, and my names are dead / and buried with my tribal soul”. The West Indian has been reduced to his marketable labour: “I am the shanty town, / banana, sugarcane and cotton man”.

Even under these conditions the representative speaker manages to make something of himself, and this poem’s close relationship with “The Fighters” becomes more apparent. There self-fashioning takes place in the arena of sport; in “Archipelago” the arena is religion (“I am a shaker and a shouter and a myal man”), the achievement is imaginative rather than physical, and as in “The Fighters” the achievement is real and effectual (“my voodoo passion swings sweet chariots low”). But in both poems the achievement, though real, is revealed to be only partial, compromised, a stopgap. Like the "tragic ferment" of the earlier poem, this "voodoo passion" produces more fire than light. So "Archipelago" moves to a new resolve for the speaker (and for the poem): the goal is to make a mark on the world, "To die or to live a man in history / my totem also on the human earth". The emphasis is on rootedness, but also on making an impression. The "tribal soul," though buried, will flourish again, and that imagery recalls the buried ancestral souls of Roach's earlier poems, whose spirits survive in monuments and singing trees. To live in history is achieved not through strength or fervour; it is intellect that will "outrun time".

Paul Breman is right to say that this poem "remains one of the most complete expressions of the middle generation of West Indian writers, intensely preoccupied with their middle position in both time and place, and in the case of Roach especially with the intricate complications of race and ancestry."[26] Yet Roach certainly would be disappointed to think he had spoken only for a generation of writers. This is the fullest realization of Roach's representative voice. From his hillock he speaks the experience he bears in his own voice, but as spokesman for the region – he is the voice through which the archipelago addresses itself.

The particular sound of this voice requires further comment. It is what Ramchand's "colonised eardrums" were responding to in the quotation at the start of this discussion, but it is also the reason why R. J. Owens described "I am the Archipelago" as "a breathless rhetorical rodomontade" in his very critical account of the state of West Indian poetry in 1961.[27] One factor in that divergence of responses is cultural. Roach's poem needs to be set in the context of the Trinidadian carnival figure known as the Midnight Robber.[28] The extravagant boasting style which characterizes the Robber is a manifestation of the widespread Caribbean taste for intentionally inflated rhetoric, an important part of the entertainment in such settings as rural toasts and orations, or the preliminary challenges between the stickfighters. It is the sound of the raging male ego, improvising almost out of control; a few lines from Faustin Charles's "The Red Robber" show how it is done: "My mother was a dragon / And my father a Griffin / I can drink a river / and belch an ocean /. . . I eat countries boiled in vinegar."[29] Gordon Rohlehr emphasizes the central position of Robber Talk in the "Oratorical" or "Sans Humanité" tradition of Trinidadian calypso, which dominated the field during Roach's youth.[30] It is in the spirit of Robber Talk that the sobriquets of calypsonians of that era lay claim to an absurdly omnipotent villainy: Bomber, Commander, Mighty Destroyer, Mighty Dictator, Hannibal, Hitler, Intruder, Mighty Viking.[31]

Swashbuckling Walter Raleigh, whose last voyage was to Trinidad and Guyana, might be imagined as the patron saint of the Robber, and that suggests an angle of approach. It may shed light on what Roach means to signify by adopting this style, if we imagine that Robber Talk is the language proper to the "adventurer" figure that keeps turning up in Roach's work, under such guises as Columbus and the Vikings. Roach has tried out several versions of "adventurer talk"; besides the Marlovian sublime in "He plucked a burning stylus" and the boasting style of "Ballad of Canga", something closer to the specific diction of the Midnight Robber appears in "Tree" (1952):

> I spearhead the nigger hope. . . .
> Regard me stalwart in the sun;
> My hope is founded on the granite
> Rock of desolation; my bone
> Holds strength from stubborn slave endurance;
> My soul is unwound from the iron wrong. (FR 86)

Traditional Robber Talk is at once self-assertive and self-mocking; here already the sound is complex, as Roach cultivates a hybrid that stands much closer to the sublime. Yet "Tree" (like "He plucked a burning stylus," or "Death Does Not") is still a projection of the romantic poet-ego; "I am the Archipelago" is Roach's greatest achievement in this vein because the voice is completely embedded in and speaking from the community. Like the image of the village as collective adventurer, this voice contributes to the domestication of the adventurer figure, the self-absorbed rapist/pillager rehabilitated for the sake of his passionate intellect and visionary action. This is the Robber with a conscience, and this is how Roach wanted to *sound*, as a poet, with this force and this immediacy of feeling. At the moment when federation seemed possible, this stance was possible; the poet poised to speak from and for the federated West Indies.

A purist might quibble about the distinctly Trinidadian model behind the diction of the poem, arguing that so enthusiastically federationist a poem ought to be couched in a generalized West Indian grapholect. But most readers recognize that federalism by nature entails a doubled identity for its participants. Speaking of this particular Federation, Lloyd Brown clearly delineates the paradox by which a shared West Indian consciousness "actually originates with the peculiarly isolated sensibility of an island environment."[32] The sea isolates, and this very isolation inspires the need for a communal identity based on common history. Nevertheless, the purist's quibble points to something more significant: "I am the Archipelago" is a very *black* poem, and to that extent at odds with its own federal ideology. Commenting on the poem, O. R. Dathorne goes so far as to claim that Roach "sees the African heritage as one that affords no compromise with other cultures."[33] That does not seem a tenable view, either in the abstract or with respect to this poem. Among other things, "I am the Archipelago" celebrates religious syncretism; the myal man who wears his Jesus on his breast already "affords a compromise" between cultures. In other poems of the same period Roach makes an analogous point of honouring the creole identity of such heroes as Columbus in "Fugue for Federation" and Cipriani in "For A. A. Cipriani". We have already encountered poems ("I Walk Abroad" and "A Reed for my Rime") in which Roach insists that West Indians are not (are no longer) Africans, and the following chapters will show him becoming quite polemical on the point in the literary debates of the 1970s.[34] That said, however, it remains quite true that Roach in this poem ignores other cultures vital to Caribbean society. His thinking is habitually in terms of black and white. The large Indian presence in Trinidadian society and politics is never addressed in Roach's poems, and is not even explicitly mentioned outside of a couple of very late unpublished poems.

The colonial heritage predisposed virtually all West Indian advocates of federation, not just Eric Roach, to elide the French and Spanish Caribbean from their archipelagic models. But urban thinkers like C. L. R. James and Derek Walcott, with a vision of multicultural city-states, saw great potential in the particular energies of *mulatez*; Roach, whose formative experience was rural, always assumed a substrate of identical black peasant culture. Roach's inclination to treat his Tobagonian village as a reference point accessible to all West Indians is consistent with that thinking. For him, federation meant moving beyond the island to embrace other *similar* islands. The assumption that the village stands accurately for all such is analogous to the assumption that federation is just individual island writ large. Federation was (rightly) grounded on assumption of shared history and of common cause. Roach, who travelled little, seems to overestimate the extent to which the islands were alike. When he thinks of the Federation he clearly thinks of islands like Tobago, Jamaica, Barbados; his obliviousness to the demographics of Trinidad, where he lived much of his life, is startling. The almost total absence of East Indians from his work, even after years of living in Port of Spain, is symptomatic of how ingrained his assumptions were. It is also symptomatic of one of the paradoxes of "nationalism" that ensued: federation appears to have a multi-cultural goal, and Roach is one who presents it as if that were the case, but the practical political implications of a West Indian Federation would have been Afro-creole domination – a serious obstacle for the East Indians populations of Trinidad and Guyana. Such anomalies in the structure of federation had profound social implications, but those did not at first come to light. The doctrine of West Indian homogeneity which the Federation embodied was largely an illusion. Federalism and "ethnic nationalism" were on a collision course in his work, and in actual events. Even in the midst of its success, "I am the Archipelago" suggests that Roach was not entirely prepared for the role of cultural differences in the failure of the Federation and the ongoing racialization of politics in Trinidad. Nor was he prepared for their role in the divergent development of Anglophone poetries a decade later, as Chapter 9 will demonstrate.

All that lay in the future. Yes, the Federation failed, and its failure pulled the foundations out from under Roach's conception of West Indian poetry, and of his own role in it. But the poems of 1957-58 mark the zenith of his confidence as a poet functioning successfully in and for his community. The notion of the village as elemental monad of any federation is the key to his vision. By enabling him to be part of something larger while staying at home on his island, Federation gives him something to stay home for, because it broadens his scope in the region, much as emigration would. Under such conditions the poet can effectually address "empty tragedy" by imaginatively joining the region into one thing, generating for his audience a recognition of identity and significance – of meaning. The invention of something called the West Indies provides a "destination" for hope that the colonial heritage of "wrath" can be driven out. Roach relies upon intellect and imagination as the appropriate tools for dealing with the burden of history, and of course sees the poet's voice as the chief instrument of those faculties. The poet envisioned and enacted in these poems is a Shelleyan legislator; he speaks from a rooted position in the black loam, but his voice is heard "everywhere", adventuring out from its root in this place to the Federation, and to the world.

Chapter 7 — Watershed

I have deferred discussion of "Caribbean Coronation Verse" (1953) until this point because Roach fortuitously published a heavily revised version of the poem (under the title "Caribbean Calypso") more than a decade later, after the failure of Federation and the dissatisfactions of Independence. A comparison of the two provides a stark indication of how deeply Roach was affected by those events, and so prepares the way for consideration of the last poems.

"Caribbean Coronation Verse" is addressed directly to Elizabeth II on the occasion of her coronation. In the first four stanzas the poet develops a parallel between her island and his own. He begins by harking back to the "rough ways" of Elizabethan England, at the very start of British colonization in the Caribbean, and then suggests a resemblance between that volatile society and the condition of the present-day Caribbean. Roach incidentally invites the inference that the West Indies may have a future as glorious as England's past, and much more specifically that great writers may emerge in the one as they did in the other, carrying on the heritage of "Shakespeare's tongue".

Shakespeare and Marlowe, however, soon yield place to Drake and Hawkins. Roach's rich language at this point acknowledges something grand in the scope of their crimes even as it condemns them; especially in the fourth stanza, the complexity of expression ("Their lustre shone and starred their fall on frantic frontiers") reminds us of the multiple valences of "adventuring" in Roach's thought. It is the source of that "viking" gene so important to his sense of distinctively West Indian identity. Thus in "The Fighters" the example of oppressors not unlike Hawkins inspires the boxers, who strive to contend with them on their own terms, and in so doing make themselves into similar monsters of violence, at once fascinating and repellent. In fact, the particular relation between the terms "arrogance" and "pride" which lies behind the progression of this poem is precisely that established in "The Fighters" (see Chapter 5).

After the first Elizabeth, Roach turns to Victoria and envisions during her reign an amelioration of Britain's relation to her subject peoples, thanks to the "freedom-minded heirs" of the original conquerors. Britain is entitled to be "prouder" as that relation becomes progressively "kinder". Having established this context, Roach in the final two stanzas presents a challenging compliment to Elizabeth II on her accession to the throne:

> now my nigger voice from the slave islands
> Proclaims her majesty in Shakespeare's tongue
> To queen a commonwealth of flowering freedoms.
> Advance Britannia. . . .
> In charity to every lesser hope
> Democracy be large; be critical
> With proper parliaments; crown justice sovereign
> As the queen, as evident as suns,
> Impersonal and equal each meridian.

The political values asserted are clear enough: Roach urges the new queen to bring about the final stage of the advance already underway, by establishing a commonwealth of representative governments ("with proper parliaments") for what had been individual "slave islands". Explicit verbal effects reinforce the poem's myth of progress. Thus "commonwealth" in the concluding passage contrasts with and supersedes the "private fief" of the opening, and similarly, Elizabeth I is described at the outset as "royal and arrogant", "personal as love, desirable as gold"; in the new "prouder empire" of this century, the real sovereign is to be justice, not a royal personage, and this sovereignty will be by contrast "*im*personal" and "equal" across the world.

This is an overtly political poem, but more significant than the message is the delivery of it. The poem's high diction sustains and justifies a statement so direct that it would be impudent if it were not so confident. Roach exploits his occasion to demonstrate (wishfully perhaps) a role for the poet of the islands in the larger forum. "Coronation Verse" is a most public and exposed poem, the work of one who conceives the poet in extraordinary proximity to power: the jester, praise singer, adviser, griot, calypsonian. Such a position is, we should recall, not at all implausible in a small, stratified society such as Trinidad. As a journalist with strong political affiliations, Roach could expect both official and unofficial access to the highest *local* circles. The crucial communication gap, for intellectuals and politicians alike, was that between the colony and England. One of the hopes for Federation was that its "proper parliament" might go a long way toward finally bridging that gap.

Unfortunately for such hopes, the Federation of the West Indies never really got off the ground. From Roach's point of view, the cynicism of Eric Williams is at the heart of this failure. Certainly Williams was adroit in juggling British and American fears of communism, Trinidadian feelings about the huge American military base leased at Chaguaramas, and an array of opinions about Independence and Federation. Even in bare summary his orchestration of the dismantling of the Federation is impressive. The call to arms was first sounded by the PNM party weekly *The Nation* (Mar 11, 1960) in an article entitled, "The Road to Independence Leads through Chaguaramas".[1] The next step was a massive PNM demonstration for independence on Apr 22, 1960, the so-called "March in the Rain" to "reclaim" the base at Chaguaramas, at which there was a public burning of the documents referred to as "The Seven Deadly Sins of Colonialism", including the constitutions of both Trinidad and the Federation, along with the Lease agreement.[2] Having thus caught the attention of the great powers, Williams in a speech of May 1960 disavowed the apparent flirtation with "Communism", a flirtation which he seems to have staged with the intention of destabilizing the relationships with England and the USA in order to make room for his political manoeuvring (the larger context included the "Red Scare" in Guyana and the return to power of Cheddi Jagan in 1958 and 1961). A few months later, in October 1960, C. L. R. James, Williams' surrogate voice for "leftist" opinions, was accused of "mismanagement", removed from the editorship of *The Nation*, and subsequently expelled from the PNM.[3] The powers were moved to negotiate, the base issue was favourably resolved by agreements of 1961, and new elections in that year resulted in a major victory for the PNM against the Democratic Labour Party (DLP), the predominantly East Indian party.

Meanwhile, in Sept 1961, the popular referendum in Jamaica voted against Federation membership. By this assertion of distinctively national identity, Jamaicans dashed the hopes even of their own Prime Minister Norman Manley (an outspoken advocate of Federation). For Roach himself, this was more than a shock to his political ideals; the referendum also called into question his long-standing assumption – fundamental to his work and to his sense of himself – that his roots in the peasantry of Tobago qualified him to speak for the Anglophone Caribbean at large. For all practical purposes, the Jamaican vote dissolved the Federation. Trinidad and Tobago became an independent nation later that year. Roach was close to these events. He had moved to Trinidad in 1961, and worked for the PNM's weekly *The Nation* in 1962-3. His hiatus as a publishing poet begins at the moment of Independence.

In the midst of these developments came an unexpected commission from England. The Poetry Book Society asked Roach to contribute to a commonwealth arts festival by providing a poem for presentation at a "festival of poetry" to be held at the Royal Court Theatre in 1965 and for publication in *Verse and Voice*.[4] It was in several respects a significant commission. Only twenty-five poets from the entire Commonwealth were invited to send their work.[5] The readings assembled under the rubric "Commonwealth Poetry Today" were important not only for encouraging the writers themselves, but for recognizing this work at a very early point. *Verse and Voice* advertises, among other commonwealth publications, the very first issue of the *Journal of Commonwealth Literature*, and Anne Walmsley describes the joint reading by Canadian and West Indian poets, as the "first corporate public reading" by West Indian poets resident in London.[6] The event served as a catalyst for the very active West Indian literary scene in London during the late 1960s. For West Indian writers living in England, these readings, discussions, and publications effectively took over the role of the now-defunct "Caribbean Voices" programme. The termination of the BBC program in 1958, however appropriate with respect to imminent independence, was a disaster for Roach (and for others in anything like his position): the sense (even if illusory) that one could indeed address the wide world, the tradition itself, was shattered. Recourse to the round of local periodicals, and even to metropolitan print anthologies, seemed an inadequate substitute for the voice that was carried on the air for anyone to hear. Several West Indian writers associated radio broadcast with the immediacy and democracy of Shakespeare's public theatre,[7] and that association is echoed in the Elizabethan milieu of "Coronation Verse", a poem which imagines for itself a very public hearing. Roach's contribution to the festival, "Caribbean Calypso", actually gained access to a public audience in the metropolis, though it was a smaller one than "Coronation Verse" imagined, more circumscribed by the old structures of power, and in a way more condescending, despite the best intentions. Some sense of imperial pageantry seems to underlie the organizers' advice that "there was no limitation of subject, but *it was suggested that each poem might reflect the landscape or the way of life of a particular country* (emphasis added)"[8] – how exotic and colourful are these fish left gasping on the strand by the withdrawing tide of empire!

For all its local colour, Roach's poem successfully resists such condescension. The first three stanzas, which together comprise the first of five sections, are drawn directly from the earlier poem, except that nearly all the lines about the queen have been removed, so that the emphasis is now on the privateering heroes, on Drake and Hawkins. The poet's orientation toward their adventures is quite transformed, however. The stanza about subduing glittering dynasties is now deleted, and three of the lines about Hawkins are also gone. Originally Roach wrote that Hawkins had "bartered and sold / and sailed home sinking with rich merchandise," and for his trouble was acclaimed by the queen. In "Caribbean Calypso" the queen has been eliminated at this point too, and the line just quoted is expanded in two ways: Roach inserts a catalogue of commodities, and amid the commodities, inserts himself: "[Hawkins] bartered, sold *me* / for indigo, molasses, cotton, spice". This is the only first person singular pronoun in the poem (first person plurals occur in sections III and IV), and it has a force equivalent to that of the phrase "nigger voice" in "Coronation". But the force is exerted to very different ends. The nigger voice that can speak to a queen in the accents of the language's greatest poet is a voice that has overcome racial prejudice without abandoning identity. The commodified "me" of "Calypso" introduces that poem's emphasis on slavery, rather than race; it locates the poet not within earshot of power, but among the people whose bondage persists, the "prisoners of history our skin and circumstance". At just that point, the end of section I, when the poet is discovered among the merchandise, the poem swerves away from its model, abandons blank verse for shorter lines touched with rhyme and slant-rhyme, and takes up new themes: the consequences of slavery, the failure (in Roach's eyes, the sabotaging) of the Federation, and the West Indian's ambivalent love for his own place.

In "Something Seen" the peasants, "beaten down and buried" by drudgery, were grotesquely "resurrected" into a zombified life of ill-paid labour. Here in Part II of "Calypso" Roach makes an effort at redemption: the peasants "buried living in the clay" are now "resurrected to the sun" thanks to their own resources ("hardihood and prayer and song"). The result of this redemptive effort is a simple, almost archetypal, vision at the poem's centre of gravity:

> The drummer and the drum
> Sprung of an ancient womb
> Crouch at the tree's root
> And are her flower and fruit

On the human scale, Roach here assimilates the musicians to the labourers: the hoeman's physical action, kneading corn into bread, associates him with the drummer, and when "reapers pluck rum from a ripe stalk" the verb associates them with the guitars. Roach's intention is plain: musicians, and likewise poets, are like other workers in the village, and verse is an integral part of life. This musical imagery of drum, guitars and dancer looks back to "The World of Islands", and to "Letter to Lamming" before it, and the unfolding of this poem might best be understood as an elaboration of the end of "World on Islands". But the idea is developed most fully here, where it functions as the main theme. From that perspective, section I functions as a prologue, while section III (on the failure of federation) and the opening of V (on a kind of nationalism) stand as episodes that colour the main theme's development.

One function of these episodes is to make it clear that the poem's apparently naive central image of rooted village musicians has been arrived at through much meditation on the failure of the experiment with federalism. Roach is left starting back at ground zero, virtually the position of the poems of 1950 but without the same hopes for the representativeness of his village and its homogeneity with others throughout the region. Thus the expectations are less lofty here than in "Letter to Lamming" or "The World of Islands". Section III pathetically celebrates how the "imprisoning sea" *would* have been overcome by the federating "seine" that *could* have gathered the archipelago into one state. But that "sweet blood brotherhood", which would have linked parish to parish across the sea, was betrayed: "asses brayed \ And the brittle dream shattered \ To shards of cays and shoals". For Roach federation had seemed the way out of bondage, confinement, isolation; in the wake of failed federation, the people are left prisoners of history, race, and narrow place. Confinement on one's own island, that "shard of land defiant of the sea", has been confirmed by events as the Caribbean condition. Roach's odd retrospective characterization of "Homestead" in 1968 as a "hut to shelter my nakedness" enacts the same rearguard action: it is a *re*-interpretation of the poem in the light of Roach's enforced retrenchment from federalism to the confines of his own "shard" of space.

Like Part III, the opening of Part V – set apart from the rest by its longer lines – functions as an intrusion. The effect is to darken the implications of the final stanza. In "Beyond", Roach had written of soaring out beyond all horizons; "Love Overgrows", en route to its optimistic expansionism, had regretted that "every dream is drowned in the shore water". In this passage he writes that, while dreams go out easily over the sea, they eventually come back home. The return from bold dreams to the "thin shard of land" is ineluctable. Roach has learned the hard lesson of Federation's failure: each island is a Petri dish, a culture unto itself, and these cultures do not travel well:

> In laboratories of islands, the sun
> Compounds chemicals of cultures, colours, tongues
> Strange everywhere but in their hothouse homes.

The reference to compounds of colour acknowledges the notion of an essentially mulatto Caribbean which in Roach's work (despite poems like "She" and "Cipriani") always has to assert itself against his more usual insistence on the pervasive "blood brotherhood" of black villages. Even in the face of the Federation experience, however, Roach still searches for a way to preserve some version of his vision of homogeneous peasantry as the foundation for West Indian identity throughout the region. Thus after the opening episode of Part V, the poem concludes by returning to the ideas and even the form of Part IV almost as if there had been no interruption. The final lines move somewhat closer to the corresponding passage in "Coronation Verse", but of course the main subject of the model – the blessings of Federation – has no place here, except in sublimated form. What remains from the previous version is a reduced claim: the region can be united not by politics, or by geography, or even by a shared culture, but specifically by *song*. While the title "Caribbean Coronation Verse" identifies the nature of that poem, the same is not true of the title of the revision. It seems very unlikely that "Caribbean Calypso" is supposed to *be* a calypso. Roach frequently uses musical terminology very loosely, but even so nothing here suggests the form: there are not enough rhymes, and of the three distinct rhythms in the poem (part I, opening of Part V, and the rest), none is typical of calypso. In the early 1960s calypso was the one characteristically West Indian musical form (reggae had not yet emerged as a contender), and Lloyd Brown rightly suggests that Roach embraces the syncretic power of that form as a kind of metaphorical substitute for Federation, capable of forging into "one melodic line" the cultural variety of the separate islands.[9]

Roach picks up from "Coronation Verse" the theme of the Caribbean poet's relation to "Shakespeare's tongue", but in this later version the point is the *transformation* of that heritage, not its acquisition: "here the songsmith tunes / The stiff Shakespearean rime /to the lilt of Cancer's seas."[10] To the extent that the 'common' language inherited from Shakespeare embodies such shared experience as there is, the shared history of colonization, this poem focuses not on the content of such language, but on the medium. There is no lofty advice here, just the assertion of this music, its authenticity and so its power (however local and circumscribed). This may be a post-federation poem, but its vision is still archipelagic. Bereft of the political apparatus he had hoped for, Roach is here retooling his ideals, investing such faith as remained to him in the musical vision of West Indian identity first proposed in "Lamming" (in response to the centrifugal pull of migration) and invoked again, in the face of even more profoundly centrifugal forces, in his last published poem, "Verse in August".

Considerable pathos attaches to the appearance "Caribbean Calypso" in the context of a Commonwealth Arts Festival. We can see all too clearly how a hopeful and even demanding poem about federation had to be rewritten in response to the failure of that hope and the booby prize of independence. Solicitation to publish in England ought to have been empowering for Roach, but when the poem appeared in print he attached the despairing autobiographical note with which my first chapter began.

Chapter 8 — Poetry and Politics II: after Independence

Chapter 6 utilized one taxonomy of Roach's themes (family, heroic figures, village). A slightly different cut highlights three other facets of Roach's poetry: nature, folk culture, history. Roach's concern with these three subjects is apparent from the earliest publications, but in the last stage of his career changes that originated in his thinking about history brought about significant changes in his treatment of the other two areas. The previously homogeneous body of his work is fractured by how he came to perceive the force of history, to such an extent that (after the silence associated with Independence) Roach's work of the 1970s entirely shifts attention to man in history rather than in nature; and what he called "the harsh comedy of history" defeats him as nature never did.[1]

As we have seen, Roach's work repeatedly depicts human aspiration and accomplishment as a matter of thriving in the face of natural forces – a rock enduring erosion ("Oh, No More Now", "At Grafton Bay"), a hawk riding the wind ("Death Does Not", "Beyond," "Frigate Bird Passing", "Transition"), a flower springing from the rock, or trees flourishing against the Trade Winds ("Oh, No More Now", "Tree", "Lady By the Sea", "Hawk Heart"). The elements of this imagery are variously combined in different poems, but their implications are constant: life springs from the most inhospitable surroundings; it is natural to resist, even triumph, in the face of buffeting weather. Roach sees this heroic quality first of all as a natural characteristic of the peasantry; he seems to have been particularly struck by the idea that folk-life is at once immemorial and unremembered. It is for this reason that the peasant simply going about his business seems to deserve (even demand) poetry. The business of the poet is then to put into words this patent but elusive character of the peasant. If he succeeds, he comes to exemplify that character in himself, and by so doing he can continue to participate in it, even as the pursuit of his poetic craft removes him from the actuality of peasant life.

An interest in the folk culture that nourishes such individual strength constitutes a second facet of his work. This shift from nature to culture is marked by increasing attention to what the peasant *does* rather than what he *is*; it is associated, too, with Roach's increasing attention to the village rather than the individual hero. With this comes an analogous conviction that the poet is not merely representative of the people he comes from, but that he plays a specific role for them. The poet's power, which at first Roach had simply celebrated, is quickly reinterpreted as a responsibility, a duty to say, "This is us", "This is our symbol" (as in "The Flowering Rock"); to name the people and the place to themselves and to the world. The expansion of his primary nature imagery to include this new aspect is explicit in passages such as the following from "Love Overgrows a Rock", where a sense of the poet as witness to "a human truth" is added to the imagery of soaring bird and jetting blood – all under the aegis of federation politics:

> The drunken hawk's blood of
> The poet streams through climates of the mind
> Seeking a word's integrity
> A human truth. So, from my private hillock
> In Atlantic I join cry:
> Come, . . . gather the islands' hills
> Into the blue horizons of our love. (FR 127)

As these lines suggest, the role of poet is hortatory, prophetic, politically engaged; he is not merely a depicter of nature or of society. We have noted repeated instances of Roach's disposition to end his poems with lengthy exhortations. Throughout his career, but especially in the era when he actively supported the establishment of a Federation of the West Indies, Roach's poems are full of imperatives. It is obvious that Roach sees the poet as an "unacknowledged legislator", linked in some active way to the processes of politics and history. Indeed, the word "history" enters any discussion of Roach's poetry without drawing much attention to itself. The myths of Imperial and regional history come into play in such overtly political poems as "I am the Archipelago", "Fugue for Federation" and "Caribbean Coronation Verse", while the African heritage, "the folktale of our grief" ("Lady by the Sea"), is a factor from very early on. Even the inaugural poem "March Trades" carries the implication that we learn from history how to handle nature, when Roach writes that it is specifically from Columbus, slavers, and pirates that one learns to bear the particular buffet of life in the trade winds of the Caribbean (the choice of examples also says 'learn by imitating those who have buffeted you most' – no boatload of settlers or refugees is mentioned).

We can trace Roach's unequal battle with "history" by way of the concept's pressure on his most persistent pattern of imagery, that early vision of burgeoning nature: flower or water bursting from the rock, trees asserting themselves in the air. In the course of deploying this imagery, however, Roach encounters the question whether the force of history acts within or upon human agents. Thus in "Something Seen" (1952) history is represented as actually a part of the blood, Roach's inner fountain of life: "some memory of history \ Like a legend's moleculed in the blood" (FR 89). As we saw earlier, however, even that relatively early poem includes an incipient image of history as an *external* force (the automobile) that most significantly (in this context) passes the village by. A conflation of the images of fountain and flourishing plant makes possible a similarly radical internalization of heritage in "The Fighters" (1953):

> . . . all our inheritance
> Was man's first heart, its springing blood,
> Its ever springing hope; . . .
> O our poor heart that sprung griefs to green rhythms. (FR 106)

That same poem, however, uncovers an *external* source behind its sequence of several versions of the familiar symbolism (water from the rock, spirit from the dark, flower from the soil): the upsurging force is living water specifically identified as coming from "the black rock of Africa", and this adds a concretely historical dimension to the poem.

I have just had occasion to mention "Something Seen", the antithetical twin to "Homestead" with which Chapter 6 began. As we now turn our attention to the late poems, it will prove useful to begin with the revised "Homestead" [C] of 1968, which stands as a comprehensive statement of Roach imaginative conception at that time – a poem about nature and culture, and about the peasant as an agent of heritage who mediates between them. The first four stanzas are virtually identical to those in the [A] version of 1952. After a few opening lines there is an unexpected and ominous modulation; the trees whose resistance to the wind makes them sing can productively "take the buffet" and "prosper in it" only until they are stripped of their leaves by drought, and "then they are tragic stands of sticks". Roach very closely identifies himself with this image of a leafless tree in poems of the mid-1950s, especially in "Tree" and the even more explicit "Hawk Heart", in which he announced: "I take this tree for symbol".

The darkest implications of this image (and of the poet's personal investment in it as an image of himself) remain undeveloped until it returns with a vengeance in "City Centre '70". Here in "Homestead", however, the minor key is sounded only briefly, and the attention of the poem at once moves beyond the trees to the distant fields, and to its central subject, the man who worked them. The version of 1968 differs most from its predecessors in the last two stanzas, and one of the changes is a return to the trees at the end. The barren trees themselves are never again at the centre of our attention, and indeed are never again literally present in the poem, but in "Homestead" [C] the tragic note struck by their mention at the outset is unobtrusively brought to resolution as the poem progresses.

First, their endurance provides a simile (in both [A] and [C]) for the peasant's own, when Roach writes that his ghost is "as tall as the tall trees" (the simile recalls a passage about another haunted ancestral plot in "The Old Man": "let the threnoding willow \ keep a tall legend of him"). But then it appears that the peasant does more than merely *resemble* the endurance of the trees; the ensuing lines (which vary only slightly from [A]) suggest strongly that he makes it *possible*. When his buried body is described as "nourish[ing] the splendour of the earth" (a revision of [A], which has instead the phrase "arteries of earth"), we are to understand that the "seven *splendid* cedars", even when stripped by the buffet of the weather, survive because nourished by the life and labour of the peasant ("splendid" is made to sound almost like a passive participle here: the peasant has "splendr'd" them). The final stanza, indeed the final line, of the poem brings about something like an apotheosis of the trees, so that their full foliage is restored – these "green boughs" appear, however, not in the course of nature's seasonal cycle, but in the perpetuity of metaphor:

> Poets and artists turn, again;
> Construct your cunning tapestries
> Upon the ages of their acres,
> The endless labour of their years;
> Still, at the centre of their world,
> Cultivate the first green graces,
> Courage, strength and kindliness,
> Love of man and beast and landscape;
> Still, sow and graft the primal good,
> Green boughs of innocence to God.[2]

This final stanza is quite different from the conclusions of [A] and [B], and the differences hint at an increasing distance between Roach and the actual life of Tobago. The revision thus drops [A]'s appeal to the farmers' sons to continue to work the land which is their heritage. In fact these true descendants of the farmers are no longer addressed at all; instead [C] concentrates all its attention on the *metaphorical* "sons", West Indian artists. Where [A] had urged "poets, painters, thinkers" to "turn again" and to learn craft and wisdom from the peasant-farmers, [C] goes further, adding the advice that artists should also make the peasant the *subject* of their work. By the end all three thematic elements have thus been accounted for: nature simply persists in the open fields (though their cultivation bears the mark of the man); the man, dead, returns as "spirit of the place"; the actual trees return in the figurative green boughs of the end. In effect the poem provides us with the map and title for Roach's imaginative homestead. It surveys the whole conceptual field of his thinking about nature (conducted in the image of the trees), about folk culture (in the emphasis on the human *genius loci*), and about history conceived as a heritage embodied in human agents.

*

In all the early instances that culminate in "Homestead" [C], "history" is the term for an accumulation of lore and experience that facilitates the struggle with nature while it gives depth and resonance to folk culture. It is the "legend" which survives (sometimes perilously) to inspire coming generations, and it is construed in very positive terms as the source of identity and pride. History is identified with whatever springs up inside the individual (or the tribe) to fortify him against hostile circumstances and environment. Soon however a crucial reversal occurs under the pressure of events; Roach begins to think of history as a process rather than a heritage. Thereafter history is associated with the externals, the devouring buffeting forces, not the internal springs of strength and resource – not an inner fountain or wellspring, but a stream that can engulf us or pass us by.[3] History becomes part of nature, *not* part of us.

Roach published his final version of "Homestead" in the midst of his nearly-complete silence as a poet in the 1960s, and it can set the stage for the strange new world of the last dozen or so poems. What moved him to publish poems again in the 1970s? There were certainly personal reasons, and the heated cultural debate that swirled around the *Savacou* anthology of 1971 also stirred him to speak – more on that in Chapter 9. But as far as the poems themselves can tell us, the incentives seem to have been primarily political. As Roach saw it, conditions in Trinidad deteriorated alarmingly during the last years of his life. The end of the 1960s brought intense social and political problems to newly independent Trinidad and

Tobago, against the backdrop of international student unrest and escalating racial confrontation in North America. During 1969 West Indian students in Canada occupied the computer centre at the University of Montreal, and students at the University of the West Indies campus in Jamaica occupied the Creative Arts Centre. Trinidad-born Stokely Carmichael was refused entry into Trinidad (as Walter Rodney had earlier been prevented from returning to his academic post in Jamaica). In Trinidad there were two complementary responses to these pressures: on the one hand increasing authoritarianism and personalization of power by Eric Williams; on the other the emergence of an improbable coalition in opposition to the policies of the PNM government.[4] In addition to the traditional base of Trinidadian opposition politics in organized labour (including of course organized East Indian sugar workers), the coalition included black power advocates gathered under the banner of the National Joint Action Congress (NJAC, founded by student leaders at UWI St. Augustine), and a cadre of intellectuals disillusioned with the PNM, especially those associated with Lloyd Best's Tapia House and its important opposition journal *Tapia* (which continues to publish as *Trinidad and Tobago Review*). Carnival in February 1970 was deeply politicized, with bands carrying portraits of Eldridge Cleaver, Malcolm X, and Stokely Carmichael; the following months brought mass marches, sporadic bombings, and violent responses from the police until, on April 21, Williams declared a state of emergency, with a curfew, and opposition leaders were taken into custody. Before the government regained control, there had been a mutiny of the Trinidad Defence Force, and British, American, and Venezuelan warships had assembled just offshore in the Gulf of Paria. In the end, there was no social revolution; on the contrary, a boycott of the general elections in 1971 put Parliament entirely in the hands of the PNM until the elections of 1976. During those years economic conditions worsened (there were 32 strikes in 1972, 84 in 1973, and unemployment ran above 15%).5 At the same time, Williams by a series of manoeuvres consolidated his personal power and distanced himself from the machinery of his own government.

Roach's eventual re-engagement with his times under these conditions is marked by a shift of focus back to individual figures (mostly politicians now) rather than the collective village. Confronted with an era of mass action, social fragmentation, repression and cynical betrayal, Roach published poems wherein the putatively heroic figures are political (and fail) and the village disperses into mass anonymity. These are bitter poems of political disenchantment and personal grief; the role of the poet as witness becomes central, but his testimony is heavily inflected with tropes of renunciation and palinode. And as we shall now see, Roach's efforts to make sense of the disasters around him – his dashed hopes for the Federation, his compounded disillusionment with the PNM, with Eric Williams, and indeed with himself – entail a curious mythologizing of "History" as the culprit.

Roach's new conception of history affects both his poetry of *nature* (as in his tree imagery) and his poetry of *culture* (representations of and about the village). Most obviously it leads to changes in how Roach uses his nature imagery. What is remarkable, whether or not it indicates (as it might) that the change in his thinking about history was very gradual, is that Roach expresses his new thinking without any appreciable resort to new imagery. Instead he modulates the images of his familiar repertory, revealing as he does so the protean potential of his archetypes. We will see several examples of this kind of transfiguration shortly, and the nature of these changes will suggest strongly that the master-trope of these last poems is *palinode*, the repudiation of earlier work employing the very forms and language in which it was originally couched. Roach's dialogue with himself, of his poems with his own poems, becomes especially prominent in late work. Roach's ideas and attitudes changed, sometimes radically, in the last decade of his life; his inclination to handle new material by the old familiar means may exemplify a continuity consistent with habit and nostalgia, but those familiar images are also undergoing a sometimes brutal deconstruction, behind which we can sense the chagrin of the disillusioned poet. To speak in terms of concrete examples: we have already seen how "At Guaracara Park", among the first of the late poems, self-consciously adapts elements of "The Fighters" to produce a parallel poem with the rough and gritty features of the model smoothed away. That is a rarity in the late poems. More typical is the way the poems "Elegy for N. Manley" and "Ballad for Tubal Butler" both repudiate the idealism of "For A. A. Cipriani". And we will soon see that by far the most important and consequential palinode is "City Centre '70", Roach's painful recantation of the poem that otherwise stands as the centrepiece of his career (and his reputation): "Homestead". Both poems are about a stand of cedars that marks a central, defining site of the poet's life and history, but in the later poem the trees are locked away in centre of sterile park, not bounding a working farm. We will take up the details in due course, but the palinodic relation between the two poems is inscribed even in the titles, which set the warmth of "homestead" against the neutrality of "city centre," rural against urban, familial against impersonal.

The relation between ideas of history and of culture in Roach's mind at this time is understandably more complex than that between history and nature. His changed view of history certainly owes a great deal to the sequence of political events in Trinidad that began with the postwar independence movement and climaxed in the turmoil of 1970. But to some extent the new sense of history seems to *derive from* the poet's perception of changes affecting the rural village which for Roach always remained the radical ground of culture. Through most of his career, Roach had freely and eloquently identified himself with the village.[6] But after the silence of the 1960s he seems to have felt a double loss. The village has been moved from its place at the cultural centre, and the poet has been removed from the village even in its displacement. These changes struck a hard blow at Roach's conceptualization of a poet's equilibrium, which depended upon a faith that the poet, though separated from peasant life by his talent, was enabled by that same talent to represent the community and so to participate in it.

Among the late poems that address the displacement of the village, "Piarco" (1972) could be considered another of the many revisions of "The Flowering Rock", a sadder look at that poem's promising young man, and at the coherence of the village from which he springs. The social *ideal* of the village is acknowledged in passing when Roach refers to it as "the green pool of home" (FR 160), but the poem is about the uprooting and dissolution of the traditional community, signified here by an emblematic displacement: one of the children is about to emigrate, and in order to ease the boy's "severing from the clan", the whole village has come in a body to the airport at Piarco – site of transience, a metaphysical nowhere (the image of the plane's "dragon breath" may be Roach's wry hint at the Renaissance cartographer's trick for filling unexplored spaces: "here be dragons").

Though the poem is not explicit about it, we feel the contrast between the villagers' heightened interior state ("their eyes are gleaming with new years of dreams") and the impression they make on a bystander: rustics huddling together in their disorientation and fussing over the boy ("cawing like poggoes").[7] Roach presents the group of villagers in language of real nobility: "They suffered centuries \ of time's distilling \ of the peasant blood, . . . in their Homeric grappling \ with the earth to gain this day, \ this font through which the son \ . . . shall name them to the world". The poet's beloved images of water from rock are reflected in that "font". But the epic of peasant life ends grotesquely in impoverishment; even after independence, the best fruit is eagerly sent abroad, like all the earlier fruits of slave labour. The promise of this single boy is lost to view as the poem's perspective expands to take in so many desperate flights to so many cities.

And when, commenting on all those hopeful departures, the poet's voice adds, "what is beyond is dreams", the change in the force of the word "dreams" drains the earlier instance of its power. To "name them to the world" – once the poet's own mission – has become hollow, one of the "dreams". In this case the "world" the boy enters is figured as a jetstream, and little Trinidad is only a way-station on the trade route from South America to the metropoles. The boy is simply swept away by the wind, as a kind of propitiatory sacrifice to the course of history (the passage recalls the ending of "For the Peasant People"). When the airplanes are said to "rest like migrant birds on our sea rock", they have taken on the attributes of the soaring, streaming migratory birds, reappropriating that imagery for *external* rather than internal forces. The poet too is an outsider here. For all his sympathy and compassion, the poet's distance from the group is palpable; it is from that distance that he concludes the poem with a glum insight not yet available to the peasants in the departure lounge:

> islands cage us
> and we long to leave them;
> the cities scorn us
> and we long to love them.
> Bite the earth's orange
> and her pips are bitter.

In "Poem for This Day" (1972) as well, Roach faces the irreversible displacement of the village engulfed by modern roads, its people transported wholesale to city slums. The alternatives for life offered in this poem are few: dilapidated village, marginalized slum, or the "bestial carnival" of engagement with the life of the city itself. Roach describes the "mouldering villages" of the countryside in a way that pointedly shrinks and degrades the world of "Homestead" and "Men":

> village labour sweats among its trees
> on the tough soil of hope
> where men grow bovine in their bovine round
> of work, feed, sleep and blind begetting
> which they can break only if they abandon home. (FR 163)

This is a chastening view of the peasant-farmers Roach had idolized since boyhood. In the earlier poems the peasant is rooted in the land amid his cedars, and at home there. He is the spirit of his place and master of the cycles of nature; his daily round leaves an impression on the very earth.

The spell of that heroic vision is broken here. By a device typical of the late poems, the depth of Roach's disenchantment is signified by the distance one of his images has shifted: the distance between his unalloyed admiration for "these tough resilient men \ who strive with hoe and shoulder \ as brothers to the ox" ("Men"; FR 84) and his recoil (in "Poem for This Day") from the men who "grow bovine in their bovine round". There was of course never any question in Roach's mind that the life of the peasant was hard; what has changed is his sense of the *value* of that life. There is, as we saw earlier, one troubled passage in "Homestead", a rhetorical question that intrudes briefly but hangs unanswered: "Is labour lovely for a man \ that drags him daily into earth \ returns no fragrance of him forth?" This is precisely the question of value, and it is answered in "Poem for This Day" with a resounding "No"; these farmers are victims of a cycle so dehumanizing that the only hope is alienation from the land. Unfortunately that means a move to the slums of the city:

giddy upon repelling slopes,
crawling like maggots into swamps,
clapboard and tin, sad prey for rains,
high winds rattling their hides like leaves,
the poor slums fester in the heart[.]

This is not the sort of airbrushed slum that Roach had invoked so portentously in "The Flowering Rock" ("this is our symbol – beauty famous in the slum"). "Poem for This Day" is urban rather than rural, but its details and representational strategy as exemplified in that quotation recall this stoical description of village life from "Despite Ancestral Rape":

Our village grips the hill,
Clings rickety to rock and laps the sea,
Whose salt breath blacks bare boards[.] (FR 54)

Amid the rigours of "Despite Ancestral Rape" Roach's values assert themselves, and (like a flower from a rock) ambition springs up in that harsh landscape. Roach in "Poem for This Day" makes no reference at all to the resilience and faith of the folk; it is a sad surprise to find that his point is the failure of *charity* towards them ("you'd think the state too stern for mercies \ or . . . that charity's atrophied") – the lack of *external* help for an otherwise helpless, "festering" people.

Roach has yet another surprise in store here, when the poem issues the following invitation:

regard these market towns and mouldering
villages we find on motoring roads . . .
not even names to us as we cruise by
in shades of opulence,
in varying degrees of cool contempt
sheltered from their sun of poverty,
sneering at their gnarled and barefoot drought.

Such a moment had first occurred (in significantly different form) in "Something Seen". Here again a peasant confronts a passing car, but this time the poet places himself (and his reader) *inside* the car, looking out at the villages overwhelmed by progress, "sneering at their gnarled and barefoot drought." The poet too has been displaced from his long-standing intimacy with the village; he now observes from the wrong side of the glass. *Now* Roach sounds like the deracinated traveller of Cecil Herbert's "Lines on a Train", as he never did before, and this alienation of the poet becomes the real subject of the poem.

The modulation of the poem's business from the dissolution of the traditional village to the poet's impotent invective against urban life is managed very strangely, by means of an arbitrary simile buried deep in a series of dependent clauses (the syntax runs like this: village labour sweats on the soil where men go through the bovine round which they can break only if they abandon home in order "to prodigal in the sour slum/ with those who've failed their hope/ *like writers their weak talents*"). The sharp lurch via "like writers" seems quite gratuitous: a paradoxically self-serving, self-absorbed, way to make room for an expression of the poet's self-contempt (this is one of many places in the late poems where we sense the revulsion and anger Roach seems to feel at what he now finds himself forced to think and say). The poem closes with a brief jeremiad against "the politician's" abuse of power, which confines the people to carnival, "the circus guarded with tear gas and guns". In the course of this attack, Roach adds a revealing detail with the line, "all that goes free are rats and roaches". There is a pattern of images involving vermin and animals throughout the poem, and this line balances the reference to "maggots" in the opening lines, just as "bestial carnival" in the final line picks up the earlier "bovine". But the wordplay can hardly be ignored. The name "Roach", which once could associate the poet with the seam of coal, the underlying black rock, now identifies him instead with something too lowly to be perceived as part of the political scene or even as part of the resistance to it. During the early years of PNM ascendancy, Roach had been able to think of himself as close to power. In the 1970s his contact with party circles was broken (he was in any case repulsed by the increasing cynicism of Eric Williams' government), and his efforts to find a place for himself among younger intellectuals and writers in opposition groups like Pivot and Tapia seem chiefly to have sharpened his sense of marginality ("Hard Drought" and other late poems suggest that he saw a refracted image of himself in the fate of old leaders like Uriah Butler, grown ludicrous in failure). This then is how "Poem for This Day" portrays the poet. He is not the insider he always aspired to be; power hems in the circus, the carnival, but the roach moves freely only because power regards it as unworthy of attention. On the other hand his mere modernity – his urban life, his car window – cuts him off from whatever is left of the village. His alienation is complete.

Why this late sense of being on the wrong side in spite of himself? "City Centre '70" provides material for an answer. The poem was written as a response to the closing of Woodford Square for some months as part of the state of emergency declared in 1970. The closing by Eric Williams' government was essentially an act of censorship; Woodford Square, directly in front of the Red House, is the traditional open forum for soapbox speeches and political gatherings, and ironically it had been the setting for the programme of lectures by Williams himself in the mid-1950s that came to be known as the "University of Woodford Square", and helped consolidate his PNM party.[8] For Roach, this Square has enormous symbolic value, since it is the urban site that most closely corresponds to the *gayelle*, the kraal, the homestead, the arena of confrontation and accomplishment, the space opened up for flourishing (as this urban space literally allows trees to spring forth amid the concrete).[9] In commenting on this poem Rohlehr notes how Roach's choice for his central image bespeaks yet another facet of the poet's isolation, his *distance* from the world-view of Trinidadian writers of the younger generation: "So rooted is Roach that even rootless and directionless movement is expressed in terms of the rootedness of trees. Having known villages, when he looks in the square he sees cedars; when Alfred Fraser, child of the city looks at the square [in "Woodford Square, Port-of-Spain"], he sees an empty fountain; Judy Miles [in "Lunch Hour"] sees chewed discarded bones."[10]

"City Centre" is especially disheartening because of its resonance: it is not just a bitter effusion arising amid the politics of the moment, but a statement of disillusionment firmly rooted in the language of a whole career. As such, it casts a long shadow. The poem brings together a variety of images from Roach's repertory to produce what amounts to a trenchant rewriting of "Homestead" – a palinode, or a Blakean song of experience to be substituted for that song of innocence. The trees, Roach's perennial symbol for the distillation of love and heritage into accomplishment, are "jailed" with the closing of Woodford Square. By this act, the "stone men" of the government reveal their true natures: "the disease of tyranny and shame's corruption".[11] Flourishing behind their fences at the heart of Port-of-Spain, the trees sustain an ambiguity about their symbolic *value* that is reflected in the mixed language of the poem, which presents them as a kind of sacred grove and yet at the same time as forlorn exiles, a bit of jailed nature. The two published versions of the poem record Roach's indecision about whether to treat the trees finally as a brave survival or an absurd irrelevance.[12] The question of the value inherent in this symbol comes to be of considerable importance, in the light of the specific interpretations of the symbol that Roach invites in the two versions. Most obviously the trees play their usual role, representing the endurance of nature under duress. But they are cultural symbols as well; the language of the following lines makes it explicit that they are also associated by the poet with the marooned villages of "Poem for this Day" and "Piarco":

> the trees condescend that we
> wayfarers in the traffic
> and in time, should see them
> with eyes cold to their beauty[.] (FR 151)

Most importantly for the development of poem, however, the trees are, as always in Roach's work, images of heroic individuals, men like the peasant of "Homestead" who "do not die \ but grow in dreams of generations". And, as he frequently does in the late work, Roach is worrying the question whether the same symbol that figures the hero can also figure the poet.

In this poem "history" (in Roach's new, sinister sense of that word) floods around the trees, as it does around the kind of individuals they represent. They are shut out of it, passed by. They are in danger of being reduced to mementoes of themselves; specimens, not presences in reality. In earlier poems, as we have seen, the challenge came from nature, and past history was a heritage that toughened men to bear it. In these late poems the buffet of nature functions as image for the buffet of human history rather than vice versa, and history is seen as ongoing process – not as heritage but as overwhelming circumstance. The particular irony that it was Williams who closed Woodford Square confirmed the disillusionment with heroes, especially with political heroes, that Roach experienced during the late 1960s. In poems written before that period, assertion in the face of circumstances is a source of strength, and though heroes die, they leave an image behind, a song, a "legend", an "impression". The ambivalence reflected in the two versions of "City Centre" is the mark of Roach's attempt to find room in a grim vision for some such positive image. Only one of the late poems, "At Guaracara Park", frankly celebrates human achievement in the old terms, depicting a runner as an unequivocally heroic figure who wins a kind of immortality. In the others, poems published *after* the first version of "City Centre", the encounter with history simply ends in exhaustion. If heroes leave any image it is piteous or repellent: a mad dog ("Ballad for Tubal Butler"), a bloody rag ("Hard Drought"), a waste of dead leaves in drought ("Elegy for N. Manley"). These poems – which will be examined more closely in a moment – depict the unequivocal defeat of once flourishing men, circumvented by the history of which they were thought to be agents. In "City Centre" it is not only the noble figures, those trees that flourish from the rock, which become marginal to malignity of history. At the same time "we" (that is, above all, the poet, Roach himself) find ourselves removed to an even worse position, cut off even from their marginality (just as in "Piarco" and "Poem for this Day"). To extrapolate from the imagery a bit: the heroes are cut off by the rushing "traffic" of history, but we are swept along *in* the traffic, as the weekend motorist is swept past the dying village – indeed, perhaps the situation of a passenger in the car, rather than the driver, is most like Roach's own.

In one sense at least Roach still strove to identify himself with the trees flourishing from urban concrete. The trees of Woodford Square in "City Centre" stand as witnesses. They stand for all those – labourers, politicians, poets – who took the buffet of the wind in their moment, whatever else happened to them. He sought to be, like them, witness to both the harsh comedy of history and the green immortality of generations. In its first published form, the poem ended with a celebration of these trees triumphing in the face of their confinement. The passage not only reiterates the opening assertion that the trees stand "witness that men do not die but grow in dreams of generations"; it also constitutes a reprise of images from deep in Roach's consciousness with notable affinities to the end of "Homestead":

> applauses, flowers, flames
> well up in silent seasonal surges;
> green fails to brown

and brownness, the earth's colour,
sinks to earth where the sweet
cycle reaffirms itself,
rejoins eternity and greens again
in the triumphant self-regenerating trees. [1970]

The first version of the poem thus insists upon the long perspective, in which the political events of 1970 diminish in their significance before the *longue durée* of the heroic trees and "their great immobile marathons", the reassuring cycles of the natural world.[13] But in the more recent version (1972) the poem ends instead with a bitter contrast. The passage just quoted is shorn of its first two lines and its final one, in other words, revised just enough to eliminate the elements of sweetness, applause, and triumph:

their green turns brown
and brownness the earth's colour
falls to earth where the great
cycle reaffirms itself,
rejoins eternity and greens again. [1972]

Thereafter an added final stanza takes a grim turn, which destroys the first version's balance between transitory political events and the persistence of the cedars. What matters to the second version is not the palliative of a cosmic vista but the here-and-now of political action. Though these trees may stand,

we cannot stand and wait:
our turbulence burst like bombs
and guns under the patient trees,
roared from our streets and homes. [1972]

The poem now ends with the February Revolution. Roach's language is so sardonic in the last poems that it is difficult to gauge the level of irony here, and in any case it would be a mistake to underestimate how provisional the choice of this ending was for him; the existence of two versions of the poem with such different conclusions testifies to the great intellectual turmoil Roach experienced in his last decade. But the dilemma he faces here – the writer's need to choose between the comforts of myth and the inelegant prose of political action – is a crucially important one. Roach's preoccupation with this question places him at the cutting edge of Caribbean intellectual life. Roach was simultaneously addressing it, on somewhat different terms and with somewhat different conclusions, in the aesthetic debates of the period, as we will see in the following chapter.

*

As a group, the poems of the 1970s are deeply embroiled in the specific politics of Trinidad; "Blues for Uncle Tom" is the exception, induced by an event that occurred outside that sphere, but had great resonance within it: the assassination of Martin Luther King, Jr., in the spring of 1968. There are some mysteries about the publication of this poem,[14] but it seems reasonable to assume that the poem was written in 1968 or 1969 at the latest (that is, soon after the assassination occurred), which would date it before the composition of either "At Guaracara Park" or "City Centre '70". If so, the death of King may have been the flash-point for the unappeasable indignation that rages through Roach's subsequent poems; "Blues" itself is a truly furious poem, sour with irony:

> we will not be satisfied
> with the vine of his rhetoric
> nor to name him in his cool idiom
> christ, lincoln, kennedy
> nor any coon preceding him on the lynching tree
> till shiloh come,
> till time or god or fate we care not which
> or the white man our nemesis enfranchises us. (FR 148)

"Blues" goes beyond even the rage and blackness of "I am the Archipelago" a decade earlier. In that connection we should note the many stylistic affinities with Kamau Brathwaite here, for example in an effect like, "in the sun's eye \ and the moon's sigh", or in the pun of the final line: "no easter morning for our mourning." The very public disputes between the two poets in the 1970s, which we will encounter in the following chapter, should not obscure the deep affinities between them. They are the pioneering poets of the Afro-Caribbean experience; there is clear evidence in the unpublished poems (most explicitly "Littering Earth's Centre") that Roach was reading Brathwaite and we know that Brathwaite had been reading and learning from Roach since the early 1950s. In any case, this poem's outrage can speak for itself; for present purposes I want to focus on Roach's deployment and development here of tropes characteristic of the earlier poems about heroic figures. This poem's lineage goes all the way back to "Shallow Underground", "The Old Man", and "Carib and Arawak":

slave blood groaning at their root,
his dripping blood this season's fruit,
his southern trees moan out the moses blues,
those tragic threnodies of tribes in trauma.

Though the setting is the American South, we recognize immediately the images of the ground saturated with unavenged blood, of the trees that stand as witness to the buried hero's "legend", of the threnodies produced by the passage of the wind through those trees. These images are employed in Roach's usual way; but there are other places here in which the new impulse to palinode is beginning to make itself felt. The following lines, for example, seem to call for a straightforward memorial to the fallen hero, on the order of Cipriani's statue, or even the witnessing stone associated with Daaga:

'i have a dream,' he cried, 'i have a dream,'
his rhetoric drumming doors of immortality,
demanding that his bloodied head
stand a stalagmite in time.

The very next line, however, rejects the idea, and initiates a sharp turn away from the familiar pieties of memory and even from the dignity of the hero:

but we have grieved past statues . . .
our pride's an ancient scarecrow
tattered by raw weathers, is poor old
uncle tom, poor featherhead
stretched dead on hope's hard bed.

It is these lines, incidentally, that finally make sense of the poem's title. "Blues for Uncle Tom" was an extremely provocative title for a poem about King in the circumstances of 1968-70, even assuming that Roach has in mind a West Indian literary audience whose view of Uncle Tom would have been affected by Brathwaite's complex recuperation of that figure in *The Arrivants*. What Roach rejects, looking beyond the person of King, is any politics of hope, and before the end of this central passage there is to be one more turn of the screw, penetrating the core of Roach's most persistent imagery:

we come from caves of history
into these ghettoes that garrotte our dreams
and burn love's hope back to its stump of stone.

The word "dream" had always carried great weight in Roach's poems; but here that weight has been invoked only to be denied (we have already noted the same manoeuvre in the later poem "Piarco"). This garrotting of the dreams retrospectively sheds an unflattering light on the opening line of this section; now the repetition which had initially seemed merely rhetorical ('i have a dream,' he cried, 'i have a dream') now sounds more like an escapist mantra, the unaccommodated man's desperate stab at accommodation – more Shakespeare's poor Tom than Stowe's. What this passage undoes is Roach's own most cherished dream. Now that he conceives us as *contained by* "caves of history" rather than vitalized by the spirit of history *within* us (the fundamental reversal underlying the late poems), he finds that there is another reversal. The film of his dream, as it were, runs backwards: the flower that should spring from the rock instead shrivels and retreats, ending back at the aphonous stone.

*

As I have said, the transformation of Roach's thinking and feeling reflected in the revision of "City Centre" antedates all the poems about West Indian political figures, which will be our concern for the remainder of this chapter. The political background of these poems is of course what Roach regarded as the cynicism of Eric Williams and the PNM. He held Williams responsible for the failure of the Federation, the bungling of Independence, and the repression that followed the February Revolution. Roach had already enunciated the standards by which he judged politicians long before, in "A Tear for Toussaint" (1953): "History reproaches those \ Who yoked rank pride and lust \ To a gross sovereignty, \ Mangled green freedom's boughs" (FR 93). The literary background, on the other hand, is "For A. A. Cipriani", which stands as parent – repudiated parent, as it turns out – to these poems about Norman Manley, Uriah Butler, Eric Williams, and the events of 1970s. It is a very welcome coincidence, then, that a brief analysis of the role of Cipriani in the *Trinidad Guardian* seems to anticipate the link between the image of the trees bypassed by traffic in "City Centre '70" and Roach's handling of potentially heroic figures in these late poems. In a *Guardian* article, Max Farquhar wrote this about Cipriani: "His leadership did not survive the evolution of the barefoot man . . . into the working class proletariat protected by trade unions. . . . His rugged individualism was soon overrun . . . and he was left stranded, a lonely monument of defiance, forgotten."[15] The key terms of that quotation – the "barefoot man" (a catchphrase of Trinidadian political discourse), the images of being overrun and stranded, the inherent oxymoron of a forgotten monument – recur in Roach's poems about politicians during the 1970s. His own poem in 1959 had celebrated Cipriani as an ideal politician, a "poet of humanity"; in the seventies that poem becomes the target of Roach's new impulse to palinode.

"For A. A. Cipriani" is Roach's idealization of a politician. The West Indian politician most worthy of idealization in the 1970s was Norman Manley of Jamaica, and like the poem for Cipriani, "Elegy for N. Manley" (1972) is framed by the idea of a monument, introduced in the very first words ("Lodge him securely, \ set him a monument") and reverted to at the end (FR 158). But we have already seen monuments radically devalued in "Blues for Uncle Tom", and this element is more than outweighed by images of decay that dominate and eventually overwhelm the poem: the sun "that bloats and rots", the worms "quick to our oblivion", the "middens" and "rotten tapestry" of slavery, the "dross of slums", the dead leaves of drought. Roach here seems at first to be setting up an argument along these lines: Manley deserves a monument that will resist decay because he did so much to overcome the decayed state of the country during his lifetime. Thus he is praised for having risen out of this setting ("the rotten tapestry \ of mastery and slavery \ was his swaddling cloth") and for having used the "hoe of hope" and the "pitchfork of politics" to "tear slave middens down, \ to plow them deep into Jamaican soil \ and seed it new with \ freedoms." But that is not, in fact, the course of the argument. Manley's career ended in failure with the failure of his dream of federation. There is a feint at the trope of the *genius loci* so common in Roach's earlier heroic poems: "his sighs were sounds of tired \ ocean rollers, . . . \ mists of his Blue Mountains \ snowed his head." But it is only a feint. The point of the final stanza (perhaps a little overstated) is that Manley's work changed nothing:

in his decrepitude
all his hope, work, faith
lay waste like dead leaves in a drought;
the barefoot black still languished,
still despised[.]

The earlier image of Manley composting the soil so as to bring forth freedoms is overruled by this image of killing drought. There can be no talk of any "legend" or "threnody" of him recorded in the landscape, in part because the trees are denuded and cannot respond to the wind. In the closing lines the idea of the monument is brought up only to be devalued, and devalued with it is Roach's cherished idea of the "worth" of leaving an "impression":

He knew all he had done
was to proffer his once handsome face
for this fine effigy for fools.

This elegy has a grim and unhappy dignity; though Roach does not intrude upon the poem, it is apparent that Manley's ideals were very close to his own.

"Elegy for N. Manley" was published together with two other poems. One is "Piarco"; the other, "Ballad for Tubal Butler", unquestionably constitutes a companion piece to the elegy, though the poems are antithetical to one another in several respects. The very titles, while parallel, communicate by way of the different implications of the literary terms "elegy" and "ballad" some of the differences of personality, style and even social class that separated Manley and Butler personally. In his prime, Butler had been the trade union leader who rose to prominence in the violent strikes of the late 1930s; it was his arrival on the scene that eclipsed Cipriani and his political style, the politics of "the barefoot man". As Roach puts it, Butler had "set a blazing torch \ to centuries rotten with our shames \ and singed the old slave tapestry" (FR 157); Roach's use of the image of the tapestry in both of these companion pieces reminds us that, in the beginning, the work cut out for two such different personalities – Manley the statesman and patron of the arts, Butler the rowdy labour agitator – was essentially the same. Yet the poem's elaboration of those events of 1937-38 undercuts the heroic element considerably, focusing not on the real social and political gains achieved, but on the lynchings of Corporal King and Sgt. Powers "by the mob \ whose rage and hatred, fear and need, \ roused to desperate bloody deeds \ flayed fat folly to awareness \ and thrust politics a theme." In addition, as Roach sees matters, the rending of the slave tapestry brings out not only the mob but the most craven sorts of leaders. In the newly opened political space, every "liar", "village lout", "city snip", and "rogue" turned orator; indeed, the poem seems to imply that Butler himself, swept up in the tide, became one of their number.

The poem begins and ends with the poet's personal knowledge of Butler, so it is all the more significant that, unlike the Manley elegy, which is framed by the image of a monument, the Butler poem is framed by the image of an old dog. "When I met him face to face", Roach writes at the outset, Butler had become "a decrepit toothless hound \ whining at his private fleas". That opening leads back to less-than-glorious memories of the glory days of 1938, but the final stanza returns to the testimony of the author ("I've heard him rant and seen him mocked") and to the dog:

history's ceaseless flood
has left him on a muddy shoal,
sometimes baying at the wind,
sometimes howling, a mad dog,
at the current in its course.

The resonance of the passage derives from its virtual allusion to the heroic figures of the trees cut off from the traffic of time in "City Centre '70", as well as from its presumably coincidental echo of Farquhar's characterization of Cipriani as "overrun" and "stranded" by the flood of history. These closing lines confirm that neither criticism nor even evaluation of Butler is the business of the poem. There is compassion for the "heroic man" now grown "decrepit" (echoing the use of the Yeatsian term "decrepitude" in the elegy for Manley), and certainly we can discern in this portrait of the old man left behind by the course of events some of the features of the artist. In this account of Butler, the villains are the lying opportunists scrambling for power and the urban mob, presented as a kind of noisome catalyst for change as it "thrust politics a theme". In "Poem for this Day", when Roach is plainly speaking about himself and his own situation, the villains are the same: he is repulsed by the mob's "bestial carnival", that antithesis of the village, and crowded out of politics by "the politician's cloven tongue". If the depiction of Manley resembles a romanticized alter ego of Roach himself, that of Butler seems something more intimate and anxious, a picture of how Roach feared he appeared to others.

Continuing along the same trajectory, the next poem in the series, "Hard Drought" (1973), considers the same political figures, identifies the same villains, and ends with a portrait of how Roach appeared *to himself* in these dark days. The very title of "Hard Drought" links it directly to the imagery of the Manley elegy; in both poems a killing drought definitively ends the cycle of "composting", of greening and blooming again, that underpins Roach's work even as late as the first version of "City Centre". The poem begins by presuming, and then almost at once rejecting, a cyclical view of the political events that punctuate Roach's own career: Butler's oilfield marches of 1938 (the year of Roach's first publications), the "March in the Rain" of 1960, at the height of Williams' popularity, and the mass demonstrations associated with the February Revolution and its aftermath during the early 1970s. As in "Ballad for Tubal Butler", however, Roach here strips every shred of idealism from the events: in the quixotic marches with Butler the participants were "mad battalions" shot at and scattered; the "janizaries" who gathered around Williams in his heyday were to be rudely disillusioned, and the marchers of 1970 were a leaderless "mob" (FR 165). After Butler's degradation and Williams' betrayal, in Roach's view only the mob and the political thugs remain.

The first thirty-one lines of the poem constitute Roach's last published meditation on political leadership. This part of the poem begins and ends with Butler, depicted as he was and as he has come to be. With considerable irony, the compromised figure of Butler thus serves as the poem's standard measure of leadership; the implication is that subsequent developments have made Butler appear relatively heroic (a "lion"), or rather that history has provided alternatives appalling enough to make Butler look attractive. One of those alternatives is the "jackals" who foul the lion's den – the unspecified group of political leaders attacked also in "Ballad of Tubal Butler" and "Poem for This Day". The poem's attention, however, is most sharply focused upon Eric Williams's betrayal of the ideals of his party and supporters – a betrayal Roach took very personally. Even the poem's picture of Williams at his height has a glitch in it:

> Williams called us
> and we thought we'd won;
> we set him on the golden stool,
> gave him kingdom upon kingdom
> of the heart.

The superficially attractive image of Williams as an Ashanti king enthroned on a golden stool seems calculated to recall the revelatory climax of Brathwaite's *Masks*, where, in the poem actually entitled "The Golden Stool", the Ashanti king Osai Tutu, having forged a federation of neighbouring peoples, is depicted in the act of cynically selling his tributaries into slavery. Moreover, behind the treatment of Williams in "Hard Drought" lies another poem entirely about Williams, "The Pharaoh's Eye", which plainly constitutes part of a set with the other poems on political figures (Cipriani, Butler, Manley, and Martin Luther King). Roach did not publish it, perhaps because it is so vituperative as to have been dangerous. There is thoughtful analysis in the poem, but that is not its main business; it concludes in curses, condemning Williams to obloquy and oblivion in very strong terms: "Shango \ of the unfailing phallus drenches him \ in faeces" (FR 195). The brief reference to Ashanti kingship in "Hard Drought" corresponds to Roach's more elaborately abusive trope in "The Pharaoh's Eye", which argues that Williams was indeed like an African king, but the African king he most resembles was the Egyptian Pharaoh, enslaver of the Chosen People.[16]

In comparison with the vigour of personal attack in "Pharaoh's Eye", "Hard Drought" appears quite restrained. Williams may have a "homing instinct" back to slave plantations, but much of the blame for Williams' behaviour is parcelled out to "history" and to the "mob" itself. It is, after all, the people, not the leaders, who are described as Samsons, pulling the place down on their own heads ("we shook the pillars of the place and wept"). Here (as in "The Fighters"), Samson is a tragic and ultimately futile figure of *induced* rage, a failure of discipline in the face of adversity. The same implication is inscribed in the *absence* of a Joshua which the poem laments: Joshua's army, acting in concert, brought down the walls of Jericho; in a parodic inversion of his achievement, the disorderly mob, braying at cross purposes, brings down its own barricades about its ears. In fact the poem is dominated by crumbling structures: Samson's pillars, Joshua's walls, the mob's barricades, "history's ruin", the pile of stones undermined by moles. The series culminates in the failure of the poem's largest and most-desired structure, "a kingdom of this world" which the poet must now confess "we shall not build".

The end of Roach's faith in humanity (he would say "man") as agent rather than victim of history is apparent also in how the poem alludes to a subtler structure, that of the *tapestry*. Roach first describes history in terms of such a worked human artifact (rather than the more spontaneously-generated "legend") when he speaks of "a sacred arras of ancestral story" as an artifact to be preserved in the poem "In Mango Shade" (1953). This notion that the weaving of communal memory is primarily the work of artists persists when he settles upon the term "tapestry" in "Homestead [C]" and "Fugue" (both published in 1958, the year of Federation). In the poems of the 1970s, however, the tapestry has become an ambivalent object in itself, and has slipped out of the hands of artists into those of political leaders. In "Hard Drought", "the rotten tapestry of slavery and mastery" which swaddled Norman Manley, "the old slave tapestry" that Butler "singed" in his prime, has been degraded even further, reduced to Butler's shabby bedding – almost his shroud: "Jackals have whinnied in the lion's lair/ . . . their rank piss/ fouled the old man's tattered sheets" (FR 165). When the poem ends with its unexpected and stunning invocation of the image of Christ on Veronica's veil the implications are rich – the "masking" of the lineaments of the individual human agent in the perennial anonymous blood of the historical process, the crucial role of the marginalized woman, so grudgingly acknowledged in "I say It was the Women". But Veronica's "napkin" is also the last remaining shred of those tattered sheets and that tapestry. It is the historical record reduced to a scrap of fabric, capable of preserving no more than the pathos and spilt blood of even the noblest human action.

Taken in conjunction with the theme of abandonment by mocking gods which "Hard Drought" shares with "Blues for Uncle Tom" (when Roach writes here "Damballa laughed \ Jehovah sneered", the first phrase looks back even further, to "Black Gods"), the force of this closing image gauges the depth and consequence of Roach's despair. Abjuring politics, Roach turns to the subject of himself, and makes that despair the central subject of the second part of the poem:

> This veteran of griefs, betrayals, shames
> snarls in the ancestral void
> where the Middle Passage flung us
> on our knees.

This is no longer the poet of the Federation joining cry from eyot to archipelago – that metaphysical entity is now seen as, replaced by, a void in which the unaccommodated Roach "snarls" (the dogs of "Butler" and "Verse in August" are just out of sight here). I have noted already several signs that Roach was reading Brathwaite at this time, and there is a plausible affinity between the passage just quoted and the conclusion of Brathwaite's "Negus", a poem which Roach almost certainly would have encountered in *Caribbean Quarterly* in 1969. The passages share not only frustrated rage, but specific details – a void, a stone, the act of flinging. The differing arrangements of these details suggest that the close verbal relation is unconscious, but the thematic relation – Roach's rejection of Brathwaite's faith – seems fully conscious. Brathwaite's stone is the paradoxically fertile one that dominates the imagery of *Islands*, the stone which like seeds, eggs, and coral contains potential for growth within its hard exterior. For Roach, however, what's been flung into the void of the Caribbean is no such seed, but "*us*", Afro-Caribbeans as they were envisioned in the opening lines of "The Fighters": "We were thrown down upon our blood and bone, \ stone heaped on broken stone in alien acres". When he wrote those lines Roach still believed in the green rhythms by which hope sprang out of the stone. But in "Hard Drought" the stones are inert; moles burrow among them undisturbed, patiently undermining the pile.

This is one of the accumulating images of crumbling structures that draw attention to some very calculated damage Roach inflicts on the poem's formal structure at this point, as a way of underscoring his abjuration of politics. "Hard Drought" has been constructed on the familiar model of which "The Fighters" and "Homestead" are the clearest instances: after the presentation of a series of exemplary figures, we reach the point in the poem where we have come to expect that Roach will offer a closing exhortation. What we get instead is severe palinode:

> Don't mock me about dreams
> I am too old.
> Don't sneer of prophecies
> count me among the numberless dead
> this grisly century.

The typical *matter* of the exhortations is here – dreams, prophecies, the building of a future – but the gesture is surrender, disillusionment, renunciation. Gone are the images of the poet as solitary bird/bard who speaks to and for his people, or as voice of the aphonous stone, or as revered ancestral figure from whom legend springs; Roach here envisions himself as leaving no mark, no "impression". His identity is lost among the untold bodies. Drunk, fed up with history ("I've eaten so much history that I belch\ boloms of years to come"), the prophet of federation and West Indian identity snarls out among the ruins one last, dismal, renunciatory prophecy: "We shall not build/ a kingdom of this world that is not ours."

*

We have seen how Roach's career insistently works within the permutations of a small group of images. One apparent exception appears at the end. In "Poem" of 1972, a serpent is in its death throes, and the poet seems to welcome the news:

> Dying, the serpent's
> writhing in its coils,
> tombing itself
> in fold on fold
> of its cold quivering flesh; . . .
>
> Who struck the coup de grace?
> No one, no one.
> The thing undid itself. . . .
>
> Well, let it die. (FR 162)

The figure of the dying serpent may at first glance seem to have no antecedents in Roach's work. Yet there are two snakes as early as "Invocation" (1949), and although one is merely part of the decor (the "scaly snake" inhabiting the "sour marshes" of his verse), the other is already linked to history: "Now from my heart draw out the adder's hate \ That counts the burning whip-weals one by one" (FR 52). These lines voice the concern expounded more extensively later in "The Fighters": the strength that comes from anger can be short-lived, difficult to control, and finally unproductive, a kind of sugar-high of the spirit. Possibly, however, the presence of this snake may be more a stroke of compositional luck than a calculated choice of imagery; that is, it may have materialized out of the wordplay: 'the *add*-er that counts one by one'. A serpent first takes centre stage in the poem "Black Gods". As the embodiment of the loa Damballa, the serpent here plays a direct, meddlesome, and self-serving role in the Haitian Revolution. The poem ends by associating him with another problematic force in human history, the serpent of Eden (Damballa also appears in "The Ballad of Canga" and in "Hard Drought", but not in the form of a snake). The snake reappears in "The World of Islands" (1962), in a passage that accumulates past images as if in preparation for the change of 1970 (this is in fact the last entirely new poem published before 1970). Flying over the eastern Caribbean, presumably after the collapse of the West Indian Federation, Roach muses on the character of the region:

> A difficult country to inherit:
> Guilt is humid in the glittering air;
> Grafted at every branch the human wood
> Blooms a bewildering scent, fruits bitter-sweet;
> Indigenous blood still stains the grass;
> Dragon's teeth still rattle under root,
> And under stone the cold snake's coiled asleep,
> Rapt in its murderous dream. (FR 147)

There is so much that burdens the ground here – not just the sedimented horrors of Caribbean history, but, in another register, the loam of Roach's own accumulated work: The blood staining the grass recalls not only the ancient blood that flowers in "Carib and Arawak", but also the blood of future violence that will one day dry on the emerald leaf in "Something Seen". The dragon's teeth sown to make trouble for some future Argonaut are related to the buried skull in "Shallow Underground". The snake, which climaxes that series of images, is recognizable as Roach's Damballa, and his dream is the course of history. A difficult country to inherit, yes. The poem goes on to insist that those who have inherited it, those fruits of the complex genetic grafting consequent on colonization and slavery, have also redeemed it; Roach will end the poem with the mulatta dancer summoning us to a new beginning in the Caribbean: "Come, come I am the phoenix Eve,\ . . . I recreate the world on islands." The final stanza, with its dancer embodying the "mingled wine of the world's grapes" and its "drummer with his father's knuckles", harks back to the particular vision with which Roach ten years earlier had tried to entice Lamming back from England, when he wrote, "Remember . . . old men goatskin drumming, \ The sun's rose ruddy in our blood, \ The wine excitement of our island women" (FR 82). A new Eden, then; but does Roach intend us to resist the thought that there may be a serpent in Eve's future? This poem was written after the failure of the Federation; the snake remains under the rock, and its dream continues.

Consistent with the sense of continuing threat in "The World of Islands", the serpent in "Poem" is at large in the world, and there is (metaphorically speaking) a sharp sting at the end of it's tail – the tense of the final verb is surprisingly *future*:

> Who grieves a serpent's death?
> No one, no one.
> It ruined paradise,
> despoiled our virgin innocence
> and *will devour*
> each pure Utopia
> we may dream. (emphasis added)

This poem has been interpreted as a response to the February Revolution and its outcome.[17] If we read the poem more broadly, however, as a treatment of Roach's late historical vision, of which the Revolution is only an instance, it is possible to recognize this serpent as a grotesque transformation of the poet's earliest wellspring imagery. We have seen that the conceptual shift from history that springs up in us to history that sweeps us away is reflected in the shift of imagery from springs to flooded rivers and *running* tides. The dying devouring serpent carries the same implications for a view of history, and draws additional expressive power from the atavistic human repulsion for serpents. This is not just an implacable natural force, but a malevolence, and a tormented one at that: a political monster grown as hideous as one of Blake's reptilian kings at the prospect of losing power.[18]

What is most horrifying in Roach's vision is his sense that somehow the serpent, though it is already dying, outlives us all, and our dreams as well (it is linked not only to images of wellsprings but also to the vengeful buried ancestors and loas). Every political or social ideal, every vision, must enter history in the form of action if it is to be anything but a myth, a comforting fiction. But to enter that serpent is to be devoured by it, to become part of its substance.[19] At the end of his career, Roach's fundamental imagery is transformed; he sees us all as inside history, swept along or swallowed up by it, not riding it like a hawk on an updraft, or emerging from it, as he had once thought, like a living spring, or like a flower from the rock.

More than one critic would share Wayne Brown's opinion that Roach "in the end lay camped at the brink of creating a mythology."[20] Why did he stop at the brink? In part because, like so many West Indian poets, he did not think well enough of his own work.[21] But there is another, odder possibility: that what failed him was not his talent but, in a way, his subject. The mythology we can see he was developing was based on the village, on its resilience, its ability to batten on history and produce human achievement. Trinidad of the 1970s seemed to be progressing in a way that cut off the village entirely, as if it were prehistoric, a cultural fossil.[22] The defeat of the village by the forces of history called into question the whole conceptual basis of his poetry, while at the same time he could not see what the new urban society was grounded on, nor how to encompass the traumatic intrusion of modernization in the frame of his work. As Rohlehr puts it, "Roach's poems after 1970 are those of a man who has lost the simplicity of his Tobago villages and can come to no real terms with Port-of-Spain."[23]

Almost twenty years earlier, Brathwaite had been worried about Roach: "The question is: will the folk society on which he is based be able to nurture and sustain him and keep him 'home', or will he, too, turn away from his sources?"[24] At the time Brathwaite wrote, migration was the pressing issue, and he was certainly most concerned with the second half of his question, but events have revealed the importance of the first half. In an unexpected sense, the village did not sustain its poet. The failure of federation was for him primarily a failure of the politicians, only confirmed by the subsequent upheaval in Trinidad, and Roach felt a real sense of *personal* betrayal by Eric Williams (hence the unrestrained attack against him in "The Pharaoh's Eye"). But there was also a kind of betrayal by the *people* of Jamaica. Their vote against federation, which brought down Norman Manley, was a blow to the very premise of the staunch federalism which Roach shared with Manley: the prospect of a common culture and common interest for inhabitants of the region who regarded themselves as "West Indians". The thinking of the Jamaican peasant-voters who swung the referendum was incomprehensible to him in some ways, and the fact that he could be so unpleasantly surprised by the sort of people he felt closest to, felt most knowledgeable about, and most in service to, confirmed for Roach his fatal alienation and remoteness, in spite of all his efforts. Roach was tormented as much by having no one to speak *for*, as by having no one to speak *to*. Social change left him with no ground upon which to address the generation of the present. He seems to have felt that the flood of history had made him, even to the marginalized youth of the February Revolution, a marginal figure, cut off from both the leaders and the followers. In the end Roach found himself borne by the current of history to an untenable, and perhaps unbearable, position: working with all his art to articulate a mythology for the first time, while he watched it become irrelevant to those it was meant to serve.

Chapter 9 — The Politics of Poetry: Roach's aesthetics and the *Savacou* debate

Roach saw himself marginalized and isolated by the tide of political events. This experience was reinforced, with devastating effect, in the arena of contemporary West Indian poetry. If the failure of the Federation shattered Roach's faith in the cultural homogeneity of the region, events in the early 1970s had a similar impact on his faith in a homogeneous West Indian aesthetic. Roach's forthright objection to the nature of the new poetry published in the *Savacou* anthology of 1971 was the most public expression of his thinking about the nexus of craft, expressiveness, and political engagement in Caribbean poetry. The ensuing debate has remained important to the development of indigenous literary criticism, and that is one reason to consider Roach's catalytic contribution to the discussion.[1] But most noteworthy for present purposes is the fact that his position vis a vis this anthology was not his only position on the nature of poetry. A divergence between theory and practice is hardly unusual; in the case of Roach the divergence is located elsewhere. In his criticism, he championed a view of the poem as a well-wrought artifact, built to endure, and with very few exceptions his own poems in fact exemplify such an aesthetic. What comes as a surprise is the conception of poetry projected *within* these poems, where the account of what a poet does, and indeed of what he is, seems quite at odds with both Roach's position as a critic and his practice as a poet. After sketching his pivotal position in the debate over the anthology, then, this final chapter will step back to consider Roach's paradoxical ideas about the nature of the poet and the poem, first as those were crystallized under the pressure of the *Savacou* debate, and then as they are implicit in the body of his published poetry.

*

The *Savacou* anthology entitled *New Writing 1970* came out early in 1971. Established figures were well represented – there was prose from George

Lamming and John Hearne, poetry from Mervyn Morris and Dennis Scott, John Figueroa, Derek Walcott, Martin Carter – but the collection was dominated by young Jamaicans (Audvil King, Bongo Jerry, Brian Meeks), and emphasized overtly political and experimental work with roots in oral poetry, reggae, and dub. It will help to recall the context of these events: against a background of campus unrest in Jamaica and the February Revolution in Trinidad, this was the era of Walcott's astringent essay "What the Twilight Says", published with his first collection of plays, of Marina Maxwell's "Towards a Revolution in the Arts", (its positive evaluation of carnival contrasting sharply with Walcott's), of Pat Ismond's account of the polarization of "Walcott vs Brathwaite", and of the lively conference in Kingston sponsored by the Association for Commonwealth Literature and Language Studies (ACLALS).[2] *New Writing 1970* appeared just after both the *Caribbean Voices* anthology and the special West Indian number of *The Literary Half-Yearly* (Mysore); in fact the very first words one encounters in the *Savacou* anthology are taken from the introduction to this issue, in which Arthur Drayton speaks of a "revolutionary questioning of West Indian values" reflected in the region's literature.[3]

If the writing in *Savacou 3/4* was predominantly Jamaican, the critical reaction was primarily Trinidadian. Roach was the first to respond, and he began with genuine surprise that a selection dominated by recent Jamaican writing would not automatically be representative of the region as a whole; surprise at how much diversity the concept of West Indian literature was going to have to accommodate. The tone of Roach's initial reaction – "It is very obvious that something is happening over in Jamaica that we in Trinidad have not a clue about"[4] – suggests that for him the evidence cast a shadow on his long-standing belief in the cultural and political unity of the West Indies as it also dimmed the "dream of wholeness" celebrated in Kamau Brathwaite's foreword to the anthology.[5] Beyond that, Roach went on to initiate debate about the anthology by raising three overlapping objections; briefly, it was too "black", too political, too inept.

The roots of Roach's criticism were complex. He spoke as a rural conservative from Tobago, as a supporter of Federation taken aback by the Jamaicanness of the anthology, as a respecter of craft incensed at the publication of what seemed to him immature and unpolished work, finally as a poet of folk life who condemned the turn to Black Power rhetoric as insufficiently indigenous, and who objected to protest poetry with the authority of one who had written many frankly political poems. For example, Roach reacted most fiercely to the suggestion that Black Consciousness constituted the thrust of West Indian writing: "To thresh about wildly like [Audvil] King and [Bongo] Jerry in the murky waters of race, oppression and dispossession is to bury one's head in the stinking dunghills of slavery."[6] But this reaction should not be misunderstood. In the 1970s it was then only the beginning of the end for the long-standing suppression of Africa in West Indian education – a fact treated explicitly in King's "The Big Wash" and Bongo Jerry's "Mabrak". Roach spoke as one of several fervent West Indian nationalists, long aware of the African heritage, who objected to the Black Power movement (and particularly to its rhetoric) on the firmly nationalistic grounds that it was a piece of the old mimicry, a slavish importation from North America of ideas that had actually originated, in more sophisticated form, in the Caribbean of Césaire, Fanon, George Padmore and C. L. R. James. In fact, Roach had frequently been praised as one of the most successful among those who took up the theme of Africa in the 1940s – not only by Wayne Brown, but by Lamming and Brathwaite.[7] For that matter, he had taken his share of criticism for being too black, too rhetorical, too "breathless".[8] Certainly the nature of the immediate political context is a governing factor in his response here. In overwhelmingly black Jamaica the rhetoric of Black Power contributed constructively in achieving national self-consciousness and self-respect. Roach's own Tobago was black and Protestant, ethnically much closer to Jamaica (or Barbados) than to cosmopolitan Trinidad. But in the Trinidad of the February Revolution, where the recent experience of Guyana with racial politics was a fresher memory, such rhetoric could appear irresponsibly inflammatory.

When Roach raised the question of the viable balance between literary and political objectives for a poet in his work, or for a particular poem, he inaugurated a general discussion of the political responsibilities (if any) of a poet in a new society. But Roach expressed his conception of the role of the poet in language that seems designed to preclude any discussion of politics: "Art is outside the fanatics [sic] scope because it engages the whole man, the totality of his life and his experience. It draws from his past, which is his tribal history and his nurture. . . Working the native clay, stone, marble or wood with the native cunning of his love, the craftsman's mind, the grace and strength of his hands, create artifacts that are the very spirit of the tribe."[9] As this choice of language makes clear, his objection was not finally political; it was an objection to artistic carelessness and compromise.

In replying to Roach, critics most frequently raised the related issues of experimentation and orality. Roger McTair, for example, noted that "Roach's main problem as a critic is an inability to recognize the validity of a committed poetry, and an experimental poetry."[10] As we have seen, Roach in fact had a strong sense of the poet's responsibility to reflect and address his own people in his own time, and many of his poems take up immediate political problems. He believed in the importance of experiment, certainly; but just as certainly he objected to the *publication* of careless work. Implicit in that attitude is an acknowledgement of print as a canonizing medium (Roach was quite willing, after all, for the BBC to broadcast poems which he never found satisfactory enough to publish). Thus questions about the status of experimental work are linked to the question whether peculiarly literary language has an inherent value.

Wayne Brown later strongly defended Roach on this point: "In his last years he waged a brief but bitter (if eventually futile) battle against the breakdown of literary standards in the islands, as evinced by a rash of publications of mostly worthless verse – publications which were nonetheless championed by certain academics as heralding a breakthrough of the oral tradition into scribal literature, and as sociologically relevant."[11] Roach himself had pursued the matter of craft more evenhandedly, coincidentally in the course of a review of Brown's poetry. In an oft-quoted passage, he identifies most of the crucial oppositions upon which the *Savacou* debate was grounded:

> The "tribe boys" claim to be creating "the New Caribbean verse," constructing a ringing rhetoric from the native patois for the new people emerging from the darkness of slavery and colonialism... They chant their rhetoric to drum beats, rapping to the brothers and sisters about tribal dispossession and the beauty of blackness... The Afro-Saxon stance is that poetry is no protest weapon... It is just poetry, art or craft... Their central concern is for the savants to say of them ... that they are among the finest poets in the English language.[12]

It is undeniable that Roach persistently identified popular culture with rural folk culture. He never came to terms with urban popular culture, with mass culture; it inspired in him a mixture of grief and disgust.[13] With that important qualification, Roach's work in every medium demonstrates profound respect for popular art and especially for fragile oral culture. Yet he could not help hearing the oxymoron in the phrase "oral literature," and would have insisted on distinguishing the art of the spoken from the art of the written word.

To the extent that *Savacou* expressed a need to suspend or broaden aesthetic standards in order to accommodate poetry that sprang from political commitment, the anthology itself seemed to set views of the poem as a crafted artifact in opposition to views of the poem as a vehicle for political expression or protest, that is, as a relatively *unmediated* expression. Roach is simply following that lead when he proceeds from the opposition between oral and written to make other equally emphatic distinctions: first between a rhetoric and a craft (that is, I take it, between improvisatory verbal skill and reflective art), and then between a transient performance and a piece of work that comes to be preserved in the tradition, in the very language itself. While Roach in his own poetry shows considerable respect for verbal performance, it seems clear from this passage that he finally ranks higher the craftsman who can immortalize verbal performance in a (relatively) permanent work of art.[14] And certainly Roach himself had no inherent objection to verse of political urgency – he had been writing it himself for decades. What infuriated him was the ready assumption that urgency and finish were in essence incompatible; that one always had to be sacrificed to the other. Such an assumption questioned the value of his life's work as a poet.

From these characterizations of the artist Roach goes on to contrast characterizations of the putative audience, conceived either in terms of the "people" or the "savants". The distinction here has to do with the poem's destination; does it go to a place in the Tradition or out to the immediate society – to the people present in the present? In other words, which is preferable: an aesthetic of the great anthology or an aesthetic of carnival?[15] In the abstract, the contrast is stark. According to the first view the poem aspires to be inscribed in the universal anthology of the tradition, standing on its own intrinsic merits (that is craft, finish, resonance), quite removed from author and circumstances – indeed valued finally for its *timelessness*. According to the other view, the ideal poem is a timely, contingent expression. It is produced by a vividly present author/speaker, the community's "man-of-words". It derives from and addresses immediate circumstances (though perhaps using "old" wisdom, memory, tradition in the process). It is ultimately valued for its *timeliness*, and so also for its inherent *timing*, for the wit of its form and conception as well as the wit of its appropriateness to the occasion.

But Roach's work draws attention to some complications here. Timeliness and timelessness are qualities largely independent of questions of medium: a memorable proverb aims at permanence and impersonal composedness; a topical newspaper poem accepts transience as price of expressive immediacy. And for some of the most anthology-oriented poets in the English tradition the operative aesthetic was not in fact one of preservation but of deserving preservation. This is especially true of the poets Roach most admired: the High Romantics, and the Yeats of poem like "Lapis Lazuli". For Roach at least, the real issue is not orality or timeliness but craft. He was not particularly objecting to the presence of oral elements in poetry; rather he maintained that it was irresponsible for printed work not to take advantage of the characteristic resources of that medium. Immediacy and vitality are the virtues of the spoken poem; density and complexity are the virtues of the written poem. Transcription is not enough. If the "oral" poem, when it moves into print, loses fire, it needs to gain polish.

Roach also implicitly reminds us that the so-called "poetry of the spoken word" is not in fact oral. The proposition that poetry should be "oral" in the West Indies comes from poets who continue to write for print. Assuming the primacy of oral practice, they wished to see the written valorized by taking on characteristics considered "oral". One initial impulse of *Savacou*, after all, was to claim a place for performance poetry *in an anthology* – publication was recognized as a way to establish that these poems had value beyond the immediate circumstances of their utterance.

Roach's implied question was pointed: if we truly want our poetry to be oral, why is it clamouring for a place on the printed page? The printed page remains a privileged space, a place of honour, the site of "literature" as such, and many poets on both sides of the debate personally aspire to find an audience among both the "people" and the "savants". Behind all the noise of the debate were two constructive impulses: to make room for people's poetry in the anthologies, and to get the production values of the anthology into poetry for the people – which, as writers like George Campbell had already demonstrated, need not be slipshod, however transient and popular. But if it seems that Roach's analysis exposes the "tribe boys" as scribal poets fully committed to print and calling for oral *style*, rather than for true oral poetry, it is worth noting that the "Afro-Saxon" Roach himself was not unaffected by the confrontation. After 1970, as we saw in the previous chapter, he wrote many poems that are overtly political, and some ("Verse in August" and the unpublished "Littering Earth's Centre") that encompass folk language and custom.

*

With the exception of these late poems, Roach's poetic practice remains consistent throughout his career. His poems bespeak a commitment to restraint and compression – very much at odds with the poetry in the *Savacou* anthology. This is most apparent in his respect for poetic form, and in his extreme parsimony with respect to imagery, vocabulary, and allusive field. After the early days, Roach generally did not work in specific traditional forms. For example, there are some early sonnets, but no more after "She" in 1949. The main exception is poems in quatrains, of which he published about a dozen, the last "The Picture" (1960). It is revealing that none rhyme after "Ballad of Canga" (1955), and of the four poems in quatrains published after 1953, the titles of three indicate some self-consciousness about the use of the form: "*Ballad* of Canga", "*Doggerel* for Adolescence", "*Notes* for a New Poem".

Yet Roach did not write free verse. His poems might be called "free" with respect to the handling of rhyme, line-length, and stanzaic pattern, but the freedom is conditional; there is usually some metrical and stanzaic norm in the background. An exception proves the rule: "Eclogue for Christmas" is genuine free verse, but that is because it is modelled closely on T. S. Eliot, and the freedom is restricted by a very strong dactylic pulse throughout, especially in the latter part of the lines. The majority of his poems invoke some stanzaic regularity. In considering Roach's practice, the term "stanza" means no more than a group of a certain number of lines; there is no implied contract about line length within or across stanzas, and no commitment to rhyme as a device for articulating the shape of the stanza. Stanza groupings of from 5 to 8 lines are most common. The 10-line stanza, supported by some rhyming in couplets, in "Homestead" is Roach's largest repeating unit. Roach has a habit of ending poems with a longer stanzaic unit than the established norm for the poem: to cite two extreme cases, "The Fighters", after five 5-line stanzas ends with a 10-line stanza; "Pray that the Poem out of Nowhere Come" follows three stanzas of 6 lines with one of 14.

Roughly half of Roach's poems have no rhyme at all; several include a few words that rhyme with one another, though with no evident intent. Such accidental rime has no structural function; the poet merely accepts a consonance that turns up in the course of composition. Truly structural rhyme does occur; Roach seems to have particularly liked the effect of pointing the final two (or three) lines of a section with rhyme as a structural marker, e.g. in "Homestead", "Lady by the Sea", "He Juggles Images", and "For A. A. Cipriani". Another favourite formal effect is to end stanzas with blank verse lines (the first part of "Black Gods" ends with a pair of them). Indeed, whatever the lineation on the page, blank verse is very often Roach's underlying rhythm, associated with a certain field of rhetoric and diction that the poet found very congenial.

Within these fairly conservative formal parameters, Roach also pared down his style, by conscious choice limiting his palette to a few very resonant images, among them the flowering rock, the black loam, the soaring bird, the aphonous stone. Is this economy of means successful? Perhaps not, if we expect the dynamic fiction of a continuous career, its products simultaneously available in a book to every reader. But Roach in his circumstances only occasionally thought himself capable of sustaining a coherent career. On the whole, Roach did not behave like the heroic figure of the poet he so often depicted in poems like "Beyond". We have seen him instead working as a maker of individual poems that stand or fall on their own, that may survive him and his memory. Roach seems also to have been motivated, in part, by a desire to produce poems that could (at least ideally) be accessible to a wider audience thanks to their limited vocabulary and range of reference. He had no illusions about actually addressing a peasant audience, but perhaps (glancing back to the model of Yeats) his poems can be said to embody a "peasant aesthetic" that values whatever is sturdy, economical, and well-made, in the hope that such simplicity and directness appeals to the aristocratic tastes of the "the savants," who in their turn recognize it as classic.

*

In extraordinary contrast to both Roach's poetic practice and his critical statements, however, his poems *depict* poetry as a matter of free expression rather than of artful composition. His earliest and most persistent images are of the poet as a kind of Aeolian harp,[16] who produces poetry as a natural effusion, almost a bodily function, when he meets the wind and makes his way through the world. After appearances in poems such as "Invocation" and "The Old Man", the High Romantic imagery of the Aeolian lyre or wind harp is at its most literal in "Homestead", where the cedars become "seven towers of song when the trades rage", and stand as symbols of the poet and of the "voluntary verse" he produces (FR 79). In "Frigate Bird Passing" and elsewhere the solitary bird is a less explicit representation of this Aeolian ideal: "Feeling the wind in his belly\ . . . He shrills his epics to the risen sun\ . . .He flies and dreams. . . " (FR 74). Poetry here is something virtually irresistible that springs, gushes, bursts forth; a proclamation, the crowing of a cock. In "Tree" (1952) it is literally an ejaculation: "I stand up siring my song / Conscious of the pride and poise of fullness" (FR 86). Because of its subject, "A Dirge for a Dead Poet" (1954) brings together several of these images: the poet is one who "crowed his cockerel light, / Pouring bright poems through / The heavy air, bright, / Jewel bright as crystal dew. / . . . O, and a bounding stag" (FR 108-109). Even the early poem "A Poet Passes" envisions the poet as a "fountain of song". It is noteworthy that in these examples the poet's output is described generically ("poetry", "song") or in the plural ("poems", "epics"). Not only is there no allowance in this conception for reflection, revision, or any exercise of craft; there is also no room for an individual poem, as a discrete finished object. The flow of song that the poet produces seems to have neither form nor content.

"A Dirge for a Dead Poet" (1954) illustrates the contrast very well. "Dirge" is a fine elegy, though quite remote from the particulars of the dead man's life (unless something biographical is behind the image of the hounded stag). The dead poet is endowed with all the attributes of Roach's lofty idealizations in the *Bim* poems: he was a "skier" (i.e., sky-er, another soaring "singing man" as in "Beyond") with "burning dreams" (as in "Transition"); he is another flowering rock, asserting himself against the odds, crowing his poems through the heavy air. The climactic celebration of the poet makes use of the same imagery that Roach explored in the central stanza of "Death Does Not":

> An arrowhead of God,
> A star clove through his soul;
> He was a prophet's rod
> Blossomed, a humming totem pole. (FR 108)

What the dirge praises is an effusive notion of poetry, yet (presumably because poetry is the subject-matter) the poem itself is obviously crafted with care. There are, for example, four classical allusions – a very unusual density of reference for Roach. Two are images associating the dead poet with Icarus ("The winged one among the stones"), and Actaeon ("a bounding stag / Hounded in beauty"). In addition a description of the new day as a "phoenix" is implicitly counterpoised with another classical pyre that ends not in rebirth but in oblivion: the fall of Troy, which Roach associated with himself (time will scatter his "ashen griefs", his tears, and "the mound of [his] days' dust" just as it scattered Troy).

If that opulence of allusion constitutes a departure from Roach's usual parsimony, the formal disposition of the poem is characteristic of Roach in his maturity: the visual impression is dominated by the regularity of five line stanzas, but the line lengths are actually quite variable. That interplay of regularity and irregularity is reproduced in the poem's system of rhymes: each stanza rhymes XBCBC except the last, which asserts its closural force by a shift to XBBBB. However, every stanza has its unrhymed first line, which no amount of subsequent rhyming can resolve (Roach has ensured that none of the "X" words rhyme with one another in the course of the poem). These devices are not obtrusive, but they have mimetic value in this text which asserts the power of art in the face of grief.

Despite such formality of surface, the *words* of these poems advocate no cult of the artifact, and (a separate issue) no discernible cult of craft. There is, however, some sense of audience. Though the emphasis is decidedly on the nobility of the *idea* of such effusion, there is some secondary interest in the effect of it on an observer, on the world – the *impression* it makes and leaves. Thus the poet is described as like a bird that sings as it flies, awakening all who hear him as his song pours "through last slow closing shutters of the soul" ("Beyond," FR 71). Elsewhere he is the high-flying, solitary hawk whose cry is nevertheless heard and attended to (Roach seems to have in mind a kind of Homeric augury). As in the following lines from "Tree", the recurrent images throughout are of abundance, exuberance, and superfluity, of passive availability rather than active service: "O world, take honey from my worth,\ . . . tap my ample heritage of strength.\ . . . Draw on my reservoir of hope" (FR 86-87). The poet is disengaged, but socially useful. He need merely be himself, and so long as he does it "gracefully" (the word occurs often, twice in "Death Does Not"), he will leave not poems, or even words, but an impression on some eye, in some mind:

soar
Like the lean hawk; . . .
How you hang gracefully
Under the dazzling sky
Some gazer's eye will mirror. . .
Stand at the precipice
At the end of the race;

Pose and leave pictures there,
The last, the best, the rare;
And like fearless diver
Leap into the air;

Plunge graceful as a swan
Into oblivion. (FR 69)

This is a *fin de siècle* tragic view of life, a celebration of the heroic individual. This springing forth of inborn and irresistible style, which Roach frequently calls "grace", has its closest relatives in the Bergsonian *élan vital* and the Renaissance *sprezzatura* that Yeats so much admired. If "Death Does Not" sounds like Yeats on art, it sounds like Unamuno on life: we should live so as to deserve immortality, whether it exists or not, so that at worst we prove worthy of more than the universe can give us. Such "grace" remains a primary value throughout Roach's career. It is still being invoked in one of his last few published poems, "At Guaracara Park", especially in the opening stanza:

the bronze god running;
beauty hurtling through the web of air,
motion fusing time and space
exploding our applauses[.] (FR 150)

This runner bears a clear family resemblance to the athletic figure in "Death Does Not", and his physical grace is characteristically associated with making an almost inadvertent impression on an audience.

There are times when Roach envisions a social role for the poet as an Adamic giver of names, as one who descries the potential symbols in nature and in his human community, and by putting them into words makes them recognizable to others, so that they can successfully function as symbols. In poems like "The Flowering Rock", Roach plays this role himself, singling out a feature of the landscape as symbolic of the character of its inhabitants. By so doing he speaks them to themselves, in words whose very artfulness constitutes a cachet of truth. But on the whole the last poems are pessimistic. In "Piarco", the peasants' devotion to the son of the village who "shall name them to the world" is presented as futile (FR 160). In "Poem for this Day", when we are invited to "regard these market towns and mouldering / villages . . . *not even names to us*" (FR 163; my emphasis), the implicit failure of the poet's naming function is included in the general collapse of society.

This conception of the social role of the poet is of salient importance in Roach's *criticism*, as we saw earlier, but within the poems it repeatedly appears only to give way to the more effusive, less responsible, view. There is a strong tendency, if not strictly a preference, to present the poet as himself more a symbol than an agent of symbolizing: as totem for the tribe, rather than shaman; not the prophet, but the prophet's blossoming rod. Thus in "Tree" (1952), the poet turns out in the end to *be* the tree he first *observed*: "I am my rooted symbol tree". As Roach imagines him here and in other poems (e.g. "The Flowering Rock" or "Frigate Bird Passing"), it seems difficult for the poet to recognize a symbol without identifying himself with it. In "At Guaracara Park" Roach follows this habit of his ideal poet: he recognizes the runner as a symbolic figure in stanza one, and by stanza four he has identified himself with his symbol (this is apparent in the shifting use of the word "our", which first links the poet with the audience as distinct from the runner, and later identifies all three). Roach associates the figure of the poet not only with the runner, but with fighters, drummers, and dancers as *enacters* of the tribe to itself.[17] Such figures occupy a place conceptually *between* shaman and totem, between agent and symbol. In each case, a highly personal style – the expression, and even the assertion, of individuality – is the ground on which value to the community is established. Graceful expression leaves an impression.

What is extremely rare in the published poems is any sense of the individual poem as an artifact, a product of skilled labour. We have encountered instances where clay and dough (the identifying media of the father and the mother respectively) are employed as images for poetry, or the poet, but these instances never achieve the prominence of such images as the flowering rock or the soaring hawk. Another case in which poetry is envisioned as an artifact occurs in "Homestead [C]". When Roach urges that the work of the peasantry deserves to be celebrated and memorialized by artists, he speaks of "cunning tapestries" to be produced by poets and artists "upon the ages of their acres, the endless labour of their years." In this passage the word "upon" is made to carry several meanings: most simply, the artists' work will be *about* the peasants, but there is a further implication that the artists' success must rest upon a culture whose foundation this unsung labour has laid. There is finally even a hyperbolic suggestion that the artists' tapestries *physically* coincide with the fields, that the land itself is transformed, through art, into what we recognize as landscape. Thus Roach exhorts poets and artists to work "at the centre" of the peasants' world, and his imperatives radically assimilate the work of poet and peasant: "*cultivate* the first green graces, . . . *sow and graft* the primal good" [my emphasis]. When the poet through his craft makes the land articulate, enables it to speak forth the man, he re-enacts and so mirrors the peasant's own labour of working the clay, labour which articulated the fields by shaping them as "monuments in stone".

But in Roach's poems there is nearly always a slide from such consciousness of craft to the earlier, simpler position. Thus "The Fighters" exhorts painter, sculptor, poet to "persist to sheer perfection in the work", but though a perfection of craft seems intended, the term is immediately defined in a different way as the statement unfolds: "like those who pit their perfect and tough sinew against arrogance and hate" (FR 107). Perfection is again something organic, a fullness of growth, the characteristic of fighters and of "dark ecstatic dancers" – heroic surrogates for the tribe as a whole. The accompanying image echoes this: perfection for the artist means that in him "the seed takes leaf and the leaf greens and flowers like fire."

This wish that formal perfection can somehow still be as kinetic as fire or a dance is worked out most thoroughly (though not very clearly) in "Poem (Pray that the Poem Out of Nowhere Come)."[18] At first poetry is described in Roach's usual way: it is something that bursts "out of nowhere" as unexpectedly as a flower from a bare bough, or water from a rock, and having made its appearance it will then "go with grace", and "sing". But the baffling last stanza struggles with a more complex idea:

> Not the gross cunning of the Doric stone,
> Those flanks and breasts amazing gods and men:
> (That form was cut for a coarse artisan
> Who was half-blind from soot in the black forge.)
> But the dancer in dreams, Cyprian in tides
> Fresh from the seafoam or gleaming at Paphos, goddess,
> Goddess, born and reborn, eternally woman,
> Eternally loved...
> And think on Shakespeare's monumented beauty;
> On Parnell's passionate wreck; on poor John Keats;
> And think on Yeats – the poem's gone to stone. (FR 105)

This passage seems to propose an opposition between the Doric statue of the goddess, laboriously cut from stone, and the goddess herself, who dances in dreams with that elation of the blossom or the spring that the poet values so highly. This opposition is complicated by a further distinction between two goddess: the true Aphrodite of the imagination, and a coarser one, unruly wife of the blacksmith Hephaestus, who (in Roach's brief myth) shamelessly modelled for storytellers and Doric sculptors. But only one of these goddesses actually plays any further role in the poem:

inasmuch as divinity corresponds to eternity, the goddess of seafoam and dreams is paradoxically timeless, and in that sense fixed, "gone to stone". Since it is shaped by her own exuberant being in space and time, this image puts to shame the Doric one, clumsy by comparison. What Roach's ideal poem aspires to is that paradoxical kind of fixity, like the shape of playing fountain, rather than the calculated, carved fixity of the sculpture.[19]

Here Roach is attempting to address an inherent friction between the implications of two key concepts, "grace" and "impression". This friction is aggravated by the two diverse senses of the word "impression": one fluent and elusive, as in "impressionism", the other rigid and inorganic, as in the impression of a mold on bronze. The very end of "Doggerel for Adolescence" is pertinent here:

> In my rough youth I could not think
> But garland you the queen of day
> With desire's rhetoric;
> You grace the evening of my dreams. (FR 126)

In these lines Roach underlines the difference between the woman's possession of grace, as an attribute that can be witnessed and that nourishes the witness and the poet's callow (and somewhat appropriative) response, which is to "garland" grace with his relatively artificial rhetoric.

This polarity comes fully to the surface only in "Pray that the Poem Out of Nowhere Come", where it is figured in the distinction between the two Aphrodites, and it is never explicitly resolved in Roach's poetry. His resort to the metaphor of dance suggests that he is looking for a reconciliation in something analogous to the performative discipline that mediates between the expressive freedom of the dancer and the impact of the dance itself as a composition (this would accord with his proposed placement of the poet somewhere between shaman and totem). But the inferiority of the Doric statue which this formulation necessitates is uncongenial to most readers, and indeed at odds with Roach's own instincts: in "Caribbean Coronation Verse" of the same year Shakespeare is unequivocally *praised* for his "cut and chiselled" verse (though that in its turn may seem a highly unusual characterization of Shakespeare's verbal texture).

In "The Picture" (1960) Roach again compares poetry with a more concrete art-form, but though he asks for Rembrandt's art to paint the woman who is his subject, what he wants to depict seems equally problematic for both media, for the framed painting as for the page-bound poem: the subject is "A moment laughing in the running moment . . . The freedom she must live, the gaiety she is" (FR 140). Again, as in "Pray that the Poem Out of Nowhere Come" and "The Fighters", he envisions exuberance somehow perfecting its own form: "A gesture like a phrase, a chord, a curve". The gesture somehow possesses classic form itself, as does the dance of Aphrodite in "Pray that the Poem Out of Nowhere Come". At the same time he seems to recognize two challenges for poetry: how to capture such gestural form in words, and how to imitate it, as a model of the compositional process – of how grace successfully leaves an impression.

*

Roach responded to these challenges; until the end, he remained sure of his raw vocation as a poet because of the kind of impression experience continued to make on him, the "bright splash on the mind" (FR 169). But by 1970 several problems developed. First, and most simply, he came to doubt his own skill; at the same time he was shaken by what seemed an absence of craft in the coming generation of poets.[20] Most profoundly, he questioned the impression he made as a poet, not particularly out of self-doubt, but because he was led to question whether any poet made an impression, whether poetry was in fact one of the heroic offices of the tribe ("what's all my witness for?") – to question, that is, the vision that had sustained him from the first. Whether the poet is to be numbered among the heroic figures of Roach's pantheon, the politicians, drummers, dancers, fighters, is argued back and forth through the late poems. "City Centre '70" and "At Guaracara Park" identify the poet with other "marathon" runners who earn (or once earned) "applauses"; there is a comparable conception in "The Blind Weavers", where the poems of Homer and Milton are said to "march . . . through each applauding generation" (FR 122). In "Elegy for N. Manley" and "Ballad for Tubal Butler" the subject is the failure of heroes, and poets are not among them, or even present in the poems, at all. In the closing lines of "Elegy for N. Manley" the idea of the monument is brought up only to be devalued, and devalued with it is Roach's cherished idea of the "worth" of leaving an "impression". In "Ballad for Tubal Butler", Roach's old idealism is ironized, the habitual image of the singing bird sardonically recast: "history's ceaseless flood / has left him on a muddy shoal, / . . . sometimes howling, a mad dog, at the current in its course" (FR 157).

In "Hard Drought" the tale of a hero ruined and bypassed by history is repeated, but its conclusion is made resonant by grim allusion to the early, idealistic image in which the heroic figure leaves an impression not of any accomplishment but of something like *style* ("grace"). Some brink is often part of Roach's visionary geography – he stands on a precipice in "Death Does Not"; "steep beneath him sleeps the green sea death" in "Frigate Bird Passing" – but in those early poems his gesture in the face of death is noble. Here it is not:

> Station by station throughout history
> the ground is bloody; the hero's face
> stamped on the woman's napkin's masked in blood. (FR 166)

A whole career falls between the naiveté of "pose and leave pictures there" and this bitter passage. These same lines at least provisionally conclude the argument about the status of the poet. The explicitly political context established in "Hard Drought" discourages any claim of the poet to the role of hero, but while the poem sharply distinguishes the two figures, it ends by identifying a place for the poet within the tale of the hero. Earlier in the poem he is associated only with dreams and prophecies, nothing tangible, but in the end he is Veronica, the chance witness who takes the impression (note the choice of "stamped") of the fall – a nobody, wholly identified with that action. Her name simply means "true icon", "true image", as if her identity begins and ends in this: simply being there, and a moment after wondering what to do with the bloody rag.

Yet in fact believers venerate the veil, not Veronica. The problem of that rag, the artifact, the tangible and enduring impression, is what lingers unresolved in Roach's work. To clarify by exaggerating: his stated aesthetic is of *action*, of Zen brushwork, the brisk single gesture that creates the work. The thing to be treasured is the dependable performer, the poet as a functionary of the tribe, and the thing that gives pleasure is the event, the process of creativity observed, more than the resulting artifact, which thus becomes a kind of evidence of activity rather than its goal. In the late poems, where testifying witness is a central concept (particularly "City Centre '70" and "Verse in August"), the emphasis is squarely on the role of the witness, the act of testifying, not on the verbal form of the testimony or the likelihood of its endurance as an artifact. As the etymology of her name indicates, Veronica is the icon she carries; here again the poet-figure is at once a symbol and an agent of symbolizing. Thus identified with the impression she takes, Veronica *is* what she *witnesses*.

As a critic, Roach remained more preoccupied with the responsibilities of the poet than with the constituents of a poem, and on the evidence of the content of the poems (as opposed to their form) his aesthetic seems quite surprisingly not one of craft, even though with a few exceptions the character of the work itself is highly crafted. Like the Yeats of "Lapis Lazuli", Roach respects the artifact as an embodiment of craft and skill, but strives to accept its fragility, so long as it is not intended to be temporary. What is important is that a poem should be built to last, whether it actually does or not. Indications are that he was more comfortable than we might assume with the aesthetic of the carnival mask, laboured over, centre of imaginative attention for months, then displayed, celebrated when the time is ripe, and at once discarded. Perhaps, finally, we should say that what interests Roach is adornment, the artist decked out in plumage of his own making, rather than the product itself alone.

A tentative conclusion brings the evidence of the poems together with a statement from the *Savacou* debate. Invoking the highly-charged image of a peasant-farmer working his soil, he had written: "Art . . . engages the whole man, the totality of his life and his experience. . . Working the native clay, stone, marble or wood with the native cunning of his love, the craftsman's mind, the grace and strength of his hands, create artifacts that are the very spirit of the tribe." Roach often wrote as if technique were an indistinguishable part of style; if what he thought he was encountering in *Savacou* was the spectre of a writer possessing the sensibility of a poet without the skill, his shock may have been primarily at the discovery of an area for self-doubt hitherto unrecognized. What had supported his writing – perhaps not quite until the end of his life – was a faith that good work deserves to survive, whatever its actual fate, because it is good, and because through what might be called its technical virtue (its "grace") it is capable of preserving the memory of its author (an "impression") as well.

*

Roach's unresolved views of poetry entailed a complex sense of himself, as a poet. He is a witness who takes the impression of some "grace", the spirit of the tribe, and then by his own "cunning, grace, and strength" leaves an impression. There are really three "impressions" here. One is an impression of what he has witnessed, the elusive spirit identified and articulated by passage through his hands. But there is also the mark, more or less enduring, left by the work, and finally the trace of the poet, of his activity, a life spent witnessing and testifying.

"Witness" is a crucial word for Roach in his last years. A witness has two pertinent attributes: he is receptive (he sees something) and he is effusive (he *testifies*). It seems to have been important to Roach's thinking that the testimony is not necessarily verbal, though as a poet his own usually was: We can testify when we simply stand up to be counted. Being there, in the past, we witnessed, being here in the present, we testify. We witness (happen to see) by inadvertent presence, we testify by intentional presence. Like the trees in Woodford Square, at the end Roach is a witness who sees, but is not then called upon to tell, and finds, moreover, that even his mute testimony, his standing there at what was supposed to be the mythic centre of Trinidadian public life, is bypassed. The artist in his carnival plumage is admired by no one, is left feeling foolish. After the death of the village as a cultural matrix, Roach seems to have sought out its successor in good faith, but he seems to have concluded that the only plausible wellspring of an urban culture was precisely the open forum that he now saw fenced and moated away with traffic. The talk, the testimony had been institutionalized, moved indoors out of sight. In the end, Roach sees the poet as a witness only, severed from politics, process, engagement, and he seems to ask (in the last poems) what is there in the present to witness, except defeat? His anxiety about his role is apparent in what are virtually his last published words: "What's all my witness for?"

Roach had begun with a very clear idea of what one was when involved in the act of poetry, as either its author or its subject: heroic, riding the contrary winds. This is of course a private, personal conception of the vocation and its rewards; what justifies it for Roach is that these acts are in the interests of one's community. The poet acts for his nation (his people and place), when he "speaks them to the world". His last published poem, "Verse in August" (1973), is yet another palinode, veering away from his usual practice in several respects. It is composed in non-standard language and in free verse, and here Roach speaks from a position he had shunned through his career, as the poet *of Tobago* in its vital specificity. He expresses the private satisfaction (and struggle) of being a poet, and a sense of his communal subject-matter as the most intimate kind of private property:

> i knew some legendary men
>   i know them still
> they're fast in file on film
>   a thought reanimates them
> whom only my death will bury
> for they're mine, they're mine
> until my body lays me down.

If it is appropriate to read this poem as a testament, Roach's private satisfaction is sure: "The days stand up to bless me as I die". But at the same time his sense of responsibility, of a public trust, has changed. "August" portrays the remembered village again, but in terms of "heroic" individuals, not really as a collective. That political initiative has been abandoned with the failure of the Federation. Here are these dead – the curmudgeon Ben Gordon, the stick-fighter Br'Angas, the fishermen "naked as fish", figures from his peasant youth – vividly present to us even now in a poem that outlives the poet's own cherishing, possessive memory.

"My life began", he writes, "among kind folk \ whose barefoot indigence was whole \ as rocks and springs". Amid the other poems of the last years, in which the peasantry is simply gone, mutated into an urban underclass, "Verse in August" memorializes the village life of his youth in some of the freest verse Roach ever wrote. It stands as a solitary achievement among the published poems, successful perhaps because addressed to Frank Collymore, his associate since the 1940s, who could be depended on to feel at home in the cultural matrix of the poem. Without the support of that sympathy Roach might not have been able to carry the poem beyond its first turn, its rueful acceptance of the fact that he cannot speak his world even to his own children:

> who'll dance my death farewell? . . .
> not my tall sons
> they have not seen nor heard
> that macabre rime of death
> and if they did
>   i could not answer their disdain
> they have inherited another season
>   in this uprooted suburb
>   of folk from villages and slums[.]

Roach speaks in this poem as the poet of Tobago, but the poem is spoken from Trinidad, from Diego Martin, a suburb of sprawling Port of Spain, which is his sons' home, not his. In the course of the poem he reanimates the film of his past, and in the course of so doing, reanimates himself for us while the poem lasts, dancing indeed his own bongo, his "death farewell". The poem ends with its great question unresolved ("is the game won or lost? \ will i know now \ at the breaking bitter last?"), but the question is dramatically posed in the preceding lines, and it is a question not just about the difference between the past and the present, their relative values, but about his personal *passage* from the past to the present. This is how he sets himself before us:

bedded on my dying century
dreaming the century's youth
        in a good place that's gone
        among the folk i loved
while my own death
howls from a mangy dog
haunting these barren streets.

These lines aim to strike a balance not between past and present, but more precisely between present reality and dreamed past. The dog is a touch of realism, one of many wandering the typically desolate streets of the Port-of-Spain suburb where "faces are tight shut". But the dog is of course also figurative, a piece of poetry, and it recalls the imagery of the howling dog in Roach's poem about Tubal Butler, the figure whose failure Roach seems to have regarded as most like his own.

Roach aimed to establish himself, first, I think, as a true poet by the standards of the craft as such. Thus the appeal for him of images that represent the poet as exercising a natural and even an involuntary faculty. In those instances, audience is not an inherent, certainly not a defining feature of the process. Audience, and therefore some acculturation of the poetic impulse, comes when the production of poetry ceases to be regarded as effusive, expressive, only, and becomes communicative. We cannot expect Roach, in black, Protestant, rural Tobago in the 1930s, to be thinking in terms of shamans and griots. But his models, after the brute natural ones, are the least bookish available to him. So he brings together what seem quite antithetical models – I mean the model of the autochthonous bard, the local poet of the local people, and on the other hand the supreme gods of the established literary pantheon: Homer, Dante, Shakespeare, Milton. Yet there is in fact a long tradition of bringing just these things together; it is just those most institutionalized authors who are thought of as "natural" geniuses, Homer and Shakespeare above all. The assumption that the greatest poets are alien creatures from another world is always part of "High Art" cultural thinking; but we must bear in mind that it is also part of the most populist and "grass-roots" views of poetry conceivable. This vatic element of "inspiration" becomes important at the extremes of the spectrum of poetic production; it is not so important – or important at all – in court poetry, coterie poetry, and the like, where the closest we get to such an indefinable essence is a much more domesticated and demystified "wit", and where judgement is primarily on the basis of craft, technique. The "coterie" need not of course be upper-class; rap is only one of the many examples that could be adduced across cultures, and at every level of social status of communities in which the ability to improvise or at least produce poetry – and often fairly formal poetry (limerick, haiku) – is regarded as an elementary social grace – of the same order as embroidery, playing the guitar, telling a story, or holding one's liquor.

In his poetry, he speaks as a West Indian of rural origins for whom literary education (and to some extent any education) was a personal accomplishment achieved against considerable odds. He is one of the few West Indian poets who genuinely resembles Walcott's Shabine, a sailor with "a sound colonial education". The voice was Roach's own, but substantially shaped by two quite different influences: his immediate experience in Tobago and his assimilation of what he and his teachers perceived as the finest models in the language he wrote. Like all West Indians, educated or not, he had a strong sense of the creole continuum and a command of its resources, but that sense comes with a corresponding sensitivity to the difference between written and spoken language. His position on poetic speech is very much at odds with the *Savacou* poets.

"Mother and Son" (1961) testifies that "peasant patois" is "on his tongue" just as intimately as his mother's bread is in his body. But this is almost never the language of his poetry. Despite Roach's intimacy with peasant life, his peasant figures are *seen* from within, but not heard. The exceptions are revealing. Canga Brown speaks "in dialect" – almost "in blackface" – for purposes of characterization and tone, not representation. The diction of the homeless in "Song of the Sleepers-Out" is sadly miscalculated. The village dancer in "The World of Islands" (1962) addresses us directly, but she is idealized, and so is her Standard English speech.

Even so, in his generation of writers, Roach's claim is greatest to legitimately represent his own people – to speak *from* as well as *for* the folk (his praising Lamming for this ability in "Letter to Lamming" is surely intended to reflect upon himself). One of the ironies in "Verse in August" is that the poet's sons, the same age as the writers of *Savacou*, don't know the folkways those poets supposedly value above all else (and, Roach suspects, neither do the poets); Roach himself does know them. Much of the shock in 1970 is his discovered estrangement from the "new" urban folk and his remoteness from the ways in which younger poets were giving speech to them.

Roach is a peasant without a village, just as, after the failure of the federation, he is a poet without a country. He does not reproduce or represent peasant voices; rather, he speaks always as a peasant – with "a sound colonial education". Roach speaks as one of them, and is free to speak his own language, formed by his experience. The view that education – in his case largely self-education – excludes one from membership of the peasantry is another face of the position voiced in the question Roach reproduces with such loathing in "Something Seen": "'Teach niggers Latin to lose good cheap labour?'" Roach created a literary language that could voice compellingly not his individuality or experience but the condition he shares; it is consistent with his goal to shape himself as a poet of the Caribbean – the place, its people, and their passage through an extraordinary stretch of history. It is with no little calculation that he speaks the Queen's own English in his "nigger voice" – a black Yeats.

End Notes

Preface

1. Trinidad and Tobago are two separate and very different islands which now form a single country, officially called "Trinidad and Tobago" but almost invariably referred to as "Trinidad". I follow this common usage except in cases where context does not ensure against ambiguity.
2. For details see Gordon Rohlehr, "A Carrion Time," *Bim* 58 (June 1975), 104.
3. See Wayne Brown's note on Roach's death in Derek Walcott, *Selected Poetry, (London*: Heinemann, 1981), 128-129.
4. See among others Derek Walcott's "The Wind in the Dooryard", *Sea Grapes* (London: Jonathan Cape, 1976), 64-66; Wayne Brown's "For Eric Roach, Drowned," in *Tapia* 4:21 (May 26, 1974); Martin Carter's "On The Death by Drowning of the Poet Eric Roach", in *Poems of Succession* (London: New Beacon, 1977), 109. The most important critical response to Roach's death is Rohlehr, "A Carrion Time", 92-109.
5. V. S. Naipaul, *A Way in the World* (New York: Alfred Knopf, 1994), 108.

Chapter One

1. This irony still reverberates. David Dabydeen and Nana Wilson-Tagoe characterize Roach as a poet of the 1960s (*A Reader's Guide to West Indian and Black British Literature*, 19). They are presumably responding to his visibility in *metropolitan* anthologies of that otherwise unproductive decade.
2. *Verse and Voice* (London: Westerham, 1965), 113.
3. J. Edward Chamberlin, *Come Back to Me My Language*, (Urbana and Chicago: University of Illinois Press, 1993), 104.
4. Walcott, "In Praise of Peasantry," *Sunday Guardian* (July 18, 1965), 9.
5. Yeats's characteristic use of present participles is familiar; the Concordance to his poems lists nearly one and a half pages of instances of the word "being", and virtually every instance is a present participle rather than a noun. Many are well-known – the refrain "beggar to beggar cried, being frenzy-struck", or Leda's "Being so caught up . . ." – but there are about ten unequivocal instances of the peculiar absolute construction imitated here in Roach; e.g. "Chance being at one with Choice" ("Solomon and the Witch"), or "Soul's beauty being most adored" (Meditations in Time of Civil War").
6. William Butler Yeats, *The Collected Poems* (London: Macmillan, 1965), 301. Subsequent citations appear parenthetically.
7. Walcott, "In Praise of Peasantry", 9.
8. Roach's contribution, in lieu of a biographical note, for *The Sun's Eye*, Ed. Anne Walmsley (London: Longman, 1968). 132.
9. Rohlehr, *Pathfinder: Black Awakening in The Arrivants of Edward Kamau Brathwaite* (Tunapuna, Trinidad: Gordon Rohlehr, 1981), 183.
10. It was Anson Gonzalez who first identified "Merton Maloney" as Roach.

11. Scott MacDonald, *Trinidad and Tobago: Democracy and Development in the Caribbean* (New York: Praeger, 1986), 63.
12. Ivar Oxaal, *Black Intellectuals and the Dilemmas of Race and Class in Trinidad* (Cambridge, Mass.: Schenkman, 1982), 64-65.
13. For a selection of work from the early magazines see *From Trinidad: An Anthology of Early West Indian Writing*, Reinhard W. Sander, ed., (London: Hodder and Stoughton, 1978).
14. Gordon Rohlehr, *Calypso and Society in Pre-Independence Trinidad* (Port of Spain: Rohlehr, 1990), 287.
15. See Reinhard W. Sander, *The Trinidad Awakening* (Westport, Conn.: Greenwood Press, 1988), especially Ch 1, "The Background: Trinidad 1919-1938" and Ch. 2, "The Magazines: *Trinidad* and *The Beacon*".
16. Texts of the poems in Sander, *From Trinidad*, 212, 209, 221, respectively.
17. A different poem with the same title appeared in the following issue.
18. Geoffrey H. Hartman, "Blake and the Progress of Poesy" and "Romantic Poetry and the Genius Loci", both in *Beyond Formalism: Literary Essays 1958-1970* (New Haven and London: Yale University Press, 1970).
19. The most familiar example is perhaps H. D. Carberry's "Nature" (*Focus* [1943], 73), which begins, "We have neither Summer nor Winter / Neither Autumn nor Spring. We have instead . . . "
20. "William Butler Yeats," *Trinidad Guardian* (Feb. 5, 1939), 23.
28. A rather hostile reviewer carps about Gomes's use of the word in the *Guardian* (Jan. 29, 1939), 30.
22. See especially the very strange "Poem" of 1949, which longs for the "crumpled ease" of the buried dead.
23. Iëre, meaning "Land of the Hummingbird", is an Amerindian name for Trinidad (not, as a rule, applied to Roach's native Tobago). It may seem "poetical" and quaint in a poem like this, but in judging the tone we need to bear in mind that "Iëre" is used frequently and without irony as a name for Trinidad in calypsos of the period. Thanks to Mary B. Campbell for pointing out that the complex intonations of the term "Eire" in Irish literature and song are closely analogous.
24. For a detailed account see Eric Williams, *History of the People of Trinidad and Tobago* (London: Andre Deutsch, 1964), 233-36.
25. MacDonald, 60.
26. MacDonald, 58.
27. Oxaal, 81.
28. Merton Maloney, "Human Progress", *The Teachers' Herald* 64 (Dec. 1938), 30.
29. *Trinidad Guardian* (Feb. 16, 1939), 13.
30. This is the text of the poem as cited in Rohlehr *Calypso*, 195; It is not included in FR. *Wisden* is the standard annual reference book for cricket.
31. See for context Rohlehr, *Calypso*, 194-200.
32. *Troilus and Criseyde*, V. 1786-92. The immediately following lines in Chaucer might seem especially pertinent to a West Indian poet: "And for there is so great diversity / In English and in writing of our tongue, / So pray I God that

none miswrite thee,/ Nor thee mismeter for default of tongue, / And read whereso thou be, or elles sung, / That thou be understood, God I beseech!" (spelling somewhat modernized in both quotations; for the original see *The Works of Geoffrey Chaucer*, ed. F. N. Robinson [Boston: Houghton Mifflin, 1961], 479).

33. *Trinidad Guardian* (Jan. 29, 1939), 30.
34. MacDonald, 63.
35. *Colonial Office Annual Report on Trinidad & Tobago 1946* (London: H. M. Stationer's Office, 1948), 7.
36. Anson Gonzalez, *Trinidad and Tobago Literature: On the Air* (Port of Spain: The National Cultural Council of Trinidad and Tobago, 1973), 35.
37. Born in Trinidad, Atwell's performance for the servicemen at Piarco marked the beginning of a very successful career playing honky-tonk piano in Britain and later Australia, with several hit recordings on the British charts.
38. The term "grace" seems somewhat mysterious, a bit tangential to the business of this poem; it seems to have implications we are not privy to, and in fact later it emerges as an important term for Roach – and so to a lesser extent does "traffic".
39. V. S. Naipaul, *A Way in the World* (New York: Knopf, 1994), 21.
40. Rohlehr, *Calypso*, 182 and 186.
41. Reinhard W. Sander, "The Thirties and Forties", *West Indian Literature*, ed. Bruce King, (London: Macmillan, 1979), 57 and Sander, *Trinidad Awakening*, 150. For the 1940s see Michael Anthony, "Growing Up With Writing", *Savacou* 2 (1970), 61-66, and remarks by Telemaque in Gonzalez, *On Air*, 36.
42. "West Indies Issue", *Life and Letters* (November, 1948) and *The Poetry of the Negro 1749-1949*, eds. Langston Hughes and Arna Bontemps (Garden City: Doubleday, 1949).
43. *Caribbean Quarterly* 5:3 (1958).
44. Gonzalez, *On Air*, 105.
45. Ramchand mistakenly prints "not be free" in the penultimate line.
46. First published in *Bronze*, (Mandeville, Jamaica: College Press, 1944), but written in 1939, according to Lindo's note in his collection *My Heart Was Singing* (1948).
47. *Sandy Lane and Other Poems*, reprint of 1945 edition (Bridgetown, Barbados: *Bim* magazine, 1985), 1.
48. "Maroon Girl" is one, while "Revelation", and Philip Sherlock's "Jamaican Fisherman" are both formal sonnets with single instances of self-conscious deformation.
49. Ramchand mistakenly prints "*Of* old continents".
50. "Anacaona" was familiar as the name of a very popular rhumba dancer who performed in Port of Spain during the 1930s; Lord Beginner sang a calypso about her in 1935 (Rohlehr, *Calypso*, 292).
51. For the text, Christopher Ricks, *Tennyson* (New York: Macmillan, 1972), 283-286.
52. *Trinidad Guardian* (Feb. 27, 1949), 10; FR prints a later version.

53. Tennyson, relying on Washington Irving's advice that "Anacaona" means "flower of gold" (Ricks, 284), calls her "The golden flower of Hayti" at the end of each of his stanzas.
54. Ricks, 49. Ricks credits William Fredeman as original observer of the importance in Tennyson of "the penultimate moment before the end, which is unrevealed" (111); "Anacaona" is specifically mentioned in conjunction with "innumerable poems by Tennyson in which the final ending is shrouded but magnetic" (50).
55. This is not the case in later versions of the poem.

Chapter Two

1. There was one regional publication which has thus far received little critical attention: the *West Indian Review*, begun in 1934 by Esther Chapman, an Englishwoman resident in Haiti and then Jamaica. The *Review* published the writings of Jamaicans and Haitians, and acknowledged African and North American literary activity. It seems, however, to have been relatively out of touch with the Anglophone Eastern Caribbean.
2. When Telemaque, in the course of introducing Roach's poems on the BBC, referred to Tobago as "the Arcadia of the Caribbean", he was voicing just this vision of the region.
3. Foreword, "A Federation of Ideas," *West Indian Review*, 1:2 (Oct. 1934).
4. On the emergence of this term see Laurence A. Breiner, *An Introduction to West Indian Poetry* (Cambridge: Cambridge University Press, 1998), 89-94.
5. For the role of cricket and of Constantine in particular in the development of West Indian nationhood the classic account is C. L. R. James, *Beyond a Boundary* (London: Hutchinson & Co., 1963).
6. "Meanings", *Savacou* 2 (Sept. 1970), 48-50.
7. Since terms like "peasant" and "folk" are not uncommonly used with glib condescension or even with alienating intent, it should be emphasized that these terms have a very strong positive valence in West Indian discourse at least since World War II. Roach in particular writes of the peasantry as an insider; his routine pronoun is unselfconsciously "we". This is the preferred terminology not only for Roach but for writers as diverse as Derek Walcott, Sam Selvon and Gordon Rohlehr. The positive valences of "folk" are cultural, as they were when the term became prominent in nineteenth century European nationalism. The preference for "peasant" is associated with connotations of dignity and self-possession, contrasted obviously with "slave", and also distinguished from seemingly more neutral terms like "farm worker" or "agricultural labourer" which could be perceived as dehumanising, a reduction of the person to an economic unit.
8. On this development see particularly Brathwaite's *History of the Voice* (London: New Beacon, 1984) and its extensive bibliographies.
9. Baugh, "Introduction", *An Index to Bim*, ed. Reinhard Sander, (Port of Spain: UWI Extra-Mural Studies, 1973), 7. By contrast, *Bim* contributors were not paid except in the very early years, and then only on the order of six-

pence for a poem (Baugh, 17; Cozier, "The Beginnings of *Bim*," *Bim* 48 [1969], 248). The difference is another small reminder of the gap between metropolitan and regional resources.

10. Telemaque's is a story of frustrated promise in its own right. See his comments and tone in a late interview with Anson Gonzalez, and his hope for a collection of his work even then (*Trinidad and Tobago Literature: On Air*, [Port of Spain, Trinidad: National Cultural Council, 1974], 33-40).
11. BBC programme transcript (Aug. 14, 1955), 1 and 3.
12. BBC programme transcript (Aug. 21, 1949), 4.
13. One might wish away the slack and superfluous line following those just quoted, "The rose of hope grows also in my garden", which weakens the otherwise effective stanza it unnecessarily extends. Perhaps, too, the line seems weak because it contains the only independent verb in the whole poem that is not imperative.
14. Dorothy and Bob Hargreaves, *Tropical Trees* (Hawaii: Hargreaves Co., 1965), 25. In Walcott's poem, "The Schooner Flight", Shabine gives a short verse-lecture on the problem of naming these trees. Are they cedar, cypress, casuarina? – "you would have to be colonial to know the difference" (Derek Walcott, *Collected Poems* 1948-1984 [New York: Farrar Straus and Giroux, 1986], 353).
15. My text here is that of the BBC transcript; like some other editors, Ramchand in FR prints "sun" instead of "sea" at this point.
16. Lloyd Brown interprets the weather here quite differently. For him, the trade winds are "the poetic imagination personified"; the force of this reading becomes a bit blurred, however, when he goes on to identify the "poetic imagination" also with "the historical landscape", and with the agency that describes it (*West Indian Poetry* [revised ed., London: Heinemann, 1984], 68-69).
17. Again, the final word is "sea" in the BBC text; "sun" in the alternatives. The overall avoidance of final vowels is managed by an unusual abundance of plurals in final position: out of the total of 59 lines in the poem's three sections (19 + 17 + 23 lines), 15 lines (0 + 7 + 8) end on plural -s.
18. A printing error in FR compounds the confusion. The poem begins on page 55, but the title is misplaced onto the top of page 56, thereby appearing to make an entire poem out of the final three stanzas, and orphaning the first seven.
19. Ramchand mistakenly has "Upon the opening ocean".
20. "The Muse of History", *Is Massa Day Dead?*, ed. Orde Coombs (New York: Doubleday, 1974) 3.

Chapter Three

1. BBC programme transcript (Aug. 21, 1949), 1.
2. Frank Collymore, "The Story of *Bim*", *Bim* 38 (1964), 68. Also Edward Baugh, "Introduction", An Index to *Bim*, ed. Reinhard Sander (Port of Spain: UWI Extra-Mural Studies, 1973), 9 and Jimmy Cozier, "The Beginnings of *Bim*", *Bim* 48 (1969), 245-248.
3. *Bim* 7 (1946), 1.
4. Baugh, "Introduction", 11.
5. These totals are approximate, since the distinction between a poetic sequence and a group of related but independent poems is often arbitrary.
6. The poem, #7 from the Egerton Ms., is widely reprinted, e.g. in *Collected Poems of Thomas Wyatt*, ed. Kenneth Muir (Cambridge, Mass.: Harvard University Press, 1950), 7. In both Roach's and Wyatt's poems the audible contrary message "seize her" complicates the texture.
7. "The Poetry of E. M. Roach: New Perspectives on his Use of Form", *Kyk-over-al* 32 (Dec. 1985), 45.
8. This is the *Bim* version, reprinted in FR. A version in the *Trinidad Guardian* differs in several details.
9. Of the eight only the first and last are at all out of the ordinary: tracery, sanctity, skeleton, tomorrow, recurrent, horizons, sunflowers, orisons.
10. The matter of the resemblance and difference between fountain and sculpture will be taken up more extensively apropos of "Pray that the Poem Out of Nowhere Come" in Chapter 9.
11. It is noteworthy that the poem's only instance of "I" occurs within this simile.
12. There is a closely related precursor of this imagery in the passage from "Colour" noted in Chapter 1: "Come poet, come, \ Up through a chasm of earth, \ Up from that darkness \ Where life sleeps and dreams, \ And breathes her great rare dreams, \ Through golden corridors, \ Whence their splendours come, \ As poets among men."
13. Edward Brathwaite, "Sir Galahad and the Islands", *Roots* (Ann Arbor: University of Michigan Press, 1993), 7.
14. Edward Brathwaite, "Timehri", *Is Massa Day Dead?*, Orde Coombs ed., (Garden City: Doubleday, 1974), 33-34.

Chapter Four

1. Roach's brother Peter is probably being referred to in this description of fishermen bringing in their nets from "At Grafton Bay" (1954): "rope-tough\ sinews, Peter's and all, hauling at ropes.\ For a seacatch of Christ, for the meal of a miracle" (FR 114). Recognizing the name makes the poem more anecdotal, and might add a touch of additional pathos to the elegy, but the personal reference is characteristically masked by the Christological imagery of the whole passage, a context which strongly directs the reader to identify Peter with the patron of fishermen (in fact, St. Peter's Day is celebrated as a fisherman's festival in this part of Tobago).

2. Derek Walcott, "What the Twilight Says", *Dream on Monkey Mountain and Other Plays* (New York: Farrar, Straus and Giroux, 1970); "Leaving School", *London Magazine* 5:6 (Sept 1965), 4-14.
3. Roger D. Abrahams, *The Man-Of-Words in the West Indies* (Baltimore: Johns Hopkins University Press, 1983); on Tobago see especially 4-10, 60-66.
4. Eric Roach, "Growing Up in Tobago", *David Frost Introduces Trinidad and Tobago*, eds. Michael Anthony and Andrew Carr (London: Andre Deutsch, 1973), 154.
5. Frost, 152, 157.
6. Frost, 157.
7. Frost, 157.
8. Especially in *The Anxiety of Influence*, (New York: Oxford University Press, 1973), and *A Map of Misprision* (New York: Oxford University Press, 1975).
9. Lloyd Brown, *West Indian Poetry*, second edition (London: Heinemann, 1984), 69.
10. Frost, 157.
11. See Edward Brathwaite, "Houses: A Note on West Indian Literature", *First World* 1 (March-April, 1977), 46-49.
12. *The Sun's Eye*, ed. Anne Walmsley (London: Longmans, 1968), 132.
13. To some extent the premise of this poem is anticipated in "Sounds Live" (*Trinidad Guardian* [Nov. 14, 1948], 10), which proposes that, since "sounds live eternally", an old house is haunted by the sounds of shoes and clothing, even the sounds of a kiss. To readers of Yeats, "The Old House" might call to mind the ghostly house of Purgatory.
14 My text is *Bim* 15 (Dec 1951), 181. This version does not appear in FR.
15. Frost, 151-2.
16. The single-spaced ellipsis is Roach's own. The version of this poem in *Caribbean Quarterly* (1958), adopted also in *Caribbean Poetry Now* (1984), has the following variants in this passage, which clarify the intended meaning: "you crawl up \ Your broken stairs like Golgotha, and all the dead \ Beckon your dying bones..... \\ I do not mourn, but all my love \ Praise life's continuity the endless year."
17. The Jamaican critic John Figueroa, praising poetry which gives the appearance of coming easily precisely as a result of hard work put into the poem, cites "To My Mother" as his example, with this comment: "E. M. Roach of Tobago, the authentic and outstanding voice of a certain kind of West Indian experience, especially the peasant experience, clearly works his verse even as his mother worked the dough, and as his peasant people work the harsh soil under the casuarinas that sing in the Trades" (in that last clause Figueroa alludes to the companion-poem "Homestead") ["Introduction", *Caribbean Voices* (London: Evans Brothers, 1970), vol. 2, 5].
18. Frost, 152.
19. It is noteworthy that the slightly earlier invocation of poets and painters in "Colour" (1947) sounds nothing like Yeats.
20. Writing in 1957, presumably on the basis of [A], Edward Brathwaite considered that "Roach's values are rural values . . . supported in the poem, . . .

with overtones of Wordsworth's Old Man symbol – a deployment, nicely executed, which gives the poem depth and power and establishes its place in the (Romantic) tradition" ("Sir Galahad and the Islands", *Roots* [Ann Arbor: Univ. of Michigan, 1993], 15). When Brathwaite comments on the [C] text more than a decade later – though like other critics he seems unaware of the extent to which the text has changed – his emphasis on the presence of "an African ancestor" is illuminating but overspecific, a reflection of cultural politics circa 1968 that ignores the clear universalizing intent of the fifth stanza ("men about their fields, world over" [C]). See Brathwaite's entry for "Roach" in *Contemporary Poets of the English Language*, ed. Rosalie Murphy (Chicago / London: St. James Press, 1970), 926-7.

21. The single-spaced ellipsis is Roach's own; it appears only in the two *Caribbean Quarterly* printings and is omitted by Ramchand.
22. Roach's juxtaposition of French "paysan" and Italian "paisano" plays a role in the universalizing drift of the passage; version [C] (in *The Sun's Eye*) introduces the misleading spelling "paisan, paisano . . ." which has been perpetuated in printings that derive from [C], and unfortunately also in FR.
23. A more explicit expression of the worry, involving the same peculiar use of "good", occurs in these lines from the contemporaneous "Letter to Lamming": "Our islands still are greener than we know them, . . . / Our ranting politicians pour foul potions / Poisoning the innocent good."
24. M. H. Abrams, *Natural Supernaturalism* (New York: W. W. Norton, 1971).
25. *The Sun's Eye*, 132; this is the autobiographical note accompanying "Homestead" [C].
26. Frost, 150.
27. Brathwaite, "Caribbean Man in Space and Time", *Savacou* 11/12 (1974), 1-11.

Chapter Five

1. Walcott has written at length about his preoccupation during the 1950s with identifying suitably West Indian protagonist figures in his essay "Meanings", Savacou 2 (1970), 45-51.
2. Derek Walcott, "What the Twilight Says", *Dream on Monkey Mountain and Other Plays* (New York: Farrar Straus and Giroux, 1970), 14.
3. "What the Twilight Says", 13.
4. "A Tear for Toussaint" is mainly concerned with contrasting Toussaint's ideals with the perversion of his revolution at the hands of his successors, but conclusive discussion is impossible because of a serious textual problem. The page containing the last part of the poem is missing from the photocopy of the BBC transcript preserved at the University of the West Indies; as a result, the final eight lines printed in FR come from a poem by Telemaque, which happened to be read next on the programme.
5. The final poem of the trilogy, "A Tear for Toussaint", reiterates this idea: "Their wild fires are ashes \ Scattered by time's wrath". Was Roach aware that the centrepiece of Christophe's coat of arms was a crowned phoenix with the

motto "I rise from my ashes" (Alejo Carpentier, *The Kingdom of This World* [New York: Collier, 1970], 146)?

6. Ramchand has "he hurled" – a mistranscription.
7. For accessible general accounts of Damballa, see Maya Deren, *The Voodoo Gods* (St Albans, Herts: Paladin, 1975), 113-114 and Alfred Metraux, *Voodoo* (London: Sphere Books, 1974), 106f.
8. Line 9 – "the serpent laughed" – connects with the much later poem "Hard Drought", for which Roach seems to have considered "Damballa laughed" as an alternative title.
9. See for example the poems "Wake", "Shepherd", "Legba", in Kamau Brathwaite, *The Arrivants* (London: Oxford University Press, 1973).
10. Metraux, 106.
11. Roach presumably would have known about both from C. L. R. James's *The Black Jacobins* (New York: Vintage, 1963).
12. See particularly George Lamming, "Caribbean Literature; The Black Rock of Africa", *African Forum* 1 (Spring 1966), 38-40; Edward Brathwaite, "Sir Galahad and the Islands", (*Roots* [Ann Arbor: University of Michigan Press, 1993], 18); Sandra Paquet, "The Fifties", in *West Indian Literature*, ed. Bruce King, second edition (London: Macmillan, 1995), 76-77.
13. There is a closely related idea in "Men" (1952), where Roach writes that the bones of West Indian peasants "were stones to an infamous house \ that time indignant broke \ from its clay foundations."
14. *Bim* 24 (Jan. - June, 1957), 223.
15. *The Black Jacobins*, 402.
16. That is how Gordon Rohlehr reads the entire poem: "Roach in considering several generations of Black heavyweight champions sees in their strength, courage and excellence the outward and visible sign of all the qualities of human excellence which have grown and continually fulfilled themselves by attacking the barriers of prejudice" ("Songs of the Skeleton", *My Strangled City and Other Essays* [Port of Spain: Longman Trinidad, 1992], 282).
17. Lamming, "Black Rock", 39-40. Subsequent quotations from Lamming in this section will be identified by page numbers in the text.
18. Apropos of "seam", it is a curiosity worth noting that the word "roach" is a term-of-art in mining for a vein or seam of coal [OED]. The poet was probably unaware of this convergence of surname and obsessive theme – Roach has almost no taste for obscure meanings or arcane words (with rare exceptions like "aphonous" and "annelid"), and does not seem to have been much of a browser in dictionaries.
19. *The Penguin Book of Caribbean Verse in English*, ed. Paula Burnett (Harmondsworth: Penguin, 1986), 407.
20. The point of the third stanza, that "the slave ships could not . . . shrivel up our hearts, but left love thundering to this running man", provides the strongest indication that the subject of the poem is specifically Keino, still recognized as it were despite the deracination of the West Indian observer. It would make sense, too, that he is animated by "the blood . . . we lost". If "he" is a twentieth-century African runner, however, it is hardly plausible (without

great interpretive ingenuity) that he would somehow be in danger of becoming a scarecrow in the canes.

21. For these details I rely on accounts of the event compiled by Michael Anthony (*Profile Trinidad* [London: Macmillan Caribbean, 1975], 107-111) and Kim Johnson (*Insight Guide: Trinidad and Tobago* [Singapore: APA Productions, 1987], 28).
22. Derek Walcott, "What the Twilight Says", 20.
23. *Caribbean Quarterly* 4:2 (1955), 167-8.
24. Michael Hughes, *A Companion to West Indian Literature* (London: Collins, 1979), 107.
25. The expression has been made familiar and fully elucidated in Henry Louis Gates, Jr., *The Signifying Monkey: A Theory of African-American Literary Criticism* (New York: Oxford Univ. Press, 1988).
26. Maureen Warner Lewis, *Guinea's Other Suns: The African Dynamic in Trinidad Culture* (Dover, Massachusetts: The Majority Press, 1991), 16 and 183.
27. Scott MacDonald, *Trinidad and Tobago: Democracy and Development in the Caribbean* (New York, Praeger, 1982), 51.
28. Ivar Oxaal, *Black Intellectuals and the Dilemmas of Race and Class in Trinidad* (Cambridge, Mass.: Schenkman, 1982), 107.
29. For "clay" see "Daaga", "The Old House", "In Mango Shade", "Mother and Son" and the autobiographical essay "Growing Up in Tobago", *David Frost Introduces Trinidad and Tobago*, eds. Michael Anthony and Andrew Carr (London: Andre Deutsch, 1973).
30. Report of Daaga's court martial in *Port of Spain Gazette*, as quoted by Michael Anthony, *Profile*, 110.
31. "The Old House", *Bim* 15 (June 1951): 181-2.
32. BBC programme transcript (July 10, 1955), 5.
33. Except where otherwise noted, in this discussion I will be quoting from the later version of the poem – "Poem (Pray that the Poem Come Out of the Dark)", *Kyk-over-al* 22 (1957), 54-5 – since it is not included in FR.
34. BBC programme transcript, 5.
35. The earlier version makes Roach's meaning clearer. The pronoun "her" refers to the mother, figured here as "dark desire", while "she" refers to the descendant who is the subject of the poem: " . . . a dark torrid passion pierced his heart \ While dark flame whirled among the jungled drums: \ Their seed was flung on islands under Cancer" ("Pray that the Poem Out of Nowhere Come").
36. We have already seen how Roach in "A Lover Speaks" (1948) declares a preference for native blackness over "all legend beauty" (including explicitly Aphrodite and Isolde) but then cannot resist one last classical allusion ("Naiad").
37. My text is that of the BBC program transcript (March 14, 1954); the poem is not included in FR.
38. Derek Walcott, "The Muse of History", *Is Massa Day Dead?*, ed. Orde Coombs (New York: Doubleday, 1974), 1-27.
39. "Adapting from Fanon, we might use the phrase 'terrified consciousness' to

suggest the White minority's sensations of shock and disorientation as a massive and smouldering Black population is released into an awareness of its power" – Kenneth Ramchand, *The West Indian Novel and its Background* (London: Faber and Faber, 1970), 225.

40. "Black Rock", 34-38.
41. Considering the subject and Roach's earlier habits, the absence of Yeats here – from the list of fools for love as from the diction and import of the closing section – is surprising.
42. *Caribbean Voices*, ed. John Figueroa (London: Evans Brothers, 1970), vol. 1, 63.
43. Judging from the syntactical parallelisms which are so much a feature of this poem's style, the first "should" in that quotation probably has the force of "had better".
44. The likelihood of homology between constructions of race and of gender underlying Roach's work is strengthened by the remarkable parallel between this passage and the following lines, from another unpublished poem, "Between Two Lives": "Africa's a slavish bitch, \ a trusting slut lascivious Europe raped; \ in dreams I fondle her with love, \ in sweating noons \ I stare at her with hatred and contempt" (FR, 177).
45. FR, 20.

Chapter Six

1. Roach's hopes are reflected in this statement from the protagonist of an unpublished autobiographical novel by staunch Federationist Phyllis Allfrey of Dominica: "I did believe that the quavering little Federation... would surpass in its capacity to blend in harmony and beat down the follies of prejudice, the rancours of historical injustice, and the stale false doctrine of race superiority, any other land." Quoted in Elaine Campbell, "'In the Cabinet': A Novelistic Rendition of Federation Politics", *Ariel* 17:4 (1986) 117-125, 121.
2. The work of two poets from St. Vincent, Daniel Williams and Owen Campbell, has nearly dropped out of sight, but during the 1950s both were included in BBC broadcasts and in the regional anthologies. The attitudes and strategies that characterize such poems as Williams's "Song of the Peasant" and "Over Here" or Campbell's "This Land", "The Washer Women", and "We" provide an excellent background against which to measure Roach's achievement.
3. Lloyd W. Brown, *West Indian Poetry* (Boston: Twayne, 1978), 77.
4. *Bim* 10 (1949), 110; broadcast on the BBC in 1949; written in 1947, according to *The Poems of Cecil Herbert*, ed. Danielle Gianetti (Port of Spain: The College Press, n.d. [1979?]), 28.
5. One finds "tragic ferment" in "The Fighters", "our tragic memory of tears" in "Reed for my Rime", the "tragic" sea-born goddess in "Lady by the Sea", the "tragic stands of trees" in "Homestead", the "empty tragedy" of "At Grafton Bay".

6. The handling of gender in this poem is consistent with the findings of the previous chapter. The initial sight of actual women is immediately deflected into a memory about men, and the poem's attention does not return to the women labouring in the field, nor is there any explicit recognition that they now carry the same burden of indignities.
7. Eric Williams quotes two different instances of planters expressing substantially this same sentiment (though in more civil diction) from public testimony before a committee of the Legislative Council as late as 1926 (*History of the People of Trinidad and Tobago* [London: Andre Deutsch, 1964], 212-214). As a private sentiment it no doubt still persists.
8. E. M. Roach, "A Type Not Found in All Generations", *Trinidad Guardian* (July 14, 1971), 8.
9. The term gains additional resonance in the Anglophone Caribbean, where "tares" is usually homonymous with the noun "tears".
10. "Despite Ancestral Rape" was revised and retitled "For the Peasant People of the Islands" two years later (1955). The revision has shorter lines and more regular form, but makes generally the same observations about the struggle for life against the elements.
11. BBC programme transcript (Aug. 14, 1955), 8.
12. This line is deleted (presumably by accident) in FR.
13. Cecil Herbert was 29 at the time Roach broadcast this poem; after his demobilization he had been active in writers' groups in Port of Spain, but he seems to have virtually stopped writing in 1949, perhaps in conjunction with the beginning of his professional life as a surveyor. It is not clear whether Gianetti attempted to collect all of Herbert's poetry in *The Poems of Cecil Herbert*, but its proportions indicate that Roach's advice was not taken: there are 20 poems written between 1946 and 1948, only 2 between 1948 and 1952, the year a booklet of his poems was published in A. J. Seymour's Miniature Poets series in Guyana, and only another two (one of which Gianetti calls a "fragment") between 1952 and 1974.
14. Roach would have heard this very poem read over BBC by Lamming (according to the BBC transcript of the broadcast, April 13, 1952). This would have given special resonance to the line "my brother's is an echo's voice". His brother poet is not only an alter ego but an actual echo, bouncing back Roach's words in the accents of a different island.
15. "Invented only in 1895, radio made it possible to bypass print and summon into being an aural representation of the imagined community where the printed page scarcely penetrated. Its role . . . generally in mid-twentieth-century nationalisms, has been much underestimated and understudied." Benedict Anderson, *Imagined Communities* (London: Verso, revised ed. 1991), 54.
16. BBC programme transcript (March 14. 1954).
17. Ramchand unaccountably inserts "my" after "take".
18. It is noteworthy that he writes "who" rather than "what". This is the only hint of another person in the poem, and under the circumstances the personal pronoun seems to suggest slavery or erotic possession.
19. The pronoun here is problematic in a way characteristic of Roach through-

out his career. The "I" of "If I go out as I came in . . ." is a trans-historical person, one who made the Middle Passage. But in the rest of the sentence "I" can only refer to the specific person of the poet.

20. *The Sun's Eye*, ed. Anne Walmsley (London: Longman, 1968), 132.
21. This is very similar to the language in which the "catholic love" of the creole Cipriani is praised, in "For A. A. Cipriani" (1959).
22. In three of those five instances, however, it was printed in a truncated version ending abruptly with line 28, at a point where the argument is about to return to the main theme from a digression.
23. Kenneth Ramchand, "Introduction", E. M. Roach, *The Flowering Rock* (Leeds: Peepal Tree, 1992), 16.
24. I am grateful to Steven Goodman for this formulation.
25. Walcott seems to have been thinking of "Archipelago" when he said of Roach that, "Whenever he 'addresses' himself to history, to the bitter memory of race, the welter of symbols becomes inchoate, the rage is not purged" ("In Praise of Peasantry: The Poetry of Eric Roach", *Sunday Guardian* [July 18, 1965], 9). When Cheryl Williams in her analysis of "Archipelago" writes that Roach "moves on to argue that there is a possibility for change" she immediately begins talking about "The Fighters" ("Eric Roach's Poetry – Part I", *Tapia* [April 28, 1974], 9).
26. *You Better Believe It: Black Verse in English*, Paul Breman, ed. (Harmondsworth: Penguin, 1973), 156.
27. R. J. Owens, "West Indian Poetry", *Caribbean Quarterly* 7:3 (Dec. 1961), 124.
28. For background see Daniel Crowley, "The Midnight Robbers", *Caribbean Quarterly* 4:3&4 (March and June 1956), 263-274.
29. *Voiceprint: An Anthology of Oral and Related Poetry from the Caribbean*, eds. Stewart Brown, Mervyn Morris and Gordon Rohlehr (London: Longman, 1989), 202.
30. Gordon Rohlehr, *Calypso and Society in Pre-Independence Trinidad* (Port of Spain: Gordon Rohlehr, 1990), 57-68.
31. Thanks to Jeremy Poynting for pointing out the several specific affinities between "Archipelago" and Martin Carter's "I Come from the Nigger Yard". A detailed study of the relationships between these two poets would be very rewarding.
32. Lloyd Brown, *West Indian Poetry*, 72.
33. O. R. Dathorne, "Africa in the Literature of the West Indies", *Journal of Commonwealth Literature* 1 (Sept., 1965), 108.
34. Cheryl Williams is insightful on the link between this ambivalence about Africa and Roach's aesthetic ambivalence, "Eric Roach's Poetry: Part II", *Tapia* (May 5, 1974), 7.

Chapter Seven

1. Scott MacDonald, *Trinidad and Tobago: Democracy and Development in the Caribbean* (New York: Praeger, 1986), 125.

2. Ivar Oxaal, *Black Intellectuals and the Dilemmas of Race and Class in Trinidad* (Cambridge, Mass.: Schenkman, 1982), 133.
3. MacDonald, 128.
4. Roach did not himself participate in the festival, but as it happens his performance of this poem on the Caedmon LP "Poets of the West Indies" (TC 1379; 1971) appears to be the only recording of his own reading of his work.
5. *Verse and Voice* (London: Westerham, 1965), 38.
6. Anne Walmsley, *The Caribbean Artists Movement: 1966-1972* (London: New Beacon, 1992), 60.
7. Holder's account of a West Indian crowd listening to the broadcast of a Walcott play is perhaps the most famous instance (*Bim* 14 [June 1951], 142).
8. *Verse and Voice*, 11.
9. Lloyd Brown, *West Indian Poetry*, revised edition, (London: Heinemann, 1984), 79. Brown's interpretation seems to move too far beyond what the text actually presents when he goes on to write in the same place that the poem "notes the calypso as the manifestation of a will to create form and life in the midst of discordance and decay. . . . [T]he calypsonian's art resembles and re-enacts that intellectual and spiritual process which enables the West Indian to reclaim a vital identity and an identifiable culture from the history of the Middle Passage. . . . [T]he calypsonian's art is identical to the poetic imagination itself".
10. The spelling "rime" perhaps calls up associations with frost; but Roach uses this spelling elsewhere (earlier in this same poem, and in the contemporaneous "Fugue for Federation") with no such intention.

Chapter Eight

1. The phrase is from "City Centre '70". On the general subject see Edward Baugh, "The West Indian Writer and His Quarrel with History", *Tapia* 7:8 (Feb. 20, 1977), 6-7 and 7:9 (Feb. 27, 1977), 6-7 & 11. Baugh however is concerned chiefly with Walcott and makes no mention of Roach.
2. *The Sun's Eye*, Anne Walmsley, ed. (London: Longman, 1968), 118.
3. The centrality of this mutation of imagery by which fountains give way to floods is apparent in Roach's posthumously published autobiographical sketch, where the theme of a world changed for the worse, dominant in the late poems, is expressed in the image of tidal movement from a morass: "Later I came to regard my journey [from his village to high school in Scarborough] as symbolic of the whole tidal movement of the Caribbean from its nineteenth-century morass of illiteracy, servitude, poverty and folk customs into the glittering, heartless, murderous menage of twentieth-century western civilization" ("Growing Up in Tobago," *David Frost Introduces Trinidad and Tobago* [London: Andre Deutsch, 1975], 157). Apart from its relation to all the "flood of history" images (the flood taking over the role of the buffeting wind in the early work), this passage particularly recalls the imagery of "flood" and "muddy shoal" in "Ballad for Tubal Butler",
4. The following account of events derives primarily from Scott MacDonald,

Trinidad and Tobago: Democracy and Development in the Caribbean (New York: Praeger, 1986) and Ivar Oxaal, *Black Intellectuals and the Dilemma of Race and Class in Trinidad* (Cambridge, Mass.: Schenkman, 1982). Oxaal offers a chronology and a narrative of the events with extensive quotation from speeches, pamphlets, fugitive publications (213-233), and a "mini-reader" of writings by participants (251-273). For a political analysis based on a narrative derived from contemporaneous accounts, see Herman L. Bennett, "The Challenge to the Post-Colonial State: A Case Study of the February Revolution in Trinidad", in *The Modern Caribbean*, eds. F. W. Knight and Colin A. Parker (Chapel Hill: University of North Carolina Press, 1989), 129-146.

5. MacDonald, 173.
6. See Gordon Rohlehr, "My Strangled City: Poetry in Trinidad 1964-1975", *Caliban* 2:1 (1976), 108-9.
7. "Poggo" is the local Tobagonian name for the yellowtail cornbird (Paula Burnett *Penguin Book of Caribbean Verse* [Harmondsworth: Penguin, 1986], 407).
8. In July 1955, during the course of series of lectures sponsored by PEM (the People's Educational Movement) in the Square and elsewhere on the island, Williams hit upon the idea of founding the "University of Woodford Square" in his lecture "Constitution Reform in Trinidad and Tobago": "With a bandstand, a microphone, a large audience in slacks and hot shirts, a topical subject for discussion, the open air and a beautifully tropical night, we have all the essentials of a university" (Oxaal, 113).
9. That Roach's emotional investment in the sacred precinct of the Square was not idiosyncratic is corroborated by V. S. Naipaul's oblique account of these days in the novel *A Way in the World* (New York: Alfred Knopf, 1994), where he refers several times to widespread reverence among Trinidadians for "the sacrament of the square" (33-38).
10. Rohlehr, "Strangled City", 109.
11. There are two different versions of this poem, one in *Studio Arts Group* 1:3 (Dec. 1970), 41, the other in *New Writing in the Caribbean*, ed. A. J. Seymour (Georgetown: Guyana Lithographic, 1972), 88-89. Unless otherwise identified, quotations are from the 1972 text, the version published by Ramchand and generally preferable when the two versions are similar.
12. Rohlehr analyzes the revision of "City Centre" as a reflection of Roach's negative response to the aftermath of 1970 ("Strangled City", 109-10).
13. It is pertinent to this survey of Roach's thinking about history that natural cycles are frequently invoked in his poems about the peasantry (for example "February", "March Trades", and "At Grafton Bay") and in his poems about death (e.g. "The White Coffin", "To My Mother", "He Juggles Images", "She Never Dies"). But there is no real evidence that Roach developed this idea about nature at all systematically in relation to his conception of the mechanisms of history.
14. The poem appeared very obscurely in a publication so ephemeral that there is confusion even about its title. The correct title is *The Black I* ("I" a pronoun, not a numeral), and the correct date is March, 1972. FR gives the title incorrectly as *The Black*, with a date of 1970 in the table of sources (215),

and 1972 at the end of the poem itself (149). Roach's subtitle says that the poem was written "on the occasion of his [M. L. King's] death", which would suggest much earlier composition, in 1968 or perhaps 1969.

15. Max Farquhar in the *Trinidad Guardian* (Feb 9, 1956), 2, quoted in Scott MacDonald, *Trinidad and Tobago: Democracy and Development in the Caribbean* (New York: Praeger, 1986), 56.
16. The high-handedness of Williams' political practice after 1970 is documented in Carl D. Parris, "Personalization of Power in an Elected Government: Eric Williams and Trinidad and Tobago, 1973-81", *Journal of Interamerican Studies and World Affairs* 25 (May 1983), 171-99.
17. Cheryl Williams, "Eric Roach's Poetry (Part II)", *Tapia* 4:18 (May 5, 1974), 6.
18. Ishmael Reed's "Dualism: in ralph ellison's invisible man", a poem written in parallel political circumstances in the United States, concludes "i am inside of \ history. its \ hungrier than i \ thot" (*Conjure: Selected Poems* 1963-1970 [Amherst, Mass.: Univ. of Massachusetts Press, 1972], 50).
19. A passage in "Hard Drought" seems to invert the conception: "I've eaten so much history that I belch \ boloms of years to come." But the humour is sardonic. The speaker has been swept along and finally victimized by political events; he may be construed as eating history in the same sense that a drowned man can be said to have drunk himself to death.
20. "Poetry of the Forties, Part 3: 'The Dilemma'", *Sunday Guardian* (Oct. 4, 1970), 11.
21. As Rohlehr suggests in "Blues for Eric Roach", *Tapia* 4:17 (April, 1974), 2.
22. V. S. Naipaul speaks of the Trinidadians' "strange time sense" circa 1960: "The England of 1914 was the England of yesterday; the Trinidad of 1914 belonged to the dark ages" (*Middle Passage* [Harmondsworth: Penguin, 1969], 45).
23. "Strangled City", 107.
24. Kamau Brathwaite, "Sir Galahad and the Islands", *Roots* (Ann Arbor: University of Michigan Press, 1993), 18.

Chapter Nine

1. On the debate see Laurence A. Breiner, "How to Behave on Paper", *Journal of West Indian Literature* 6:1 (July 1993) 1-10.
2. For chronicles of this period, see Edward Brathwaite, "Love Axe/l: Developing a Caribbean Aesthetic 1962-1974", in *Reading Black: Essays in the Criticism of African, Caribbean, and Black American Literature*, ed. Houston A. Baker, Jr. (Ithaca: Cornell Univ. Press, 1976), 20-36 and Gordon Rohlehr, "My Strangled City: Poetry in Trinidad 1964-1975", *Caliban* 2:1 (1976), 50-122. For an illuminating chronological list of the notable articles appearing in these years see Jeannette B. Allis, *West Indian Literature: An Index to Criticism*, 1930-1975 (Boston: G. K. Hall and Co., 1981), 329-49.
3. Arthur Drayton, as quoted in Edward Brathwaite, "Foreward", *Savacou* 3/4 (March, 1971), 5.
4. Eric Roach, "A Type Not Found in All Generations", *Trinidad Guardian* (July 14, 1971), 6.

5. "The miracle is . . . that despite the racial/colour/class biases and stereotypes on which our society is built, explorations of it, by West Indians, have on the whole, been conducted in the most humane and generous context imaginable. This is because the dream of wholeness has (so far) dominated over the fragments, the pebbles, the divided islands of the selves" (Brathwaite, "Foreward", 6).
6. Roach, "A Type Not Found in All Generations", 8.
7. Wayne Brown, "Poetry of the Forties, Part 5: The Mulatto Question", *Sunday Guardian* (Oct. 11, 1970), 11; George Lamming, "Caribbean Literature: The Black Rock of Africa", *African Forum* 1:4 (1966), 32-52; Edward Brathwaite, "Sir Galahad and the Islands", *Bim* 25 (1957), 8-16.
8. R. J. Owens, "West Indian Poetry", *Caribbean Quarterly* 7:3 (Dec. 1961), 120-127. Cheryl Williams notes that "to the end Roach remains a poet of blackness, oppression, etc.; the same aspects he so summarily dismissed in his younger colleagues", and illustrates the resemblance between Roach's objection to King and Jerry in 1971 and Walcott's critique of Roach himself in 1965 ("Eric Roach's Poetry: Part I", *Tapia* 4:17 [April 28, 1974], 3-4, 9).
9. Roach, "A Type Not Found in All Generations", 6.
10. Roger McTair, "A Critic Criticized", *Trinidad Guardian* (Aug. 18, 1971), 12. This critique is developed even by Roach's most sympathetic readers, including Gordon Rohlehr (especially in "A Carrion Time", *Bim* 58 [June 1975], 92-109) and Cheryl Williams: "in the debate Roach had confused his desire for craft (a true mark of the poet) by locating that craft solely in the European tradition" ("Eric Roach's Poetry: Part II", *Tapia* 4:18 [May 5, 1974], 7). Gordon Rohlehr sensibly emphasizes the need for plural standards to respect generational and even (sub-)cultural differences within the region, in what is still the most substantial review of the anthology and of the reaction to it, "West Indian Poetry: Some Problems of Assessment", *Bim* 54 (1972), 80-88 and 55 (1972), 134-44.
11. Notes to "The Wind in the Dooryard" in Derek Walcott, *Selected Poetry*, ed. Wayne Brown (London: Heinemann, 1981), 129.
12. Eric Roach, "Conflict of West Indian Poetry: Tribe Boys vs. Afro-Saxons", Trinidad *Guardian* (Jan. 12, 1973), 4. Kamau Brathwaite has documented the prominence of the term "Afro-Saxon" in the work of the New World group during the 1960s, and identified its earliest printed occurrence in *New World Quarterly* (March 1963), 7 (*Contradictory Omens* [Mona: Savacou Publications, 1974], 73).
13. This is most explicit in "Poem for this Day", *Tapia* 2:11 (Dec. 17, 1972), 14.
14. See Gordon Rohlehr's discussion of this point in "My Strangled City," 110-12.
15. The throwaway aesthetic of carnival embodies its tradition in the memories of its participants and so gives them control over the tradition. But when carnival masks begin to be preserved in a museum (out of the desire to articulate a heritage), a kind of secondary authority necessarily grows up; the preserved relics begin to assert themselves as standards. The making of the museum need not in itself affect the aesthetic, which can still continue as if all the masks were discarded every season. But as in any clash between scribal

and oral cultures, the living tradition embodied in individual memories and skills becomes vulnerable to the authority of history embodied in the museum of its own past inventions.

16. On the wind harp see Erika von Erhardt-Siebold, "Some Inventions of the Pre-Romantic Period and their Influence upon Literature", *Englische Studien* 66 (1931-2), 347-63.
17 For example, these are the implicit parallels for the poet in "The World on Islands", *Bim* 34 (1962), 81.
18. "Poem (Pray That the Poem out of Nowhere Come)", *Bim* 19 (1953), 179. A later version of this poem introduces more of Roach's most familiar imagery: "She is the dancer in dreams, the grace in the tides, / The flower of foam that gleamed at Paphos, goddess, / Goddess, eternally woman, legend and living" [my emphasis]. "Poem (Pray that the Poem Come Out of the Dark)", *Kyk-over-al* 22 (1957), 54-5.
19. In "For A. A. Cipriani" (1959) there is a similar contrast between the energetic politician and his rigid memorial; the description in "City Centre '70" of the trees as "statued living in eternity" enacts the same interplay of burgeoning nature and static art.
20. See Gordon Rohlehr, "Blues for Eric Roach", *Tapia* 4:17 (April, 1974), 2.

A Note on the Text of the Poems

As a rule, Roach's poetry is cited from the only collection of the poetry, that edited by Kenneth Ramchand (with the assistance of Danielle Gianetti): E. M. Roach, *The Flowering Rock: Collected Poems 1938-1974* (Peepal Tree Press, 1992).

Citations of this edition appear in my text in the form "FR plus page number."

Ramchand's is an invaluable work, but it does not pretend to be a critical edition, and a number of poems or variants of poems are not included in the collection for one reason or another. This present book in turn is not a bibliographic study, but in the discussions of individual poems I have identified and sometimes cited alternative sources. Apart from periodicals the most important source is the transcripts of the BBC "Caribbean Voices" programmes, photocopies of which are preserved in the libraries of the University of the West Indies. In quotations from the poetry I have made an effort to correct any errors of which I am aware. Since most of Roach's poems were published only once, I have silently restored the punctuation of the original publication where Ramchand's divergence from it seems unjustified and perhaps inadvertent (many of the sources at his disposal are poor photocopies of typescripts). In cases where Ramchand is plainly correcting a typesetter's error, I have accepted his emendation – again, without comment. On any more substantive points my departures from Ramchand are explained in a note.

BIBLIOGRAPHY

[A comprehensive bibliography of Roach's writings is attached to Gianetti, 1984]

[Anon.], "Purest Poet of them All, A Profile of Eric Roach", *Sunday Guardian*, (Jan. 8, 1961): 7.

——, "Three More Deaths in the South", *Trinidad Guardian* (Apr. 18, 1974): 11.

——, "Body on Beach Identified as Playwright's", *Trinidad Guardian* (Apr. 23, 1974): 1.

——, "Eric Roach", *Trinidad Guardian* (Apr. 23, 1974): 8.

——, "Police Probe Death", *Express* (Apr. 23, 1974): 3.

——, "Roach Was Man of Great Integrity", *Express* (Apr. 23, 1974): 3.

——, "He Devoted Life to Writing", *Trinidad Guardian* (Apr. 24, 1974): 4.

——, "The Poem That Foretold Death", *Sunday Guardian* (May 5, 1974): 1.

Abrahams, Roger D, *The Man-of-Words in the West Indies*, Baltimore: Johns Hopkins University Press, 1983.

Anthony, Michael, "Roach's Death a Blow", *Trinidad Guardian* (Apr. 23, 1974): 1.

Baugh, Edward, *West Indian Poetry 1900-1970, A Study in Cultural Decolonisation*, Kingston, Jamaica: Savacou Publications, 1971.

——, "The West Indian Writer and His Quarrel with History", *Tapia* 7:8 (Feb. 20, 1977): 67 and *Tapia* 7:9 (Feb. 27, 1977): 6-7 & 11.

Brathwaite, Edward Kamau, "Sir Galahad and the Islands", In Brathwaite, *Roots,* Ann Arbor: University of Michigan Press, 1993, 7-27.

——, "Eric Roach", In *Contemporary Poets of the English Language*, ed. R. Murphy. Chicago and London, 1970, 62-67.

——, "The African Presence in Caribbean Literature", *Daedalus* 103:2 (1974): 73-109.

——, "Love Axe/l: Developing a Caribbean Aesthetic 1962-1974", In *Reading Black: Essays in the Criticism of African, Caribbean, and Black American Literature*, Ed. Houston A. Baker, Jr. Ithaca: Cornell Univ. Press, 1976. 20-36

——, *History of the Voice: The Development of Nation Language in Anglophone Caribbean Poetry*, London: New Beacon, 1984.

Breiner, Laurence A, "The Ambivalent Aesthetic of Eric Roach", *Ariel* 19:2 (April, 1988) 319.

——, "History, Nature and People in the Poetry of Eric Roach", *The Journal of Commonwealth Literature* 23:1 (August, 1988) 43-60.

——, "How to Behave on Paper", *Journal of West Indian Literature* 6:1 (July 1993) 1-10.

Brother, Newton, "He was a man [poem]", *Trinidad Guardian* (Apr. 23, 1974): 4.

Brown, Lloyd W., *West Indian Poetry*, Boston: Twayne, 1978. Second edition, London: Heinemann, 1984.

Brown, Wayne, "Poetry of the Forties, Part 3: 'The Dilemma'", *Sunday Guardian* (Oct. 4, 1970): 11.

——, "Poetry of the Forties, Part 5: The Mulatto Question", *Sunday Guardian* (Oct. 11, 1970): 11

——, "For Eric Roach, Drowned", *Tapia* 4:21 (May 26, 1974); Revised as "Quinam Bay", In Brown, *Voyages,* Port of Spain: Imprint Caribbean, 1989. 90-91.

Carew, Jan, "BWI Poets", *Phylon* 14:1 (1953): 7-23.

Carter, Martin. "On The Death by Drowning of the Poet Eric Roach", *Poems of Succession*. London: New Beacon, 1977, 109.

Chamberlin, T. Edward, *Come Back to Me My Language*, Urbana and Chicago: University of Illinois Press, 1993.

Coulthard, G. R. *Race and Colour in Caribbean Literature*, London: Oxford University Press, 1962.

Dathorne, O. R., "Africa in the Literature of the West Indies", *Journal of Commonwealth Literature* 1, (1965): 95-116.

Drayton, Arthur. "The European Factor in West Indian Literature", *Literary Half-Yearly* 11:1 (1970): 71-94.

——, "West Indian Consciousness in West Indian Verse", *Journal of Commonwealth Literature* 9 (1970): 66-88.

Forde, A. N., "Eric Roach Poet With Soul", *Bajan* 247 (June, 1974): 16.

Fraser, Fitzroy, "A Talk With Eric Roach", *Sunday Gleaner*, (Jan.29, 1961): 14, 20.

Gianetti, Danielle, "The Life and Poetry of Eric Roach" [unpublished thesis], University of the West Indies, St. Augustine, 1984.

——, "The Poetry of E. M. Roach: New Perspectives on his Use of Form", *Kyk-over-al* 32 (Dec. 1985): 40-47.

Gonzalez, Anson, *Trinidad and Tobago Literature: On the Air*. Port of Spain: The National Cultural Council of Trinidad and Tobago, 1973.

Hughes, Michael, "Eric Roach", *A Companion to West Indian Literature*, (London: Collins, 1979), 78.

James, Louis, *The Islands in Between*, London: Oxford University Press, 1968.

King, Bruce. *West Indian Literature*, London: Macmillan, 1979.

Lamming, George, *The Pleasures of Exile*, London: Michael Joseph, 1960.

——, "Caribbean Literature: The Black Rock of Africa", *African Forum* 1:4 (1966): 32-52.

Lowhar, Syl, "Painful Unravellings", *Trinidad Guardian,* (July 17, 1971): 8.

———, "Don't Take it All Too Literally", *Trinidad Guardian* (July 18, 1971): 12.

———, [untitled column on death of Roach], *Tapia* 4:17 (April 28, 1974): 1.

MacDonald, Scott, *Trinidad and Tobago: Democracy and Development in the Caribbean,* New York: Praeger, 1986.

McTair, Roger, "A Critic Criticized", *Trinidad Guardian* (Aug. 18, 1971): 12.

———, "Bongo Jerry Come Alive Loud", *Trinidad Guardian* (Aug. 21, 1971): 8.

Mitchum, J, "Vivid Carnival Article by Eric Roach", *Trinidad Guardian* (Apr. 27, 1974): 8.

Owens, R. J., "West Indian Poetry", *Caribbean Quarterly* 7:3 (Dec. 1961): 120-127.

Oxaal, Ivar, *Black Intellectuals and the Dilemmas of Race and Class in Trinidad*, Cambridge, Mass.: Schenkman, 1982 (reprint of *Black Intellectuals Come to Power* (1968) and *Race and Revolutionary Consciousness* (1971), with updated epilogue).

Pantin, Dennis, [no title], *Tapia* 21 (Oct. 3, 1971): 3.

Pouchet-Paquet, Sandra, "The Fifties", In *West Indian Literature*, ed. Bruce King, London: Macmillan, 1979). 63-77.

Ramchand, Kenneth, "Parades, Parades: Modern West Indian Poetry", *The Sewanee Review* 87 (1979): 96-118.

——, "Introduction", In E. M. Roach, *The Flowering Rock: Collected Poems 1938-1974,* Leeds: Peepal Tress Books, 1992. 11-20.

Roach, Eric M., "Masks – A Homecoming with a Taste of Aloes", *Sunday Guardian* (Oct. 12, 1968): 6.

——, "The Panthers, Their Test is Yet to Come", *Sunday Guardian – Independence Supplement* (Aug. 30, 1970): 4.

——, "Meritorious Achievement", *Trinidad Guardian* (June 16, 1971): 6.

——, "A Type Not Found in All Generations", *Trinidad Guardian* (July 14, 1971): 6, 8.

——, "No Excuse for Verse", *Sunday Guardian* (July 18, 1971): 12.

——, "'Breaklight' Puts Focus on Poetic Unity in W. I.", *Trinidad Guardian* (Dec. 9, 1971): 6.

——, [review of *Score*], *Trinidad Guardian* (Mar. 22, 1972): 6.

——, "Conflict of West Indian Poetry: Tribe Boys vs. AfroSaxons", *Trinidad Guardian* (Jan.12, 1973): 4.

——, "Why Tobago is so Different", *Trinidad Guardian* (Aug. 5, 1973): 4.

——, "Growing Up in Tobago", In *David Frost Introduces Trinidad and Tobago*, London: Deutsch, 1975.

——, "Introducing Caribbean Poetry to North Americans", *Sunday Guardian* (Mar. 17, 1974): 6.

Rohlehr, Gordon, "West Indian Poetry: Some Problems of Assessment", *Bim* 54 (1972): 80-88 and 55 (1972): 134-44; an earlier version of this essay appeared in *Tapia* in 1971.

——, "Blues for Eric Roach", *Tapia* 4:17 (April, 1974): 2.

——, "A Carrion Time", *Bim* 58 (June 1975): 92-109.

——, "My Strangled City: Poetry in Trinidad 1964-1975", *Caliban* 2:1 (1976): 50-122.

——, *Pathfinder: Black Awakening in the Arrivants of Edward Kamau Brathwaite*, Tunapuna, Trinidad: Gordon Rohlehr, 1981.

——, *Calypso and Society in Pre-Independence Trinidad*, Port of Spain: Gordon Rohlehr, 1990.

Sander, Reinhard W., *The Trinidad Awakening*, Westport, Conn.: Greenwood Press, 1988.

Telemaque, Harold M. and A. M. Clarke, *Burnt Bush*, Port of Spain, 1948; rpt. Nendeln: Kraus, 1973.

Walcott, Derek, "In Praise of Peasantry: The Poetry of Eric Roach", *Sunday Guardian* (July 18, 1965): 9.

——, "Time to Separate Politics from Good Verse", *Trinidad Guardian* (Mar. 17, 1966): 5.

——, "The Wind in the Dooryard", In Walcott, *Sea Grapes*, London: Jonathan Cape, 1976. 66-68.

——, "Why Belle Fanto has Survived", *Sunday Guardian* (Aug. 22, 1976): 6.

Walmsley, Anne, *The Caribbean Artists Movement 1966-1972,* London and Port of Spain: New Beacon Books, 1992.

Williams, Cheryl, "Eric Roach's Poetry: Part I", *Tapia* 4:17 (April 28, 1974): 3-4, 9.

——, "Eric Roach's Poetry: Part II", *Tapia* 4:18 (May 5, 1974): 7.

Williams, Eric, *History of the People of Trinidad and Tobago*, London: Andre Deutsch, 1964.

INDEX

ABOUT THE AUTHOR

Larry Breiner is Professor of English at Boston University. He has been a Visiting Professor, American Studies, University of Tokyo (2004); Rockefeller Fellow, Center for Study of Black Literature and Culture, UPenn (1991-92); ACLS Grant-in-Aid (1984); NEH Research Fellow (1980-81); ACLS/Social Science Research Council Fellow (1976-77). He is the author of the widely praised *Introduction to West Indian Poetry* and numerous scholarly articles in Caribbean Literature.

NEW FROM PEEPAL TREE

Tourist, Traveller, Troublemaker, Essays on Poetry
ISBN: 9781845230531; pp. 340; £16.99

This isn't a conventional book of academic essays, though these pieces on Caribbean, African, British and American poets are always scholarly and intellectually rigorous. They are particularly rewarding as the work of a practicing poet writing about those of his peers whose work he admires. There are essays on major Caribbean figures, on Walcott, Brathwaite and Martin Carter, and on the major African poets Niyi Osundare, Jack Mapanje and Femi Oyebode, but there are also pieces on less well-known poets such as Frank Collymore, Ian McDonald and James Berry that, without any agenda, bring to view work that ought to be taken far more seriously. As the editor of major anthologies of Caribbean poetry, Stewart Brown is more than usually aware of the new directions that Caribbean poetry has taken, and pieces on Olive Senior, Linton Kwesi Johnson and Kwame Dawes indicate some of these.

How other societies are perceived has long been a preoccupation of Stewart Brown's own poetry and critical writing, and essays on the work of poets who have travelled frame this collection. Here he explores his own and other writers' work to make distinctions between the discourses of tourist, traveller and troublemaker.

One subtext of the collection is a mistrust of the academic industry of postcolonial criticism. Here it is always the poem that matters (although the essays are alert to social, political and cultural contexts) and the emphasis is on close and sensitive reading rather than theory.

A good many of these essays began as papers for oral delivery. One of their great pleasures is that they retain a flavour of the speaking voice: enthusiastic, generous and respectful of the presence of listeners, and now readers.